WE NOW HAVE THE ANSWERS!

Ever since the very first "alleged" saucer sighting there has been a growing concern over the UFO phenomenon—and a growing suspicion that we were not being told all there was to know.

This history-making document will end that suspicion and clear up the UFO picture better than anything that has gone before.

Readers will be startled by the facts concerning the UFOs themselves, as well as the exhaustive way the Air Force spent American tax dollars to investigate the UFO mystery, employing top scientists, the FBI, the CIA, and special Armed Forces investigators.

Here are actual interviews, photographs, reports, and transcribed conversations.

After thirty classified years, the information is ours!

Project Blue Book

The Top Secret UFO Findings Revealed

Edited by Brad Steiger

BALLANTINE BOOKS • NEW YORK

ISBN 0-345-34525-8

This edition published in association with
ConFucian Press, Inc.

Manufactured in the United States of America

First Edition: November 1976
Seventh Printing: March 1989

Cover photo by Dan Esgro/The Image Bank

Contents

Introduction: An Exercise
in Charting a Phenomenon

Throughout the 1950s and '60s, retired Marine Corps major Donald E. Keyhoe charged the U.S. Air Force with deliberately censoring information concerning UFOs. As a director of the National Investigations Committee on Aerial Phenomena (NICAP), Keyhoe regularly repeated his accusations that, while the Air Force had been seriously analyzing UFO data in secret, it maintained a policy of officially debunking saucer stories for the press and ridiculing all citizens who reported sightings.

The official Air Force rejoinder was that the reason for the Top Secret and Classified designations on UFO investigations was solely to protect the identities of those individuals who made reports of mysterious, unidentified "somethings" in the skies. The essence of all research, Air Force spokesmen insisted, was always released to the communications media. Nothing of national interest was being withheld.

But men like Major Keyhoe and most of the membership of the civilian UFO research groups (of which there were once as many as fifty) never bought the Air Force's claims of serving the greater public interest by releasing all pertinent details of their studies and investigations. In the January 1965 issue of True magazine, Keyhoe struck out at the Air Force for its establishment of a regulation that seemed designed to stifle the truth about UFOs. According to Keyhoe: "The tactic is total suppression of news. By a strict Air Force order, entitled AR 200-2, Air Force personnel are forbidden to talk in public about UFO sightings, and information about UFO's is to be withheld from the press unless the thing seen 'has been positively identified as a familiar or known object.'"

In the True article Keyhoe went on to accuse the Air Force of censoring information about events that the public deserved to know. Among them: Four "spacecraft of unknown origin" cruised up to the two-man Gemini space capsule on April 8, 1964, when it was on its first orbit, inspected it, then blasted off; on January 10, 1961, a UFO flew so close to a Polaris missile that it botched up the radar for fourteen minutes; there was a possible "recharging" operation of UFOs near Canberra, Australia, on May 15, 1964.

On March 28, 1966, after a saucer "flap" in Michigan, Keyhoe was once again repeating his charges that the Pentagon had a top-level policy of discounting all UFO reports and "over the past several years has used ridicule to discredit sightings."

On March 30 spokesmen for the Air Force called a press conference to insist that they kept an open mind about UFOs and to deny any "hushing" of saucer reports. In the case of recent Michigan sightings, a spokesman said, "marsh gas was pinpointed as the source of colored lights observed by a number of people."

But by 1966, public-opinion surveys indicated that over fifty million Americans believed in the existence of UFOs. Perhaps in 1956 the majority of men and women were willing to laugh along with official disclaimers and professional flying-saucer debunkers, but ten years later the UFO climate had become considerably warmer.

In the August 1976 issue of UFO Report, Dr. J.

Allen Hynek, who for more than two decades served as an astronomical consultant to Project Sign and Project Blue Book, expressed his blunt opinion that he had been a "complete jerk" in his early dismissal of the UFO enigma as just so much nonsense. He had been teaching astronomy at Ohio State University in Columbus, which is not far from Dayton, where Wright-Patterson Air Force Base—the home of the now defunct Project Blue Book—is located. Dr. Hynek told interviewer Timothy Green Beckley:

At the time the government was trying like mad to determine whether it was the Martians or the Russians who were responsible for the elusive discs being tracked in our atmosphere. To put it bluntly, they needed a competent astronomer to tell them which cases arose out of the misidentification of planets, stars, meteors, and so forth.

Personally, I was dead sure that the entire affair could be accounted for in mundane terms—that it was a cut-and-dried case of post-war nerves, and people had to have something to occupy their minds . . . In all honesty, however, looking back there were several dozen hard core episodes which I'm sorry to say I neglected on the general hypothesis that it cannot be—therefore it isn't.

Certainly when I started getting involved, I would have taken bets that by 1952, at the very latest, the whole mess would have been forgotten. I was convinced it was a phase that would quickly pass. Of course, I was dead wrong!

On top of this, just like everyone else, I felt positive flying saucers were an acute American fad. Never did I suspect in my wildest dreams that it would turn out to be a global phenomenon.

As early as 1953, though, Dr. Hynek wrote an article for the **Journal of the Optical Society of America,** suggesting that there might well be some important data that the government investigators were overlooking. In 1956 he went to the Smithsonian Institution in Washington, D.C., and convinced officials there to establish a satellite-tracking network, in which he completely immersed himself for about five years.

In spite of such serious efforts to zero in on the UFO phenomenon, Dr. Hynek freely admits that "nobody enjoyed busting holes in a wild story and showing off more than I did. It was a game and it was a heck of a lot of fun."

But the famous sightings in Michigan in March and April 1967, the ones that got Dr. Hynek dubbed "Dr. Swamp Gas," demonstrated to "Blue Book's tame professor" that there was a "backlash of public sentiment." For the first time, Dr. Hynek told Beckley, he became aware that "the tide was slowly turning."

Project Blue Book, begun as Project Sign in 1947, produced what the Air Force considered a satisfactory explanation for most of the nearly 13,000 sightings reported through 1969. Of the unexplained UFO incidents, the official statement is: "The description of the object or its motion cannot be correlated with any known object or phenomenon."

The staff of Project Blue Book was assigned to carry out three main functions: to try to find an explanation for all reported sightings of UFOs; to determine whether the UFOs pose any security threat to the United States; and to determine if UFOs exhibit any advanced technology which the U.S. could utilize.

Blue Book officers were stationed at every Air Force base in the nation. They were responsible for investigating all reported sightings and for getting the reports in to Blue Book headquarters at Wright-Patterson Air Force Base. The bulk of the investigations, as interpreted by field officers, led Blue Book officials to decide that most people see, not extraterrestrial spacecraft, but bright stars, balloons, satellites, comets, fireballs, conventional

4

aircraft, moving clouds, vapor trails, missiles, reflections, mirages, searchlights, birds, kites, spurious radar indications, fireworks, or flares.

On the basis of Blue Book reports, therefore, the Air Force concluded:

1. No UFO has ever given any indication of threat to the national security.

2. There is no evidence that UFOs represent technological developments or principles beyond present-day scientific knowledge.

3. There is no evidence that any UFOs are "extraterrestrial vehicles."

Neatly arranged evidence and skeptical space scientists to the contrary, many trained observers agreed with Donald Keyhoe and civilian UFO-investigation groups that the Air Force was not telling all that it knew.

The flying-saucer story begins on June 24, 1947, when a young businessman named Kenneth Arnold sighted nine discs near Mount Rainier in the state of Washington. Arnold described the motion of the unidentified flying objects as looking like "a saucer skipping across the water." In subsequent reports and later sightings, the description was condensed to "flying saucers." The Boise, Idaho, businessman had coined a term that would become known in most languages of the world.

The Air Force immediately denied that they had any such craft, and at the same time officially debunked Arnold's claim of having spotted unidentified flying objects. The civilian pilot had improperly sighted a formation of military planes or a series of weather balloons. Donald H. Menzel, Professor of Astrophysics at Harvard, who was later to become a professional saucer-skeptic and debunker, said that Arnold had been fooled by tilting snow clouds or dust haze reflected by the sun.

Arnold, however, stuck fast to his story, and the item made the front-page of newspapers across the nation. For UFOlogists, it was the birth of an era.

During the period June through December 1947 there was no specific organization responsible for investigating and evaluating UFO reports. At this time everyone had an expert opinion. Even within the military structure, there were those who expressed their own feelings and beliefs as to what UFOs actually represented.

The wide news coverage of public reports of "flying discs or saucers" created sufficient concern at high military echelons to authorize the Air Material Command to conduct a preliminary investigation into these reports. Early belief was that the objects reported were of aircraft more advanced than those possessed by the U.S. Armed Forces.

A letter, September 23, 1947, from Lt. General Twining of AMC to the Commanding General of the Army Air Forces, expressed the opinion that there was sufficient substance in the reports to warrant a detailed study.

On December 30, 1947, a letter from the Chief of Staff directed AMC to establish a project whose purpose was to collect, collate, evaluate, and disseminate all information concerning UFO sightings and phenomena in the atmosphere to those interested agencies. The project was assigned the code name "Sign." The responsibility for "Project Sign" was delegated to the Air Technical Intelligence Center which was then part of the AMC.*

The next classic case in the chronicle of UFO sightings was the tragic encounter of Captain Thomas Mantell with a flying saucer over Godman Field Air Base in Kentucky on January 7, 1948.

At 1:15 P.M., the control tower at the base received a telephone call from the Kentucky State Highway Patrol inquiring about any unusual aircraft that might be being tested in the area. Resi-

* Project Blue Book.

dents at Marysville, Kentucky, had reported seeing an unfamiliar aircraft over their city. Flight Service at Wright-Patterson told Godman Field that there were no flights of test craft in the area.

Within twenty minutes, Owensboro and Irvington had reported a strange aircraft, which residents described as "circular, about two hundred fifty to three hundred feet in diameter."

At 1:45 P.M. the tower operators on the base had seen it. They satisfied themselves that it was not an airplane or a weather balloon and called the base operations officer, the base intelligence officer, and several other high-ranking personnel.

At 2:30 P.M. they were still discussing what to do about the object when four P-51s were seen approaching the base from the south. Captain Mantell, the flight leader, started in pursuit of the UFO after the tower asked him to take a closer look at the object in an attempt to identify it.

Mantell was still climbing at ten thousand feet when he made his last radio contact with the tower: "It looks metallic and it's tremendous in size. It's above me and I'm gaining on it. I'm going to twenty thousand feet."

Those were Mantell's last words. His wingmen saw him disappear into the stratospheric clouds. A few moments later, Mantell crashed to the earth and was killed. The Air Force issued an official explanation of the incident, which would have been ludicrous had not the death of a brave man been involved. The experienced pilot, they claimed, had "unfortunately been killed while trying to reach the planet Venus."

That was what the officers in the control tower had been watching for all that time—the planet Venus. And that pesky planet was what had lured Captain Mantell to his death. The pilot had thought that he was pursuing something "metallic and tremendous in size" directly above him when, in reality, he was aiming his F-51 at Venus.

As farfetched as the Air Force's official explanation sounded, it was not without precedent. During World War II, the battleship New York, while headed for the Iwo Jima campaign, sighted a strange object overhead. Officers on the bridge studied it and couldn't make out what it was. It was round, silver-colored, and about the size of a two-story house.

The three-inch guns were brought into action, but they couldn't seem to touch the great silver balloon. The New York's destroyer escort opened fire with their five-inch guns. Their marksmanship proved to be no better.

About that time, the navigator, who had been awakened by the barrage, came to the deck. Through sleep-fuzzed eyes he watched the shells zoom up and fall short of their target. He continued to observe the strange action for a few minutes; then, scratching his head sleepily, he walked back to his quarters to make some calculations.

"Sir," he reported to the commander a bit later, "if it were possible to see Venus at this time of the day, you would see it at exactly the same position as the silver balloon."

On the evening of July 24, 1948, an Eastern Airlines DC-3 took off on a scheduled flight to Atlanta from Houston. Twenty miles southwest of Montgomery, pilots Clarence S. Chiles and John B. Whitted reported a UFO with "two rows of windows from which bright lights glowed." The underside had a "deep blue glow," and a "fifty-foot trail of orange-red flame shot out the back." Chiles and Whitted were positive that it was not the planet Venus that they had seen.

George F. Gorman, a twenty-five-year-old second lieutenant in the North Dakota Air National Guard, was waiting his turn to land at Fargo on October 1, 1948, when a bright light made a pass at him. When he called the tower to complain about the errant pilot, he was informed that there were no aircraft in the vicinity besides a Piper Cub, which was just landing, and Gorman's own F-51. Gorman could still see the mysterious light off to one side, so he decided to investigate. Within moments he found himself on a collision course with the strange light, and he had to take the F-51 into a dive to escape the unswerving globe of light. The UFO repeated the attack, and once again Gorman just managed to escape collision. When the UFO at last disappeared, pilot Gorman was left shaken and convinced that "its maneuvers were controlled by thought or reason."

After these three "classic" cases in 1948, as well as numerous other less dramatic sightings, many Air Force pilots were reminded of the weird "foo fighters" which several Allied personnel had seen in World War II. Often while on bombing missions, crews noticed strange lights that followed their bombers. Sometimes the "foos" darted about. Other times they were seen to fly in formation. Several pilots reported seeing the "foo fighters" during combat.

Barracks and locker-room scuttlebutt had classified the "foo fighters" as another of the Nazis' secret weapons, but not a single one of the glowing craft was ever shot down or captured. And, Allied pilots had to agree, if the Germans had come up with another military invention, it was certainly harmless enough—especially when compared to the buzz bomb. Outside of startling the wits out of greenhorn pilots, there is no record of a "foo"'s ever damaging any aircraft or harming any personnel.

The "foos" were spotted in both the European and Far Eastern theaters, and it came as something of a surprise to thousands of pilots when the Air Force officially decreed that the mysterious lights had never actually existed at all—or were hallucinations at best. Many Allied pilots, however, had kept quite an account of the "foos," and had begun to theorize that the things operated under

9

intelligent control. It came as no shock to these pilots when waves of "foos" were sighted over Sweden in July 1946. A kind of hysteria gripped Sweden, however, and the mysterious "invasion" was reported at great length in the major European newspapers. Some authorities feared that some new kind of German "V" weapon had been discovered and unleashed on the nation that had remained neutral throughout World War II. Others tried to explain the unidentified flying objects away as meteors—peculiar meteors that disappeared and reappeared and made an infernal roaring, but meteors nonetheless.

Too many eyewitness reports were appearing in the newspapers to make either theory tenable. If they had been some new kind of V-2 or buzz bomb, they surely would have caused great destruction in Sweden. Then, too, who would have been launching the bombs? The Nazi war machine had been destroyed, and the Allies were busy dividing Berlin, conducting atrocity trials, and recruiting German scientists for their respective space programs. As for their being meteors, bolides simply do not maneuver in circles, stop and start, or look like metal cigars.

Because of the large-scale interest in the objects which had been generated in Europe, the London **Daily Mail** sent reporter Alexander Clifford to interview Swedish and Danish military personnel and conduct his own investigation. Clifford's report listed certain facts upon which all eyewitnesses to the Swedish "ghost rockets" had agreed: The objects were shaped like cigars; orange or green flames shot out of their tails; they traveled at an altitude of between three hundred and a thousand meters; their speed was about that of an airplane; they made no noise, except, perhaps a slight whistling.

In February, 1949 "Project Sign" completed its evaluations of the 243 UFO reports which had been submitted to the project. The report concluded that: "No definite and conclusive evidence is yet available that would prove or disprove the existence of these UFOs as real aircraft of unknown and unconventional configuration."

"Project Sign" was changed to "Project Grudge" on December 16, 1948 at the request of the Director of Research and Development. Project Grudge completed their evaluations of 244 reports in August, 1949. The conclusions of the Grudge reports were as follows:

Evaluations of reports of UFOs to date demonstrate that these flying objects constitute no threat to the security of the United States. They also concluded that reports of UFOs were the result of misinterpretations of conventional objects, a mild form of mass hysteria or war nerves, and individuals who fabricate such reports to perpetrate a hoax or to seek publicity.

Project Grudge also recommended that the investigation and study of reports of UFOs be reduced in scope, as had the Project Sign Report.

The UFO project continued on a reduced scale and in December, 1951 the Air Force entered into a contract with a private industrial organization for another detailed study of the UFO cases on file. The report, which was completed March 17, 1954, is commonly referred to as Special Report #14. Reports one through thirteen were progress reports dealing with administration. Special Report #14 reduced and evaluated all UFO data held in Air Force files. Basically, the same conclusions were reached that had been noted in both the preceding Sign and Grudge Reports.

It was during the early 1950's that the national interest in reported sightings increased tremendously. With the increased volume of reports, a Scientific Advisory Panel on UFOs was established in late 1952. At a meeting held during January 14–18, 1953, all available data was examined. Conclusions and recommendations of this panel were published in a report, and made public. The panel concluded that UFOs did not threaten the national security of the United States and recommended that the aura of mystery attached to the project be removed.

In March, 1952 Project Grudge became known as Project Blue Book. From this time to the present, the project concerned itself with investigation of sightings, evaluation of the data, and release of information to proper news media through the Secretary of the Air Force, Office of Information (SAFOICC).

It may have been an Air Force officer who remembered the "foo fighters" who gave the order on July 26, 1952, to "Shoot them down!" when dozens of UFOs suddenly converged on Washington, D.C.

Several prominent scientists, including Albert Einstein, protested the order to the White House and urged that the command be rescinded, not only in the interest of future intergalactic peace, but also in the interest of self-preservation: Extraterrestrials would certainly look upon an attack by primitive jet firepower as a breach of the universal laws of hospitality.

The "shoot them down" order was withdrawn on White House orders by five o'clock that afternoon. That night, official observers puzzled over the objects, visible on radar screens and to the naked eye, as the UFOs easily outdistanced Air Force jets, whose pilots were ordered to pursue the objects but to keep their fingers off the trigger.

Although the Air Force was flippantly denying the Washington flap within another twenty-four hours and attributing civilian saucer sightings to the usual causes (hallucinations, seeing planets and stars), the national wire services had already sent out word that for a time the Air Force officials had been jittery enough to give a "fire at will" order.

On May 15, 1954, Air Force Chief of Staff general Nathan Twining told his audience at Amarillo, Texas, that the "best brains in the Air Force" were trying to solve the problem of the flying saucers. "If they come from Mars," Twining said, "they are so far ahead of us we have nothing to be afraid of." The general's assurances that an ultra-advanced culture would automatically be benign or disinterested did little to calm an increasingly bewildered and alarmed American public. And on December 24, 1959, after important people had begun to demand that the Air Force end its policy of secrecy, the much-discussed Air Force Regulation 200-2 was issued to all Air Force personnel.

Briefly, AR 200-2 made a flat and direct statement that the Air Force was definitely concerned with the reporting of all UFOs "as a possible threat to the security of the United States and its forces, and secondly, to determine technical aspects involved." In the controversial paragraph 9, the Secretary of the Air Force gave specific instructions that Air Force personnel were not to release reports of UFOs, "only reports . . . where the object has been definitely identified as a familiar object."

Early in 1959, John Lester of the Newark **Star-Ledger** had reported that a group of more than fifty airline pilots, all of them with at least fifteen years of experience, called the Air Force censorship policies "absolutely ridiculous." Each of these pilots had seen at least one UFO and had been interrogated by the Air Force. Their consensus was that they were completely disgusted with Air Force procedures and policies. One of the men said that any pilot who failed to maintain secrecy after sighting a UFO could face up to ten years in prison and a fine of ten thousand dollars.

"We are ordered to report all UFO sightings," complained another pilot, "but when we do, we are usually treated like incompetents and told to keep quiet.

"This is no fun, especially after many hours of questioning—sometimes all night long. You're

13

tired. You've just come in from a grueling flight, anxious to get home to the wife and kids. But you make your report anyhow and the Air Force tells you that the thing that paced your plane for 15 minutes was a mirage or a bolt of lightning. Nuts to that. Who needs it?"

On February 27, 1960, Vice Admiral Robert Hillenkoetter, USN, Ret., former head of the Central Intelligence Agency, rocked the Air Force when he released to the press photostatic copies of an Air Force directive which warned Air Force Commands to regard the UFOs as "serious business."

The Air Force admitted that it had issued the order, but added that the photostatic copy which Hillenkoetter had released to the press was only part of a seven-page regulation, which had been issued to update similar past orders, and made no substantive changes in policy.

The official Air Force directive indicated the remarkable dual role which the Air Force appeared to play in the unfolding UFO drama.

Unidentified flying objects—sometimes treated lightly by the press and referred to as "flying saucers" —must be rapidly and accurately identified as serious USAF business . . . As AFR 200-2 points out, the Air Force concern with these sightings is threefold: First of all is the object a threat to the defense of the U.S.? Secondly, does it contribute to technical or scientific knowledge? And then there's the inherent USAF responsibility to explain to the American people through public-information media what is going on in their skies.

The phenomena or actual objects comprising UFOs will tend to increase, with the public more aware of goings-on in space but still inclined to some apprehension. Technical and defense considerations will continue to exist in this era.

. . . AFR 200-2 outlines necessary orderly, qualified reporting as well as public-information procedures.

This is where the base should stand today, with practices judged at least satisfactory by commander and inspector:

Responsibility for handling UFOs should rest with either intelligence, operations, the Provost Marshal or the Information Officer—in that order of preference, dictated by limits of the base organization;

A specific officer should be designated as responsible;

He should have experience in investigative techniques and also, if possible, scientific or technical background;

He should have authority to obtain the assistance of specialists on the base;

He should be equipped with binoculars, camera, Geiger counter, magnifying glass and have a source for containers in which to store samples.

What is required is that every UFO sighting be investigated and reported to the Air Technical Intelligence Center at Wright-Patterson AFB and that explanation to the public be realistic and knowledgeable. Normally that explanation will be made *only* by the OSAF Information Officer. . . .

Quite a statement for an organization that repeatedly claimed that UFOs are nonexistent; that anyone who sees one is suffering from a hallucination or is ignorant of the true natural phenomenon (planets, stars, swamp gas) he is observing; and that even if they do exist they are absolutely unimportant and unworthy of study!

Obviously, in spite of official dismissals, the Air Force was very much aware of the UFOs—aware and actively investigating.

In the 1976 **UFO Report** interview, Dr. Hynek said that two factions definitely existed in Project Blue Book:

There were those individuals who were extremely concerned over the radar trackings and the close approaches made by UFOs to civilian and military air-

15

craft. They conjectured that their pilots were being truthful and were not concocting far-out tales. They wanted to check all the possibilities. Hopefully, clues could be gathered which would lead to an eventual solution as to how UFOs accomplished such drastic right-angle turns and accelerations without apparent harm to either craft or occupants. The possible method of propulsion also intrigued them.

These were the more scientifically oriented, for as Hynek noted, "Most of the top brass, however, thought of themselves as being down to earth. They couldn't understand for a split second why any of their colleagues would bother to take the subject seriously."

A memorandum dated September 28, 1965 from Major General LeBailly requested that a working scientific panel composed of both physical and social scientists be organized to review Project Blue Book. The product of this request was the Special Report of the USAF Scientific Advisory Board Ad Hoc Committee. Their primary conclusion was that the present program could be strengthened by providing the opportunity for an in-depth scientific study of selected UFO sightings.

After sightings in Michigan in March 1966, Dr. Hynek told reporters that "when good solid citizens report something puzzling, I believe we have an obligation to do as good a job as we can. I regard our 'Unidentifieds' as a sort of blot on the escutcheon. Somehow we scientists should be able to come up with answers for these things."

Major Hector Quintanella, then director of Project Blue Book, agreed that it was "impossible to prove that flying saucers do not exist," and that the Air Force should persist in investigating UFO sightings. "We are spending millions to get our spacecraft to the moon and beyond. Imagine what a great help it would be to get our hands on a ship from another planet and examine its power plant."

On April 5, 1966, Dr. Harold Brown, Secretary of the Air Force, told the House Armed Services Committee that there was no evidence to support the claim that UFOs are spaceships. The formal hearing on UFOs was prompted by a rash of sightings in Michigan that March.

"You might call the study of UFOs a study in puzzlement," Dr. Brown said as he credited the Michigan saucers to "marsh gases." He concluded by saying: "The Air Force is hiding nothing."

Nothing? When Hynek held a press conference to dismiss the Michigan sightings as will-o'-the-wisps in a swamp, he was honest enough to add this disclaimer: "Scientists in the year 2066 may think us very naive in our denials."

Recently Hynek, for twenty years Project Blue Book's consultant in astronomy, said that in spite of its occasional pretensions to heavy scientific investigation—and there was some fine research undertaken and some excellent papers prepared—not once was he able to have a serious high-level scientific discussion.

The attitude of the board members was absolutely adamant. There were personnel in high places who really wondered and appeared troubled by what was going on, but they couldn't admit it. Not publicly!

The procedure was just about always the same— they [the serious investigators] were usually transferred to another line of work . . . I saw this happen time after time . . .

Orders were passed down from the top office in the Pentagon—the Secretary of the Air Force. On several occasions, I was called in to see Secretary Harold Brown. Never once was I asked my opinion as an astronomer. I was always *told*, 'That was a balloon,' or 'That was a flock of geese!' It was clear that *Project Blue Book* was a finger exercise.

In July, 1966, the Commander of FTD initiated a QRC request through Project White Stork to provide an in-depth evaluation of some fifty UFO cases for the purpose of identifying procedural changes that should be made in Blue Book methodology. In addition, it was decided with sponsor approval, that the investigating group include an assessment of the entire UFO situation. Results of the evaluation of selected cases did not reveal any evidence of extraterrestrial vehicles nor anything that might be considered beyond the range of present day scientific knowledge. The most probable explanation for the unidentified cases would have to be cast in terms of man made objects, natural phenomena, or psychological cause. Of their recommendations they stressed the fact that immediate steps should be taken to educate the public to the sensational but insidious exploitation of UFO reports, by releasing official books, reports, and news items. Also, the extent of public concern and opinion regarding UFOs for use in determining long range requirements should be determined. If results should indicate that public concern has been overestimated, then consideration should be given to dropping all official (government) interest in UFOs.

The history of Project Blue Book alone has shown that the UFO phenomena is mainly that of a public relations problem. The fringe of believers in extraterrestrial visitation continues to grow. UFO hobby clubs are a constant critic of Air Force policies—the majority of these clubs profess to be studying the phenomena scientifically.

However, it should be recognized that the public could be expected to *accuse the Air Force of withholding information* on UFOs since their *investigation* has been assigned to Air Force Technical Intelligence.

Initial classification of the UFO project and continuous association with the intelligence community has contributed to constant public criticism. The major criticism, that of withholding information, could be expected because of Blue Book's long intelligence association. With continued government involvement, the Air Force must announce and maintain a standard policy of releasing information to the public. The public must be continually informed of all matters regarding the UFO phenomena.

A recent nationwide Gallup survey of the American people on the UFO subject, revealed that more than five million Americans claim to have seen something they believed to be a "flying saucer." Nearly half of the U.S. adult populus believe that these frequently reported flying objects, while not necessarily "saucers," are real—29 per cent of the population believe them to be a product of the imagination.

This represents quite a change in public attitudes toward the creditablility of "flying saucers" since a Gallup survey conducted almost twenty years ago revealed that forty per cent of the populus called the saucers either a hoax or the product of the imagination.

What can be the reasons for this public belief? We can attribute this to several things:

(1) The Air Force should capitalize on the belief of 50 million Americans in the existence of UFOs.

(2) Announce and maintain a scientific investigation policy to satisfy public interest.

(3) Initiate positive programs oriented at establishing contact with extraterrestrial life.

We must establish a new image for Project Blue Book and we believe this can be done by acceptance of these recommendations.

But Project Blue Book was never able to clean up its image in the eyes of the UFOlogists and those who had participated in UFO sightings. Some assessed the Air Force procedures as the kind of busywork "finger exercises" to which Dr. Hynek referred. Others saw the project as a sinister cover-up.

There is no question that certain Air Force officers have always taken UFOs very seriously. Some saw the UFO as, according to one memo, "a devilishly clever psychological warfare weapon of the Commies to continuously disrupt the Air Force." The memo went on to argue: "The Commies **do** sit up nights thinking up new ideas how to confuse us." Captain Edward Ruppelt, a director of Project Blue Book, struck this note heavily in 1952 in his argument for continuing the project:

The hyothesis that since nothing hostile has been discovered in the past nothing hostile will be discovered in the future can be followed and the project discontinued. However, with the present day technological advances, this hypothesis may involve a certain degree of risk in the future.

Continuing Expanded Project

(1) If the project is to continue it must be expanded in scope. This would require a limited increase both in the amount of funds and of personnel. Reports now being received are not thoroughly analyzed. Many sources of information that are available have not been utilized due to the limited scope of the project. The possibility that any definite conclusions as to the nature of the objects being reported will ever be reached is extremely doubtful under the present operations.

(2) At the present time the objects that have been reported apparently present no threat to the United States. However, sometime in the future some unfriendly nation might conceivably develop unconventional weapons that would appear similar to the objects that are presently being reported and it is apparent from the past five years history of this project that present operations could not adequately cope with such an occurrence.

(3) There are still "incredible reports by credible observers" that have not been and should be thoroughly explained.

(4) An enemy could use the present flying saucer

report as a psychological weapon and if an organization is not available to cope with such reports (i.e., the mere existence of such an organized project would be a counter-weapon) a certain degree of panic could result.

(5) It is thought possible that all the reports of unidentified objects are due to misinterpretation of known objects. The continuance of an expanded project will provide the necessary data to arrive at more definite conclusions as to this possibility.

From the very inception of a governmental investigative branch for UFOs, there have been certain officers who feared the threat of hostile aliens from an unknown source in "outer space" or who felt that a benevolent or aloof intelligence was taking its time in making an extensive evaluation of our planet. Ruppelt would one day join the ranks of those who believed in the theory that an extraterrestrial intelligence was responsible for the unidentified flying objects in our skies.

The transfer of the responsibility of UFO research to the University of Colorado in 1969 served to terminate the Air Force's official involvement in the UFO mystery, but the annoying residue of suspicions and outright accusations of cover-up and censorship has never been dissipated. It is to be hoped that this book (which is really a kind of historical document, edited for digestibility) will answer a good many of those paranoid charges and, at the same time, reveal details never before published about certain of the classic UFO encounters.

Quite likely most readers will be startled to learn just how extensively the Air Force spent tax dollars to investigate every angle of the UFO enigma, employing top scientists, the FBI, the CIA, and special Armed Forces investigators. Now, for the first time, we can read for ourselves the actual interviews, reports, and transcribed conversations of witnesses to UFO activity—including those who experienced an interaction with alleged UFO occupants.

For nearly thirty years the Air Force kept its UFO files classified. Now, at last, we will be able to gain a much clearer picture of what they were up to during those years.

Chapter One: Kenneth Arnold and the Sighting That Started It All

On June 24, 1947, at 2 P.M., Kenneth Arnold took off from the Chehalis, Washington, airport in his personal plane and headed for Yakima, Washington. Arnold's trip had been delayed for an hour by a search for a large Marine Corps transport aircraft that supposedly went down near or around the southwest side of Mount Rainier. After takeoff Arnold flew directly toward Mount Rainier at an altitude of approximately 9,500 feet, which is the approximate elevation of the high plateau from which Mount Rainier rises. He made one westward sweep of this high plateau, searching ridges for the Marine ship, and flew to the west near the ridge side of the canyon, where Ashford is located. Unable to see anything that looked like the lost plane, Arnold turned above the town of Mineral, started again toward Mount Rainier, and climbed to an altitude of 9,200 feet.

Arnold subsequently reported that the air was so smooth that it was a real pleasure flying, and, as most pilots do when the air is smooth and they are at a high altitude, he trimmed out the aircraft and simply sat in his plane, observing the sky and terrain. The sky was as clear as crystal.

Arnold reported that there was a DC-4 to his left and rear at approximately 14,000 feet. He hadn't flown more than two or three minutes of his course when a bright flash reflected on his airplane. He couldn't find where the reflection came from, but to the left and north of Mount Rainier he did observe a chain of nine peculiar-looking objects flying from north to south at approximately 9,500 feet. They were approaching Mount Rainier very rapidly, and he assumed that they were jet aircraft. Every few seconds two or three of the objects would dip or change course slightly, just enough for the sun to reflect brightly off them. The objects being quite far away, he was unable to make out their shape or formation. As they approached Mount Rainier he observed their outline quite clearly. Arnold stated that he found it very peculiar that he couldn't find their tails, but nonetheless assumed they were some type of jet aircraft. The objects were observed to pass the southern edge of Mount Rainier, flying directly south to southeast down the hogback of a mountain range. The elevation of the objects was estimated to have varied approximately a thousand feet one way or another, but they remained very near the horizon, which would indicate that they were near the same elevation as the witness. Arnold stated that the objects flew like geese, in a rather diagonal chainlike line, as if they were linked together. They seemed to hold a definite direction, but swerved in and out of the high mountain peaks. The witness estimated the distance between him and the objects to be approximately 25 miles. Using a Zeus fastener, or cowling tool, he estimated the size of the objects to be approximately two thirds that of a DC-4. He observed the UFOs passing a high snow-covered ridge between Mount Rainier and Mount Adams and reported that as the first object was passing the south crest of this ridge the last one was entering the northern crest. This ridge, measured later, is approximately 5 miles, so it was estimated the chain of objects was 5 miles long. Mr. Arnold timed the objects between Mount Rainier and Mount Adams and determined that they crossed this 47-mile-stretch in 1 minute and 42 seconds. This is equivalent to 1656.71 miles per hour.

In an interview subsequent to the sighting,

Arnold described the objects as appearing like saucers skipping on water. This description was shortened to "flying saucers" by newspapermen and resulted in the popular use of that term.

It was the Air Force's conclusion that the objects of this sighting were due to a mirage. Arnold's statement concerning how smooth and crystal clear the air was is an indication of very stable conditions which are associated with inversions and increase the refraction index of the atmosphere.

PENDLETON ORG JULY 12 1233A

COMMANDING GENERAL
    WRIGHT FIELD   DAYTON OHIO

DEAR SIR: YOU HAVE MY PERMISSION TO QUOTE GIVE OUT OR REPRINT MY WRITTEN ACCOUNT AND REPORT OF NINE STRANGE AIRCRAFT I OBSERVED ON JUNE 24TH IN THE CASCADE MOUNTAINS IN THE STATE OF WASHINGTON. THIS REPORT WAS SENT TO YOU AT REQUEST SOME DAYS AGO. IT IS WITH CONSIDERABLE DISAPPOINTMENT YOU CANNOT GIVE THE EXPLANATION OF THESE AIRCRAFT AS I FELT CERTAIN THEY BELONGED TO OUR GOVERNMENT. THEY HAVE APPARENTLY MEANT NO HARM BUT USED AS AN INSTRUMENT OF DESTRUCTION IN COMBINATION WITH OUR ATOMIC BOMB THE EFFECTS COULD DESTROY LIFE ON OUR PLANET. CAPT. _____ CO-PILOT STEVENS OF UNITED AIR LINES AND MYSELF HAVE COMPARED OUR OBSERVATIONS IN AS MUCH DETAIL AS POSSIBLE AND AGREED WE HAD OBSERVED THE SAME TYPE OF AIRCRAFT AS TO SIZE SHAPE AND FORM. WE HAVE NOT TAKEN THIS LIGHTLY. IT IS TO US VERY SERIOUS CONCERN AS WE ARE AS INTERESTED IN THE WELFARE OF OUR COUNTRY AS YOU ARE.

KENNETH ARNOLD
    BOISE IDAHO PILOTS LICENSE_____

24 333487.

Some Life Data on Kenneth Arnold

I was born March 29, 1915 in Subeka, Minnesota. I was a resident of Minnesota until I was six years old when my family moved to Scobey, Montana, where they homesteaded. My grandfather also homesteaded in Scobey, Montana, and became quite prominent in political circles along with Burton K. Wheeler, the famous Montana senator.

I went to grade school and high school at Minot, North Dakota. I entered scouting at twelve years of age and achieved the rank of Eagle scout before I was fourteen. My former scout executive was H. H. Prescott, now a regional commissioner for the Boy Scouts in Kansas City, Kansas.

As a boy, I was interested in athletics and was selected as an all-state end in 1932 and 1933 in the state of North Dakota. I entered the U. S. Olympic trials in fancy diving in 1932; I was a Red Cross Life Saving Examiner during the years of 1932, '33 and '34. I taught swimming and diving at scout camp and the municipal pool in Minot, North Dakota. I went to the University of Minnesota, where I swam and did fancy diving under Neils Thorpe, and also played football, under Bernie Bierman, but upon entering college I was unable to continue my football career because of an injured knee. My high school football coach was Glenn L. Jarrett, who is now the head football coach of the University of North Dakota. I had little or no finances, and my ambition in furthering my education in college was through my athletics. As a boy in Minot, North Dakota, I did a good deal of dog sled racing, placed first with my dog in 1930 in the Lions Club Dog Derby.

In 1938 I went to work for Red Comet, Inc. of Littleton, Colorado, a manufacturer of automatic fire fighting apparatus. In 1939 I was made district manager for them over a part of the western states, and in 1940 I established my own fire control supply known as the Great Western Fire Control Supply. I have been working as an independent fire control engineer since, and I handle, distribute, sell and install all types of automatic and manual fire fighting equipment in the rural areas over five western states.

My flying experience started as a boy in Minot, North Dakota, where I took my first flying lesson from Earl T. Vance, who was originally from Great Falls, Montana. Due to the high cost at that time, I was unable to continue my flying and did not fly of any great consequence until 1943. I was given my pilot certificate by Ed Leach, a senior CAA inspector of Portland, Oregon, and for the last three years have owned my own airplane, covering my entire territory with same and flying from forty to one hundred hours per month since. Due to the fact that I use an airplane entirely in my work, in January of this year I purchased a new Callair airplane, which is an airplane designed for high altitude take-offs and short rough field use.

In the type of flying I do, it takes a great deal of practice and judgment to be able to land in most any cow pasture and get out without injuring your airplane; the runways are very limited and the altitude is very high in some of the fields and places I have to go in my work. To date, I have landed in 823 cow pastures in mountain meadows, and in over a thousand hours a flat tire has been my greatest mishap.

The following story of what I observed over the Cascade mountains, as impossible as it may seem, is positively true. I never asked nor wanted any notoriety for just accidently being in the right spot at the right time to observe what I did. I reported something that I know any pilot would have reported. I don't think that in any way my observation was due to any sensitivity of eye sight or judgment than what is considered normal for any pilot.

On June 24th, Tuesday, 1947, I had finished my work for the Central Air Service at Chehalis, Washington, and at about two o'clock I took off from Chehalis, Washington, airport with the intention of going to Yakima, Wash. My trip was delayed for an hour to search for a large marine transport that supposedly went down near or around the southwest side of Mt.

27

Rainier in the State of Washington and to date has never been found.

I flew directly toward Mt. Rainier after reaching an altitude of about 9,500 feet, which is the approximate elevation of the high plateau from which Mt. Rainier rises. I had made one sweep of this high plateau to the westward, searching all of the various ridges for this marine ship and flew to the west down and near the ridge side of the canyon where Ashford, Washington, is located.

Unable to see anything that looked like the lost ship, I made a 300 degree turn to the right and above the little city of Mineral, starting again toward Mt. Rainier. I climbed back up to an altitude of approximately 9,200 feet.

The air was so smooth that day that it was a real pleasure flying and, as most pilots do when the air is smooth and they are flying at a higher altitude, I trimmed out my airplane in the direction of Yakima, Washington, which was almost directly east of my position, and simply sat in my plane observing the sky and the terrain.

There was a DC-4 to the left and to the rear of me approximately fifteen miles distance, and I should judge, at 14,000 foot elevation.

The sky and air was as clear as crystal. I hadn't flown more than two or three minutes on my course when a bright flash reflected on my airplane. It startled me as I thought I was too close to some other aircraft. I looked every place in the sky and couldn't find where the reflection had come from until I looked to the left and the north of Mt. Rainier where I observed a chain of nine peculiar looking aircraft flying from north to south at approximately 9,500 foot elevation and going, seemingly, in a definite direction of about 170 degrees.

They were approaching Mt. Rainier very rapidly, and I merely assumed they were jet planes. Anyhow, I discovered that this was where the reflection had come from, as two or three of them every few seconds would dip or change their course slightly, just enough for the sun to strike them at an angle that reflected brightly on my plane.

These objects being quite far away, I was unable for a few seconds to make out their shape or their formation. Very shortly they approached Mt. Rainier, and I observed their outline against the snow quite plainly.

I thought it was very peculiar that I couldn't find their tails but assumed they were some type of jet planes. I was determined to clock their speed, as I had two definite points I could clock them by; the air was so clear that it was very easy to see objects and determine their approximate shape and size at almost fifty miles that day.

I remember distinctly that my sweep second hand on my eight day clock, which is located on my instrument panel, read one minute to 3 P.M. as the first object of this formation passed the southern edge of Mt. Rainier. I watched these objects with great interest as I had never before observed airplanes flying so close to the mountain tops, flying directly south to the southeast down the hog's back of a mountain range. I would estimate their elevation could have varied a thousand feet one way or another up or down, but they were pretty much on the horizon to me which would indicate they were near the same elevation as I was.

They flew like many times I have observed geese to fly in a rather diagonal chain-like line as if they were linked together. They seemed to hold a definite direction but rather swerved in and out of the high mountain peaks. Their speed at the time did not impress me particularly, because I knew that our army and air forces had planes that went very fast.

What kept bothering me as I watched them flip and flash in the sun right along their path was the fact I couldn't make out any tail on them, and I am sure that any pilot would justify more than a second look at such a plane.

I observed them quite plainly, and I estimate my distance from them, which was almost at right angles, to be between twenty to twenty-five miles. I knew they must be very large to observe their shape at that distance, even on as clear a day as it was that Tuesday.

In fact I compared a zeus fastener or cowling tool I had in my pocket with them, holding it up on them

29

and holding it up on the DC-4 that I could observe at quite a distance to my left, and they seemed smaller than the DC-4; but, I should judge their span would have been as wide as the furtherest engines on each side of the fuselage of the DC-4.

The more I observed these objects, the more upset I became, as I am accustomed and familiar with most all objects flying whether I am close to the ground or at higher altitudes. I observed the chain of these objects passing another high snow-covered ridge in between Mt. Rainier and Mt. Adams, and as the first one was passing the south crest of this ridge the last object was entering the northern crest of the ridge.

As I was flying in the direction of this particular ridge, I measured it and found it to be approximately five miles so I could safely assume that the chain of these saucer like objects [was] at least five miles long. I could quite accurately determine their pathway due to the fact that there were several high peaks that were a little this side of them as well as higher peaks on the other side of their pathway.

As the last unit of this formation passed the southern most high snow-covered crest of Mt. Adams, I looked at my sweep second hand and it showed that they had travelled the distance in one minute and forty-two seconds. Even at the time this timing did not upset me as I felt confident after I would land there would be some explanation of what I saw.

A number of news men and experts suggested that I might have been seeing reflections or even a mirage. This I know to be absolutely false, as I observed these objects not only through the glass of my airplane but turned my airplanes sideways where I could open my window and observe them with a completely unobstructed view. (Without sun glasses)

Even though two minutes seems like a very short time to one on the ground, in the air in two minutes time a pilot can observe a great many things and anything within his sight of vision probably as many as fifty or sixty times.

I continued my search for the marine plane for another fifteen or twenty minutes and while searching for this marine plane, what I had just observed kept going through my mind. I became more disturbed, so after taking a last look at Tieton Reservoir I headed for Yakima.

I might add that my complete observation of these objects, which I could even follow by flashes as they passed Mt. Adams, was around two and one-half or three minutes, although, by the time they reached Mt. Adams, they were out of my range of vision as far as determining shape or form. Of course, when the sun reflected from one or two or three of those units, they appeared to be completely round; but, I am making a drawing to the best of my ability, which I am including, as to the shape I observed these objects to be as they passed the snow covered ridges as well as Mt. Rainier. When these objects were flying approximately straight and level, they were just a black thin line and when they flipped was the only time I could get a judgment as to their size.

These objects were holding an almost constant elevation; they did not seem to be going up or to be coming down, such as would be the case of rockets or artillery shells. I am convinced in my own mind that they were some type of airplane, even though they didn't conform with the many aspects of the conventional type of planes that I know.

Although these objects have been reported by many other observers throughout the United States, there have been six or seven other accounts written by some of these observers that I can truthfully say must have observed the same thing that I did; particularly, the descriptions of the three Western Air Lines (Cedar City, Utah) employees, the gentleman (pilot) from Oklahoma City and the locomotive engineer in Illinois, plus Capt. _____ and Co-Pilot _____ of United Air Lines.

Some descriptions could not be very accurate taken from the ground unless these saucer-like disks were at quite a great height and there is a possibility that all of the people who observed peculiar objects could have seen the same thing I did; but, it would have been very difficult from the ground to observe these for

31

more than four or five seconds, and there is always the possibility of atmospheric moisture and dust near the ground which could distort one's vision.

I have in my possession letters from all over the United States and people who profess that these objects have been observed over other portions of the world, principally Sweden, Bermuda, and California.

I would have given almost anything that day to have had a movie camera with a telephoto lens and from now on I will never be without one, but, to continue further with my story, when I landed at the Yakima, Washington, airport I described what I had seen to my very good friend, Al Baxter, who listened patiently and was very courteous but in a joking way didn't believe me.

I did not accurately measure the distance between these two mountains until I landed at Pendleton, Oregon, that same day where I told a number of pilot friends of mine what I had observed and they did not scoff or laugh but suggested they might be guided missiles or something new. In fact several former Army pilots informed me that they had been briefed before going into combat overseas that they might see objects of similar shape and design as I described and assured me that I wasn't dreaming or going crazy.

I quote _____, a former Army Air Force pilot who is now operating dusting operations at Pendleton, Oregon, "What you observed, I am convinced, is some type of jet or rocket propelled ship that is in the process of being tested by our government or even it could possibly be by some foreign government."

Anyhow, the news that I had observed these spread very rapidly and before the night was over I was receiving telephone calls from all parts of the world; and, to date I have not received one telephone call or one letter of scoffing or disbelief. The only disbelief that I know of was what was printed in the papers.

I look at this whole ordeal as not something funny as some people have made it out to be. To me it is mighty serious and since I evidently did observe something that at least Mr. John Doe on the street corner or Pete Andrews on the ranch has never heard about, is no reason that it does not exist. Even though I openly invited an investigation by the Army and the FBI as to the authenticity of my story or a mental or a physical examination as to my capabilities, I have received no interest from these two important protective forces of our country; I will go so far as to assume that any report I gave to the United and Associated Press and over the radio on two different occasions which apparently set the nation buzzing, if our Military Intelligence was not aware of what I observed, they would be the very first people that I could expect as visitors.

I have received lots of requests from people who told me to make a lot of wild guesses. I have based what I have written here in this article on positive facts and as far as guessing what it was I observed, it is just as much a mystery to me as it is to the rest of the world.

My pilot's license is _____. I fly a Callair airplane; it is a three-place single engine land ship that is designed and manufactured at Afton, Wyoming as an extremely high performance, high altitude airplane that was made for mountain work. The national certificate of my plane is _____.

/s/ Kenneth Arnold
Boise, Idaho

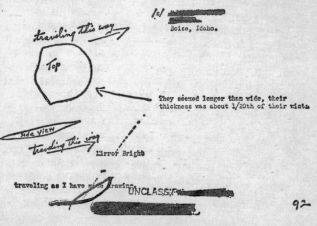

/s/ ████████
████
Boise, Idaho.

traveling this way →

Top

← They seemed longer than wide, their thickness was about 1/20th of their width.

Side view
traveling this way
Mirror Bright

traveling as I have made drawing.
UNCLASSIFI████

9?

Incident #17—Mt. Rainier, Washington—24 June 1947

There appears to be no astronomical explanation for this classic incident, which is the prototype of many of the later flying saucer stories.

It is impossible to explain this incident away as sheer nonsense, if any credence at all is given to Mr. Arnold's integrity. However, certain inconsistencies can be pointed out in the facts as reported:

Arnold's attention was first drawn to the objects by a bright flash on his plane, which was followed by numerous other similar flashes. If these were something like the flash one gets from a distant mirror, it means that the reflection was specular, or direct. For a direct reflection, the angle between the observer, sun, and object must be "just right," and at such distances as 20 or 25 miles, the chance of a series of direct reflections is extremely small. If the object was a diffuse reflector—that is, scattering the sunlight falling on it, much as the moon or a balloon does—then at such a distance it seems quite unlikely that Mr. Arnold would have been startled, or that our attention would have been called to it, unless the objects reflecting were extremely large.

The supersonic speeds called for if the estimated distance is correct also throw suspicion on the original calculations; by computation (see below) it can be seen that, considering the detail which Arnold observed in the objects, at least one of his estimates must have been erroneous:

Arnold states that the objects seemed about 20 times as long as wide. Let us assume that the thickness was just discernible, which means that the object was just at the limit of resolution of the eye. Now, the eye cannot resolve objects that subtend an angle of appreciably less than 3 minutes of arc, and, in general, for any detail to be seen at all, the angle subtended must be much greater. Even if we assume the limiting resolution of 3 minutes, then, if

34

the distance was 25 miles, elementary calculations show that each object must have been at least 100 feet thick, and if, as Arnold's drawing indicates, the object was some 20 times longer than wide, it must have been about 2000 feet long.

Looking at the matter in another way and assuming that Arnold's estimate of distance as 20 to 25 miles (12,000 feet) and his estimate of length as 45 to 50 feet are both correct, then it can be shown that the object will subtend an angle of only about 80 seconds of arc, which is definitely below the limit of resolution of the eye.

If Arnold actually saw the objects, and if his estimate of distance is correct, that of size cannot be, and *vice versa*. It seems most logical to assume that his estimate of distance is far too great. In fact, assuming a reasonable limiting size to the objects of 400 feet, in order to show the detail that Arnold's drawings indicate, the distance must have been not over roughly six miles. At this distance the objects would have travelled 11 miles (rather than 47 miles) in 102 seconds, or at a rate of approximately 400 MPH. (Arnold's original estimate is also incorrect; if the objects had travelled 47 miles in 102 seconds, they would have been travelling at a rate of approximately 1700 MPH, not 1200.)

In view of the above, it appears probable that whatever objects were observed were travelling at subsonic speeds and may, therefore, have been some sort of known aircraft.

Kenneth Arnold Case

Arnold made drawings of objects showing definite shape and stated that objects seemed about 20 times as long as wide, estimating them as 45–50 feet long.

He also estimated the distance as 20–25 miles and clocked them as going 47 miles in 102 seconds. (1700 MPH)

If the distance were correct, then in order for details to be seen, objects must have been of the order of 100 × 2000 feet in size.

If we adopt a reasonable size, Arnold's own estimate, in fact, of 50 feet long, hence about 3 feet wide, the objects must have been closer than a mile, obviously contrary to his statement.

If we adopt a reasonable limiting size to the objects of 20 × 400 feet, objects must have been closer than six miles to have shown the detail indicated by Arnold. At this distance, angular speed observed corresponds to a maximum speed of 400 MPH.

In all probability therefore, objects were much closer than thought and moving at definitely "sub-sonic" speeds.

Note: Observational data taken from original Arnold files.

J. Allen Hynek

Memorandum for the Office in Charge: 16 July 1947

1. On 12 July 1947, a call was made at the newspaper office of the "Idaho Daily Statesman," Boise, Idaho. The aviation editor of the paper, Mr. David M. Johnson, was interviewed in regard to how well he knew Mr. Kenneth Arnold of Boise, Idaho, and as to the credibility of any statement made by Mr. Arnold. The purpose of this interview was an attempt to verify statements made by Mr. Kenneth Arnold on 26 June 1947 to various national news services to the effect that he, Mr. Arnold, had seen 9 objects flying in the air above the Cascade Mountain Range of Washington. These objects were subsequently referred to as flying saucers or flying disks and will here-in-after be referred to as such in this report. Mr. Johnson stated that he had known Mr. Arnold for quite a period of time, having had relations with Mr. Arnold on various occasions, due to the fact that both he, Mr. Johnson, and Mr. Arnold were private fliers and frequently got together to talk shop. Mr. Johnson stated that as far as he was concerned anything Mr.

Arnold said could be taken very seriously and that he, Mr. Johnson, actually believed that Mr. Arnold had seen the aforementioned flying disks. Mr. Johnson stated that after Mr. Arnold reported having seen the flying disks, that the editor of the paper had assigned him, Mr. Johnson, the assignment of taking the airplane belonging to the newspaper and exhausting all efforts to prove or disprove the probability of flying disks having been seen in the northwest area. The results of this assignment to Mr. Johnson and what he subsequently saw is put forth in a sworn statement signed by Mr. Johnson attached to this report as Exhibit B.

AGENT'S NOTES: Mr. Johnson is a man of approximately 33 to 35 years of age. From all appearances he is a very reserved type of person. Mr. Johnson has logged 2800 hours of flying time in various types of airplanes up to and including multi-engine aircraft. During part of the war years, Mr. Johnson was the first pilot of a B-29 type aircraft being assigned to the Twentieth USAAF and stationed on Tinian Island, in the Pacific. It is the personal opinion of the interviewer that Mr. Johnson actually saw what he states that he saw in the attached report. It is also the opinion of the interviewer that Mr. Johnson would have much more to lose than gain and would have to be very strongly convinced that he actually saw something before he would report such an incident and open himself for the ridicule that would accompany such a report.

1 Incl: Exhibit "B"

FRANK M. BROWN, S/A, CIC 5th AF

Statement of David N. Johnson at Boise, Idaho, July 12, 1947

To Whom It May Concern:
On the sixth day of July, 1947, I received from James L. Brown, general manager of the Statesman

Newspapers, incorporated in Idaho as The Statesman Printing company, an assignment which was in substance:

"Conduct an aerial search of the northwest states in an effort to see and photograph a flying disc. Conduct this patrol for so long a time as you believe reasonable, or until you see a flying disc."

In accordance to these instructions, I took the Statesman's airplane, and with Kenneth Arnold as passenger, flew a seven and one-half hour mission on the seventh day of July, 1947. This mission was without result. It covered an area embracing the confines of the Fanford plant in Washington, and territory between and around Mr. Rainier and Mt. Adams, where Arnold first reported seeing objects hence forth described as saucers or discs.

On the eighth day of July, 1947, I took an AT-6 of the 190th Fighter squadron, Idaho National Guard, of which I am a member, and flew to northern Idaho, into northwestern Montana briefly, to Spokane, Washington, and back to Boise by way of Walla Walla, Washington, and Pendleton, Oregon. This search also was negative.

On the ninth day of July, 1947, I continued the search, again using a national guard AT-6, this time centering my efforts over the Owyhee mountains west and southwest of Boise, a portion of the Mountain Home desert on a track southeast of the Mountain Home army air base, thence into the Sawtooth mountains, and back in the general direction of Boise on a line carrying me well to the north of the Shafer butte forest service lookout station, into the Horseshoe Bend area, and thence back in a southwesterly direction to a point between Boise and the village of Meridian, west of Boise a few miles.

During this search, which lasted approximately two and one-half hours, I flew under and around rapidly forming cumulus clouds over that area known as the Camas Prairie, east of Boise. The clouds were near the village of Fairfield in that valley, and Fairfield is 75 miles airline distance east of Boise. At that time I saw nothing in the vicinity of these clouds.

38

At the time I reach the point between Boise and Meridian, I was flying at an altitude of 14,000 feet mean sea level, which would be a mean average of 11,000 feet above the earth in this area, not considering errors in the altimeter induced either by barometric changes since my takeoff, or by the temperature at that altitude.

I turned the aircraft on an easterly heading, pointing toward Gowen Field, and had flown on that course for perhaps a minute when there suddenly appeared in the left hand portion of my field of vision an object which was black and round.

I immediately centered my gaze on the object. At that time, due to its erratic movement, I thought I was seeing a weather balloon. I called the CAA's communication station at Boise, and asked if the weather station had recently released a balloon. The reply from communicator Albertson was that the bureau had not. I do not remember his exact words; I am under the impression he said "not for several hours" or gave me the exact time of the previous release, which was around 0830 that day.

Upon hearing this response, I turned the aircraft broadside to the object, pulted back the plexiglass covering to avoid any distortion, took my camera from the map case, and exposed about 10 seconds' duration of eight millimeter motion picture film. During the time the camera was at eye level, I could not see the object because of minuteness of scope introduced by the optical view finder with which the camera, an f.1.9 Eastman, was equipped.

Taking the camera away and once again centering my gaze on the object, I observed it to roll so that its edge was presented to me. At this time it flashed once in the sunlight. It then appeared as a thin black line. It then performed a maneuver which looked as if it had begun a slow roll, or a barrel roll, which instead of being completed, was broken off at about the 180-degree point. The object rolled out of the top of the maneuver at this point, and I lost sight of it.

This entire performance was observed against the background of clouds previously forming over the

Camas Prairie. The object appeared to me, relatively, as the size of a twenty-five cent piece. I do not know how far away it was. I do not know, nor can I truthfully estimate, its speed. I can only say it was not an airplane, and if it was at a very great distance from me, its speed was great, taking into consideration that apparent speed is reduced to the viewer if an object is a very great distance away.

I forgot to look at my clock to determine the exact time I saw the object. The CAA's log of radio contacts shows my first contact to have been made at 1217 hours. But a few seconds elapsed between the time I first saw the object and the time I called the CAA's station.

I subsequently related over the radio a description of what I saw, and communicator Albertson may remember it. The contsrol tower may have a recording of the conversation. I have not checked to determine that.

The purpose of my relating over the air what I saw was to enable rapid transmission of the report to the newspaper, for at that time I was on assignment and my energies thenceforth were devoted to (1) transmitting the information and (2) conducting a further search, which I did after landing for fuel and to make some telephone calls.

The next search, begun within half an hour after landing from the first one, consumed another two hours, but was negative. I explored thoroughly the region where I saw the object.

Immediately after sighting the object, I asked if there were other aircraft in the area. There was a P-51 of the 190th squadron practicing maneuvers in the vicinity of Kuna, but that was behind me. A C-82 passed over Boise, but I saw that aircraft go beneath me by some 2,000 feet.

The P-51 in the vicinity of Kuna proceeded to the area where I saw the object, at my request, and conducted a search. It was negative. During the afternoon, flights of P-51s were sent out to cover the area, and some of them flew high altitude missions on oxygen. These searches were negative.

I was subsequently informed that personnel on both

the United Air Lines side of Gowen Field, and on the national guard side, observed a black object maneuvering in front of the same cloud formation, which by now had grown so that the clouds reached a probable height of 19,000 or 20,000 feet from a mean base of 13,000 or 14,000 feet, mean sea level. Three of these men were national guard personnel and I talked to them, asking them to describe what they saw, before telling them my story, in order to avoid suggestion or inference of a leading nature. They saw the object (from the ground) while I was on my second search. They believed the time to have been 1400 hours. The object performed in the same erratic manner, they said, as I observed.

The above is the extent of the story, and information concerning myself is now in order.

I have approximately 2800 hours of flying time in equipment ranging from primary trainers to B-29s. Of course, that does not increase my powers of observation except as to those practiced daily by an airman. It does not make my eyesight any sharper except again as to the incidental demands upon the eyes of a pilot.

At the time of the experience related above, I had flown fourteen and one-half hours on an assignment to find a disc and if possible to photograph it. In all frankness, I was tired. I may have been suffering, although slightly, from want of oxygen.

Prior to sighting the object, I had concluded there was no point in pressing the search, that I probably would never see the disc-like objects referred to by Arnold and by Captain _____ of United Air Lines.

At all times during the search, both on that day and the two preceding days (particularly when I was with Arnold) I had literally talked to myself to keep beating into my head that I would not fall victim to the power of suggestion or self-hypnosis arising from a naturally very intent desire to find a disc and bring success to the assignment given me.

I therefore do not believe that I was the victim of suggestion or hypnosis. I am familiar with the optical illusion of a fixed object beginning to move after it is

41

watched a sufficient length of time. I know what tricks the eyes will play as to moving bodies, and have learned of this particularly during night formation flying.

I saw the object appear suddenly. If it had moved in a jerky fashion (as it did at first) for the full length of time I observed it, I would not be so strong in saying that I saw something not an aircraft, not a balloon, and not a corpuscle moving across the retina of either eye. The maneuver described by the object when its edge was presented to me convinces me that I saw an object actually performing in an erratic flight path.

The question remains, of course, whether I saw it. The motion picture film, developed and processed by R. W. Stohr in the Eastman laboratories at 241 Battery Street, San Francisco, showed no trace of any object. Stohr says that if it was more than a mile distant from me at the size I described, the object would not have registered sufficiently on the film to be shown. He said it probably was too far away to be apparent even though great enlargement in that case is limited because of the size of the film and the fact I did not have any telescopic equipment on the lens. The exposure was f.16, stop set at infinity, at a speed of 16 frames per second.

I have worried over this matter a great deal since seeing it. I "took myself aside" and said, "Come now, Johnson, don't be stupid." But I cannot bring myself to the point of thinking I did not see anything. The impression of the moment was too vivid, too realistic, and I knew in the air when I saw that partial slow roll or barrel roll, that I was not a victim of illusion.

I trust this matter will be of help to those investigating the flying disc phenomena which have been reported.

A chart is attached depicting the movements of the object as I saw it.

This statement is made voluntarily and freely, in response to the request of Mr. Brown and Captain Davidson, who called on me this morning.

/s/ David N. Johnson

Subscribed and sworn to before me, a notary public,
this 12th day of July, 1947.

/s/ _____

Notary public for
Ada county Idaho.

Chapter Two: UFOlogy's First Martyr

The story is well known about the former war
correspondent's interview with an Air Force major
who on V-E Day told a number of journalists about
Allied experience with what he termed "flying
saucers." It is interesting to note that this B-17
pilot with fifty missions under his belt used the
term "flying saucers" two years before the Kenneth Arnold sighting near Mount Rainier, when the
term was supposed to have been coined.

"Suddenly they'd be on our wing, six or eight of
them, flying pefect formation," the major told the
skeptical newsman. "You turn and bank, they turn
and bank; you climb, they climb; you dive, they
dive—you just couldn't shake 'em. Little, dirty
grey aluminum things, ten or twelve feet in diameter, shaped just like saucers; no cockpits, no
windows, no sign of life . . . when the things got
tired of the game, they would just take off into
space and disappear, flying at the most incredible
speeds, five thousand miles an hour or more."

Although the war correspondent was skeptical
of the major's story, he later discussed "flying
saucers" with a man who had been the SHAEF G2
(Supreme Headquarters, Allied Expeditionary Force,
intelligence officer) in Paris near the end of the
war. This man told him that SHAEF had known all

about the pilots' reports of flying saucers. "They were considered so secret they were in the 'eyes only' file . . ."

It would seem, then, that in the pre-Arnold days Air Force pilots were quite voluble about flying saucers. We have here a paradoxical reversal: During the closing days of the Second World War, it was members of the Air Force who were going around trying to convince people that its pilots were seeing flying saucers. Then, post-1947, the Air Force became the official debunker and scoffer in regard to civilian sightings of UFOs.

Official Air Force policy that flying saucers were "hallucinations" did not deter Captain Thomas Mantell from going in pursuit of the UFO that had been hovering over Godman Field Air Base on January 7, 1948.

The strange case of Captain Mantell was sketched in the Introduction. The pilot's last words: "It looks metallic and it's tremendous in size. It's above me and I'm gaining on it. . . ." set off a controversy which still rages today. There are reports of a closed-casket funeral because of mysterious wounds on Captain Mantell's body; there are reports that no body could be found in the wreckage of the P-51. Whatever the truth of the matter, the Air Force had once again found itself dramatically involved in the enigma of flying saucers.

Now, for the first time, we are able to examine the extent of the Air Force's investigation into this perplexing case. We can judge for ourselves whether Captain Mantell became UFOlogy's first martyr while pursuing the planet Venus.

The Mantell Case

On 7 January 1948, at 1320 (1:20 pm) hours, the tower crew at Godman Field, Kentucky sighted a bright disc shaped object which they were unable to identify. The presence of this object was brought to the attention of the Base Operations Officer, Base Intelligence Officer, and eventually the Base Commander, but the object remained unidentified. At 1445 (2:45 pm), a flight of five * P-51's flew over Godman Field. The object was still visible, and the Flight Commander, Captain Mantell, stated he was on a ferry mission, but would investigate. Captain Mantell then started a spiraling climb to 15,000 feet, then continued to climb on a heading of 220°, the approximate direction of the UFO from Godman Field. At 15,000 feet the wing men turned back because they were not completely outfitted for flights requiring oxygen. The wing men attempted to contact Captain Mantell by radio but were unsuccessful. Captain Mantell made a transmission at 15,000 feet to the effect that he had the object in sight, and was still climbing to investigate. The 15,000 foot transmission was the last known of Captain Mantell.

It is the [Air Technical Information Command] opinion that Captain Mantell lost consciousness due to oxygen starvation, the aircraft being trimmed continued to climb until increasing altitude caused a sufficient loss of power for it to level out. The aircraft then began a turn to the left due to torque and as the wing drooped so did the nose until the aircraft was in a tight diving spiral. The uncontrolled descent resulted in excessive speed causing the aircraft to disintegrate. It is believed that Captain Mantell never regained consciousness. This is born out by the fact that the canopy lock was still in place after the crash, discounting any attempt to abandon the aircraft. The UFO was in no way *directly* responsible for this experienced pilot conducting a high altitude flight without the necessary oxygen equipment.

There were two conceptions as to the identity of the object; Venus, one of the brightest objects in our heavens, or a large balloon used for high altitude experimental flights and known as "sky hooks." These

* Documents following generally state four—ed.

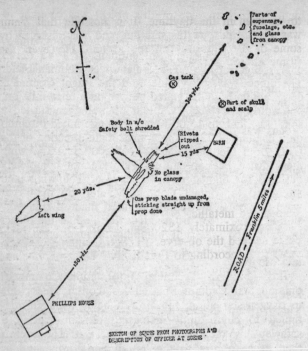

N

8 ⊙ ; Parts of
fuselage, etc.
and glass
from canopy

Gas tank
⊗

⊗ Part of skull
and scalp

Body in a/c
Safety belt shredded

Rivets
ripped
out
— 15 yds. —

BARN

No glass
in canopy

20 yds.

One prop blade undamaged,
sticking straight up from
prop dome

Left wing

ROAD — Franklin 5 miles

150 yds.

PHILLIPS HOUSE

SKETCH OF SCENE FROM PHOTOGRAPHS AND
DESCRIPTION OF OFFICER AT SCENE

balloons fly at altitudes in excess of 60,000 feet and reach diameters of approximately 100 feet.

During the period of this sighting the Navy was conducting a program utilizing "sky hook" balloons. The Navy program was classified at this time and therefore these balloon flights were known only to those with a "need-to-know." It was subsequently determined that on the date of the Godman sighting a balloon was released by the Navy from Clinton County airport in Ohio. The release time of the balloon was related to a wind plot for 7 January 1948, and it revealed that the balloon would have been in the area of Godman at the time of the sighting.

On 7 January 1948, at the time of the sighting, Venus was also in a directional position which coincided with that of the UFO. This planet's angular distance from the sun was rather small but bright enough to be seen in the daytime. It is possible that Venus was also a cause to this sighting, and was observed by some of the witnesses on the ground. However, the prime culprit is believed to have been the sky hook balloon released by the Navy. Captain Mantell was attempting to close in on this balloon which was still more than 40,000 feet above him.

It is the Air Force conclusion in this case that Venus was probably the original cause of the sighting since the object remained in the area for a long period of time and was relatively stationary. The object pursued by Captain Mantell is believed to have been the sky hook balloon, and this object was probably seen by other witnesses who described the object as pear shaped and metallic.

At approximately 1320 Sgt. Cook from the CO's office notified the observer (T/Sgt. Quinton A. Blackwell) that according to Fort Knox Military Police and "B" Town State Police,* a large circular object about 250 to 300 feet in diameter was over *Mansville, Kentucky*. Advised him to check with Army Flight Svc. They advised negative but shortly thereafter reported object over *Irvington, Kentucky,* then *Owensboro, Kentucky*. Object first sighted by Blackwell about 1345 to 1350 over south Godman Field.

Verification:
1st Lt. Orner (Detachment Commander)
Captain Carter (Operations Officer)
Colonel Hix (CO) sighted it about 1420

At approximately 1430 to 1440, four P-51's approached Godman f/south enroute f/Marietta, Georgia to Standiford Field, Kentucky. Blackwell asked Flight Leader NG 869 to attempt to identify object. Accompanied by two other planes he proceeded south f/Godman. Fourth plane proceeded to Standiford Field alone.

About 1445, flight leader (NG 869) reported sighting object "ahead and above—still climbing." At 15,000 feet he reported "Object directly ahead and above and moving about half my speed." Again "it

---

* T. Sgt. Blackwell's statement says "E" Town State Police—ed.

appears metallic of tremendous size." Still later "I'm still climbing—object is above and ahead moving about my speed or faster—I'm trying to close in for better look." This was about 1515. Five minutes later the other two ships turned back. NG 800 reported "it appeared like the reflection of sunlight on an airplane canopy." Shortly afterward this same pilot (NG 800) resumed search going to 33,000 feet, 100 miles south but did not sight anything.

Unknown object first reported by Military Police at Fort Knox, approximately 1400 CST, vicinity of Maysville. Later over *Irvington and Owensboro, Kentucky*. Sighted, Godman, by Blackwell, Chief Control Tower. Lieutenant Orner then left office of CO, proceeding to Control Tower where he sighted a small white object in the southwest sky. It appeared stationary. Could not determine if object radiated or reflected light. Through binocs it appeared partially as parachute with bright sun reflecting from top of the silk, however, there seemed to be some red light around the lower part of it. Three P-51's alerted to pursue object. Took a course of around 210°. Approximately 5" later object sighted. NG 861 (flight leader reported it "high and traveling about ½ his speed at '12 o'clock'." Later he stated he was "closing in to take a good look." This was his last message. NG 800 then reported high and ahead of wing men at approximately 18,000 to 20,000 feet and wing men at approximately 15,000 feet. Wing men (NG 800) returned for fuel and resumed pursuit going to altitude of 33,000 feet but did not sight object. At about 1654 Lieutenant Orner left tower.

Later, Lieutenant Orner returned to Control Tower (about 1735 CST and perceived bright light at a position of about 240° aximuth and 8° elevation. It was a round object and did not resemble a star. Although there was a base the object remained visible and did not disappear until it went below the level of the earth in manner similar to the sun or moon setting. This object was viewed and tracked with the Weather Station theoelite from the hanger roof.

RELIABILITY: a. Verified by Commanding Officer,

48

Operations Officer, S-2 and Executive Officer. However, these officers were apparently present when second sighting took place.

b. It is doubtful that Venus could be observed by the unaided eye from the ground or 15,000 feet as it would probably be hidden by the high degree of sky brightness due to its proximity to the Sun.

c. Jupiter is the only other planet within ±90° of the Sun during this period and its magnitude of brightness is only −1.4 as compared with −3·4 of Venus, making it impossible to observe with the unaided eye. However, the following figures on the Moon are submitted for your information:

Time Local	Altitude	Azimuth
10:00	28°00+	197°
10:30	26°00+	204°
11:00	23°00+	211°
11:30	20°00+	217°
12:00	17°00+	223°
12:30	13°00+	228°

J. C. HARVELL VSB
Colonel, ASAF VLB/md
Chief, Equipment 25136
Laboratory
Engineering Division Bldg. 45

Report of Unusual Incident

At approximately 1400E, 7 January 1948, Kentucky State Police reported to Ft. Knox Military Police they had sighted an unusual aircraft or object flying through air, circular in appearance approximately 250–300 feet in diameter, moving westward at "a pretty good clip." This in turn was reported to the Commanding Officer, Godman Field, Ft. Knox, Kentucky, who called Godman Tower and asked them to have Flight Service check with Flight Test at Wright Field to see if they had any experimental aircraft in that area. Captain Hooper at Flight Test Operations stated,

"We have no experimental aircraft in that area, however we do have a B-29 and an A-26 on photo missions in that area." This information was relayed to Godman Tower by dispatcher on duty and a verification on report was asked for.

Godman Tower later called back and stated first report was by radio to Ft. Knox Military Police and followed by telephone call to same from State Police.

Information on P-51's and further reports are reported as follows by Captain Arthur T. Jehli, Supervisor of the 1600E–2400E shift.

"When the 1600E–2400E shift reported for duty we were advised that a 'disc,' or balloon, or some strange object was seen hovering in the vicinity of Godman Field. This object was seen by the Commanding Officer and Operations Officer of Godman Field who advised that they would attempt to send aircraft to ascertain the size and shape of the object.

"At this time there was a flight of 4 P-51's enroute from Marietta, Georgia to Standiford Field, Louisville, Kentucky. The lead ship was NG 3869, pilot Mantell. The Commanding Officer, Godman Field contacted this pilot and requested that he investigate the object overhead.

"One of the ships of the formation, NG 336 pilot Hendrichs, landed at Standiford Field. The 3 other aircraft started to climb toward the object.

"At 22,000 feet pilot Hammond, NG 737, advised Clements, NG 800, that he had no oxygen equipment. Both pilots then returned to Standiford Field; pilot Mantell, NG 3869, continued climbing.

"Pilot Clements, NG 800, refueled and went back up to 32,000 feet but did not see either the strange object or the aircraft NG 3869 again, and so returned to Standiford Field.

"At 1750E, Standiford Field advised that NG 3869, pilot Mantell, crashed 5 miles SW Franklin, Kentucky at approximately 1645C.

"We then sent an arrival of 1500C for the 3 aircraft, NG 336, NG 737, and NG 800, also notified Maxwell Flight Service Center that NG 3869 had crashed.

"Maxwell Flight Service Center made a long distance call to Franklin, Kentucky and spoke to police officer Joe Walker, who took charge at the scene of the accident.

"Officer Walker stated that when he arrived the pilot's body had been removed from the aircraft. Upon questioning eye witnesses, Officer Walker learned that the aircraft had exploded in the air before it hit the ground, but, that the aircraft did not burn upon contact with the ground.

"The wreckage was scattered over an area of about one mile, and at that time the tail section, one wing, and the propeller had not been located.

"Lt Tyler, Operations Officer at Standiford Field, departed Standiford Field for Bolling Green, Kentucky in NG 8101 to investigate the accident—Also at our suggestion an investigation party and Military Police were dispatched from Godman Field to the scene.

"So much for the accident—now hold on to your hat!

"Godman Tower again contacted us to report that there was a large light in the sky in the approximate position of the object seen earlier. Then Lockbourne Tower and Clinton County Tower advised a great ball of light was traveling southwest across the sky.

"We then contacted Olmsted Flight Service Center and gave them all the information available to deliver to the Air Defense Command at Mitchel Field, Hempstead, New York.

"Later we received a call from St. Louis Tower advising that a great ball of light was passing directly over the field—Scott Tower also verified this.

"We then received a call from Air Defense Command through Olmsted Flight Service Center advising us to alert Coffeville, Kansas, Ft. Smith, Arkansas, and Kansas City, Missouri, and that they had plotted the object as moving WSW at 250 miles per hour.

"We then received information from Maxwell Flight Service Center that a Dr. Seyfert, an astronomer at Vanderbilt University, had spotted an object SSE of Nashville, Tennessee that he identified as a pear shaped

51

balloon with cables and a basket attached, moving first SSE, then W, at a speed of 10 miles per hour at 25,000 feet. This was observed between 1630 and 1645C.

"Olmsted Flight Service Center then advised us to instruct Godman Field to forward a complete report of the whole incident to Air Defense Command at Mitchel Field, Hempstead, New York as soon as possible.

"The Military Police at the scene of the accident called back and advised Godman Field that someone at Madisonville, Kentucky had observed, through a Finch telescope, an object described as cone shaped, 100 feet from top to bottom, 43 feet across, and 4 miles high proceeding SW at 10 miles per hour.

"All this time the weather observer at Godman Field was spotting the object with a Theodolite and keeping a record of times, elevations and azimuths.

"St. Louis ATC advised of an article printed in the 'Edwardsville Intelligencer,' Edwardsville, Illinois, describing an object, over the town at 07200, of aluminum appearance without apparent wings or control surfaces which was moving southwest. This object remained visible for about 30 minutes. This article went on to describe the amazement and wondering of the editor regarding this object—and you can bet that he was no more confused than I am at this moment."

315 AF base
Godman Field, Fort Knox, Kentucky

9 January 1948

At approximately 1420, 7 Jan 48, I accompanied Lt. Col. E. G. Wood to the Godman Field Control Tower to observe "an object hanging high in the sky south of Godman."

Shortly after reaching the tower, Col. Guy F. Hix, Commanding Officer, was summoned; it was at that time that I first sighted the bright silver object.

Approximately five minutes after Col. Hix came into the tower, a flight of four F-51's flew over Godman. An officer in the tower requested that the Tower Operator call this flight and ask the Flight Leader to investigate this object if he had sufficient fuel. The Flight Leader (Capt. Thomas F. Mantell) answered that he would, and requested a bearing on this object. At that time one member of the flight informed the leader that it was time for him to land and broke off from the formation. This A/C was heard requesting landing instructions from his home field, Standiford, in Louisville.

In the meantime the remaining three F-51's were climbing on the course given to them by Godman Tower towards this object that still appeared stationary. The Tower then advised the Flight Leader to correct his course 5 degrees to the left; the Flight Leader acknowledged this correction and also reported his position at 7,500 feet and climbing. Immediately following the Flight Leader's transmission, another member of the Flight asked "Where in the hell are we going?" In a few minutes the Flight Leader called out an object "twelve o'clock high." Asked to describe this object, he said that it was bright and that it was climbing away from him. When asked about its speed, the Flight Leader stated it was going about half his speed, approximately 180 M.P.H.

Those of us in the Tower lost sight of the flight, but could still see this object. Shortly after the last transmission, the Flight Leader said he was at 15,000 ft, and still climbing after "it," but that he judged the speed to be the same as his. At that time a member of the flight called to the leader and requested that he "level off," but we heard no reply from the leader. That was the last message received from any member of the flight by Godman Tower.

"CERTIFIED A TRUE COPY"

James F. Duesler, Jr.
Captain, USAF

The undersigned was on duty at Godman Field 7 Jan. 48 as Operations Officer.

At approximately 1400 hours and 7 minutes, 7 Jan 48 I received a call from Lt. Orner, AACS Detachment Commander, that the Tower had spotted an unidentified object and requested that I take a look. Lt. Orner pointed out the object to the southwest, which was easily discernible with the naked eye. The object appeared round and white (whiter than the clouds that passed in front of it) and could be seen through cirrus clouds. After looking through field glasses for approximately 3 or 4 minutes, I called Col. Hix's office, advising that office of the object's presence. Lt. Col. Wood and Capt. Duesler came to the tower immediately. Col. Hix followed them.

About this time a flight of four P-51 aircraft were noticed approaching from the south. I asked Tec. Sgt. Blackwell, Tower Operator to contact the planes and see if they could take a look at the object for us. The planes were contacted and stated they had sufficient gas to take a look. One of the planes proceeded on to Standiford, the other planes were given a heading of 230°. One of the planes said he spotted the object at 1200 o'clock and was climbing toward it. One of the planes then said, "This is 15,000 ft., let's level out." One [of] the planes, at this point (apparently the plane who saw the subject) estimated its speed (the object's) at 18 CM.P.H. A few seconds later he stated the object was going up and forward as fast as he was. He stated that he was going to 20,000 feet, and if no closer was going to abandon the chase. This was the last radio contact I heard. It was impossible to identify which plane was doing the talking in the above report. Later we heard that one plane had landed at Standiford to get fuel and oxygen to resume the search.

The undersigned reported to Flight Service a description, position of the object while the planes searched for it.

Gary W. Carter
Captain, USAF

9 January 1948

Statement of T Sgt Quinton A. Blackwell

I, T. Sgt. Quinton A. Blackwell, AFI8162475, was on duty as chief operator in the Control Tower at Godman Field, Ky. on the afternoon of January 1948. Up until 1315 or 1320 matters were routine. At approximately that time I received a telephone call from Sgt. Cook, Col. Hix's office, stating that according to Ft. Knox Military Police and "E" Town state police, a large circular object from 250 to 300 feet in diameter over Mansville, Ky. and requested I check with Army Flight Service to see if any unusual type aircraft was in that vicinity. Flight Service advised negative on the aircraft and took the other info, requesting our CO verify the story. Shortly afterward Flight Service gave Godman Tower positions on an object over Irvington, Ky. then Owensboro, Ky. of about the same size and description. About 1345 or 1350 I sighted an object in the sky to the South of Godman Field. As I wanted verification, I called my Detachment Commander, 1st Lt. Orner, to the Tower. After he had sighted the object, he called for the Operations Officer, Capt. Carter, over the teletalk box from the Traffic Deck. He came up stairs immediately, and looked at the objects through field glasses in the Tower. He then called for the CO, Col. Hix. He came to the tower about 1420 (approx) and sighted the object immediately. About 1430 to 1440 a flight of four P-51's approached Godman Field from the South, enroute from Marietta, Ga. to Standiford Field, Ky. As they passed over the tower I called them on "B" channel, VHF and asked the flight leader, NG 869, if he had enough gas and if so, would he mind trying to identify an object in the sky to the South of Godman Field. He replied in the affirmative and made a right turn around with two planes and proceeded South from Godman Field. The fourth plane proceeded on to Standiford Field alone. The three ship formation proceeded South on a heading of 210°, climbing steadily. About 1445 the flight leader, NG 869, reported seeing the object "ahead and above, I'm still climbing." To which a wing man retorted, "What the

Hell. are we looking for?" The leader reported at 15,000 ft. that "The object is directly ahead of and above me now, moving about half my speed." When asked for a description he replied "It appears metallic object of tremendous size". At 15,000 ft., the flight leader reported, "I'm still climbing, the object is above and ahead of me moving at about my speed or faster. I'm trying to close in for a better look." This last contact was at about 1515. About 5 minutes afterward, the other two ships in the flight turned back. As they passed over Godman NG 800 reported "It appears like the reflection of sunlight on an airplane canopy." Shortly afterward, the same pilot and plane took off from Standiford and resumed the search. He went to 33,000 feet one hundred miles South and did not sight anything. I left the Control Tower shortly afterward.

Statement of PFC Stanley Oliver   9 January 1948

I, Pfc. Stanley Oliver, was on duty in the Control Tower at Godman Field on the afternoon of 7 January 1948. When first heard of the object in the sky about 1320 CST, we received a phone call from Colonel Hix's office that a large object was sighted at Mansville, Kentucky, the supposed object supposed to be about 250 feet to 300 feet in diameter at 1330 CST or more.

Sgt. Blackwell sighted an object to the southwest of Godman Field and he asked me if I saw it. I saw the object but thought I was imagining I saw it and Sgt. Blackwell told me to look again. This time I was really sure I saw an object and then we called Lt. Orner, who came to the Control Tower and he too saw the object. Lt. Orner then called Captain Carter who after coming to the Control Tower, also saw this object. Captain Carter called Colonel Hix who came to the Control Tower and he too saw the object. We all then attempted to figure out just what it could be and to me it had the resemblance of an ice cream cone topped with red.

At or about 1445 CST we sighted five (5) P-51 aircraft coming on from the southwest and as they came over the Control Tower someone suggested contacting the aircraft. Sgt. Blackwell contacted them on "B" channel (VHF) and aircraft acknowledged his call. Someone suggested they try to overtake the object and we requested the planes to try and the flight leader stated he would. The call sign of this ship was NG869. They turned around and started toward the southwest again. One pilot in the formation told the flight leader that he would like to continue to Louisville with the leader giving his permission to do so. We kept in contact with the flight leader for about twenty-five (25) minutes. The last contact we had with the flight leader was when one of his wingmen called and said "what the hell are we looking for." Flight leader stated he had the object in sight and he was going up to see what it was. He said at present he was at 15,000 feet and was still climbing. Those were the last words I believe we heard from him. Other pilots in the formation tried to contact him but to no avail.

In about another ten or fifteen minutes another P-51 took off from Standiford Field to look for the object. He gave me a call and asked if we still had the object in sight. He was told that at present the object was behind a cloud formation but he said he would try and locate it and in the meantime he tried contacting his flight leader but was unable to do so. He then reported he was unable to see the object and was coming back in when he came over the Control Tower.

I received a call from Standiford Operations that the plane had crashed and the pilot was killed at Franklin, Kentucky.

Incident #33, a–g—Godman Field, Fort Knox, Kentucky—7 January 1948 and discussion of all incidents reported for this date

Incidents #30, 32, 33, and 48 all occurred on 7 January 1948, with #33 involving the death of Lieutenant Mantell. Detailed attention has therefore been given to say possible astronomical body or phenomenon which might serve to identify the object or objects crossroad. The four incidents are considered together here.

Although the several reports differ considerably in regard to the bearing and motion of the object (assuming for the moment that the afternoon and evening sightings refer to the same phenomenon), they are generally consistent concerning the time, manner, and place of its disappearance over the horizon. Hour and azimuth are given as 1906 CST, about 250°, by observers at Godman Field; 1955 EST, west southwest, by those at Lockbourne Air Base; and 1955–2000 EST, about 210°, by those at Clinton County Air Base (there are, as is to be expected, slight differences in individual reports). Uusing this for the focal point of attack, one notes immediately that all these times and bearings agree closely with the time and place of the setting of Venus. Furthermore, all accounts except one agree that the object was low in the southwest before the time of disappearance. Reports vary as to details of its motion, but the overall motion was southwest and then over the horizon. Those facts taken together preclude any question of coincidence. Furthermore, simultaneous observation from scattered locations proves that the object had negligible parallax, or, in short, that it was a very great distance away. All other statements concerning the object must, it seems to this investigator, be weighed in terms of the overwhelming evidence of the manner of disappearance over the horizon.

The stellar magnitude of Venus on January 7 was −3.4, which makes it 30 times brighter than the bright star Arcturus. Venus, were [it] as bright as this and shining through interstices in a host of clouds, could very easily give the effect of a flaming object with a tail. Concerning the erratic motion reported by some witnesses, this can be said: motion of clouds past the object could give the illusion of rapid movement, as when clouds scud by the moon; the effect could have been a psychological illusion; a third possibility, remote but based on a rarely-observed phenomenon, is that, owing to thermo-inversions in the atmosphere, stars near the horizon have been known to jump about erratically through arcs of two or three times the moon's apparent diameter. Venus, when very close to the horizon, has been known to twinkle brilliantly with rapidly oranging colors.

It appears to the present investigator, in summing up the evidence presented, that we are forced to the conclusion that the object observed in the early evening hours of January 7, 1948, at those widely separated localities, was the planet Venus. To assume that a terrestrial object could be located so high as to be visible simultaneously over a wide area, could be of such intrinsic brightness (of incredible brightness, far surpassing any known man-made light), and would so placed essentially at the very position of Venus in the sky over an interval of more than half an hour, would be incredible.

Incident #33 is the only one of the four that includes the daytime observation of presumably this same object. The importance of the incident is, however, paramount, for it was in tracking down the mysterious object that Lieutenant Mantell lost his life. Again it is possible that the object observed was the planet Venus, although the evidence is by no means as definitive as that for the sightings made later that day. First, the bearings of the object as reported by various witnesses differ considerably; where one says southwest, another says south, for the same instant. However, integrating all the evidence, one is again struck with the coincidence of the object's position with that of Venus. The following short table of sightings *vs* the position of Venus shows the general agreement of the two in azimuth:

CST	OBJECT	VENUS
1330 (PFC Oliver)	SW of field	Almost due S: 174°
1345 (Sgt. Blackwell) (PFC Oliver)	South of field	178°
after·1400 (Lt. Orner)	SW	from due S (180°) at 1400, moving westward 195°
1445 (Capt. Mantell) (Col. Hix)	210° 215°	

A more pertinent question is that of whether it would have been possible to see Venus in the daytime on that day. All that can be said here is that it was not impossible to see the planet under those conditions. It is well known that when Venus is at its greatest brilliancy, it is possible to see it during the daytime when one knows exactly where to look, but on January 7, 1948, Venus was less than half as bright as it is when most brilliant. However, under exceptionally good atmospheric conditions and with the eye shielded from the direct rays of the sun, Venus might be seen as an exceedingly tiny bright point of light. It can be shown that it was definitely brighter than the surrounding sky, for on the date in question Venus had a semidiameter of 8 seconds of arc, or a total apparent surface area of approximately 125 square seconds. Assuming that a square second of sky would be a trifle brighter than the fourth magnitude, a portion of the sky of the same area presented by Venus would be about −1.4 magnitude. Since the planet, however, was −3.4, it was 6 times brighter than an equivalent area of sky. While it is thus physically possible to see Venus at such times, usually its pinpoint character and the large expanse of sky makes its casual detection very unlikely. If, however, a person happens to look toward a point on the sky that is just a few minutes of arc from the position of Venus, he is apt to be startled by this apparition and to wonder why he didn't see it before. The chances, of course, of looking at just the right spot are very few. Once done, however, it is usually fairly easy to relocate the object and to call the attention of others to it. However, atmospheric conditions must be exceptionally good. It is improbable, for example, that Venus would be seen under these circumstances in a large city.

It can be said, therefore, that a possible explanation for the object sighted in the daytime in incident #33, a–g, is that it too was the planet Venus. In the absence of exact measures, however, it is impossible to establish that it was or was not. (It is unfortunate that theodolite measures of the afternoon observations were evidently not made.) *

It has been unofficially reported that the object was a Navy cosmic ray balloon. If this can be established, it is to be preferred as an explanation. However, if one accepts the assumption that reports from various other locations in the state refer to the same object, any such device must have been a good many miles high— 25 to 30—in order to have been seen clearly, almost simultaneously, from places 175 miles apart.

It is entirely possible, of course, that the first sightings were of some sort of balloon or aircraft, but that when these reports came to Godman Field, a careful scrutiny of the sky revealed Venus, and it could be that Lieutenant Mantell did actually give chase to the planet, even though whatever objects had been the source of the excitement elsewhere had disappeared. At the altitudes that the pilot reached, Venus would have been very much more easily observed than from the ground, and it might even be that he did not actually pick it up until he was at a considerable altitude. The one piece of evidence that leads this investigator to believe that at the time of Lieutenant Mantell's death he was actually trying to reach Venus is that the object appeared essentially stationary (or moving steadily away from him) and that he could not seem to gain on it.

In summing up, this can be said: the evening sightings reported in incidents #3o, 32, 33, and 48 were undoubtedly of the planet Venus. Regarding the daylight sighting from Godman Field and other places in Kentucky, there seems so far to be no single explanation that does not rely greatly on coincidence. If all reports were of a single object, in the knowledge of this investigator no man-made object could have been large enough and far enough away for the approximately simultaneous sightings. It is most unlikely, however, that so many separate persons should at that time have [fixed] on Venus in the daylight sky. It seems, therefore, much more probable that more than

* But, see p. 52—ed.

one object was involved: the sightings might have included two or more balloons (or aircraft); or they might have included both Venus (in the fatal chase) and balloons. For reasons given above, the latter explanation seems more likely. Such a hypothesis does, however, still necessitate the inclusion of at least two objects other than Venus, and it certainly is coincidental that so many people would have chosen this one day to be confused (to the extent of reporting the matter) by normal airborne objects. There remains one possible, very plausible explanation for this fact, however: was the original report by any chance broadcast by local radio stations? If so, with the general public on the alert, even the commonest aircraft might suddenly have appeared to be strange celestial objects.

In any event, since it seems possible that at the time of Lieutenant Mantell's death, he was actually giving chase to Venus (and since, certainly, during the evening sightings, persons assumedly well acquainted with objects of the sky were alarmed by the appearance of the planet), it might be wise to give information about this incident wide circulation among air force personnel, so that tragic mistakes will not occur in the future.

Chapter Three: Dogfight over Fargo

In February 1968, when I heard him relate the following account, Lieutenant Colonel Howard C. Strand, Base Commander of the Detroit Air National Guard, had over seven thousand military hours flying time, more than half of it in jets. Strand impressed me as an honest, straight-from-the-shoulder military man. He seemed a soft-spoken gentlemen-officer of the old school. He most certainly did not appear to be the sort of man to fabricate a UFO yarn to bring attention to himself.

On a clear spring day in 1953, Strand encountered a number of UFOs while flying over Detroit. At that time he was on active duty in the Air Force, flying F94-B aircraft, and was stationed at Selfridge Air Force Base, Michigan. He had not been a "believer" in flying saucers prior to that sighting, and even today he devotes no time to UFOlogy, other than to do selective reading on the subject. Strand has had only that single experience in 1953, but it is a particularly impressive sighting. Here is his story:

Approximately ten A.M. one morning in March 1953, I was scrambled on a routine patrol mission. We were expecting the Navy to try and penetrate our air defenses in the local area for practice purposes. After about twenty minutes of flight, the radar site controlling our flight gave us a target to our left at about the eight o'clock position. Upon visual checking, my airborne radar operator and I could see tiny specks in the sky which appeared as a ragged formation of aircraft. Our position at the time was approximately thirty miles northwest of downtown Detroit. The targets appeared to be over the city's central section.

The objects were a little lower than our aircraft, so we were in a slight downhill run at full military power, without afterburner, on the intercept. I can recall thinking more than once that I should be able to start identifying the aircraft any second—but I couldn't. Their tailswings and aircraft features just didn't seem to 'pop out' as they normally do when you close in on an aircraft to identify its type.

All the while we were on a quartering head-on intercept, my radar operator in the back seat was trying to pick up the targets on our airborne radar. The ground radar had both our aircraft and the unknowns painted as good strong targets, but we were still unable to get any positive identification, and the objects seemed to be getting a little larger all the time.

About this time, the radar operator in the back seat started receiving some returns on his scope and thought that he was picking up the targets. I was watching the objects until I looked in the cockpit, trying to inch out a little more speed without going into afterburner. When I looked up again—after no more than two to four seconds—the objects were gone!

I had estimated the number of the UFOs to be between twelve and sixteen. We had been expecting to see and to identify Navy fighter-type aircraft. But now, nothing. Every last one of the objects had disappeared from sight.

Immediately I asked the ground radar controller where they were and he told us the targets were still there—loud and clear.

We continued to fly the headings given by the controller, right into the center of the targets.

We flew and turned in every direction, but there was still nothing in sight.

Gradually the targets disappeared from ground radar after we had been amongst them for three or four minutes, as close as two thousand feet, according to radar. Our airborne radar had picked up nothing after the initial fleeting contact before the objects had disappeared from visual sight.

No UFO report was submitted by the air crew for one reason. This was the era when it seemed the Air Force was denying even the possibility of UFOs and was attempting to make everyone who thought that there had been such objects look silly or stupid.

In retrospect, I have personally come to two conclusions about my sighting:

Number one: that I could not identify the objects as aircraft, because they weren't—there were no wings or tails to 'pop' into sight for identification as aircraft. At the time I had no thoughts of flying saucers; therefore, I made no efforts to identify them as such. If I had even so much as thought of it at the time, I never would have taken my eyes off them.

I can say definitely that the objects were not conventional or jet aircraft, due to the fact that no aircraft could have turned around or 'gotten away,' so to speak, in the two or four seconds I was looking in the aircraft cockpit. Remember, all the while we were bearing down on the objects at approximately five hundred mph in a quartering head-on pass.

Number two: that the objects went straight up, out of sight to me and my airborne radar operator, but still visible as targets on the ground radar. Other sightings have been made where UFOs have gone straight up for tens or hundreds of thousands of feet in one or two seconds, then hovered or moved slowly at that new altitude.

At the time of the sighting, I had seventeen hundred hours flying time, accrued in nine years. Today I still feel the sighting on that perfectly clear day in 1953 was valid, that it was no figment of the imagination or trick of the eyesight. I have had no other sightings since that time.

Second Lieutenant George F. Gorman of the North Dakota Air National Guard was known as a serious young man, not given to "figments of the imagination or tricks of the eyesight." Would this well-trained, disciplined pilot have engaged an illusion in a loop-the-loop dogfight?

On that day of October 1, 1948, while he was waiting his turn to land at Fargo, Gorman was startled when a bright light made a pass at him. When he sought to investigate in his F-51, he was forced to use all his skill to avoid being struck by the bright object. Could an astronomical phenomenon have been responsible for the unnerving aerial combat over Fargo?

Incident a, b, c—Fargo, North Dakota—1 October 1948

There is no conceivable astronomical explanation for this much-examined and much-discussed incident.

Analyses by a psychologist and a meteorological expert would be of importance here.

It seems significant to this investigator that other witnesses of the incident did not observe the complex tactics reported by Lieutenant Gorman, although they were presumably seeing the same thing. It is possible, then, that the pilot "took on" a lighted weather balloon? (See report on incident 207 for further discussion.)

HEADQUARTERS
NORTH DAKOTA AIR NATIONAL GUARD
HECTOR AIRPORT
Fargo, North Dakota

23 October 1948

CERTIFICATE

I hereby certify that the following facts concerning my experiences with an unidentified object in the vicinity of Fargo, North Dakota on or about 2900 to 2127 hours 1 October 1948, are true and correct to the best of my knowledge and belief.

This statement is supplementary to my previous testimony and its purpose is to clarify certain points as follows:

Upon my initial approach the object became aware of my presence at about five hundred yards (500).

I am convinced that there was definite thought behind its maneuvers.

I am further convinced that the object was governed by the laws of inertia because its acceleration was rapid but not immediate and although it was able to turn fairly tight at considerable speed, it still followed a natural curve. When I attempted to turn with the object I blacked out temporarily due to excessive speed. I am in fairly good physical condition and I do not believe there are many if any pilots who could withstand the turn and speed effected by the object, and remain conscious.

The object was not only able to out turn and out-speed my aircraft (F-51 V-1650-7) but was able to attain a far steeper climb and was able to maintain a constant rate of climb far in excess of my aircraft.

GEORGE F. GORMAN
2nd Lt.
North Dakota Air Nat'l. Guard

Witness by:

Captain Ernest Winterquist
Lt. Donald M. Serlie

Statement of an interview conducted by Major Donald C. Jones, Commanding Officer 178th Fighter Squadron and 2nd Lt. George F. Gorman, Pilot in the above organization pertaining to the witnessing of an Aerial Phenomenon by Lt. Gorman.

Q. How did you happen to first notice the object in question?

A. Flying in circles to the left over the city of Fargo at 270 miles an hour, I noticed a cub circling the Football Field on the North end of Fargo. At almost the same time I noticed the object travelling from East to West between the tower at Hector Airport and the Football Field. The time was 2100.

Q. How did the object first look to you?

A. At first observation it appeared to be the rear navigation light on an aircraft except that it had no glare and was blinking on and off.

Q. What did you then do?

A. My first reaction was to keep it in sight and circle with it. At the time the object was making a circle around the city of Fargo at approximately 1000 feet travelling at the same rate of speed as I. Putting it in the light of the city, myself above it, I checked it for wings and fuselage but it appeared to have none. I could distinguish the outline of the cub distinctly.

Q. Did you have any conversation with the tower

regarding the position of any aircraft in the air?

A. Yes.

Q. What was the gist of this conversation and the time it occurred?

A. My first call occurred at 2107 at which time I asked the tower if any other aircraft were in the air besides the cub and myself.

Q. What was the tower's response?

A. They knew of no other local aircraft.

Q. What did you do then?

A. I contacted the tower, gave them my position, the position of the object, and notified the tower that I was peeling off and going to give chase.

Q. How near did you estimate that you got to the object during the chase?

A. The closest time I got to the object was in a head-on pass at which the object passed over me at less than 500 feet.

Q. How large did the object appear when it passed over you?

A. It appeared to me from 6 to 8 inches in diameter.

Q. Can you describe the object?

A. The object was white light with no apparent glare and clear cut edge.

Q. Did the object have any depth?

A. Apparently no.

Q. Could you describe it as merely a ball of light?

A. No, it seemed to be flat.

Q. How long were you able to keep the object in view?

A. Twenty-seven (27) minutes.

Q. Can you describe briefly what occurred during these 27 minutes?

A. After the initial peel off, I realized the speed of the object was too great to catch in a straight chase, so I proceeded to cut it off in turns. At this time my fighter was under full power. My speed varying between 300 and 400. The object circled to the left, I cut back to the right for a head-on pass. The pass was máde at apparently 5000 feet, the object approaching head-on until a collision seemed inevitable. The object veered and passed apparently

68

500 feet or less over the top above me. I chandelled around still without the object in sight. The object made a 180 degree turn and initiated a pass at me. This time I watched it approach all the way and as it started to pull up, I pulled up abruptly trying to ram the object until straight up with me following to apparently 14,000 feet, I stalled out at 14,000 feet with the object apparently 2000 feet above me circling to the left. We made two circles to the left. The object then pulled out away from me and made another head-on pass. At this time the pass started and the object broke off a large distance from me heading over Hector Airport to the Northwest at apparently 11,000 feet. I gave chase circling to the left trying to cut it off until I was 25 miles Southeast of Fargo. I was at 14,000, the object at 11,000 when I again gave the aircraft full power [trying] to catch it in a diving turn. The object turned around and made another head-on pass. This time when pulling up, I pulled up also and observed it travelling straight up until I lost it. I then returned to the field and landed.

Q. Did the object at any time change its appearance?
A. Yes.
Q. In what way?
A. When the object was travelling slow, the light varied in intensity [blinking] on and off.
Q. Did the light ever remain steady?
A. Yes.
Q. At what time?
A. When the object increased its speed, the light increased in intensity and became steady.
Q. What did you estimate its fastest speed to be?
A. Somewhere above 600 miles per hour.
Q. Did the object appear to be opaque?
A. No.
Q. At any time did the light change color?
A. No.
Q. Did the light also appear the same even in turns?
A. Yes.
Q. Did the light at any time have an elliptical shape?
A. No.

Q. Did you have the impression that the object was controlled?

A. Definitely, there was thought behind the maneuvers.

Q. How was the weather especially the visibility at the time of this engagement?

A. CAVU.

Q. Were you conscious of the Northern lights?

A. Yes, I had observed them low on the North Eastern horizon through my flight.

Q. Are you willing to certify that this is a true and accurate statement to the best of your knowledge?

A. Yes, I so certify to the best of my powers of observation, that every statement herein is true.

A Statement by Doctor ———
October 1st at 11:20 P.M.

A gentleman and myself took off from Skye Ranch Flying Field, which is five (5) miles South of Hector Airport, at eight-forty (8:40) P.M. to do a little night flying. We were in a two-way radio connection with the tower at Hector Airport. I was doing the flying and _____ was using the phone and while circling the Football Field at the A.C. at 1600 feet, the Fargo tower advised us there was a 51 in the air and a few moments later asked who the third plane might be. We had noticed the 51, and when we were over the North side of Hector Field going West a light seemingly on a plane flared above and to the North moving very swiftly toward the West. At first we thought it was the 51 but we then saw the lights of the 51 higher and more over the field. We landed on runway three (3) and taxied into the Ad building and went up to the tower and listened to the calls from the 51 which seemed to be trying to overtake the plane or lighted object which then went southward and over the city. The plane was moving very swiftly, much faster than the 51. Tried to get a better view with a pair of binoculars but couldn't follow it well enough. The 51 landed and we took off just ahead of Northwest plane and landed at Skye Ranch and registered on the flying sheet at 10:20 P.M. I saw the light and the 51 at the same time. The lights seemed to be outside of the circle made by the 51.

A TRUE COPY   /3/Doctor _____

Donald C. Jones
Major, AF, NDNG
Commanding

                                        6 October 1948

MEMORANDUM
SUBJECTS: Incident #172, Fargo, N. Dakota,
            dated 1 Oct '48
TO: Mr. _____

   1. Per your request for telecon condensation:
      a. Command Representatives interrogated witnesses involved in Incident #172 on the 3 Oct '48.
      b. Newspaper reports confirmed as being substantially correct.
      c. Summary of witness testimony reveals that one object was observed over a period of 27 minutes; that it consisted only of a small round ball of clear white light with no physical form or shape attached, about 6–8 inches in diameter which at times traveled faster than the F-51 and performed maneuvers in both evasive and *aggressive* manners. When first sighted the object was traveling at about 250 MPH at 1,000 feet altitude. Under this condition the light was not continuous but blinked off and on. At higher performance the white light was continuous. Possibilities of other aircraft, meteorological balloon releases, Canadian Vampire Jets having been in immediate vicinity have been discredited. Geiger check now being performed on F-51

for comparison survey with unaffected aircraft. Technical studies are being initiated.

Robt. R. Sneider
Captain, USAF
Project Officer

ATI FIELD OFFICE
INTELLIGENCE DEPARTMENT
HEADQUARTERS AIR MATERIEL
COMMAND
Wright-Patterson Air Force Base
Dayton, Ohio
4 October 1948
INTERROGATION REPORT NO. 2
INTERROGATION OFFICER:
Major Paul Kubala

Personal History of Person Interrogated:
    NAME: Gorman, George F.
    AGE: Twenty-five years.
    ADDRESS: Building 18, Federal Housing Project, Fargo, N.D.
    OCCUPATION: Manager of construction work.
    MARITAL STATUS: Married, one child.
    EDUCATION: Two and one-half years college—mechanical engineering and physics.

Military History of Person Interrogated:
    RANK: 2nd Lieutenant.
    SERIAL NUMBER: AO943873.
    UNIT: North Dakota Air National Guard.
    NUMBER YEARS SERVICE: Two years with the National Guard.
    WAR ASSIGNMENT: Pilot instructor for French military students.

Evaluation of Person Interrogated:
    2nd Lt. Gorman did not make the impression of

being a dreamer. He reads little, and only serious literature. He spends 90% of his free time hunting and fishing; drinks less than moderately; smokes normally; and does not use drugs. He appears to be a sincere and serious individual who was considerably puzzled by his experience and made no attempt to blow his story up.

Summary of Interrogation:

Lt. Gorman had been with his squadron on a cross-country flight. When the squadron returned at approximately 2030 hours, Lt. Gorman decided to remain in the air inasmuch as he wanted to do some night flying. He flew west as far as Valley City and returned to Fargo to watch the football game from the air, his altitude being approximately 1500 feet at the time. Circling the football field, he saw about 500 feet beneath him a Piper Cub. At approximately 2100 hours he decided to return to the field. He called the tower to find out if all was clear, and was told that one other ship was in the air, the aforementioned Piper Cub, which was flown by Dr. Cannon of Fargo, North Dakota.

Subject:
Project "Sign"

TO: MCIAXO—3 _____ From: MCIA
         Date 23 Dec 48   Comment #4

1. A review of Lt. Gorman's statement and facts presented, which were considered highly reliable by interrogation from this Hqs, suggests the following comments regarding comment 2 by MCIAXS:

   a. The positive statement that the aerial object sighted by Lt. Gorman was a piloted aircraft is unjustified and may lead to serious complications. Although the object apparently performed in a superior manner and as though human thought was involved, nothing was reported to indicate or permit assumption that the object was an aircraft, as the term is accepted today.

b. Reference paragraph 1a, the assumption regarding errors and deficiencies of observation and that Lt. Gorman failed to perceive the configuration is also not justified. The official report, see pages 2 and 3 of enclosed exhibit "E", testimony obtained by Major D. C. Jones (Gorman's Commanding Officer at Fargo), states quite definitely the configuration of the aerial object encountered by Lt· Gorman. The evaluation of Lt. Gorman by interrogating officer, Major Paul Kubala, is excellent, see page 1, exhibit "A." Therefore, there seems to be no justification to assume or distort the aerial object other than as described by Lt. Gorman.

c. A check with MCIA personnel involved in this case and project "Sign" disclosed that their concept of the configuration was spherical or "ball-like." Furthermore, it was officially reported and recorded as such. Actually, the configuration is round, but *flat* or "disc-like." Major Kubala stated that according to the direct question and answer interrogation, by Major Jones, NDNG, Commanding Officer, that the disc-like or round-flat configuration would have to be accepted in lieu of the apparently indirect and assumed "ball-like" shape. This error on the part of the Intelligence Department could cause some serious embarrassment and repercussions.

d. The centrifugal force formula presented in comment 2, par. 2, is correct, but application to show normal "g's" in example of par. 3 is not justified in view of Lt. Gorman's own statement that he did perform turns that imposed extreme acceleration forces on him even to the point of black out.

2. It is recommended that (1) the entire comment 2 from MCIAXS be disregarded and not made a matter of official record of the subject incident No. 172; (2) the records be corrected regarding the "understood" configuration of a ball to that of a

74

flat round disc or that further investigation be made to correct this one important point.

		A. C. LOEDDING
1 Incl	ACL/jr	Technical Assistant
n/c	66322	Technical Intelligence Div.
	P 201C	Intelligence Department
	B 288	

HEADQUARTERS
AIR MATERIEL COMMAND
Wright-Patterson Air Force Base
Dayton, Ohio

MCIAXO
SUBJECT: Project "Sign"

MCIAXO–3/HWS/rm
January 7, 1949

TO: Commanding General
Hq North Dakota Air National Guard
—Hector Airport
Fargo, North Dakota

1. Reference is made to incident of an unidentified flying object which occurred near your base 1 October 1948, and to subsequent investigations by personnel of this Command.

2. During analysis of evidence, certain points were brought out on which clarification is desired. It is requested that all witnesses to subject incident, particularly Lt. Gorman, be interviewed again concerning the following matters:

a. As to the exact shape of the object seen. Did object appear symmetrical and what was its shape as seen from various angles—in turns, from head-on, from the rear, from either side, above and below? Did shape appear to vary while being viewed from any one aspect? Give details of shape as it appeared from all angles. Include three dimensional sketches by each witness.

b. As to the size and range of object as viewed from Lt. Gorman's plane and from the ground. Lt. Gorman states object appeared to be six to eight inches in diameter and that its closest proximity to his aircraft was apparently five hundred feet. There is great difficulty in estimating size and distance of an object when neither the normal size is known, and where there is no object of known size at equal range to the unknown object for comparison. Was object estimated to be actually six to eight inches in diameter or was this the area of space it occupied on Lt. Gorman's windshield? Did size of object (in respect to area occupied on windshield) vary in proportion to apparent variance in range, or did it appear to the eye in constant dimensions? Was object only seen through windshield, or was it seen also through the canopy, to the sides and rear of the F-51?

c. As to luminosity of the object, Lt. Gorman states there were no visible projections or unlighted sections to the object, and that he observed the object while it passed between him and the lights of Fargo. How intense was the light of the object, in comparison to city lights? Was object lost to view for instantaneous periods while it eclipsed bright city lights?

4. It is requested these questions be reviewed, answered carefully and returned together with any additional pertinent information to the Commanding General, Headquarters, Air Materiel Command, Dayton, Ohio, attention MCIAXO–3.

FOR THE COMMANDING GENERAL:

H. M. McCOY
Colonel, USAF
Chief,
Intelligence Department

BASIC: Ltr Hq AMC 7Jan49 Subj: Project "Sign" to CG NDNG Fargo, NDak·

1st Ind

OFFICE OF THE COMMANDING OFFICER, North Dakota National Guard, Hector Airport, Box 1952, Fargo, North Dakota 30 January 1949.
TO: Commanding General, Air Material Command, Wright-Patterson Air Force Base, Dayton, Ohio.

In compliance with your request for additional information from Lt. Gorman the following information is submitted:

a. (1) Object was symmetrical
   (2) Shape:
      (a) in turn-around, symmetrical
      (b) head-on—same
      (c) rear—same
      (d) either side—same
      (e) above & below—same
   (3) Shape did not vary
   (4) Appeared to be a round ball at all times, though appearance of a ball at times gives a flat-plate effect.
b. (1) Object estimated to be six or eight inches in diameter. This diameter *not* as area covered on windshield.
   (2) Size did vary in respect to size on windshield.
   (3) Object seen through windshield, canopy and to sides and rear of F-51.
c. (1) Object was about the same intensity in light as were the lights of the city.

77

(2) Object was lost to view for instantaneous periods while it eclipsed bright city lights.

DONALD C. JONES
Major, AF, NDNG
Commanding.

Chapter Four: Mystery of the Lubbock Lights

The famous mystery of the Lubbock Lights, two strange formations like "strings of beads in crescent shape," was given much greater credence than many other sightings in those early, confusing days of UFO investigation because of the high caliber of the witnesses.

Four Texas Technical College professors observed the August 1951 aerial enigma, and their sighting was substantiated by the testimonies of yet another professor and a graduate student working toward his Ph.D. In addition, the witnesses asked a professor of astronomy to assess their account. Then, too, there was excellent photographic evidence to supplement the expert testimonies of the highly educated witnesses. Critics could not brush the sightings away because they had been made by untutored and unsophisticated laymen.

W. L. Ducker, head of the Tech Petroleum engineering department, admitted that if there had not been confirming witnesses present, he probably would not have reported the UFO sighting. According to Ducker, he and Dr. A. G. Bert, Professor of Chemical Engineering, were relaxing at the home of Dr. W. I. Robinson, Professor of Geology, when the illuminated "string of beads" whipped across the sky.

"We felt no shock waves, such as an object moving at such high speeds in the lower atmosphere would give off," Ducker commented. "And the absence of such waves would indicate the formation was flying in the stratosphere, fifty thousand feet above the Earth or higher."

The professors agreed that the passage of the "beads" across the sky required about three seconds. At that remarkable pace, Ducker said, "We figured the speed must have been eighteen hundred miles per hour if the objects were a mile high. If they were at fifty thousand feet, the speed must have been about eighteen thousand miles per hour."

The professors remarked that they were unable to determine the shape of the objects because of the speed, but they stressed that each gave off a glow of reflected light.

In the reports which follow, all gleaned from Air Force files, the names of the professors and all other witnesses were censored. Although contemporary news accounts provide their names, an editorial judgment was made to present the reports as they exist in the Project Blue Book records. In the case of the Lubbock lights, it is the high quality of the testimonies which is important, not the names and personalities of those who gave them.

Appendix I
Lubbock, Texas—25 August 1951

The first of a series of sightings related to this incident occurred the evening of 25 August 1951 at approximately 2110 CST. Four Texas Technical College professors were sitting in the backyard of one of the professor's homes observing meteorites in conjunction with a study of micrometeorites being carried out by the college. At 2110 they observed a group of lights pass overhead from N to S. The lights had about the same intensity as a bright star but were larger in area. The altitude was not determined but they traveled at a high rate of speed. The pattern of the lights was almost a perfect semi-circle containing from 20 to 30 individual lights. Later in the evening a similar incident was observed and during a period of about three weeks a total of approximately twelve (12) such flights were observed by these men.

The group of men included:

a. The Head of the Petroleum Engineering Department
b. Professor of Geology, has Ph.D.
c. Professor of Physics, has Ph.D.
d. Professor of Chemical Engineering, has Ph.D.

Besides the above four men the following have observed the incidents:

a. Professor of Mathematics, has Ph.D.
b. Graduate student working on Ph.D.

In addition, a Professor of Astronomy was consulted on the incident, but he did not observe any of these flights.

The above mentioned men took a personal interest in the phenomena and undertook a study of the objects. Attempts were made to obtain an altitude measurement by laying out a measured base line perpendicular to the usual flight path of the object and placing angle measuring devices at the end of the base line, however, all their attempts failed because the objects did not appear on the nights the observers were waiting for them.

From the series of observations, the following facts were obtained:

a. The angular velocity of the object was very nearly 30° of arc per second.

b. There was no sound that could be attributed to the object.
c. The flight path of the object was from N to S in the majority of the flights.
d. There were two or three flights per evening.
e. The period between flights was about one hour and 10 minutes.
f. The color of the lights was blue-green.
g. There were from 15 to 30 separate lights in each formation.
h. The first two flights observed were a semi-circle of lights but in subsequent flights there was no orderly arrangement.
i. The object always appeared at an angle of about 45° from horizontal in the north and disappeared at about 45° in the south. The object did not gradually come into view as would an aircraft approaching from a distance, neither did it gradually disappear.
j. There was no apparent change in size as the object passed overhead.
k. The "angular span" was estimated to be 10°.

Attempts were made to obtain the relative height of the objects in respect to clouds. However, these attempts were also unsuccessful due to the fact that the objects passed between widely scattered clouds.

Attempts were made to determine whether or not there was any form between the lights by trying to see stars between the lights. These also were unsuccessful due to the short time the object was in view.

This phenomena was observed by at least one hundred people in and around Lubbock, Texas. Some of these people were of the opinion that the objects were birds reflecting lights from the city.

On the evening of 31 August 1951 at about 2330 CST, a college freshman from Texas Tech observed a flight of the unidentified objects pass over his home. The flight was observed through an open window. Upon observing the first flight of the objects, the observer obtained his camera and went into the backyard of his home in an attempt to get photographs of additional flights of the object. (Comment: This would be logical as by 31 August 1951 these flights of the objects, and the fact that several flights might occur in an evening, was well known.) Two more flights of the object allegedly did occur and were photographed. Two photos of one flight and three of another were obtained. ATIC has four of the negatives but the other one was lost or misplaced by the photographer. The photographs show a V-shaped formation of lights. In one photo a single V of lights appear, while on three photos there is a double V. The separate lights, which appear to be pinpoint light sources, vary in intensity.

(See Appendix II for possibly related incidents.)

II. Status of the Investigation

A. Trip to Lubbock, Texas

A trip was made to Lubbock, Texas, on 6–9 November 1951 to obtain more details on the incident. Many people who had seen the object or who were involved in the incident were interrogated. A conference was held with the college professors and they prepared a signed statement describing the objects they observed.

The photographer was interrogated, in conjunction with OSI, in regard to the photographs of the objects. His account of the incident seemed logical, and there were no obvious indications of a hoax. The photographer had previously been interrogated by the Lubbock newspaper and the photos inspected by Associated Press and Life magazine representatives. It was their opinion that the photos were not obviously a hoax. The college professors were doubtful as to whether or not the photographs were of the same objects that they had observed because:

1. They had never observed a V-shaped formation of lights. This is not too significant, however, as the arrangement of the lights that they observed varied and since there were several flights the college professors possibly did not see the flights that were pho-

tographed. In addition, the photographer states that the object appeared to be U-shaped but when he developed the negatives, the object was V-shaped.

2. The objects that the professors observed were, in their opinion, not bright enough to be photographed. This is, however, an estimate and could be in error.

It was found that one school of thought of the people in the Lubbock area was that the objects were some type of migratory birds reflecting light from the city. Several people reported that they definitely know the objects were birds because they could see wings "flapping." It is very possible that some of the people who were looking for the object did see ducks as there were duck flights passing over during the period.

The college professors do not believe the theory that the objects were birds, but they are giving the possibility more thought. If they were birds, they would have to be relatively low to give the illusion of high speed. An occasional flight of birds might pass low over a city on a clear night but it is highly doubtful if they would continue to do this for several nights. Migratory birds usually try to keep away from cities.

The Federal Wild Life Game Warden was visited and although he was not familiar with the incident he doubted if the objects were birds. He stated that they could have been, however. The most likely suspect, if it is a bird, is a member of the Plover family which has a pure white breast, but unless there was a sudden influx of the birds into the Lubbock area, the game warden doubted if there would be enough of these birds to make up as many flights as were observed.

If the photos are authentic, the objects very probably are not ducks because an experienced photographer from the Lubbock Avalanche Newspaper attempted to get photos of ducks using both natural light and flash, but failed.

B. Analysis of Photos by Wright Air Development Center

The Photographic Reconnaissance Laboratory of WALC made a preliminary analysis of the photographs. The analysis was made by inspecting the negatives in a comparator microscope. Their conclusions were:

1. The images on the negatives were caused by light striking unexposed film (i.e., the negatives were not retouched).

2. The individual lights in the "formation" varied in intensity.

3. The intensity was greater than any surrounding stars as the stars did not register. (The photos were taken under CAVU conditions.)

4. The individual lights changed position in the "formation."

C. Reinterrogation of the Photographer

A trip to Lubbock, Texas, will be made during January. Arrangements are being made to have a Project Grudge consultant and a physicist accompany Project Grudge personnel. If the photographs are authentic, they are important in that:

1. They will give an accurate measurement of the "angular mean."

2. The light source, although it appeared to be of low intensity to the eye, was highly actinic.

3. The movement of the individual lights in the formation can be studied further.

4. Density comparison tests can be made.

A Visit with the Photographer

Mr. _____ was interviewed on the evening of 7 November 1951 at his home by Lt. Ruppelt and Mr. H. N. Bossartt of the Reese AFB OSI detachment. (A description of Mr. _____ is given in OSI report.)

The purpose of the visit was to obtain further data on the photos taken by Mr. _____ and to attempt to determine the authenticity of the photos. Mr. _____ was again questioned as to the events leading up to taking the photos and how he took them. [. . .]

84

In addition several other facts were obtained. Upon seeing the objects _____ rushed into the house and got his camera. He had experience in taking pictures at night as he had experimented with star shots. He realized that he would have to give the objects as much light as possible so he "opened it up", f3.5 at $\frac{1}{10}$ of a second, the "fastest" combination for a Kodak 35.

The object appeared at about 30° from the horizontal. _____ stated that they appeared just over a tree top, and the angle was measured to be very close to 30°. The direction was NNE. The objects went a little to his right and disappeared at about 30° from the horizontal at SSE. This gives an arc of very close to 120°. During this time he "panned" his camera (i.e. followed the object with the camera.) During this process he took two pictures during each flight. The procedure was duplicated by Mr. _____ and timed. It took 4 seconds, timed by the sweep second hand on a wrist watch. This comes out to be 30° per second. (Note: This is the same time obtained by Prof. _____.)

The interrogating officer, Lt. Ruppelt, has been an amateur photographer for 14 years and all the data and procedures given by _____ were accurate and very logical.

No progress was made in attempting to determine whether or not the photos were faked. _____'s story could not be "picked apart" because it was entirely logical. He was questioned on why he did certain things and his answers were all logical, concise, and without hesitation. He was visibly nervous but this could be due to the fact that he knew Mr. Bossartt was from OSI and Lt. Ruppelt from W-P AFB. This nervousness at no time caused him to falter in his story.

_____ stated that the object appeared to be about brighter than the brightest star in the sky. He compared it to Venus in the early evening.

Additional info on _____ in the interview with the newspaper people and college professors.

Mr. Jay Harris, Managing Editor of the Lubbock Morning Avalanche and William Hans, Photographer

Mr. Bossartt of the RAFB Detachment of the OSI and Lt. Ruppelt interviewed the Managing Editor of the Lubbock Morning Avalanche, Mr. Harris, on the evening of 7 November 1951.

Mr. Harris gave the following information before the interrogation began:

On the evening of 25 September 1951 he was at the news desk of the paper when a Prof. _____ of Texas Tech College called him on the phone. _____ reported he had just seen an aerial phenomena that would be worth a story. He continued to tell about the "string of beads" that he and two other college professors had seen in the sky. Harris at first was not interested. _____ then said he felt it was important and that by running the story they might be able to contact others who had seen the phenomena. Harris said o.k. if he could use _____'s name. _____ said he wasn't sure about this and ended the conversation. A few minutes later he called again and said that it would be o.k. to use his name and the names of Prof. _____ and _____ who were with him at the time and also saw it. It would first, however, have to be o.k'd by the college public relations people. This was done and the story was printed on 26 August 1951. No further reports came in until a few days later.

On Friday, 31 August 1951, a photographer who does work for the paper and is highly regarded by Mr. _____ called and said a young man (Mr. _____) had just developed some negatives in his studio and he thought the paper might be interested in them. They advised _____ to bring them over which he did. Mr. _____ and his head photographer, Mr. _____ looked them over and were dubious about using them because of the possibility of a hoax. They examined the negatives very carefully, however, and decided to use them. Mr. Harris then called _____ on the phone and again asked them if it were a hoax which he denied. Harris then in his approximate words

86

"raised hell with him" and told him all the consequences if it were a hoax. He threatened to "run him out of town" if it were. This did not faze _____ and his only reply was that the pictures were of something flying over Lubbock and that if they were afraid to use them o.k., he didn't care. As far as payment was concerned anything would be all right. (He finally received $7.50–$10.00 for them.) Prior to this, _____ had taken a few photos for the paper and was regarded as an honest, conscientious person trying to pick up a little extra money on photos. He was not obnoxious as a lot of amateurs are, always trying to sell photos, but would occasionally take a good photo and attempt to sell it.

It was then decided by Mr. Harris to put the photos "on the wire service" with a story. _____ was called in on this discussion and again "read the riot act" on any possible fraud. This time it was stronger because the photo was going out all over the U.S. Again he stuck to his story, and the photo went out.

The negatives were sent to AP in Ft. Worth to be checked. *Life* magazine also looked at the photos but rejected them because they claimed to have many photos of "flying saucers." The photos and story went out on the wire service. It is unknown which papers used it but some did.

At this point in the interview Mr. Hans, head photographer and Asst. Managing Editor, was called in and gave this information. When the story of V-shaped lights came out some people immediately branded them as ducks or some type of migratory fowl. Later when _____'s photos were printed, the argument as to whether or not they were migratory fowl came up. Mr. Hans decided to try to get a picture himself so he stationed himself on top of the Lubbock Avalanche Building with a 4 x 5 Speed Graphic loaded with a tungsten ASA 80 film and a GE #22 flashbulb in a concentrating reflector. He normally uses this same equipment to photograph night football games. He can get a normal negative by shooting f16, at $\frac{1}{100}$ of a second and developing twice the normal time in DK-60 a developer. This night he sat on the roof and had his camera set at f4.7 at $\frac{1}{10}$ of a second. He waited some time and a flock of some type of birds flew over. They were visible in the light of the sodium vapor street lights used in Lubbock. He shot as the flock was overhead. He also stated that he knew they were birds before he took the pictures because he could see them dimly outlined. They were in a *ragged* V-formation and silent, which is unusual for ducks or geese, if they were ducks or geese. He developed his negatives and found the image so weak he could not print them. On the next night he attempted the same thing using a Kodak Reflex at f3.5 at $\frac{1}{10}$ with Super XX film, a #22 bulb and the concentrating reflector; the results were the same. Mr. Hans assumed that with his experience he should know that he was in a position in the city to get a maximum of light on any birds flying over him. From this, he is convinced that whatever _____ took a picture of was many times as bright as the birds he unsuccessfully attempted to photograph.

Mr. Hans added that some time back he had attempted to photograph an eclipse of the moon. He ran into difficulty getting enough exposure, further indicating that _____'s shots were of a bright object. (This was later disproved by taking test photos of the moon. It is possible his statement was misinterpreted.)

Mr. Harris impressed the interviewers as a typical newspaper editor. He made it very plain that he was not one to have someone use his paper to perpetrate a hoax. He has thoroughly checked both the photos and reports and believes the people have seen something and the photos are not faked (i.e. something flying over Lubbock.) Other sources confirmed this fact and stated that he has a reputation of making very sure what he prints is true. He stated he purposely played down the articles because he felt that the object was possibly some Air Force project, he was more sure when the AF did not investigate. (We knew nothing about it for several weeks.)

He believes the people who saw this object were not seeing birds. Some people did see birds because there was some bird flight activity in the area. His observation on a great many reports was that the people who saw ducks knew they were ducks because they could see them. The people who saw V lights knew they couldn't be ducks. At least one experienced duck hunter who saw them threw out the duck idea. Therefore, his idea was that a lot of people were conscious of the lights, were looking, and saw ducks and knew they were ducks. Others saw the real thing and knew they weren't ducks.

Harris' statement on _____ was that he has seen a lot of fakes in his time and if _____ is a fake he is the best in the business and wasting his time in college.

In answer to a query about sightings in areas without a large concentration of lights such as larger cities, Mr. Harris stated that they had received calls from many people in small towns and in the country. All reports were about the same as those reported in the newspapers.

a. The objects were migratory birds.
b. The objects were a group or string of light traveling from N to S at a high speed.

Another instance mentioned by Mr. Harris occurred several nights after, 25 August 1951. An Air Force Capt. from Reese AFB called to tell of the object he had seen. He stated he had read about the objects in the newspaper and did not believe it. However, a few minutes before he had called, he had seen the same phenomena as was mentioned in the newspaper and was now convinced it was true. He stated that he had flown jets and had been around them and that this object was much faster than a jet. He said he couldn't give his name but would be glad to clear the story through the base PIO. This was never done, however, as the editor was not running any more stories on the incident and all records of the captain's name were gone.

Mr. Harris had been in the newspaper business about 20 years. Some of this time was spent as a PIO during WW II. He has a reputation of being very honest and will print nothing unless he is personally sure it is accurate. This is brought out by his very complete investigation of the authenticity of the "string of beads" stories.

Mr. Hans is considered one of the best photographers in Lubbock. He has had a studio for many years before coming to the newspaper. All the time he had a studio, he worked for the newspaper on a part-time basis.

Federal Wild Life Game Warden

On the afternoon of 8 November 1951 Lt. Ruppelt and Capt. Parker contacted the Federal Wildlife Game Warden at the Post Office Building in Lubbock. The purpose was to determine the habits and description of Plover.

It was determined that there are several kinds of Plover. Several types have white breasts and are found in West Texas. The bird is about 8" long and has a wing span of about 1'. It will fly at night and in groups but the groups are usually not larger than 5 or 6 birds. They are known to migrate south from late August till the middle of November. Also they have been seen in the Lubbock locality recently although not in great numbers. They fly at about 1,000' or lower at a maximum of 50 mph.

The game warden had not read the articles about the "objects" in the paper so was unfamiliar with the description of the objects, but tended to doubt if they were Plover. He added that they might be ducks but not geese because geese continually "honk" as they fly over populated areas.

Meeting with Texas Technical College Professors

On the evening of 8 November 1951 Lt. Ruppelt and Capt. Parker met with four professors of the Texas Technical College to discuss the aerial phenomena they observed over a period of time from 25 August

90

1951 until about 15 October 1951. Those present were:

a. _____, Ph.D. in Geology but also well versed in all fields of science. The meeting was at his home.
b. _____, Ph.D., Professor of Chemical Engineering
c. _____, Ph.D. in Physics, presently head of the Texas Tech Seismograph Station and has previously spent several years at The University of Alaska studying the aurora.
d. Prof. _____, Head of the Petroleum Engineering Department.

On the evening of 25 August 1951, _____, _____, and _____ were sitting in Dr. _____'s yard discussing a project on micro-meteorites that _____ is conducting at Texas Tech. They were counting meteors when the first object passed over the yard. They stated they were surprised at the sight and began discussing it. They agreed that if another object came over they would attempt to find out some of its characteristics and about an hour later one did come over, one man listened while the other two timed it. This object, and the first one, was a semi-circle, about 160° arc, of lights. There was no discernible noise and the angular velocity was very close to 30° per second. The direction was about N to S, and they passed 15°–20° west of the Zenith. The men could not agree on the color except that it was yellowish to white. It varied in intensity and was somewhat larger in area than a star. All men agreed it appeared to have its own light source. Since 25 August 1951 these men and several others have seen more flights, approximately twelve. They all were of the same nature as the first except there was no regular arrangement or formation. Others who have seen the objects well in the presence of the original three men are:

a. _____, Ph.D. in Geology.
b. _____, Mathematics Professor.
c. _____, Studying for Ph.D.

Dr. ———, Astronomer from Texas Tech., has not observed the phenomena but has been present at all the investigations.

Several characteristics of the object have been noticed by the observers. The lights always appear at about 50° in the S or SW. They never gradually come into view or gradually disappear. Its "span angle" from the ground was about 7°–8°. They follow a rough schedule beginning about 2120 and appearing every hour and 10 minutes until three flights pass overhead. The men have attempted to determine whether or not there is any form between the lights by trying to observe stars between the lights. They have been unsuccessful, however, due to the great speed of the object. Once they thought they observed stars between the objects but could not be sure.

The group is confident of the angular velocity of the object of 30°/second from measurements of several flights. Stop watches and protractors were used to measure time and angles. Several attempts have been made to measure the altitude. On only one occasion has there been any clouds and these were widely scattered. The objects appeared but did not pass close enough to a cloud to obtain a relative altitude.

Several other attempts to determine the altitude were made by using triangulation from a measured base line. On the first occasion an eleven mile base line was used with home-made angle measuring devices set up at each end of the base. Radios were used for communication from one end of the base line to the other. Another night a shorter base line was used. On the first night, neither party observed the flights although two of their wives saw them from the city. On the second night only one party thought they saw the object but they were not able to get a measurement. The object appeared to be very low over the city of Lubbock.

A third attempt was made by Dr. ———, the astronomer. He questioned three people who saw the object as to their position and the angle of observation. This technique is used in plotting the path of meteors. He arrived at an altitude of between 2,000 and 3,000 feet. However, one of the observers was doubtful as to the time she made observation so it could have been another object she saw, consequently, they are not putting any reliability on this altitude measurement.

Two other incidents took place which the group would not mention at first but finally did. They qualified the incidents with the statement that they are so absurd they have never mentioned them. The first incident happened to Mrs. _____, who according to several people is a very calm woman. Prof. _____ stated that she came running into the house one evening just at dusk very excited. Due to her usually calm manner, the excitement was very apparent. She said she had seen a very large wing type aircraft, making no sound, go over the house. She could offer no more description. Prof. _____ could not remember exactly when it took place as he had passed it off as being too fantastic. (Note: Nearly identical to 25 August 1951 sighting in Albuquerque, New Mexico.)

The next incident was observed by Prof. _____ and Dr. _____ and has been titled "_____'s Horror." The men were sitting in the yard waiting for the "9:20," a term coined for the first object of the evening to pass over the observers. (Strangely enough, there was a remarkable amount of regularity to the flights of the objects.) All of a sudden a group of yellowish lights came across the yard very low, and according to Prof. _____ they had a "wiggling" motion. It upset Dr. _____ considerably, consequently the name "_____'s Horror." Again the instance was dropped because no one else in the neighborhood saw it and it was very low.

At this point in the conversation the unusual meteor activity in the SW United States was brought up. The group, with Dr. _____, the astronomer, has already attempted to associate the formation of lights with this activity, however, they could find no association between the two. Dr. _____ mentioned the fact that the series of events terminating with the large meteor that fall in Oklahoma on the morning of 7 November

1951 was very odd. They did not follow the general pattern of meteors. An expedition from several Southwestern Colleges is now being formed to attempt to find the one that is supposed to have fallen in Oklahoma.

Several meteors were reported to have fallen in the Lubbock area during the period Lt. Ruppelt was there. In two instances people reported crashed aircraft, and Lt. Ruppelt was present when B-25s were sent out to search. Later the locations where these "crashes" were reported were examined by Texas Tech people. They picked up some material that allegedly came from the object. A piece of this material has been obtained and will be analyzed. It may be ash from the many cotton gins located in the Lubbock area. According to Texas Tech chemists, if it is, the potassium content will be high.

The above named men together with Dr. _____, an astronomer at Texas Tech, have developed a very great interest in their objects. Their genuine interest is brought out by the fact that they devoted an entire evening discussing the matter with Lt. Ruppelt and Capt. Parker, and they previously have had many meetings between themselves. They refuse to recognize any sightings not witnessed by at least two of the group although they admit many other reputable people have seen the objects. Thus the figure of twelve sightings is conservative. Their term is twelve "official sightings." They have made every effort to investigate all possibilities as to what the objects might be. It is apparent after listening to them review what they have done that they are deeply interested in the phenomena.

They had dropped their investigation by the time Lt. Ruppert arrived because they had come to the conclusion that the object was some kind of a new weapon belonging to the U.S. and that they would only be prying into something that was none of their business. They also reasoned that if such an aircraft was far enough along to be flight tested they would probably hear something about it soon anyway. It is very apparent that their interest is again aroused and that they will attempt more research on the incident.

They are rather firmly convinced that the object is not a flock of birds. This is due to the great speed at which they travel. If the birds did have an apparently great speed, they would have to be very low. The lights these people saw gave the appearance of being very high, except for "_____'s Horror." Another doubtful point is the nearly perfect geometric pattern of the first two formations. Birds could not do that. The men did state that now that they know that the Air Force is interested, they will thoroughly discuss the possibility of birds in hopes that it is birds or some other such thing that can be explained. It is apparent that they were concerned when they found out it wasn't an Air Force project, which they had assumed when no Air Force personnel came to investigate the incident.

The professors were asked why they and their friends were the only ones who had seen so many while most people only saw them on one or two nights just after the newspaper articles came out. They said that they had thought of that and their explanation was that the other people had lost interest. They and their friends were interested in the objects and continued to look for them. They stressed the fact that they were not readily apparent unless you were looking for them. (This can be borne up by the fact that on the morning of 7 November the very bright meteor mentioned above was visible from Reese AFB. Lt. Ruppelt was in front of the Officer's Club with several other people. Only those of the group who were looking directly at the meteor saw it, and it was considered to be extremely bright.)

Report on Night Flying Objects

The first observations of these objects were made by Messrs. _____, _____ and _____ at about 9:20 P.M. on August 25, 1951. Two flights were observed and were about five minutes apart. These observers have agreed that:

95

(1) The objects were traveling from northeast to southwest and passing slightly southeast of overhead of the City of Lubbock.

(2) Each flight consisted of a series of lights in an arcuate formation which covered about 10° in the sky.

(3) It was apparent that the arcs were not continuous. Individual objects could not be clearly distinguished, but rather they appeared as scintillating points of bluish-green color, clearly and plainly visible but not brilliant, and having approximately the same illumination as high cirrus clouds on a clear moonlight night.

(4) Immediately after the flights it was estimated that the velocities of the flights were thirty degrees per second through an arc of ninety degrees beginning forty-five degrees below the zenith to forty-five degrees beyond the zenith.

(5) Both flights were identical in size, shape, velocity, and course.

(6) No sound was associated with the flights.

During the following week the same observers witnessed five flights between the hours of 9 and 12 P.M., each passing through the sky from north to south. Additional details are:

(1) On September first (Saturday) the above three were joined by Messrs. _____ and _____. On that night two flights were seen similar to those previously seen but not in the clean arcuate form above described, but rather more irregularly grouped, and with definite and individual objects present in the formation.

(2) The apparent number of objects in these succeeding flights has been variously estimated as being from fifteen to thirty.

(3) The most unusual flight was observed at 12:17 A.M. on September second by the five people who had met for the purpose of making observations. This flight passed directly overhead

in the general direction of north to south, and was seen by each member of the group.

Mr. ———— observed that in the case of this flight, an irregularly shaped yellow light appeared in the rear. The formation included dark diffuse areas, and the arc itself quivered or pulsated in the direction of its travel.

Mr. ———— first sighted this flight, and described it as a group of individually distinct yellow flames, approximately twelve or fifteen in number, traveling at an extremely high velocity, each with an angular magnitude that would be the equivalent of twelve inches across at a distance of thirty or forty feet and in violent agitation.

Mr. ———— described this flight as having the appearance of a group of from twelve to fifteen pale objects in the shape of a quadrant of a circle, producing a pale yellow blinking light, and moving noiselessly.

The two other observers, Mr. ———— and Mr. ————, agreed to the above descriptions in their essential details.

The startling characteristics of this one flight made calm observation difficult to impossible.

The members of this group have seen a total of ten or twelve flights of these objects between August 25 and about November 1, 1951.

Submitted by

————
Professor and Head of Department of Petroleum Engineering

————
Professor of Geology
Department of Geology

————
Professor of Chem. Eng.
Department of Chemistry and Chemical Engineering

————
Professor and Director
Seismological Observatory

Test Report No. WCEFP-2-4, Physics Branch, Sensitometry Unit 29 Nov 1951
Subject: Evaluation of 35 mm. Negatives

FACTUAL DATA

1. Four negative frames were submitted from the Air Technical Intelligence Center for photographic evaluation by the Sensitometry Unit. These negatives were exposed at approximately 2330 CST, 30 Aug. 1951, at Lubbock, Texas. The camera was the familiar Kodak 35 with coupled range-finder and a 50 mm (2 inch) f/3.5 Anastor Kodak lens. The Plus X film was exposed for $\frac{1}{10}$ sec with lens aperture wide open, presumably with the camera hand-held and the film was processed in Panthermic 777 developer for 15 min. An interpretation of the configuration of spots was requested, in addition to general sensitometric notes.

2. A preliminary microscopic examination of the negatives disclosed the presence of patterns of spots, the patterns on the four frames being generally similar. Roughly 20 spots were visible on each negative in a flat "V" formation. In 3 negatives the formation consists of two rows, while the fourth shows all spots lined up in a single row. All negatives show evidence of camera motion during exposure, since the spots all are similarly blurred on the same negative, and the blur shape is different for each negative.

3. To resolve the formations and detect internal motion of the spots, each negative was examined on a large comparator microscope. The rectangular coordinates of each spot, relative to a convenient origin of coordinates, were read and then plotted on coordinate paper. It is emphasized here that the resulting plot is erect, but a mirror image, from left to right, of the actual object photographed.

4. Little significance, other than brightness variations, can be found from the negatives separately. When the charts were superimposed, however, it was readily apparent that the two rows of spots behaved differently. One row shows only slight variation from a precise "V" formation throughout, whereas the other

row appears to pass from above the first row, through it to a position below. The spacings of this second row vary irregularly in the 3 frames plotted, while the first row holds a fairly precise formation. The first frame, No. 4, was not plotted because of extreme blurring, but frames 5, 7 and 8 were plotted as Charts I, II and III respectively. Chart IV is a composite of Charts I, II and III. In it the spots from the previous charts, that appear relatively fixed in the formation, are shown as heavy black ink spots. The relatively moving spots are shown in light pencil—the first position of these shifting spots is light red, as in Chart I; the second position, spaced between the heavy spots, is in black pencil, as from Chart II; and the final position is shown in light green.

5. According to the microscopic examination, spot brightness range could be expressed as weak, average, and bright, corresponding to faint, average, or heavy spot densities. The faint spots in the moving row are underscored, while the bright spots are circled. Only those spots in the fixed row that are alike in all three negatives are indicated in the same way.

6. There is the appearance of two extra spots, outside the regular rows. One spot is to the lower right in all three charts, while the spot shows[6] only faintly in the No. 7 negative and was missed in plotting Chart II; it appears in position at the left end of the moving row in Chart III.

CONCLUSIONS

7. There is relative movement within the formation of spots, so that they are not lights on a fixed object. The relative motion is such that it appears unlikely that they are co-planar and photographed from different angles. Furthermore, it is unlikely that the moving spots are in any kind of straight line.

8. The angular size of the formation, at the camera lens, is very nearly the same in all cases. The formation is, however, slightly larger in Chart II, or Frame 7, than in the others. The angular size corresponds to an object size of 310 ± 30 ft., seen by the camera 1 mile away. The actual size of the formation may be

calculated from this ratio, if the actual distance from the camera can be determined. This image size is actually 0.12", formed by a 2" focal length lens in the camera used.

9. Although the image size in Frame 8 is about 2% less than in Frame 7, suggesting that the objects are receding from the camera, the aspect of the "V" formation does not correspond to a horizontal "V", travelling parallel to the earth's surface unless at an enormous altitude. Such motion at conventional altitudes would require the "V" to flatten, eventually becoming a straight line, but the "V" in Frame 8 is a slightly smaller angle than in Frame 7.

10. The orientation of the "V" formation is the same on all negatives. If the formation did actually pass directly over the camera station, all photographs were taken either before or after, but not both. It is obvious that the image would be inverted on two successive negatives if they were taken on an approaching and then a receding slant angle.

11. The pattern of spot brightness is such as to prove conclusively that all 3 frames—5, 7 and 8—were exposed to the same object pattern of spots. However, the relative positions of these spots varies, as described above.

RECOMMENDATIONS

12. In the event that further assistance is required of this Laboratory, exposure tests should be made under identical conditions to determine the spot nature required to produce the observed densities, and to determine the amount of camera blur produced by an experienced photographer in "panning", to track a moving target at night.

Chapter Five: Of Monsters, Little Green Men, and the UFO Insignia at Socorro

"It looked worse than Frankenstein," was the way Mrs. Kathleen May described the alien being that she and seven other Flatwoods, West Virginia, residents had seen on September 12, 1952.

Mrs. May had had her attention called to the saucer by a group of excited children, including her sons, Eddie, thirteen, and Fred, twelve. The children were at a nearby playground with Gene Lemon, Neil Nunley, Ronnie Shaver, and Tommy Hyer when they spotted a "saucer spouting an exhaust that looked like balls of red fire." According to the boys, the saucer had landed on a hilltop above the May house.

Gene Lemon, a husky seventeen-year-old, found a flashlight and said that he was going to investigate. At the urging of her children, Mrs. May agreed to accompany the teenager, and they and the children set out into the night.

After about half an hour of tramping through the brush that covered the narrow uphill trail, Gene Lemon's courage left him in a long scream of horror. The intrepid band of saucer hunters fled in panic from the sight that Lemon's flashlight had illuminated.

When Lemon had flashed the beam on the glowing green spots, he had thought them the eyes of an animal. Instead, the flash had spotlighted an immense, manlike figure with a blood-red face and greenish eyes that blinked out from a pointed hood. Behind the monster was "a glowing ball of fire as big as a house" that grew dimmer and brighter at intervals.

Later, Mrs. May described the monster as having "terrible claws." Some of the children, however, had not noticed any arms at all. Most agreed that the being had worn dark clothing, and fourteen-year-old Neil Nunley specified the color as "dark green." Estimates of the creature's height ranged from seven feet to ten feet. The party was in definite agreement about one characteristic of the alien, however: the sickening odor that it seemed to emit. Mrs. May told reporters that it was "like sulphur," but really it was unlike anything that she had ever encountered before.

A. Lee Stewart, Jr., of the Braxton (West Virginia) Democrat, arrived on the scene moments ahead of Sheriff Robert Carr. Although most of the party were too frightened to speak coherently and some were receiving first aid for cuts and bruises received in their pell-mell flight down the hill, the newsman persuaded Lemon to accompany him to the spot where they had seen the being.

Stewart saw no sign of the giant space traveler or the pulsating red globe of light, but he was able to inhale enough of the strange odor to declare it "sickening and irritating." He later wrote that he had developed a familiarity with a wide variety of gases while serving in the Air Force, but he had never been confronted by any gas with a similar odor.

Each of the party later testified that the monster had been moving toward them, possibly because they were between the creature and the large, globular object that evidently served as its spacecraft.

Neil Nunley said the alien "didn't really walk. It just moved. It moved evenly: it didn't jump."

On the evening of August 21, 1955, aliens allegedly made the backwoods jump again when they visited Kelly-Hopkinsville, Kentucky. The landing and the subsequent sighting of two to five aliens was witnessed by eight adults and three children.

The Air Force, local authorities, the police, and area newspapers conducted an extensive and well-documented investigation of the incident.

The adults involved were rather staid, reserved people, hardly likely to have invented the entire adventure simply for the sake of sensational publicity. Some even went so far as to leave town when the curiosity seekers and cultists began to arrive, and they remained consistently reluctant to speak about the ordeal with Air Force officials and other investigators.

It was a Sunday evening, and company had gathered at Gaither McGehe's farm, which had been rented by the Sutton family. Teenager Billy Ray Sutton left the farmhouse to get a drink from the well. As he drank the cool, refreshing water from a chipped cup, he was startled to see a large bright object land about a city block away from the farmhouse.

Billy Ray's announcement of the strange arrival was met with a pronounced lack of response. The family's interest was considerably heightened, however, when, according to several reports, they saw "little men, less than four feet tall with long arms and a large, round head" approaching the farmhouse.

The Suttons testified that the creature's eyes had a yellow glow. The orbs were extremely large and seemed very sensitive to light. It was the outside lights of the farmhouse that seemed to prevent the creatures from advancing into the home rather than the bullets from the farmers' rifles, which were fired in great abundance.

"Bullets just seemed to bounce off their nickel-plated armor," said one of the witnesses.

Although several direct hits were made on the aliens, they seemed to "pop right up again and disappear into the darkness, away from the light."

A man named Taylor told investigators: "I knocked one of them off a barrel with my .22. I heard the bullet hit the critter and ricochet off.

103

The little man floated to the ground and rolled up like a ball. I used up four boxes of shells on the little men."

Billy Ray Sutton blasted one of them point-blank with his shotgun. The alien simply somersaulted and rolled off into the darkness.

As with the monster at Flatlands, West Virginia, the witnesses claimed that the aliens did not walk, but "seemed to float" toward them.

The farmers battled the seemingly invulnerable creatures for nearly four hours before they drove in panic to the Hopkinsville police station for reinforcements. Chief Greenwell was convinced by the hysteria of the three children and the obvious fright of the eight adults that they had definitely been battling **something** out on that farm. And everyone knew that the Suttons "weren't a drinking family."

Led by Chief Greenwell, more than a dozen state, county, and city police officers arrived to investigate and, if need arose, do battle with the little supermen. On the way to the farm, the officers noticed a "strange shower of meteors that came from the direction of the Sutton farmhouse." One officer testified later that the meteors had made a "swishing sound" as they passed overhead.

The investigators found no trace of a space ship or the little men, but they found "several peculiar signs and indications" that something extremely strange had taken place that evening on the Sutton's farm. Whatever had invaded, the bullet holes in the walls bore mute testimony that the farmers had deemed the creatures real enough to shoot at.

Such cases as these gained a great deal of public notoriety, but were given very short shrift by Air Force investigators. The official files contain little more than newspaper clippings and cursory judgmental comments concerning the mental stability of the witnesses.

It was not until he wrote **The UFO Experience**

(1972) that Dr. J. Allen Hynek presented his UFO category "Close Encounters of the Third Kind," which describes confrontations between humans and alleged aliens from landed unidentified vehicles. "Currently we have an estimated 800 sightings of this sort on file," Dr. Hynek told **UFO Report** (August 1976). "These encounters constitute what is probably the most incredibly bizarre aspect of the UFO enigma."

Hynek admitted that when he had first heard of such episodes, while a Project Blue Book consultant, his natural prejudices told him to throw them out. But the "little-green-man syndrome" has never ceased to exist in UFOlogy, and Hynek now concedes that "no scientist should discard data simply because he doesn't like it."

Hynek acknowledged that he had been "building toward a positive attitude for years" when John Fuller presented the fascinating account of Betty and Barney Hill, the couple who claimed to have been medically examined aboard a UFO. The case of Hickson and Parker, two Mississippi fishermen who also claimed to have been taken aboard a UFO and subjected to a physical examination, altered Hynek's thinking "completely."

"I don't know what makes me want to automatically look down upon these creature cases," Dr. Hynek pondered for **UFO Report**:

Maybe this involves an atavistic fear of the unknown, or of rivalry with another species. There is, upon closer scrutiny, another factor which I find difficult to sort out. It is odd that the creatures seen coming from these craft should resemble our own *Homo sapiens* race so closely. It is also peculiar that they would be able to adjust to our gravitational pull or breathe our air so easily. This could only mean that they are mechanical creatures—robots—or they originate from a habitat whose environment is very similar to ours here on Earth.

105

In the Socorro, New Mexico, case of April 24, 1964, Air Force investigators were presented with a witness whose testimony could not be cracked, the apparent landing of a UFO, and the sighted presence of two UFOnauts. If the Hill case helped to build a positive attitude for humanoid entities in Dr. Hynek's mind, in the following pages we can see his opinion of "creatures" definitely moving toward the point of readiness at which he could experience complete alteration with the Hickson-Parker case. It would also seem that the Socorro sighting began to plant strong seeds of belief in the minds of several Air Force personnel —belief that the UFO mystery most certainly presented something beyond misinterpretation of natural phenomena, bizarre hallucinations, and mental aberrations.

On April 24, 1964, a Socorro, New Mexico policeman, Mr. Lonnie Zamora, reported sighting an object about a mile south of the town at approximately 5:45 p.m., in an unpopulated area full of hills and gullies and covered with sagebrush. Following is a summary of his report to Air Force investigators:

Mr. Zamora reported that while chasing a speeding car north on US 85, he heard a roar and saw flames in an area where a dynamite shack was known to be located. He abandoned chase of the auto and proceeded to where he believed an explosion had occurred. After traveling a little-used road and experiencing considerable difficulty in trying to drive his car up a gravel-covered hill, he said he then observed what he thought was an overturned car standing on end. At this point he was about 800 ft. distant from the object and his car was at the crest of a hill with the object ahead of him in a gully. He reported that during this first glance he saw one or two figures in coveralls whom he assumed to be occupants of the object. This is the only time he saw these figures; he did not see them again. After radioing to Police Headquarters at Socorro that he was proceeding to investigate what he believed to be an auto accident, he drove to a point about 150 ft from the gully where the object rested and stopped the car to proceed on foot. He said the object was white, egg or oval-shaped and apparently supported on girderlike legs. He said he heard a roar and saw smoke and flame coming from the bottom of the object. At this point, Mr. Zamora believed that the object was about to explode and he became frightened, turned, and ran to shield himself behind the police car, bumping his leg and losing his glasses on the way. He said that he crouched down, shielding his eyes with his arm while the noise stopped and he glanced up. He reported that the object had risen to a point about 15–20 feet above the ground and the flame and smoke had ceased. At this point, he reported, he noted a design on the object which he described as markings in red about 1 to 1½ ft in height, shaped like a crescent with a vertical arrow and horizontal line underneath. He stated that the object remained stationary for several seconds and then flew off in a southerly direction following the contour of the gully.

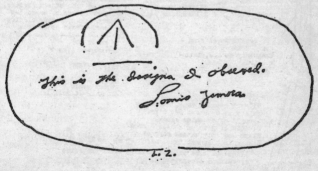

OBSERVED "INSIGNA" LOCATED APPROXIMATELY AT CENTER OF OBJECT AS SEEN FROM ABOVE SIDE.

This is the insignia I observed.

Lonnie Zamora

L. Z.

Within moments afterward, Sgt Chavez of the New Mexico State Police arrived on the scene in response to Mr. Zamora's earlier radio call. He observed no object, but he reported that there were some slight depressions in the ground and apparently burned brush in the area where Mr. Zamora had reported seeing the object. The brush was cold to the touch. Sgt Chavez reported the incident to local military authorities who conducted the initial investigation.

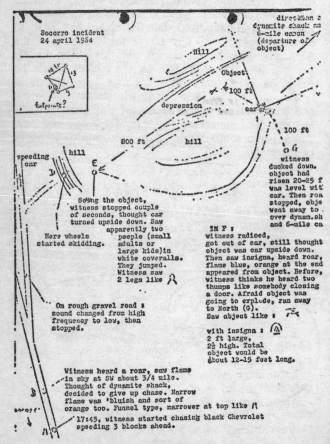

Socorro incident
24 april 1964

footprints?

direction of dynamite shack an 6-mile canon (departure of object)

Hill

Object
← 100 ft

depression

car

100 ft

800 ft   hill

speeding car

hill

witness ducked down. object had risen 20-25 f was level wit car. Then roa stopped, obje went away to over dynam.sh and 6-mile ca

Seeing the object, witness stopped couple of seconds, thought car turned upside down. Saw apparently two people (small adults or large kids)in white coveralls. They jumped. Witness saw 2 legs like

Here wheels started skidding.

IN F :
witness radioed, got out of car, still thought object was car upside down. Then saw insigna, heard roar, flame blue, orange at the end appeared from object. Before, witness thinks he heard two thumps like somebody closing a door. Afraid object was going to explode, ran away to North (G). Saw object like :

On rough gravel road : sound changed from high frequency to low, then stopped.

with insigna :
2 ft large,
2½ high. Total object would be about 12-15 feet long.

Witness heard a roar, saw flame in sky at SW about 3/4 mile. Thought of dynamite shack, decided to give up chase. Narrow flame was bluish and sort of orange too. Funnel type, narrower at top like

17:45, witness started chasing black Chevrolet speeding 3 blocks ahead.

108

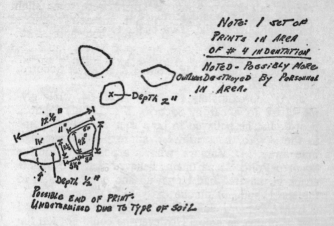

FOOTPRINTS.
— IN SOFT SAND

NOTE: 1 SET OF PRINTS IN AREA OF # 4 INDENTATION NOTED — POSSIBLY MORE OUTLINES DESTROYED BY PERSONNEL IN AREA.

X — DEPTH 2"

12¼"
11"
11"

DEPTH ½"

POSSIBLE END OF PRINT. UNDETERMINED DUE TO TYPE OF SOIL.

The Air Force sent investigators from their project office at Wright-Patterson AFB, Ohio. The investigation discolsed the following facts:

No other witnesses to the object reported by Mr. Zamora could be located.

There were no unidentified helicopters or aircraft in the area.

Observers at radar installations had observed no unusual or unidentified blips.

There was no unusual meteorological activity; no thunderstorms. The weather was windy but clear.

There was no evidence of markings of any sort in the area other than the shallow depressions at the location where Mr. Zamora reported sighting the object.

Laboratory analysis of soil samples disclosed no foreign material or radiation above normal for the surrounding area.

Laboratory analysis of the burned brush showed no chemicals which would indicate a type of propellant.

There was no evidence presented that the object was extraterrestrial in origin or represented a threat to the security of the United States.

The Air Force is continuing its investigation and the case is still open.

For several days following this report, other sightings were reported in the New Mexico area. In each case the sighting was determined to be a known object or natural phenomena. Two of the reports were determined to be hoaxes.

1. The following is a resume on the unidentified flying object sighted by Mr. Lonnie Zamora, of Socorro, New Mexico.

a. At approximately 1745, 24 April 64, while giving chase to a car in Socorro, Mr. Lonnie Zemora heard what he believed to be a roar and saw a flame in the sky to the southwest, approximately one half mile away. Mr. Zamora, who is a policeman for the Socorro Police Department, believed that a dynamite shack in the area had blown up and decided to go to the shack and not pursue the speeding automobile.

b. Mr. Zamora claims that the flame was bluish and sort of orange in color. However, he could not tell the size of the flame which was slowly descending. The flame was of a narrow type and streamed down into

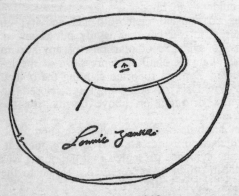

SKETCH OF OBJECT
FROM MY POSITION-
AT APPROXIMATELY 103 ft.-

sort of a funnel shape. At this time he was still driving his car and did not pay too much attention.

c. Mr. Zamora traveled slowly on the gravel road westward toward the object. He noted nothing for a while and he went slowly looking for the shack; he could not recall exactly where the shack was located. He suddenly noted to the south of his position a shiny object which was off the road. At first glance it appeared as a car upside down. He thought some kids might have turned it over. At this point he saw the people in white coveralls, quite close to the object. One of these persons seemed to stop and look straight at him and seemed startled. At this point Mr. Zamora was traveling with the idea of helping them. The object was like aluminum-white, smooth, but not like chrome. Object was oval shape and at first glance appeared to look like an overturned white automobile. The only time that Mr. Zamora saw the two people in white coveralls was when he stopped, probably two seconds or so. The two persons appeared to be normal in shape. At this point Mr. Zamora proceeded towards the object and radioed the sheriff's office at Socorro of a possible accident. He informed the Socorro office that he would be busy and out of his car, checking the object.

2. Attached is a listing of sightings reported to the Air Force and might be attributed to the Socorro, New Mexico sighting.

For The Commander
ERIC T de JONCKHEKRE
Colonel, USAF
Deputy for Technology
    and Subaystems
    Listing
    1, Atch

For SCFTC RE your SCFTC 16-6-13. The possibility of a research vehicle being involved in the Socorro sighting has been investigated. The army liaison office at FTD has been contacted and the case has been discussed with them at great length; however, they have no knowledge of an army research vehicle which would leave marks such as those found at Socorro. Lt. Col Conkey and Maj. H. Mitchell of the AFMDC have also been contacted and the case has been discussed with them. Both of these officers were aware of the case before our discussion; however, neither one of them has any knowledge of a vehicle in the Holloman area, such as described in the report. Bell Aircraft Co. has been queried regarding their research on a lunar landing vehicle which would leave impressions on the ground such as those found in Socorro. One such vehicle has been delivered to the Air Force at Edwards AFB: However, this vehicle is not operational and is not scheduled for tests until the latter part of June. Fifteen letters were written to industrial companies asking them for their research status on lunar landing modules. Thus far, information received from these companies has not been useful in solving case. NASA in Wash. D.C. was contacted by SAFOI and they have received no reply. Col. Conkey, while on a recent visit to FTD, remarked that security in Holloman is extremely tight. Re SCFT Assistance. Still believe that tenant organizations at Holloman hold key to sighting. Could SCFT ask Holloman Base Commander to grant audience to FTD/UFO Project Officer (Capt. Quintanilla) [sic] in order to discuss details of Socorro sighting. Significant developments have been nil since Dr. Hynek's briefing to HQ AFSC.

29 September 1964

Dr. Donald H. Menzel
Harvard College Observatory
Cambridge 38, Massachusetts

Dear Don:

Thank you for your letter of September 10, and I'm glad that you liked the review.

With respect to the Socorro case, I wish I could

substantiate the idea that it was a hoax or a hallucination. Unfortunately, I cannot. I have talked at length with the principals in the sighting, and unless my knowledge of human nature is utterly out of phase, I would feel that [he] is incapable of perpetrating a hoax. He is simply a good solid cop whose two early comments are in themselves quite revealing. The first was to ask his superior whether he should first talk to his priest and his second was that he resented the whole thing because it prevented him from getting his quota of speeders that day: He is not imaginative, sticks solidly to the business, and is far from talkative. His superior, Sergeant Chaves, is much more articulate.

Major Quintanilla is convinced that the Socorro sighting is neither a hoax nor a hallucination, but he feels that perhaps some sort of test object (war games, etc.) might have been going on. However, there is no record of such even though he has tried to track this down through White Sands, Holloman Air Force Base, and a few others. I would like to go along with the hallucination idea if it weren't for the marks and the burned patches. I arrived there several days afterwards, of course, but the marks had been preserved, and I have the word of nine witnesses who saw the marks within hours of the incident, who tell me that the center of the marks were moist as though the topsoil had been freshly pushed aside. The four marks when plotted out lie such that the diagonals intersect at exactly ninety degrees, which may or may not be significant.

Then, of course, we have the testimony of the tourist who stopped by a gas station (I talked to the filling station man in detail) who while waiting for his change remarked, "Your airplanes fly awfully low around here, one liked to knock me off the road just south of town."

Whereupon the attendant replied, "Oh, we have a lot of helicopters flying around here."

To which the tourist replied, "If that was a helicopter it's the damndest helicopter I ever saw. It seems he was in some sort of trouble because he

113

landed just over the hill, and a little later I saw a police car going out toward it."

I checked the times on all these, and they jibe well within human error of time estimates. Furthermore, I talked with all the townspeople I could get hold of, including the baggage man at the station, the priest, and several people who have known him since he was in knee britches. This baggage man at the station, (baggage men have a way of knowing everything about everybody in town) gave him one of the cleanest bills of health I've ever heard from anyone. Furthermore, one of my astronomy undergraduates did a term paper on the Socorro case since he comes from Socorro and his aunt essayed to gather a great deal of raw materials for him. She personally visited and went up and down the town fishing out what she could. In her talk with _____ she quotes _____ as saying, _____ "just gave himself up to God." The term paper was complete with geologic map, road maps, etc. and while I asked the student undertaking the term paper to do everything he could to find an obvious natural explanation of the sighting, he was unable to do so. I think it's time for H. M. and Lyle Boyd to get in the act to solve this mystery! I'm stuck.

Furthermore, I revisited Socorro on my way to Las Cruces a month ago just to check the pulse. I thought perhaps that if I talked to _____ and the other again, they would certainly have had some afterthought about the thing after this many months had passed. _____, if anything, is more reticent than before and, although I tried to find negative character references for _____ or some sort of medical history, I met nothing but a wall of good character references. The guy doesn't drink, cavort with women, or recite poetry. He captures speeders. In fact, as you know, he was chasing a speeder when the incident occurred. He was in uniform, on duty, and this is a situation hardly conducive to an isolation hallucination or what-have-you. He is the sort of cop who when he chases a speeder has a one track mind and wants to get his speeder and make up his quota for the day. It was, I think, only because he heard this noise and report-

114

edly saw a flash of light out near the mayor's dynamite shack (he is apparently beholden to the mayor for his job) that he swerved aside from his normal course of duty to respond to what he thought was a higher call, namely to do a good turn for the mayor and his dynamite shack. Also the fact that when he first saw the object in the distance, he stated that he thought it was an overturned auto, doesn't sound like the start of a hallucination. He first saw it from a distance of a good quarter mile—more like a half mile and then of necessity lost sight of it for a couple of minutes while he drove around hillock which obscured his sight. It was not until he rounded the hillock and came onto the small mesa that he was confronted with the object a bare 200 feet away from him. I reenacted the crime with him, along with stopwatch, etc. and throughout the whole thing, he had none of the marks of the crackpot as I found, for instance, in my interview with _____. Just a solid cop. So, you come up with an answer please.

Sincerely yours,
Allen

Officer Zamora's Own Account

_____, Socorro NM, _____, Officer Socorro PD about 5 years, office phone 835-0941, now on 2:00 P.M. to 10:00 P.M. shift.

About 5:45 P.M. 4/24/64 while in Socorro 2 Police Car (64 Pontiac white) started to chase a car due south from west side of Court House. Car was apparently speeding, and was about 3 blocks in front. At point on Old Rodeo Street (extension of Park St. south) near George Morillo residence (about ⅛ mile south of Spring Street, the _____ chased car was going straight ahead toward rodeo grounds. Car chased was a new black Chevrolet (it might have been _____ boy about 17). Chased car still about 3 blocks ahead. _____ alone.

At this time heard a roar and saw a flame in the

sky to the southwest some distance away—possibly a ½ mile or a mile. Came to mind that a dynamite shack in that area had blown up, decided to leave chased car go.

Flame was bluish and sort of orange too. Could not tell size of flame. Sort of motionless flame, slowly descending. Was still driving car and could not pay too much attention to the flame. It was a narrow type of flame. It was like a "stream down"—a funnel type—narrower at top than at bottom. Flame possibly 3 degrees or so in width—not wide.

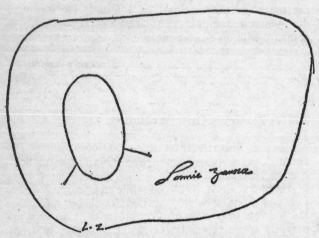

FIRST VIEW OF THE OBJECT FROM APPROXIMATELY .15 MILES LOOKING DOWN ON IT

Flame about twice as wide at bottom as top, and about four times as high as top was wide. Did not notice any object at top, did not note if top of flame was level. Sun was to west and did not help vision. Had green sun glasses over prescription glasses. Could not see bottom of flame because it was behind the hill. No smoke noted. Noted some "commotion" at bottom—dust? Possibly from windy day—wind was blowing hard. Clear sunny sky otherwise—just a few clouds scattered over area.

Noise was a roar, not a blast. Not like a jet. Changed from high frequency to low frequency and then stopped. Roar lasted possibly 10 seconds—was going towards it at that time on the rough gravel road. Saw flame about as long as heard the sound. Flame same color as best as recall. Sound distinctly from high to low until it disappeared. Windows both were

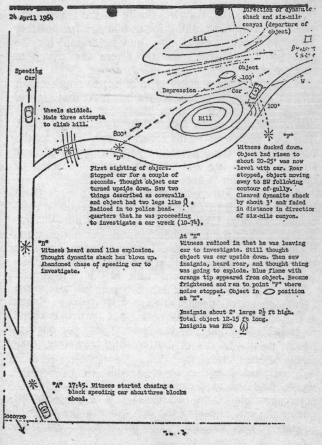

24 April 1964

Direction of dynamite
shack and six-mile
canyon (departure of
object)

Hill

Speeding
Car

Object
100'

Depression

Car

100'

W.

Wheels skidded.
Made three attempts
to climb hill.

Hill

800'

"C"

"D"

First sighting of object.
Stopped car for a couple of
seconds. Thought object car
turned upside down. Saw two
things described as coveralls
and object had two legs like
Radioed in to police headquarters that he was proceeding
to investigate a car wreck (10-74).

"F"

Witness ducked down.
Object had risen to
about 20-25' was now
level with car. Roar
stopped, object moving
away to SW following
contour of gully.
Cleared dynamite shack
by about 3' and faded
in distance in direction
of six-mile canyon.

At "E"
Witness radioed in that he was leaving
car to investigate. Still thought
object was car upside down. Then saw
insignia, heard roar, and thought thing
was going to explode. Blue flame with
orange tip appeared from object. Became
frightened and ran to point "F" where
noise stopped. Object in ⬭ position
at "E".

"B"
Witness heard sound like explosion.
Thought dynamite shack has blown up.
Abandoned chase of speeding car to
investigate.

Insignia about 2' large 2½ ft high.
Total object 12-15 ft long.
Insignia was RED

"A" 17:45. Witness started chasing a
black speeding car about three blocks
ahead.

Socorro

down. No other spectators noted—no traffic except the car in front—and car in front might have heard it but possibly did not see it because car in front was too close to hill in front, to see the flame.

After the roar and flame, did not note anything, while going up the somewhat steep rough hill—had to back up and try again, two more times. Got up about half way first time, wheels started skidding, roar still going on, had to back down and try twice and rock. While beginning third time, noise and flame not noted.

After got to top, traveled slowly on the gravel road westwardly. Noted nothing for awhile . . . for possibly 10 or 15 seconds, went slow, looking around for the shack—did not recall exactly where the dynamite shack was.

Suddenly noted a shiny type object to south about 150 to 200 yards. It was off the road. At first glance, stopped. It looked, at first, like a car turned upside down. Thought some kids might have turned over. Saw two people in white coveralls very close to the object. One of these persons seemed to turn and look straight at my car and seemed startled—seemed to quickly jump somewhat.

At this time I started moving my car towards them quickly, with idea to help. Had stopped about only a couple seconds. Object was like aluminum—it was whitish against the mesa background, but not chrome. Seemed like O in shape and I at first glance took it to be overturned white car. Car appeared turned up like standing on radiator or on trunk, at this first glance.

The only time I saw these two persons was when I had stopped, for possibly two seconds or so, to glance at the object. I don't recall noting any particular shape or possibly any hats, or headgear. These persons appeared normal in shape—but possibly they were small adults or large kids.

Then paid attention to road while drove towards scene. Radioed to sheriff's office "Socorro 2 to Socorro, possible 10-44 (accident), I'll be 10-6 (busy) out of the car, checking the car down in the arroyo."

Stopped car, was still talking on radio, started to get

out, mike fell down, reached back to put up mike, then replaced radio mike in slot, got out of car and started to go down to where knew the object (car) was.

Hardly turned around from car, when heard roar (was not exactly a blast), very loud roar—at that close was real loud. Not like a jet—knows what jets sound like. Started low frequency quickly, then roar rose in frequency (higher tone) and in loudness—from loud to very loud. At same time as roar saw flame. Flame was under the object. Object was starting to go straight up—slowly up. Object slowly rose straight up. Flame was light blue and at bottom was sort of orange color. From this angle, saw what might be the side of object (not end, as first noted). Difficult to describe flame. Thought, from roar, it might blow up. Flame might have come from underside of object, at middle, possibly a four feet area—very rough guess. Cannot describe flame further except blue and orange. No smoke, except dust in immediate area.

As soon as saw flame and heard roar, turned away, run away from object but did turn head towards object. Bumped leg on car—back Fender area. Car facing southwest. Glasses fell to ground, left them there. Ran to north—car between him and object.

Object was oval in shape. It was smooth—no windows or doors. As roar started, it was still on or near ground. Noted red lettering of some type (see illustration). Insignia was about 2½′ high and about 2′ wide I guess. Was in middle of object . . . Object still like aluminum-white.

After fell by car and glasses fell off, kept running to north, with car between me and object. Glanced back couple of times. Noted object to rise to about level of car, about 20 to 25 feet guess—took I guess about six seconds when object started to rise and I glanced back. I ran I guess about half way to where I ducked down—about fifty feet from the car is where I ducked down, just over edge of hill. I guess I had run about 25 feet when I glanced back and saw the object about level with the car and it appeared about directly over the place where it rose from.

I was still running and I jumped just over the hill —I stopped because I did not hear the roar. I was scared of the roar, and I had planned to continue running down the hill. I turned around toward the object and at same time put my head toward ground, covering my face with my arms. Being that there was no roar, I looked up, and I saw the object going away from me. It did not come any closer to me. It appeared to go in straight line and at same height— possibly 10 to 15 feet from ground, and it cleared the dynamite shack by about three feet. Shack about eight feet high. Object was traveling very fast. It seemed to rise up, and take off immediately across country. I ran back to my car and as I ran back, I kept an eye on the object. I picked up my glasses (I left the sun glasses on ground), got into the car, and radioed to Nep Lopez, radio operator, to "look out the window, to see if you could see an object." He asked what is it? I answered "It looks like a balloon." I don't know if he saw it. If Nep looked out his window, which faces north, he couldn't have seen it. I did not tell him at the moment which window to look out of.

As I was calling Nep, I could still see the object. The object seemed to lift up slowly, and to "get small" in the distance very fast. It seemed to just clear the Box Canyon or Six Mile Canyon Mountain. It disappeared as it went over the mountain. It had no flame whatsoever as it was traveling over the ground, and no smoke or noise.

Feeling in good health. Last drink—two or three beers—was over a month ago. Noted no odors. Noted no sounds other than described. Gave directions to Nep Lopez at radio and to Sergeant M. S. Chavez to get there. Went down to where the object had been and I noted the brush was burning in several places. At that time I heard Sgt. Chavez (N.M. State Police at Socorro) calling me on radio for my location, and I returned to my car, told him he was looking at me. Then Sgt. Chavez came up, asked me what the trouble was, because I was sweating and he told me I was white, very pale. I asked the Sgt. to see what I saw, and that was the burning brush. Then Sgt. Chavez and I went to the spot, and Sgt. Chavez pointed out the tracks.

When I first saw the object (when I thought it might be a car) I saw what appeared to be two legs of some type from the object to the ground. At the time, I didn't pay much attention to what it was—I thought it was an accident—I saw the two persons. I didn't pay any attention to the two "legs?" The two "legs" were at the bottom of the object, slanted outwards to the ground. The object might have been about three and a half feet from the ground at that time. I just glanced at it.

Can't tell how long [I] saw object second time (the "close" time), possibly 20 seconds—just a guess—from time got out of car, glanced at object, ran from object, jumped over edge of hill, then got back to car and radio as object disappeared.

As my mike fell as I got out of car, at scene area, I heard about two or three loud "thumps," like someone possibly hammering or shutting a door or doors hard. These "thumps" were possibly a second or less apart. This was just before the roar. The persons not seen when I got up to the scene area.

Just before Sgt. Chavez got to scene, I got my pen and drew a picture of the insignia on the object.

Socorro Revisited

On Saturday August 15, I drove with _____ whose car I had rented for the day, to Socorro from Las Cruces, New Mexico. We left Las Cruces shortly before 7:30 in the morning, and arrived in Socorro about 10:30 A.M.

The object of this visit was to obtain an overview of the feelings and opinions in Socorro about the Zamora's sighting of April 24th, after several months had passed, and to find out if the principals had any afterthoughts or changes which they wished to make in their story, how they were now regarded by the townfolk, and what if any was the official opinion.

The net results of the visit which involved talking once again with Zamora, Sergeant Chavez, Captain Holder, the editor of the local paper, and seven other townspeople, was much the same as before. Zamora, if anything, is more reticent and withdrawn. The more articulate Sgt. Chavez still firmly believes in Zamora's story, and I found no contradictions between his partial retelling of the story and the original telling of his story in late April. Although I made a distinct attempt to find a chink in Zamora's armor, I simply couldn't find anyone, with the possible exception of a _____ who has a house fairly near the site of the original sighting, who did anything but completely uphold Zamora's character and reliability, and I again talked with people who had known him since childhood.

I revisited the site: the markings are still there, but very much obliterated, and this time I was able to take stereo photographs of the general terrain. I was impressed more than before with the illogical nature of the landing site. If an ordinary aircraft had been in trouble it could have landed on the quite flat mesa just to the side of the gully, and no pilot, unless his craft were completely disabled, would have chosen to land in the rocky and uneven gully. If he had been that disabled, he certainly would not have been able to take off shortly thereafter.

Returning to the chronological account: when I arrived, neither Chaves or Zamora was available, having been on duty most of the night. I talked with the radio dispatcher and a "cowboy type" townsman who said that he spent much of his time in mountains around the country. Both of these men were very curious about what the Air Force had found, and both volunteered that things had quieted down very much, but that there was still a big belief in Zamora's story. Apropos of the Air Force's story, my statement throughout the day was always the same: the Air Force is still interested and working on it; they had not found as yet a specific, logical explanation, and the results of the chemical analysis (everybody was curious about that) was that the rocks were ordinary minerals unaffected by the landing, and that the charred materials showed only results of conventional combustion. Considerable surprise throughout the day was expressed that the Air Force had not made a more detailed analysis of the possible fuel or mechanism of the burning of the bushes, and also, incidentally, why the Air Force had not made compression tests of the ground in the area to see how much downward thrust would have been necessary to produce the observed markings.

Once again coming to the chronological story: I armed myself with about a dollar's worth of dimes and started to make telephone calls, but first _____ and I visited the office of the local newspaper, the _____. Both the owner, _____, and the editor, were there, and we looked up the back numbers of papers around that time, and especially what was said after I had left. The editor remarked that there had been several UFO officials who had come to visit them, and that one had remarked, "What sort of line of bull has Hynek and the Air Force been handing you?" He also stated that they had received many letters, one from as far away as Spain. Naturally, he wanted a statement mentioned above. The editor made one statement to the effect that they could still give full credence to Zamora's story, despite the fact that there had been some opinion in town that it shouldn't be taken seriously. But, both the owner and editor said that they would continue to believe the story unless it were proved otherwise. Of course, it is to their advantage to give full credence to the story, since it sells more papers.

* * *

My story was that I was passing through, going from Boulder to Las Cruces, and that since I was passing through, I stopped to say hello and to see if there had been any recent developments. At lunchtime I lined up a number of interviews by phone for the afternoon. The results will follow:

We first talked to _____, who is the grandmother of _____, the latter of whom was a student in my astronomy class this spring. He chose as his term paper topic "The Socorro Flying Saucer," and it was his grandmother, _____, who browsed around the town and picked up a lot of additional information. She had a long talk with _____ and _____ told us again yesterday afternoon that _____ firmly believed that _____ had been very thoroughly frightened and that he had seen something supernatural. Visiting at the _____ home (the _____ family is apparently one of the recognized and older families in town, and they live in quite a hacienda), a local parish priest was also visiting at the time, and from him in the course of conversation, we got perhaps one of the best bits of character reference on Zamora. The Father stated that in all his experience, he had not come across one person who cast any aspersion on _____, which, he remarked, was very unusual for Socorro. _____ herself is obviously a very level-headed, established woman in the society of Socorro, and when she went about investigating the Zamora case, it appeared that she had immediate access to anyone she wished. Various members of the faculty of the New Mexico School of Mines, for instance, came to her immediate assistance in answering various questions, as did Sgt. Chaves and various townspeople. One thing that she mentioned which bears on the character reference of Zamora should be noted: the baggage master at the station, a man in his sixties who apparently acts as a depository of character references for all people in town, stated that he had known Zamora for all of Zamora's life and that he was one of the most dependable people whom he'd ever known. In short, if I had any hopes of finding some chinks in Zamora's character armor, I was certainly unable to do so.

After we left the _____s, we then went to talk to Chaves, who was then on duty, and I talked to him privately for five or ten minutes after which time, by prearrangement, _____ came in. Chaves was just about the same as he was originally, still quite articulate about the thing, and when we stated that one of the main points that continued to impress us about the whole situation was the consummate fright that

124

Zamora had experienced (which everybody continued to tell us about), Chaves admitted that Zamora had been frightened, but indicated that perhaps part of that was prudence on Zamora's part—after all, if you think that something is going to explode, it is only expedient to make yourself scarce.

After a lengthy conversation which really added very little new to the original story, he radioed for Zamora to come in from his rounds and, in a few minutes, Zamora was with us. He seemed much more reticent than previously and never actually completed a full sentence. I think that there are at least two possible interpretations here, one being that, deep in his own mind, he may have realized that he overstated the case originally, or perhaps has even solved it, but, in view of the ingrained fear of possible ridicule, etc., he is keeping it to himself, or, I feel more probably, he is simply tired of the whole thing and rather wishes that it had never come up in the first place. At least nothing that he said would indicate that he does not continue to believe that something really unusual happened.

By this time the sun was over the yardarm, and we retired to a nearby bar, where we found the editor of the _____. We had a long discussion with _____ there who stated again his basic faith in the story and in Zamora's character, although he did say that, for a while there, Zamora did seem to be enjoying some of the publicity. This, however, is contrary to most of the other evidence about Zamora's reaction to the publicity.

_____ offered to go with us to see Mr. _____, the operator of the _____ Gas Station, and we heard the story of the itinerant tourist from _____ himself. The time was shortly before 6 o'clock, because _____ said that he was hurrying to get to the bank before it closed at 6 P.M. on that Friday. He stated that this was one of the reasons why he did not pay more attention to the tourist's story. However, he said that the tourist said something to this effect: "Your planes fly awfully low here—one of them liked to knock me off the road just about when I was passing your sign

125

coming into town." The _____ gas sign is almost in line with the gully where the craft landed, and the logical direction from which it would have come, considering markings, etc. The tourist said that he thought that it might be a craft in trouble, and figured this was so because he saw a police car going out toward where it had landed. This would have placed the time of the craft over the tourist's car at approximately 5:35 or 5:40 P.M. This coincides, as well as we can see, with the time that _____ was chasing a speeder. It indicates that the craft did not remain in the gully very long, and therefore could not have been disabled to any major extent. _____ said then to the tourist that there are a lot of helicopters flying around the place, to which the tourist answered that, if this was a helicopter, it certainly was a strange one. _____ promised to keep his eyes open for the tourist, but the chances of this is small.

After visiting _____, _____ and I went to the original site at approximately the same time of day that the original sighting occurred, and we went over the remaining marks and took some photographs, etc. We also photographed the apparent size of a man seen from the point along the road where Zamora first stated that he had sighted the object which he thought was an overturned car. We also took photographs of how a large car would look from that direction. _____ was particularly impressed with the fact that the marks remained after three and a half months of weathering, and it was he who wondered whether compaction tests had been made of the soil.

We then returned to have coffee with Captain Holder, the uprange commanding officer for White Sands, to see whether he had anything to add after this many months had passed. Captain Holder is still quite enthusiastic and really fairly enamoured of the idea of strange crafts. It was Captain Holder, you will remember, who, with Mr. Burns of the FBI, made the original measures between the markings, and we call recall that although the figure was drawn poorly, when it was redrawn according to dimensions given, it was found that the diagonals of the quadrilateral intersected at exact right angles. _____ pointed out that there is a well known theorem which states that if the diagonals of any quadrilateral intersect at right angles, then the points lie on a circle, the center of which is called the mean center of the figure. _____ also pointed out that one of the burned marks was directly at this mean center.

Captain Holder was particularly interested in what the Air Force had flown in 41 states, and is also an instructor in flying. She comes into the picture only because, in the course of discussions with her, she turned up a UFO story of June 2, 1960 which was duly reported to the Air Force and should be in our files. I append as Exhibit A her rather interesting and extensive writeup in the _____. Both _____s are "true believers" after their sighting which, however, I feel must have been an optical phenomenon in view of the projectory and acceleration.

Before we left, we called _____, the retiring president of the _____ School of Mines, who had nothing further to offer. Before our visit with Captain Holder, on coming back from the site, we visited a _____ who lives fairly close to the site of the alleged landing. _____ had been in his back yard just over the hill from the sighting place, and maintains that he heard no loud roar and has remained skeptical about the whole thing. He claimed that if there had been an explosion such as Zamora claims to have heard, he _____ certainly would have heard it. However, this does not necessarily follow, because _____ was directly down wind from the gully, there was a very strong southwest wind blowing, and the gully is on the opposite side of the hill from where _____ was listening. This, of course, can make a tremendous difference in ability to hear. Further, there are trucks passing along the highway quite close to _____'s house, and he undoubtedly is used to hearing backfires, and truck roars of one sort or another. He was the only person whom we talked to, however, who tended to disbelieve Zamora's veracity, indicating that it probably was a hoax. This solution is not acceptable to the present writer, because there are just too many

127

bits of evidence that militate against this hypothesis.
———— and I arrived back in Las Cruces at 12:30 A.M. on Sunday morning, August 16th.

Report on the Trip to Socorro—Albuquerque—Socorro, March 12–13, 1965

Left Las Cruces 7:45 A.M., Friday, March 12. Arrived Socorro 10:30 A.M. and had an immediate conference with Mr. Ted Ralpor, Editor of the *El Defensor Chieftan*, the Socorro newspaper. Our first subject was the movie that had been made by the Empire Films whose address in Hollywood is 7417 Sunset Blvd. A name connected with it is Morry Malkin; a phone number is AC 213, 876-6800. Malkin is coming back to Socorro in a few weeks to arrange for the world premiere of the UFO movie in Socorro. This will be a white tie affair probably! Do you think the Air Force official consultant should be present at this world premiere? He does not think so. It would be exciting, but it would also give needless significance and importance to the picture. I think we had at best ignore it.

However, I learned through the grapevine that the picture is to have a Washington, D.C. preview in about three or four weeks and that Senator Symington is interested in it. We had better get Maston Jacks office, or whoever is running the show now, on to this if at all possible. That is one preview that I should attend if at all possible. The scuttlebutt has it that the picture contains movies taken in Milan, Italy of a UFO landing with a little man getting out of it. Rumor also has it that the Empire Film Studios paid $40,000 for that Milan, Italy filmstrip. Apparently they have sunk quite a bit of money into this picture and expect to have it shown in many movie houses throughout the country and then shortly thereafter to release it for TV use. The film runs 86 minutes.

I found the situation in Socorro largely unchanged. Zamora is still generally believed, but the current feeling seems to be that there is no question that he saw something real, but that it was most likely a super-secret device being tested. I was asked many times whether I was really sure that the U.S. government didn't have a super-secret project. I pointed out that if this were the case, that it would be unlikely that we would be testing it on a global basis and the UFO phenomenon, apart from the Socorro case, is certainly not limited to the United States.

After these discussions in the editorial offices, Raynor and I went out for lunch and asked Sgt. Chaves to join us. While we were waiting for him, I showed Raynor the letter from Menzel and his comments about parts of it were, "Childish." But we went over it point by point, and likewise Chaves did. Chaves' reaction to the letter was rather strange. He had sort of a resigned, almost pathetic look on his face, and said, "I really feel sorry for Lonnie. He's had to take an awful lot."

Then he told of a recent case where Zamora was arresting a kid for speeding, and the kid said, "What do you want to give me a ticket for? Don't you know a flying saucer might come right down on us now?" (or something like that.)

I asked him what the whole movie situation had been concerning Zamora and how it had affected him. He said that Zamora had not wanted to be in the picture, but it was at the Mayor's insistence, via his boss, that he consented to do so. I can't quite believe this myself. When I talked to Zamora later, he seemed to be reasonably pleased about being in the movie. Clearly, with a world premiere in Socorro, it would be a strange human who did not get some kick out of a thing like that.

I will come back to the Menzel letter later because I discussed it with Dr. La Paz, who knows Menzel well. That was the next day in Albuquerque.

I purchased five newspapers which had various stories about the movie or about related matters. The papers were for Tuesday, February 9; Thursday, February 25; Tuesday, March 2; Tuesday, March 9; and Thursday, March 11. The first one I think you have; it states, "Socorro Part of Film on UFO's Com-

129

pleted; Zamora's Account Jibes With Sixteen Verified Sightings." The February 25th issue contains a front page story on a UFO sighted over Gallup which, as far as I can see, is nothing more than a meteor. The March 2nd issue contains a lovely story about "Scientist Indicates Why UFO's Choose Areas for Landing." One Chan P. Thomas of Los Angeles, "a former government scientist," is supposed to be the scientific advisor to Empire Film Studios. His theories as to why UFO's land in New Mexico lack, shall we say, a scientific solidity in my opinion as he is not listed in the *American Men of Science,* and I have no knowledge of him personally. There was some question as to whether he should be asked to come to Socorro to give a public lecture on the general subject. Unfortunately my advice was asked, and I strongly urged that they not do so unless they find out considerably more about the gentleman's qualifications first. His principal reason for selecting Socorro seems to be the following: "The main one can be directly attributable to the subsurface geology. I would suspect there is a multiplicity of faults, or—areas wherein sedimentary strata have been tilted to the vertical with the interlayer demarcations being plains largely in the north-south direction. The effects such subsurface deceptions have upon the energy distributions between the earth's core and the Van Allen radiation belt gives the key to the answer." He also states that he has stumbled onto many answers of heretofore unanswerable riddles: What is gravity; Why do planets orbit and rotate; Why do stars burn in nuclear fires; Is the speed of light really a velocity boundary; Can a ship be built which would do everything people who claim they have seen flying saucers say that those vehicles do?" I hardly need say more.

The same issue, however, contains a story about "UFO Sighted Streaking Over City." "The observer, a Socorro woman who asked that her name be withheld (I have her name, however, a Mrs. Williams,) said the 'perfectly round object' with deep yellow or gold light traveled at tremendous speed. She saw the object as it came over Socorro Mountain, and as it passed southeast over the city, it did not seem far above the street light." I was unable to get in touch with this woman, but according to Raynor, this did not have a trail. It seemed to be just a light.

Would you be kind enough to send about ten blank forms to Mr. Ted Raynor, Editor, Socorro *El Defensor Chieftan,* Socorro, New Mexico, and he can send one of these forms to Mrs. Williams to fill out. The results will be, probably, a meteor. I tried to get in touch with her the next day, but she seemed to be at some sewing circle.

March 9 issue has a story "Film Studios Praise Cooperation Here in Film on UFO's." The letter received from Mr. Michael Mustow, a letter sent to Mayor Holm O. Burson, stated, *"Phenomena 7.7 is now completed. It will be viewed by countless millions of people throughout the world. It will open the door to facts heretofore shrouded in secrecy. It will prepare the entire human race for a better knowledge of the universe and possible neighbors who may have been observing our earth for centuries."*

Finally, the Thursday, March 11, issue has a short article on "Zamora Saw a UFO, Not Flying Saucer." This was in response to a request by Zamora to please say in the paper that he never saw a flying saucer land, only a UFO. In part the article states, "Zamora says he was trying to cooperate with persons who asked him about the UFO, which he described as egg-shaped, and he wishes that they would not ask him about a flying saucer which he says he has never seen and cannot describe. The policeman says that the account here stands unchanged from that he gave on April 24 and the following day." Raynor showed me a letter from Rev. Guy J. Cyr S.M. (Society of Mary) Sacred Heart Rectory, Lawrence, Mass. dated November 26, 1964. It is a long letter concerned with intelligence on other planets and trying to make out a case for civilization on the moon. The letter was rightfully published.

I left for Albuquerque about 2:30 P.M., arriving at the Institute of Meteoretics, where Dr. Lincoln La-Paz was waiting for me, at 4:00 P.M.

I gave LaPaz a copy of Vallee's book and also the Menzel letter which he took home and by the next morning had completely read the manuscript and the letter. LaPaz is still very concerned about the green fireball incident. Another one was sighted this last Christmas night. According to LaPaz, the official investigation never satisfactorily cleared up the question of why these peculiar uranium green fireballs should have chosen New Mexico to fly over and avoid being seen in other states and why they were so peculiarly grouped. LaPaz is thoroughly convinced that both the green fireballs and Zamora's sighting were observations of tests of advanced vehicles being produced by some project, even more secret that the Manhattan Project. I am afraid that LaPaz is unshakable from the hypothesis. His primary criticism of Vallee's book was that Vallee has ignored the green fireballs which, as far as LaPaz is concerned, represent the most important part of the UFO phenomenon. It is always just a matter of viewpoint!

LaPaz showed me his excellent meteorite collection and spent much time in general conversation.

He was engaged for the evening, and we met again early the next morning during which time we took the opportunity to meet with the President of the University of New Mexico, Dr. Pokejoy, and to establish good relations between astronomy at Northwestern and astronomy at New Mexico.

Although LaPaz was impressed with Vallee's book, he felt that his impressive list of references was padded with too many references to unpublished articles or statements. He feels that it is not really a scientific book on the subject (I guess that about in the year 1980 I will have to write a really scientific book on the subject).

Coming now to the Menzel letter, I will consolidate the opinions of LaPaz, Chaves, and of Raynor. I did not show the letter to Zamora because I think it merely would have upset him.

Page 1. I asked Zamora about the reported flame when he first heard the explosion, when he was still on the highway. He denies ever having said anything about a flame at that time, only at the time when he saw it rise from the ground. As a matter of fact, he never mentioned anything like that to me, originally, but this did appear in Captain Holder's original report, and he purportedly got this in conversation with Zamora. However, I think this was in the original newspaper writeup. I will have to agree with Menzel that this part of Zamora's evidence is very mixed up and suggests some embroidery of the original sighting either by Zamora or by Captain Holder when excitement was running high.

Page 2. I can't agree with Menzel here. When he wears his glasses, his vision is okay. He had the glasses on when he saw the flame at the time the object was preparing to rise. Now this whole question of the "burning bush": I visited the site again on Saturday, with Raynor and Shrode, the owner of the radio station, and at no time was any bush or grass seen to be burning, and nobody seems to confirm any actual smoke. All that they seem definitely to agree on is that the green snakeweed and the green greasewood, which are notoriously hard materials to ignite, showed evidence of having been charred, as though they had been seared by a hot flame and not burned in an ordinary fashion.

As far as kids having it in for Zamora, there is ample evidence that this is the case. But it was also pointed out to me by Opelgrinder and his assistant and by several others, that it is a national phenomenon for teenagers to hate "fuzz" and the statement by Wesley Johnston, a high school senior who works at Opelgrinder's, is particularly significant. He said that many of the high school kids didn't like Zamora, but that he, Zamora, was not important enough to do anything about it. He said that if the kids wanted to get even with Zamora they would simply thrash him or do something to his car, but that an elaborate hoax would not be the way they would get even with him. One should remember that before the time of the sighting there had been no talk in the Socorro region of unidentified flying objects. This would not have suggested itself as a means of getting back at Zamora.

133

Apparently the Socorro teenagers are much more direct in their methods of reprisal for the "fuzz." As far as the cardboard is concerned, Menzel's conjectures here fall completely flat. The cardboard was portions of very old and weathered corrugated paper from a packing box. There are many samples of this all over the region. There is a city dump not too far away, and when the wind, which blows tumbleweeds all over the place, gets hold of some of this stuff, it scatters the papers pretty well all over the whole region. Many of the bushes, I noticed particularly this time, have papers caught on their underneath side. In any case, some of this paper was still there, and I shall send Menzel a sample of what this cardboard really looks like. I would say that the cardboard had been there through many rains and had suffered successive dryings. The original piece I picked up was definitely charred. This was the piece I sent to you along with soil samples, you will remember.

One rather interesting item is that the burning bush has recently exuded some sap, and one of the movie people took this to Los Angeles to have it analyzed and found it radioactive: I have also obtained some of the sap which I shall send to you, and maybe Moody can try it out on his super-duper counter. It is odd that no one seemed to have bothered to have checked this area originally for radiation. Or did they?

Menzel's idea that the speeder was a deliberate decoy, who signaled to the hoaxers by walkie-talkie who then released a balloon with a cardboard or aluminum flying saucer attached thereto simply does not hold water. Although some of the students do have walkie-talkies, the fact of the matter is that the wind was from the south, and the object went west. A balloon released at that time would have gone directly over town. Furthermore, they would have had to release it after Zamora got there and have watched the object on the ground for a short time. A previous release would simply have had it well over town by the time Zamora got to the spot.

The dynamite shack does not have legs.

There would have been a place for hoaxers to have hidden over on the other side of the knoll, particularly had they lain prone.

None of the people I talked with gave any credence to the hoax hypothesis, generally considering it to have been far above the capabilities and motivations and provocation of the hoaxers. Chaves says that Zamora never described the thing as looking like a balloon. Zamora knows exactly where the dynamite shack is. It is plainly visible from the site of the sighting, but about 500 feet to the west.

Zamora does not have any particular schedule for patroling the town. He has the run of the whole town.

There is no UFO Club in town.

No paraphernalia of a hoax were ever found. It would be rather hard to have done away with all tell-tale evidence, such as tubes of helium, release mechanism, etc. Finally, it was LaPaz's feeling that had it been a hoax, it surely would have leaked by now. He told me of an elaborate hoax that was played on one of the geologists at Ohio State University when he taught there. The students had it in for this guy and contrived an explosion in a nearby town, and the crater which it produced was reported then as a meteorite crater. It had everybody excited for a while and would have succeeded except those who got away with it were so pleased with themselves that they began to brag a bit and got caught. I do not believe that the Socorro high school students could have kept a secret this long. Furthermore, it would seem that any youngsters that hated Zamora sufficiently to have gone to all this trouble to perpetrate a hoax would now be very envious of the glory he is getting in a movie and all the publicity he has received and would certainly burst his bubble right now. Finally, there is the matter of the tourist who reported a strange object to Opelgrinder. This could not very well have been part of the hoax since the tourist was a complete stranger just passing through. Furthermore, if Zamora is to be believed at all, the object rose vertically and took off horizontally to the west and was observed as it passed

135

well over the dynamite shack and disappeared over the pearlite mill. This is entirely too big a hoax for high school students to perpetrate.

Perhaps I spent too much time on this matter, but the letter was a very convenient device for re-discussing the whole situation. Sgt. Chaves indicated that Menzel should have been a science fiction writer. Actually Lyle Boyd has done some of this, and I believe also Menzel has.

I left Albuquerque in the late morning on Saturday and arrived in Socorro about 1:00 P.M. Raynor, Shrode, and I visited the site and took some more samples, particularly of the sap, and I took a few more pictures, particularly of the dynamite shack to show Menzel. Then I went back to the radio station and tried to call the Empire Film Studio, but it was closed.

In view of the fact that the prevailing opinion in the town still is that what Zamora saw was not the result of hallucinations or of a hoax, but a secret test vehicle, what has become of my suggestion to have this left as "an exercise for the students"? It would be a marvelous exercise for neophyte intelligence officers.

There is also the opinion expressed in Socorro, and expressed to me a number of times in the past, by several people (and also by LaPaz), that I am merely a part of a super-smoke screen and so is FTD and Wright Field, and that the whole Project Bluebook is a grand coverup for something the government does not want discussed. Best way to give a lie to this, of course, is to point out that if this were the case, the U.S. government should also have been responsible for the sightings in France, Brazil, Spain, and in England. Maybe the U.S. government has really gone global! On that happy thought I conclude my report.

Sincerely yours,
J. Allen Hynek

P.S. I now have a slightly infected finger from the thorns on the bush that was originally charred. The bush drew blood when I attempted to get some soil

136

samples. Undoubtedly, the finger will now wither away from radiation burns. Unfortunately, I do not have interplanetary Blue Cross coverage!

Chapter Six: The Nights UFOs Buzzed the White House

Six Army Signal Corps engineers looked out the windows of their offices in downtown Washington, D.C., at the request of one of their group, who had observed some strange spots in the sky.

It was 4:20 P.M. on January 11, 1965. The offices were located in the Munitions Building, and the engineers had a chance to observe the spots, which were reflecting the low afternoon sun, long enough to agree on the number and approximate shape of the objects and to estimate their altitude at between 12,000 and 15,000 feet.

As the engineers watched, the discs zigzagged easily across the sky toward the Capitol Building, moving from north to south. Suddenly two delta-wing jets burst onto the scene and began chasing the discs, but the objects outran their pursuers, seemingly without effort.

Two of the engineers, Paul M. Dickey and Ed Shad, reported seeing a commercial airliner make a regular approach to the National Airport in about the same area of the sky.

The incident was one of many reported around the nation's capitol in January 1965. The press, eager for an explanation of the discs and the presence of the two jet pursuit planes in the area, tried to squeeze a statement out of the Defense Department. The official reaction was: "There was no such incident. It just didn't happen."

As if regimented by some unspoken law, officials of the military installation around Washington gave exactly the same reply to reporters' inquiries.

This unyielding position prompted one newspaper in the Washington area to run the headline PENTAGON CAN'T SEE SPOTS IN SKY over the story of the incident.

The rare official who did comment on the sightings blamed them on meterological illusions, wild imaginations, and the like.

But the presence on a radar screen of a solid object moving at speeds greater than that of any known jet requires a more sophisticated explanation.

The first sighting officially occurred on December 29, 1964, but some independent investigators speculated that the actual radar sighting took place ten days before but leaked out to the public only on the later date.

Three objects were detected by the radar screens—first one alone, then two together—all traveling at an estimated speed of 4800 miles per hour. Weeks after the sighting had taken place, official Air Force sources blamed defective equipment for the presence of the objects on the radar screens.

In the countryside surrounding Washington, sightings of UFOs occurred both before and after reports were made in the city itself. Horace Burns, a gunsmith of Grottoes, Virginia, reported a fantastic experience on December 21, 1964.

While driving along U.S. Highway 250 between Staunton and Waynesboro, he was startled to see a huge cone-shaped object float into view. It glided across the road in front of him; at one time, the outline of its shape more than filled the windshield in front of him. Without any warning of engine trouble, he said, he felt "some sort of force" that caused his car to stop.

The strange-looking craft settled easily in a

meadow about a hundred yards from the highway as Burns climbed out of his stalled car. The gunsmith counted six concentric circular rings that diminished in diameter toward the top of the cone-shaped object. The top was crested with a dome, and the entire object emitted a bluish glow.

He watched the craft for a period of time which he estimated to be a minute and a half. Then the craft took off at a "square angle," building up great speed instantaneously. Burns estimated the UFO to be 75 feet high and about 125 feet at the base. It had no observable openings or seams.

Although the Air Force did not bother to make an immediate investigation, Ernest Gehman, a professor at Eastern Mennonite college, was curious enough to do a little investigating on his own. Taking a Geiger counter to the reported place of landing, he found the radiation concentration was about 60,000 counts per minute.

With the use of his Geiger counter, the professor could trace the outline of the landing spot, and it checked with Burns's original estimation of the size of the craft. Two Du Pont engineers checked the area and found that their readings agreed with Gehman's.

Over three weeks after the reported landing, the Air Force investigated the case. By that time, the area had been subjected to rain, snow, and the trampling feet of many curiosity seekers. The official opinion finally released was that the sightings were mirages.

The "mirages" were not content with a single manifestation, however, On January 23, 1965, two men traveling on U.S. Highway 60 near Williamsburg reported that they had sighted a hovering cone-shaped object. Although the men were in separate cars and were traveling in different directions, both their cars had stopped as they approached the object.

One report described the object as aluminum-colored and cone-shaped. It had hovered over a cornfield next to the stalled motorist for twenty or thirty seconds before it vanished straight up into the air.

The driver traveling the opposite direction on U.S. 60 described a similar object, likening it to an inverted ice cream cone. He estimated the height at 75 feet and described a "swishing" sound that he heard when he stepped out of his car. As in the first sighting, the object had disappeared straight upward at a great velocity.

Dempsey Broton, chief of Satellite Tracking on NASA's Wallops Island, Virginia base, was standing in front of his house on January 5, 1965, waiting for the appearance of an artificial earth satellite, when a bright object appeared over the southwest horizon. It traveled at tremendous rate and gave off a yellowish-orange glow as it streaked through the sky. Several residents near the Wallops Island base confirmed Bruton's sighting by independently reporting it to the NASA installation.

Exactly one week later, on January 12, a bright yellow-orange object streamed out of the sky and appeared to be heading right for a NASA public relations staff member. The light seemed to streak directly for the woman and her husband as they walked toward their house.

The NASA base had been the scene of even more UFO activity earlier. An incident in October 1964, which had received little publicity, was brought to light. Three technicians and an engineer observed a triangular-shaped object move over the base and execute a ninety-degree turn. They all agreed that the object moved faster than any conventional jet aircraft and that the abrupt turn was impossible for an ordinary aircraft of any variety to execute.

A group of citizens of Marion, Virginia, went on an excursion to investigate the reported sighting of a UFO on January 25. Woody Darnell, a Marion policeman, claimed that he and his family and several policemen watched a glowing object that hovered over them for several minutes before it took off in an explosion and a shower of sparks. The investigators did not find the UFO, but they did find a number of trees that had had their tops bent over, and one green tree on fire in the area where the object had been reported. At Byrd Field, Virginia, Tactical Air Command officials had quickly come up with the explanation that the object was a plane equipped with a new arc light. Though this did not explain the fire, a thoughtful forestry official suggested that the "dead" tree had been set on fire by a hunter trying to claim a squirrel. These explanations were too farfetched for anyone on the scene to consider.

Exactly twenty minutes after the Marion sighting, nine persons near Fredricksburg, 275 miles from Marion, reported a UFO which they described as a "Christmas sparkler." It appeared to be spinning at a great velocity and spewing sparks from the bottom as it glided over the Rappahannock Valley.

On January 26, the UFOs again visited Marion, but this time they were seen by many residents. Local radio stations and police were swamped with calls. All sightings were of similar fire-spewing or spark-shooting objects.

The Reverend H. Preston Robinson described a UFO that gave off a buzzing sound and had a round-shaped bottom, "from which several lights showed." The craft seemed to eject a ball of fire as it accelerated away from witnesses.

This was not the first time the UFOs had visited Washington. A wave of sightings in 1952 caused the biggest military press conference since the Second World War.

Memorandum for Record   23 July 1952
Subject: ATIC Participation in the Investigation of
          Washington Incident of 20 July 1952.

1. The first notification of this incident was on the morning of 22 July 1952 when Col. Bower and Capt. Ruppelt were eating breakfast and read it in the Washington papers. They had been out at Andrews AFB the previous day and had not heard of it. They had contacted people from the D/I of MATS who also did not know of it.

2. Upon reporting to the Pentagon on the morning of 22 July 1952 they met Lt. Col. Teaburg, D/I Estimates Division, who stated that a Capt. Berkow, D/I of Headquarters Command at Bolling, was coming in with the report of the incident. This was about 0900. At about 0930 Capt Berkow arrived and briefed Col. Bower, Capt. Ruppelt, Major Linder of ATIC, and others on the incident. He stated that a full report would be ready, and would be delivered to Col. Bower by 1700. During the day several phone calls were received by Capt. Ruppelt on this sighting. One was from the White House. They were advised that an investigation would be made.

3. Before the afternoon was over it appeared that this was going to be a "hot" incident. Capt. Ruppelt called Col. Bower in Lt. Col. Teaburg's office and offered to stay over in Washington to get the investigation started but was advised that this should not be done.

Memorandum for Record   28 July 1952
Subject: Telephone Call from a Washington News-
             paper

At approximately 2130 on the night of 27 July 1952, a Washington newspaper, the name of which is unknown (the caller identified himself but the name of the newspaper could not be remembered), called Capt. E. J. Ruppelt at his home. The caller was advised that Capt. Ruppelt could make no statement for the press. He advised the caller that all public statements for the press had to come from PIO in Washington. The gentleman from the newspaper was very insistent and rather indignant about the fact that he had received a "run around" all afternoon. Capt. Ruppelt stated that he was sorry about this but that he could still make no comments. The gentleman asked whether or not we had received a report about the Washington sighting that occurred on the night of 26 July 1952. He was advised that we had been advised of the sighting but could make no comment on it. The gentleman said that he believed the Air Force was withholding information that was vital to the press. Capt. Ruppelt said that he didn't know whether this was true or not and that he was sorry that he could not give them any information. The man then asked what could be the cause of radar returns like that. Capt. Ruppelt said that he had nothing to say about the Washington sighting although as previously had been announced in all of the newspapers, ATIC had reports of radar sightings but that he would make no comment on them. The gentleman stated that he had no knowledge of radar and assumed since there was a radar pickup there must be something there. Capt. Ruppelt said again that he could not make any statement but that it was a well-known fact that radar images could be caused by weather, by birds, by malfunctions in the radar set, from interferences of two radar sets, and many other reasons and just the fact that there was a return on a radar scope did not mean a great deal unless that return could be evaluated. The gentleman asked next how soon it would be before we had an evaluation on the Washington incident. Again he was informed that we could make no statement. He asked what Capt. Ruppelt's affiliation with the project was and he was advised that the full details were in Look Magazine and that, as they quoted, Capt. Ruppelt was the Project Officer. He was advised that nothing else could be said and the conversation was terminated.

Chief, Facility Operations Branch, 1-547
Chief, Washington Center—9
Unidentified Targets, July 20, 1952

Attached is a copy of the report written by the Senior Controller on duty, _____, from approximately 2330E July 19, to 0800E July 20, 1952.

Parts of this report have been given to Major Williams of Air Force Intelligence, Lt. Col. Searless, Office of Public Information, Department of Defense and to Mr. ———, W-41.

———

WWT/eb
cc: W-1
    USAF Hdqtrs.

At 2340E (19th) Controller Nugent called my attention to several targets observed on the VC-2 scope. Eight of them were counted and, although an occasional strong return was noted, most of the targets would be classified as fair to weak. After we had checked carefully on the movement (about 100 to 130 mph) and confirmed our findings with what the Tower saw on the ASR, I called MFS and reported it. This was about midnight EST. MFS later advised that the nearest military base was supposed to handle these matters and to call the BOF Intelligence Officer or AO. There was some confusion for a while as to whether Andrews or Bolling was going to make the report, but it was finally determined that ADW would handle.

I called ——— and asked if they could see them and was advised they saw nothing. Our HEW Maintenance then checked the equipment very carefully and advised that it was functioning satisfactorily and confirmed it with a fellow worker. (This lad tells me he has been working on this equipment for five years, so guess he knows what he is doing.) The targets were noticed east and south of ADW so we asked the ADW tower to look and see if they saw anything, also asked ADW approach control to check scope. ADW had a lad on the roof with glasses who spotted an object that looked to be orange in color and appeared to be just hovering in the vicinity of ADW. They saw others as time went on with varying descriptions. Most of this

144

information was given to _____ and MFS with the expectation that they would run an intercept.

The impression received from _____ was to the effect that more information was needed to order an intercept. I told them our equipment was giving us good readings so we would be able to do any vectoring that might be necessary but they seemed to be leaving it all up to Smoke Ring. As time wore on, pilot reports were received—P807 saw 7 of the objects between Washington and Martinsburg variously described as lights that moved very rapidly, up and down and horizontally as well as hovering in one position and SP160 saw one come in with him from around Herndon and follow him to within 4 miles of touch-down. This was substantiated by Tower and Center radar.

In my conversation with MFS, ADW and the men on duty, we reached the point where we wondered just how much of this could go on and for how long before something could be done about it. I contacted Smoke Ring finally about 300 EST. They were doing nothing about it so I asked if it was possible for something like this to happen, even though we gave them all this information, without anything being done about it. The man who was supposed to be in charge and to whom I had been talking, said he guessed so. Then another voice came on who identified himself as the Combat Officer and said that all the information was being forwarded to higher authority and would not discuss it any further. I insisted I wanted to know if it was being forwarded tonight and he said yes, but would not give me any hint as to what was being done about all these things flying around Washington. He tried to assure me that something was being done about it. I asked too how he was getting his information. He said they would get it from Thorndyke and ADW. We were then told by ADW that they had no way of forwarding it to them. Smoke Ring then said that they were not really concerned about it anyway, that somebody else was supposed to handle it.

MFS then said that ADW was supposed to have forwarded it to Intelligence but when I checked with ADW (0505E) they said the AO had gone back to bed and the report would go in later. They confirmed the above by saying that they could not give it to any-one tonight.

It would be extremely difficult to write this so that it is in a logical sequence due to the confusion that seems to have existed throughout the whole affair. For example, ADW called us and asked what we wanted them to do with the information we had given them. (This took place after 0505E.) At about 0530E Controller Ritchey reported seeing 10 targets in the vicinity of ADW which was confirmed by the other man in radar and I went in and counted 7 or 8 in scattered positions which indicated a very rapid movement if they were the same ones seen near ADW. This report was forwarded to both ADW and MFS. It was at this time that MFS advised they had determined that none of the information we had geen giving the ADW was forwarded in accordance with procedures. MFS advised, however, that they were following up with their own report.

At 0540E 7 targets counted in area.

Washington, D.C.—
Night of 26-27 July 52

(Partially witnessed by Maj. Fournet and Lt. Holcomb AFOIN-205; remainder as reported to them)

General:
This incident involved u/i targets observed on the radar scopes at the Air Route Traffic Control Center and the tower, both at Washington National Airport, and the Approach Control Radar at Andrews AFB. In addition, visual observations were reported to Andrews and Bolling AFB and to ARTC Center, the latter by pilots of commercial a/c and one CAA a/c. Two flights of interceptors were dispatched from New-castle, Del., but their official reports have not been received by this office; comments on their conversations with ARTC Center personnel are included herein.

It has been impossible to collect all facts for a single report. The Base Intelligence Officer, Bolling AFB, is submitting a report covering the Bolling and Andrews aspects of the incident. This report covers the facts obtained from Washington National A/P personnel, the USAF Command Post and the AFOIN Duty Officer log. As yet, the commercial and ACC pilots who reported visuals have not been contacted, nor have other potential sources been investigated. Such action will not be possible by this office.

1. Varying numbers (up to 12 simultaneously) of u/i targets on ARTC radar scope. Termed by CAA personnel as "generally, solid returns," similar to a/c return except slower. No definable pattern of maneuver except at very beginning about 2150 EDT, 4 targets in rough line abreast with about 1½ mile spacing moved slowly together (giving about a 1″ trace persistency at an estimated speed of less than 100 mph) on a heading of 110. At the same time 8 other targets were scattered throughout scope. ARTC checked Andrews Approach Control by telephone at 2200 EDT and ascertained that they were also picking up u/i targets. U/i returns were picked up intermittently until about 27/0100 EDT, following which weak and sporadic (unsteady) returns were picked up intermittently for another 3½ hours. Washington National Tower radar crew reports only one target positively u/i. This return was termed a "very good target" which moved across the scope from West to East at about 30 to 40 mph. However, the radar operators stated that there could have been other u/i targets on their scopes, particularly outside their area of a/c control, which they would not have noticed or would have assumed to be a/c under ARTC Center control. However, they noticed no other unusual (i.e., very slow or erratic) returns. ARTC Center controllers also report that a CAA flight inspector, Mr. _____, flying a/c # NC-12, reported at 2246 EDT that he had visually spotted 5 objects giving off a light glow ranging from orange to white; his altitude at time was 2200′. Some commercial pilots reported visuals ranging from "cigarette glow" (red-yellow) to "a light"

147

(as recorded from their conversations with ARTC controllers). At 2238 EDT the USAF Command Post was notified of ARTC targets. Command Post notified ADC and EADF at 2245, and 2 F-94's were scrambled from Newcastle at 2300 EDT. ARTC controlled F-94's after arrival in area and vectored them to targets with generally negative results (flew through "a batch of radar returns" without spotting anything). However, one pilot mentioned seeing 4 lights at one time and a second time as seeing a single light ahead but unable to close whereupon light "went out" (these comments from ARTC controllers). One ARTC controller worked a USAF B-25 (AF 8898 ?) for about 1 hr. 20 mins. about 2230 EDT. B-25 was vectored in on numerous targets and commented that each vector took him over a busy highway or intersection. Maj. Fournet (AFOIN-2A2) and Lt. Holcomb (USN, AFOIN-2C5) arrived at ARTC Center about 27/0015 EDT. Lt. Holcomb observed scopes and reported "7 good, solid targets." He made a quick check with airport Weather Station and determined that there was a slight temperature inversion (about 1°) from the surface to about 1000'. However, he felt that the scope targets at that time were not the result of this inversion and so advised the Command Post with the suggestion that a second intercept flight be requested. (2nd intercept flight controlled by ARTC, but no strong targets remained when they arrived. They were vectored on dim targets with negative results.) Maj. Fournet and Lt. Holcomb remained in ARTC Center until 0415, but no additional strong targets were picked up: many dim and unstable targets (assumed due to temperature inversion) were observed throughout the remainder of the period.

2. Intermittently between 26/2150 and 27/0100 EDT July 52. Periods of observation vary.

3. Electronic: VC-2 radar (ARTC) and ASR-1 radar (Tower). Others visual from air (details unknown).

4. Radar located at Washington National Airport, Washington, D.C. (Alexandria, Va.) a/c/ #NC-12 believed in vicinity of Aberdeen/Baltimore, Md., com-

mercial a/c reporting visuals located in general area vicinity Washington National A/P.

5. ARTC Center radar crew and controllers:

Austin M. Stapf	All are CAA employees with vary-
Lloyd Sykes	ing levels of experience (ARTC
James M. Ritchey	radar installed Jan. 52). All ap-
Harry Barnes	peared to be serious, conscientious
James M. Copeland	and sincere although somewhat
Stewart Dawson	vague about details of their ex-
Phil Ceconi	perience on 26/27 July. Considered
Mike Senkow	fairly reliable.
Jerome Biron	

Washington Tower radar operators:

——— (2 yrs. radar)	Conscientious and sincere.
——— (1½ yrs. radar)	Direct manner, Appeared sure of themselves. Considered very reliable.

Observer in a/c #NC- ———, Mr. ———, reliability unknown.
Pilots of commercial a/c: unknown.

6. Weather clear, scattered thins (alt. unknown). Temperatures at 26/2200Z as reported by Washington National Weather Station:

Surface	25°C	
800′	26	
3,500	20	
4,800	20	
10,000	7 ⎫	Steady drop
15,000	0 ⎬	
22,000	—17 ⎭ ⎫	Constant
22,800	—17 ⎬	
23,000	—20 ⎭	

7. See 6. Others negative.
8. Negative
9. See 1. Official reports not received.
10. Normal commercial traffic inbound and outbound Washington National Airport plus some USAF a/c—all known and identified.

Remarks:

ARTC crew commented that, as compared with u/i returns picked up in early hours of 20 July 52, these returns appeared to be more haphazard in their actions, i.e., they did not follow a/c around nor did they cross scope consistently on same general heading. Some commented that the returns appeared to be from objects "capable of dropping out of the pattern at will." Also that returns had "creeping appearance." One member of crew commented that one object to which F-94 was vectored just "disappeared from scope" shortly after F-94 started pursuing. All crew members emphatic that most u/i returns were "solid." Finally, it was mentioned that u/i returns have been picked up from time to time over the past few months but never before had they appeared in such quantities over such a prolonged period and with such definition as was experienced on the nights of 19/20 and 26/27 July 52.

A transcript of a conversation between the towers at Washington National and Andrews which took place at 2130 EDT 26 July is attached. The "Center" mentioned is the ARTC Center at Washington National. The number of the National Airlines flight referred to is unknown.

Director of Intelligence
Hqs. Tenth Air Force AFXOI FLYOBRPT 5-52

1. On 20 July 1952 at 0555 CAPTAIN CASEY _____ of CAPITAL AIRLINES was in the cockpit of his DC-4 aircraft performing a check list prior to take-off from WASHINGTON NATIONAL AIRPORT, WASHINGTON, D. C. The aircraft was on the parking ramp heading 020°. CAPTAIN _____ looked up and observed a clear bluish white light travel from 150° to 010° at a 30° angle above the horizon in horizontal flight until it disappeared in the distance. CAPTAIN _____ stated that he had to turn his head slowly through a 45° quadrant in order to observe the object while in its flight and estimates that he observed it for five (5) seconds or less. CAP-

TAIN _____ states that he did not attach any significance to this light until later events demanded attention to it.

2. Immediately after performing his check list, CAPTAIN _____ took off from WASHINGTON NATIONAL AIRPORT on a heading of 180° and climbed to 1200′ before making a right turn on course 330°. Upon gaining 1200′ and course 350°, CAPTAIN _____ stated that he switched over from Tower Control to AIRWAY TRAFFIC CONTROL CENTER (ATCC) at WASHINGTON NATIONAL AIRPORT. At this time ATCC informed him that their radar scope indicated two or three objects on the screen traveling at high speeds ATCC instructed CAPTAIN _____ to steer 290° so as to intercept the objects which were approximately nine (9) miles ahead of him. At this time CAPTAIN _____'s rate of climb was approximately 600′ per minute and his altitude was between 3500′ and 4000′.

3. Immediately after ATCC instructed CAPTAIN _____ to steer course 290° he stated that the following events occurred within 5–8 minutes in the order in which presented and at the approximate time intervals as indicated:

a. 3–5 minutes after take-off, ATCC informed pilot that objects were five (5) miles distant dead ahead.

b. 3–5 seconds later, ATCC informed pilot that objects were four (4) miles distant dead ahead.

c. 1–3 seconds later, ATCC informed pilot that objects were at ten (10) o'clock. At this time pilot stated he plainly observed a DC-4 type aircraft at ten (10) o'clock level proceeding in the opposite direction. This information he reported to ATCC.

d. 4–5 minutes later, COPILOT _____ observed one (1) object bluish white in color in a twenty-five degree (25°) dive from northeast to southwest traveling at a tremendous rate of speed. The copilot told CAPTAIN _____ that he could neither estimate from what altitude the object began its descent nor at what altitude it faded. CAPTAIN _____ stated that at this time his altitude was 6000′ and he could look

151

down almost vertically and see CHARLES TOWN, WEST VIRGINIA.

e. Immediately upon sighting CHARLES TOWN, CAPTAIN _____ and his copilot observed a brilliant bluish white flash past from high over his left and disappear in level flight dead ahead traveling at a tremendous rate of speed and appeared to be outside the earth's atmosphere.

f. Next CAPTAIN _____ and his copilot observed a brilliant bluish white light reappear where the last light had disappeared and flash past from right to left at approximately 30° above the horizon and traveling at a tremendous rate of speed. This light also appeared to be outside the earth's atmosphere.

4. CAPTAIN _____ stated that he may have seen as many as seven (7) objects during as many minutes but due to the fact that things were happening so fast he had no way of keeping an accurate account of the number of objects.

TENTH AIR FORCE DIRECTOR OF INTELLIGENCE COMMENT:

1. The interrogators, LT. JANCZEWSKI and M/SGT. TAYLOR, are of the opinion that CAPTAIN _____ is reliable and conscientious. He has been a pilot for twenty-four (24) years and has piloted for CAPITAL AIRLINES for seventeen (17) years. CAPTAIN _____ stated that during all his years as a pilot he has never seen anything that would compare with the objects mentioned in this report. He further stated that he is thoroughly convinced that the objects he observed were traveling at such tremendous speeds that he would not attempt to estimate the rate of their speeds.

2. CAPTAIN _____ stated that the ATCC at WASHINGTON NATIONAL AIRPORT had the objects on the radar scope. Due to such an unusual circumstance there is a possibility that scope photographs were made providing the equipment was available.

3. CAPTAIN _____ also stated that ATCC contacted the tower at BOLLING AIR FORCE BASE and queried them of any knowledge of the objects.

It is not known if any such targets had been plotted by BOLLING AIR FORCE BASE.

4. The following is offered as a suggestion:

Due to the tremendous speeds of the objects and the inability of the observers to determine the exact altitudes or even if the objects observed were in the earth's atmosphere there is a possibility that there is some connection between a previous report (AFXOI FLYOBRPT 4-52) and this report since they occurred at approximately the same time.

5. Weather: 0500Z 19 July, WASHINGTON, D. C.
Ceiling—Unlimited
Visibility—10 miles
Clouds—Negative
Winds:
Surface—230°/04 knots
5,000'—360°/20 knots
10,000'—350°/16 knots
20,000'—310°/25 knots
30,000'—310°/42 knots
40,000'—290°/46 knots

GEORGE H. JANCZEWSKI
2nd Lt.   USAF
Director of Intelligence

Chapter Seven: Deriving a Model UFO from Twelve Top Cases of "Unknowns"

Out of the 434 OBJECT SIGHTINGS that were identified as UNKNOWNS by the data reduction process, there were only 12 that were described with sufficient detail that they could be used in an attempt to derive a model of a "flying saucer." The following is a summary of the 12 good UNKNOWN SIGHTINGS:

Case I (Serial 0573.00)

Two men employed by a rug-cleaning firm were driving across a bridge at 0955 hours on July 29, 1948, when they saw an object glide across the road a few hundred feet in front of them. It was shiny and metallic in construction, about 6 to 8 feet long and 2 feet wide. It was in a flat glide path at an altitude of about 30 feet and in a moderate turn to the left. It was seen for only a few seconds and apparently went down in a wooded area, although no trace of it was found.

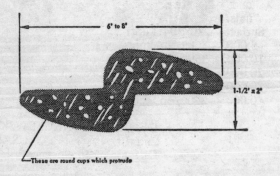

These are round cups which protrude

Case II (Serial 4508.00)

A naval aviation student, his wife, and several others were at a drive-in movie from 2115 to 2240 hours on April 20, 1952, during which time they saw several groups of objects fly over. There were from two to nine objects in a group and there were about 20 groups. The groups of objects flew in a straight line except for some changes in direction accomplished in a manner like any standard aircraft turn.

The objects were shaped like conventional aircraft.

The unaccountable feature of the objects was that each had a red glow surrounding it and was glowing itself, although it was a cloudless night.

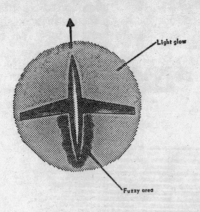

Case III (Serial 2013.00, 2014.00, and 2024.01)

Two tower operators sighted a light over a city airport at 2020 hours on January 20, 1951. Since a commercial plane was taking off at this time, the pilots were asked to investigate this light. They observed it at 2026 hours. According to them, it flew abreast of them at a greater radius as they made their climbing turn, during which time it blinked some lights which looked like running lights. While the observing plane was still in its climb turn, the object made a turn toward the plane and flew across its nose. As the two men turned their heads to watch it, it instantly appeared on their other side flying in the same direction as they were flying, and then in 2 or 3 seconds it slipped under them, and they did not see it again. Total time of the observation was not stated. In appearance, it was like an airplane with a cigar-shaped body and straight wings, somewhat larger than a B-29. No engine nacelles were observed on the wings.

Case IV (Serial 4599.00)

A part-time farmer and a hired hand were curing tobacco at midnight on July 19, 1952, when they looked up and saw two cigar-shaped objects. One hovered while the other moved to the east and came back, at which time both ascended until out of sight. Duration of observation was 3 to 4 miles. Both had an exhaust at one end, and neither had projections of any kind. It was stated that they appeared to be transparent and illuminated from the inside.

Lighted

Exhaust

Case V (Serial 0565.00 to 0565.03)

A pilot and copilot were flying a DC-3 at 0340 hours on July 24, 1948, when they saw an object coming toward them. It passed to the right and slightly above them, at which time it went into a steep climb and was lost from sight in some clouds. Duration of the observation was about 10 seconds. One passenger was able to catch a flash of light as the object passed. The object seemed powered by rocket or jet motors shooting a trail of fire some 50 feet to the rear of the object. The object had no wings or other protrusion and had two rows of lighted windows.

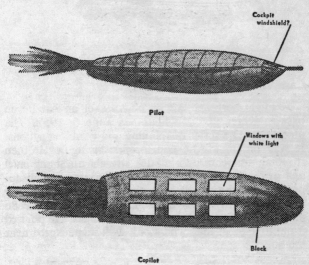

Cockpit windshield?

Pilot

Windows with white light

Black

Copilot

Case VI (Serial 4822.00)

An instrument technician, while driving from a large city toward an Air Force base on December 22, 1952, saw an object from his car at 1930 hours. He stopped his car to watch it. It suddenly moved up toward the zenith in spurts from right to left at an angle of about 45°. It then moved off in level flight at a high rate of speed, during which maneuver it appeared white most of the time, but apparently rolled three times showing a red side. About halfway through its roll it showed no light at all. It finally assumed a position to the south of the planet Jupiter at a high altitude, at which position it darted back and forth, left and right alternately. Total time of the observation was 15 minutes. Apparently, the observer just stopped watching the object.

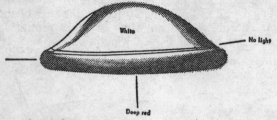

White

No light

Deep red

Case VII (Serial 2728.00)

A Flight Sergeant saw an object over an Air Force base in Korea at 0842 hours on June 6, 1952. The object flew in a series of spinning and tumbling actions. It was on an erratic course, first flying level, then stopping momentarily, shooting straight up, flying level and again tumbling, then changing course and disappearing into the sun. It reappeared and was seen flying back and forth across the sun. At one time an F-86 passed between the observer and the object. He pointed it out to another man who saw it as it maneuvered near the sun.

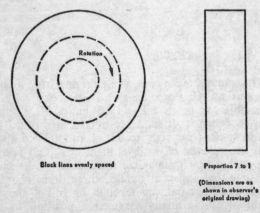

Rotation

Black lines evenly spaced

Proportion 7 to 1

(Dimensions are as shown in observer's original drawing)

Case VIII (Serial 0576.00

An electrician was standing by the bathroom window of his home, facing west, at 0825 hours on July 31, 1948, when he first sighted an object. He ran to his kitchen where he pointed out the object to his wife. Total time in sight was approximately 10 seconds, during which the object flew on a straight and level course from horizon to horizon, west to east.

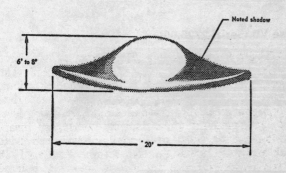

Noted shadow

6' to 8'

20'

Case IX (Serial 0066.00)

A farmer and his two sons, aged 8 and 10, were at his fishing camp on August 13, 1947. At about 1300 hours, he went to look for the boys, having sent them to the river for some tape from his boat. He noticed an object some 300 feet away, 75 feet above the ground. He saw it against the background of the canyon wall which was 400 feet high at this point. It was hedge hopping, following the contour of the ground, was sky blue about 20 feet in diameter and 10 feet thick, and had pods on the side from which flames were shooting out. It made a swishing sound. The observer stated that the trees were highly agitated by the craft as it passed over. His two sons also observed the object. No one saw the object for more than a few seconds.

Side view

End view

Case X (Serial 1119.00)

An employee in the supersonic laboratory of an aeronautical laboratory and some other employees of this lab were by a river, 2½ miles from its mouth, when they saw an object. The time was about 1700 hours on May 24, 1949. The object was reflecting sunlight when observed by naked eye. However, he then looked at it with 8-power binoculars, at which time there was no glare. (Did glasses have filter?) It was of metallic construction and was seen with good enough resolution to show that the skin was dirty. It moved off in a horizontal flight at a gradually increasing rate of speed, until it seemed to approach the speed of a jet before it disappeared. No propulsion was apparent. Time of observation was 2½ to 3 minutes.

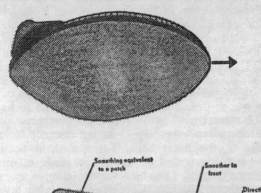

No propulsion

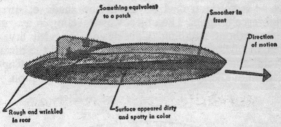

Something equivalent to a patch

Smoother in front

Direction of motion

Rough and wrinkled in rear

Surface appeared dirty and spotty in color

Case XI (Serial 1550.00)

On March 20, 1950, a Reserve Air Force Captain and an airlines Captain were flying a commercial airlines flight. At 21:26, the airline Captain directed the attention of the Reserve Air Force Captain to an object which apparently was flying at high speed, approaching the airliner from the south on a north heading. The Reserve Air Force Captain focused his attention on the object. Both crew members watched it as it passed in front of them and went out of sight to the right. The observation, which lasted about 25 to 35 seconds, occurred about 15 miles north of a medium-sized city. When the object passed in front of the airliner, it was not more than ½ mile distant and at an altitude of about 1000 feet higher than the airliner.

The object appeared to be circular, with a diameter

of approximately 100 feet and with a vertical height considerably less than the diameter, giving the object a disc-like shape. In the top center was a light which was blinking at an estimated 3 flashes per second. This light was so brilliant that it would have been impossible to look at it continuously had it not been blinking. This light could be seen only when the object was approaching and after it had passed the airliner. When the object passed in front of the observers, the bottom side was visible. The bottom side appeared to have 9 to 12 symmetrical oval or circular portholes located in a circle approximately ¾ of the distance from the center to the outer edge. Through these portholes came a soft purple light about the shade of aircraft fluorescent lights. The object was traveling in a straight line without spinning. Considering the visibility, the length of time the object was in sight, and the distance from the object, the Reserve Air Force Captain estimates the speed to be in excess of 1000 mph.

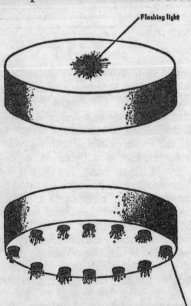

Flashing light

Portholes

Case XII (Serial 3601.00)

At 0535 on the morning of August 25, 1952, a musician for a radio station was driving to work from his home when he noticed an object hovering about 10 feet above a field near the road along which he was driving. As he came abreast of the object, he stopped his car and got out to watch. Having an artificial leg, he could not leave the road, since the surrounding terrain was rough. However, he was within about 100 yards of it at the point he was standing on the road. The object was not absolutely still, but seemed to rock slightly as it hovered. When he turned off the motor of his car, he could hear a deep throbbing sound coming from the object. As he got out of the car, the object began a vertical ascent with a sound similar to "a large covey of quail starting to fly at one time." The object ascended vertically through broken clouds until out of sight. His view was not obscured by clouds. The observer states that the vegetation was blown about by the object when it was near the ground.

Description of the object is as follows:

It was about 75 feet long, 45 feet wide, and 15 feet thick, shaped like two oval meat platters placed together. It was a dull aluminum color, and had a smooth surface. A medium-blue continuous light shone through the one window in the front section. The head and shoulders of one man, sitting motionless, facing the forward edge of the object, were visible. In the midsection of the object were several windows extending from the top to the rear edge of the object; the midsection of the ship had a blue light which gradually changed to different shades. There was a large amount of activity and movement in the midsection that could not be identified as either human or mechanical, although it did not have a regular pattern of movement. There were no windows, doors or portholes, vents, seams, etc., visible to the observer in the rear section of the object or under the object (viewed at time of ascent). Another identifiable feature was a series of propellers 6 to 12 inches in diameter spaced closely together along the outer edge of the object. These propellers were mounted on a bracket so that they revolved in a horizontal plane along the edge of the object. The propellers were revolving at a high rate of speed.

Investigation of the area soon afterward showed some evidence of vegetation being blown around. An examination of grass and soil samples taken indicated nothing unusual. Reliability of the observer was considered good.

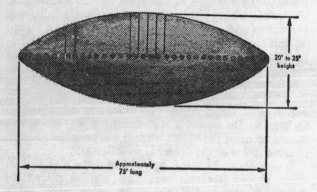

20' to 25°
height

Approximately
75' long

These 12 sightings can be classed into four categories on the basis of their shapes, as follows:

(1) Propeller shape—Case I
(2) Aircraft shape—Cases II and III
(3) Cigar shape—Cases IV and V
(4) Elliptical or disc shape—Case VI to XII

The criterion for choosing the above sightings was that their descriptions were given in enough detail to permit diagrams of the objects to be drawn. It might be noted here that in all but one of these cases (Case XI) the observer had already drawn a diagram of what he had seen.

The object of this section of the study was the conceiving of a model, or models. The requirements that the description be detailed is an important one, and was the easiest to determine in the re-evaluation program. However, a good model ought to satisfy the following conditions as well:

(1) The general shape of the object and the maneuvers it performed should fit the reports of many of the UNKNOWNS and thus explain them.

(2) The observer and the report should be reliable.

(3) The report should contain elements which should have been observed with accuracy, and which eliminate the possibility that the sighting could be ascribed to a familiar object or to a known natural phenomenon.

(4) The model should be derived from two or more good UNKNOWNS between which there is no essential conflict.

It can be shown that it is not possible to deduce a model from the 12 cases that will satisfy all of these conditions. The following case-by-case discussion of the 12 good UNKNOWNS will illustrate this point:

(1) Case I does not satisfy Conditions 1 and 4. The reported shape of this object is not duplicated in any of the other UNKNOWNS.

(2) Case II does not satisfy Conditions 1 and 3. There are very few UNKNOWNS in the aircraft shape classification. In addition, the unusual characteristic of this sighting (i.e., the red glow) could have been reflection of the lights of Flint from the objects if they were either birds or aircraft.

(3) Case III does not satisfy Condition 1. It also does not satisfy Condition 4 when Case II is eliminated as a good UNKNOWN.

(4) Case IV does not satisfy Conditions 1 or 2. There are few cigar-shaped or rocket-shaped objects reported in the literature. In addition, this observer is not considered to be well-qualified technically.

165

(5) Case V does not satisfy Condition 1. It also does not satisfy Condition 4 when Case IV is eliminated as a good UNKNOWN.

It might be argued here that many of the UNKNOWNS might actually have shapes similar to these good UNKNOWNS. It will be noted, however, that each of these five cases does not satisfy one of the other three conditions.

(6) Case VI does not satisfy Condition 2. In the description of the object, it was stated that at certain times there was no light seen from the object. Apparently, the "band of no light," as diagrammed by the observer, was an attempt to explain this. However, if the object were constructed as shown in the diagram, light should have been seen at all times. Because of this conflict the drawing is not considered reliable, and without the drawing, there is not enough detail in the description to make it useful for this study.

(7) Case VII violates Conditions 1 and 4. Although the shape is disc-like, the maneuvers performed by the object are unique both among the UNKNOWNS and among the good UNKNOWNS.

Cases VIII to XII satisfy Conditions 1 through 3, but they do not satisfy Condition 4. The features which make them different from each other are as follows:

(8) Case VIII. The object is smooth, with no protrusions or other details.

(9) Case IX. The object had rocket or jet pods on each side that were shooting out flames.

(10) Case X. The object had a fin or rudder.

(11) Case XI. The object had a series of portholes, or windows, on its under side.

(12) Case XII. The object had windows in its top

and front and its top midsection. It also had
a set of propellers around its waist.

It is not possible, therefore, to derive a verified model
of a "flying saucer" from the data that have been
gathered to date. This point is important enough to
emphasize. Out of about 4,000 people who said they
saw a "flying saucer", sufficiently detailed descriptions
were given in only 12 cases. Having culled the cream
of the crop, it is still impossible to develop a picture
of what a "flying saucer" is.

In addition to this study of the good UNKNOWNS,
an attempt was made to find groups of UNKNOWNS
for which the observed characteristics were the same.
No such groups were found.

On the basis of this evidence, therefore, there is a
low probability that any of the UNKNOWNS represent
observations of a class of "flying saucers". It may be
that some reports represent observations of not one
but several classes of objects that *might have been*
"flying saucers;" however, the lack of evidence to confirm even one class would seem to make this possibility
remote. It is pointed out that some of the cases of
KNOWNS, before identification, appeared fully as
bizarre as any of the 12 cases of good UNKNOWNS,
and, in fact, would have been placed in the class of
good UNKNOWNS had it not been possible to establish their identity.

This is, of course, contrary to the bulk of the
publicity that has been given to this problem. The
reason for the nature of this publicity was clearly
brought out during the re-evaluation study. It is a
definite fact that upon reading a few reports, the
reader becomes convinced that "flying saucers" are
real and are some form of sinister contrivance. This
reaction is independent of the training of the reader
or of his attitude toward the problem prior to the initial
contact. It is unfortunate that practically all of the
articles, books, and news stories dealing with the phenomenon of the "flying saucer" were written by men
who were in this category, that is, men who had read
only a few selected reports. This is accentuated by the

fact that, as a rule, only the more lurid-sounding reports are cited in these publications. Were it not for this common psychological tendency to be captivated by the mysterious, it is possible that no problem of this nature would exist.

The reaction, mentioned above, that after reading a few reports, the reader is convinced that "flying saucers" are real and are some form of sinister contrivance, is very misleading. As more and more of the reports are read, the feeling that "saucers" are real fades, and is replaced by a feeling of skepticism regarding their existence. The reader eventually reaches a point of saturation, after which the reports contain no new information at all and are no longer of any interest. This feeling of surfeit was universal among the personnel who worked on this project, and continually necessitated a conscious effort on their part to remain objective.

Conclusions

It can never be absolutely proven that "flying saucers" do not exist. This would be true if the data obtained were to include complete scientific measurements of the attributes of each sighting, as well as complete and detailed descriptions of the objects sighted. It might be possible to demonstrate the existence of "flying saucers" with data of this type. *IF* they were to exist.

Although the reports considered in this study usually did not contain scientific measurements of the attributes of each sighting, it was possible to establish certain valid conclusions by the application of statistical methods in the treatment of the data. Scientifically evaluated and arranged, the data as a whole did not show any marked patterns or trends. The inaccuracies inherent in this type of data, in addition to the incompleteness of a large proportion of the reports, may have obscured any patterns or trends that otherwise would have been evident. This absence of indicative relationships necessitated an exhaustive study of selected facets of the data in order to draw any valid conclusions.

A critical examination of the distributions of the important characteristics of sightings, plus an intensive study of the sightings evaluated as UNKNOWN, led to the conclusion that a combination of factors, principally the reported maneuvers of the objects and the unavailability of supplemental data such as aircraft flight plans or balloon-launching records, resulted in the failure to identify as KNOWNS most of the reports of objects classified as UNKNOWNS.

An intensive study, aimed at finding a verified example of a "flying saucer" or at deriving a verified model or models of "flying saucers" (as defined on Page 1), led to the conclusion that neither goal could be attained using the present data.

It is emphasized that there was a complete lack of any valid evidence consisting of physical matter in any case of a reported unidentified aerial object.

Thus, the probability that any of the UNKNOWNS considered in this study are "flying saucers" is concluded to be extremely small, since the most complete and reliable reports from the present data, when isolated and studied, conclusively failed to reveal even a rough model, and since the data as a whole failed to reveal any marked patterns or trends.

Therefore, on the basis of this evaluation of the information, it is considered to be highly improbable that any of the reports of unidentified aerial objects examined in this study represent observations of technological development outside the range of present-day scientific knowledge.

Chapter Eight: The Findings of Project Sign

Foreword

Project "Sign" was initiated by the Technical Intelligence Division, Air Material Command, and assigned Project Number XS-304, 22 January 1948, under authority of a letter from the Deputy Chief of Staff, Material, USAF. This letter is referenced C/S, USAF, 30 December 1947, subject "Flying Disks."

Assistance in analyzing the reported observations has been provided by other Divisions of Air Material Command in accordance with Technical Instructions TI-2195, Addendum No. 3, dtd 11 February 1948, subject: "Project Sign—Evaluation of Unidentified Flying Objects".

Analysis of the reported incidents, as an effort to identify astro-physical phenomena, is being accomplished by Ohio State University under contract with Air Material Command.

A special study has been initiated with the Rand Project in accordance with Air Corps Letter No. 80-10 dtd 21 July 1948 to present information that would serve to evaluate the remote possibility that some of the observed objects may be space ships or satellite vehicles.

Members of the Scientific Advisory Board to the Chief of Staff, USAF, have also supplied their services in a consulting capacity.

Summary

The results of the study reviewed in this report are based on data derived from reports of 243 domestic and thirty (30) foreign incidents. Data from these incidents is being summarized, reproduced and distributed to agencies and individuals cooperating in the analysis and evaluation. Distribution has so far been accomplished on the summaries of 172 incidents and more are in process of reproduction at this time.

A check list of items to be noted in reporting incidents has been prepared and distributed to government investigative agencies. The data obtained in reports received are studied in relation to many factors such as guided missile research activity, weather and other atmospheric sounding balloon launchings, commercial and military aircraft flights, flights of migratory birds, and other considerations, to determine possible explanations for sightings.

Based on the possibility that the objects are really unidentified and unconventional types of aircraft a technical analysis is made of some of the reports to determine the aerodynamic, propulsion, and control features that would be required for the object to perform as described in the reports. The objects sighted have been grouped into four classifications according to configuration:

1. Flying disks, i.e., very low aspect ratio aircraft.
2. Torpedo or cigar shaped bodies with no wings or fins visible in flight.
3. Spherical or balloon-shaped objects.
4. Balls of light.

The first three groups are capable of flight by aerodynamic or aerostatic means and can be propelled and controlled by methods known to aeronautical designers. The fourth appears to have no physical form attached, but the means of support may not have been seen by the observer.

Approximately twenty percent of the incidents have been identified as conventional aerial objects to the satisfaction of personnel assigned to Project "Sign" in this Command. It is expected that a study of the incidents in relation to weather and other atmospheric sounding balloons will provide solutions for an equivalent number. Verbal statements by an astro-physicist at Ohio State University and by psychologists of the Aero-Medical Laboratory of this Command indicate the possibility of solving an appreciable number of the sightings as a result of their investigations. Elimination of incidents with reasonably satisfactory explanations will clarify the problem presented by a project of this nature.

The possibility that some of the incidents may represent technical developments far in advance of knowledge available to engineers and scientists of this country has been considered. No facts are available to personnel at this Command that will permit an objective assessment of this possibility. All information so far presented on the possible existence of space ships from another planet or of aircraft propelled by an advanced type of atomic power plant have been largely conjecture. Based on experience with nuclear power plant research in this country, the existence on Earth of such engines of small enough size and weight to have powered the objects described is highly improbable.

Reports of unidentified flying objects are not peculiar to the present time. In "The Books of Charles Fort" by Tiffany Taylor, published in 1941 by Henry Holt & Co., New York, similar phenomena are described as having been sighted during past centuries. In the last war, numerous sightings of "balls of fire" in the air were reported by bomber crews.

Recommendations

Future activity on this project should be carried on at the minimum level necessary to record, summarize, and evaluate the data received on future reports and to complete the specialized investigations now in progress. When and if a sufficient number of incidents are solved to indicate that these sightings do not represent a threat to the security of the nation, the assignment of special project status to the activity could be terminated. Future investigations of reports would then be handled on a routine basis like any other intelligence work.

Reporting agencies should be impressed with the necessity for getting more factual evidence on sightings, such as photographs, physical evidence, radar sightings, and data on size and shape. Personnel sighting such objects should engage the assistance of others, when possible, to get more definite data. For example, military pilots should notify neighboring bases by radio of the presence and direction of flight of an unidentified object so that other observers, in flight or on the ground, could assist in its identification.

Discussion

Organization of Data on Incidents

Approximately 243 domestic incidents have been reviewed at the present time. In each incident, the observers have been interrogated by investigators and the results have been analyzed by technical personnel.

Condensed summaries have been prepared for the list of incidents in sufficient quantity to make the basic information easily available to individuals or agencies having an authority or an interest in the project. (See Appendix A.)

A detailed check list, compiled by technical personnel, indicating the basic elements of information, necessary for analysis of the individual incident, has been prepared and distributed to appropriate government agencies.

In order to identify ordinary and conventional objects that have probably been included in the list of reported incidents, graphical methods have been applied so as to present the basic data in such form that overall facts, implicit in the grouped data, will be made apparent. (See Appendix B.)

The prepared graphical data includes:

(a) Charts concerning unidentified aerial objects, to indicate:

1. Type of object observed
2. Vicinity in which particular type of object was observed
3. Direction of flight
(b) Locations of guided missiles, research and related centers
(c) Locations of airlines, airfields, both military and commercial
(d) Locations of radio beacon stations
(e) Known or projected radar stations from which reports and assistance may be derived
(f) Meteorological stations from which balloon release data, radiosonde or theodolite readings may be obtained
(g) Past, current, and projected celestial phenomena
(h) Flight paths of migratory birds

Conclusions

No definite and conclusive evidence is yet available that would prove or disprove the existence of these unidentified objects as real aircraft of unknown and unconventional configuration. It is unlikely that positive proof of their existence will be obtained without examination of the remains of crashed objects. Proof of non-existence is equally impossible to obtain unless a reasonable and convincing explanation is determined for each incident.

Many sightings by qualified and apparently reliable witnesses have been reported. However, each incident has unsatisfactory features, such as shortness of time under observation, distance from observer, vagueness of description or photographs, inconsistencies between individual observers, and lack of descriptive data, that prevents definite conclusions being drawn. Explanations of some of the incidents reveal the existence of simple and easily understandable causes so that there is the possibility that enough incidents can be solved to eliminate or greatly reduce the mystery associated with these occurrences.

Evaluation of reports of unidentified objects is a necessary activity of military intelligence agencies. Such sightings are inevitable, and under wartime conditions rapid and convincing solutions of such occurrences are necessary to maintain morale of military and civilian personnel. In this respect, it is considered that the establishment of procedures and training of personnel is in itself worth the effort expended on this project.

Psychological Analysis

A psychological analysis of the reported data is being prepared by Aero-Medical Laboratory, A.M.C., for the purpose of determining those incidents that are probably based upon errors of the human mind and senses. A preliminary verbal report from the professional psychologists indicates that a considerable number of incidents can be explained as ordinary occurrences that have been misrepresented, as the result of human errors.

The condition of "vertigo," well known to airplane pilots, as well as others, is considered to be an important factor in some of the reported incidents. "Vertigo" is defined from a medical viewpoint by Webster's Dictionary as "Dizziness or swimming of the head; a disturbance in which objects, though stationary, appear to move in various directions, and the person affected finds it difficult to maintain an erect posture. It may result from changes in the blood supply of the brain or from disease of the blood, eyes, ears, stomach, or other organs."

Accelerations, resulting from airplane maneuvers, together with space-orientation difficulties at night in an airplane, due to the lack of or strangeness of visual references, makes a condition of "vertigo" more likely to appear in personnel in night-flying aircraft than under more normal conditions. The fact that both pilot and co-pilot may report the same impressions is not complete proof of accuracy, since both individuals have experienced the same maneuvers and accelerations and have viewed the same lights and surroundings under the same optical conditions (including the same windshield and canopy glass).

A more complete discussion of psychological factors is expected to be provided in a future status report. Quite probably, some of the incidents of fast, highly maneuvering "lights," reported by both air and ground observers, are the result of "vertigo" or optical illusions.

Strictly speaking, no engineering analysis of an incident should be initiated until the psychological analysis has been made and has shown that psychological factors cannot explain the observation.

Agencies, Outside Air Material Command, Supplying Information and Analysis

Specialist services, supplementary to those of Air Material Command technical offices, are being provided by a number of agencies.

The Air Weather Service has reviewed the list of incidents and has provided the information that twenty-four of them coincide, both with respect to location and time, with the release of weather balloons.

The Ohio State University has contracted with Air Material Command to supply astronomical services in an effort to identify meteors, planetoids and associated phenomena. Professor Hynek, Ohio State University Astro-Physicist, and head of the University Observatory, has undertaken to review the incident summary sheets. While this work has not yet been completed, Professor Hynek has reported verbally that he is satisfied that a number of the reported observations represent astro-physical phenomena.

Members of the Scientific Advisory Board to the Chief of Staff, USAF, who have provided consultant services to Project "Sign," include Dr. Irving Langmuir, Chief, General Electric Research and Dr. G. E. Valley of MIT.

A preliminary type of interview has been held between Dr. Langmuir and personnel of Project "Sign" during early stages of the project. It is intended to consult further with Dr. Langmuir in an effort to supplement present technical efforts toward identifying the reported objects.

Dr. G. E. Valley has displayed an active interest in Project "Sign" to the extent of reviewing the reported incidents and writing an overall type of analysis in which he groups the various objects and then analyzes each group from the standpoint of scientific feasibility. This analysis is provided as Appendix (C) to this report.

Inasmuch as various surmises have been advanced that some of the reported observations may have represented "space ships" or satellite vehicles, a special study has been initiated with the Rand Corporation, under the Rand Project, to provide an analysis from this standpoint and also to provide fundamental information pertaining to the basic design and performance characteristics that might distinguish a possible "space ship."

As a preliminary undertaking, the Rand Project has submitted a study by Dr. Lipp in which the possibility is explored of any planet in the known universe being in a physical and cultural position to allow the development and use of the "space ship." This study has been prepared in the form of a report that is presented as Appendix (D).

The Weather Bureau Library of the Department of Commerce has supplied information on "ball lightning." This was requested because of the belief by some persons that some of the observations may have represented "ball lightning." It appears that the subject of "ball lightning" occupies an undetermined status and authorities are not at all convinced that such a phenomena actually exists.

The Federal Bureau of Investigation has assisted Project "Sign" in a number of instances, both by investigations of the character and reliability of witnesses of incidents and by providing other investigative services.

Considerations Affecting Analysis and Evaluation

OPERATIONAL

Inasmuch as there is a distinct possibility that a number of the reported incidents represent domestic projects of a security-classified nature, the list of incidents has been submitted to higher echelons for review.

Since weather balloons, blimps, airplanes of unusual size or configuration, and guided missiles test vehicles may represent some of the observations, action has been taken to obtain information concerning schedules and flights of such craft from the appropriate agencies.

In connection with the psychological studies being performed, extensive investigations concerning the character and reliability of the reporting witnesses have been made.

TECHNICAL

A certain proportion of incidents appear to be real aircraft, though of unconventional configuration. In order to investigate the credibility of their existence the following factors must be considered in any technical analysis.

Aircraft
  Method of Support (lift)
    Wings
    Fuselage Lift (Wingless)
    Rotor
    Vertical Jet
    Magnus Effect (rotating cylinder, cone or sphere, subjected to relative translational air velocity)
    Aerostatic (lighter-than-air craft)
  Method of Propulsion (thrust)
    Propeller-reciprocating engine combination
    Jet, rocket, ramjet (utilizing conventional fuels and oxidants or possibly atomic energy)
    Aerodynamic (Katzmayer Effect—oscillating airfoils developing negative drag [thrust])

If an atomic energy powered engine were available, a small mass flow at a large velocity could accomplish the required lift and propulsive forces and the large energy expenditure would be of small importance.

However, the heat exchange requirements for the atomic-powered engine appear to demand physical dimensions of inordinate size that presently would preclude the use of this power plant for aircraft.

In addition, manned aircraft would require an excessive percent weight of shielding for human protection, unless configurations of extremely large size were used. If unshielded craft were in operation, existing detection means would probably have indicated their presence.

Metallurgical limitations to date limit the rate of converting the heat energy of the atomic source to useful propulsive work to such an ineffective order to magnitude that such a power system is quite unlikely from the standpoint of size and weight.

Stability
- Aerodynamic (both static and dynamic through the use of aerodynamic surfaces and weight distribution).
- Servo-mechanism (gyro or accelerometer—servomotor system)

Control
- Movable surfaces in airflow or jet
- Jet (flow control or swiveling types)

Possible Spaceships
- World knowledge, techniques and resources are considered to be presently adequate for the development of spaceships.
- Distinguishing design and performance parameters are expected to be supplied as a special study by the Rand Project.

Probable Natural Phenomena
- Astrophysical (meteors, comets, planetoids, etc.)
- Astrophysical analysis is expected to be performed by personnel of Ohio State University Research Foundation.

Electromagnetic (ball lightning, St. Elmo's Fire, Phosphorescence, corona, etc.)

Ordinance Items

While this analysis considers the reported objects largely from the standpoint of aircraft with requirements for speed and substantial duration of flight and range, it is entirely possible that the configurations reported in small sizes could serve as very useful ordnance items to take the place of (or supplement) such short-range weapons of ground (infantry) warfare as the trench mortar, hand grenade, etc. The small saucer-like, spinning, disks, reportedly under development by the USSR with the aid of German scientists, having explosive edges and launched by a compressed air catapult (perhaps in the manner of clay pigeons projected by a trap mechanism), could possibly be ordnance articles. Also, such devices could be used by aircraft in attacking enemy airplane formations. In such cases, only a modest speed, short range, and limited flight duration would be required, hence the aerodynamic efficiency of the design would not be of very much importance.

Insufficient Information for Even 'Possible or Hypothetical Type Determination'.
Discredited Reports
Erroneous (See Discussion, Psychological Errors)
False

TECHNICAL ANALYSIS OF VARIOUS CONFIGURATIONS

The extreme lack of data for each of the incidents that have been reported makes it presently impossible to accurately identify any of the reported craft with respect to design and performance. Technical analysis must be made by considering possibilities and probabilities, which are expected to be proved or disproved only when complete data or physical specimens of aircraft (crash) are available. Unidentified aerial objects appear to be grouped as follows:

(1) Flying disks (saucers)
(2) Torpedo or Cigar Shaped Bodies (no wings or fins visible in flight)
(3) Spherical or Balloon-Shape Objects (capable of hovering, descending, ascending or travelling at high speed).
(4) Balls of light (no apparent physical form attached). Capable of maneuvering, climbing and travelling at high speed.

The first three groups of objects are capable of flight through the atmosphere by means of aerodynamic and propulsion designs (to produce the required lift and thrust) that are readily conceivable by aeronautical designers. The stabilizing and control features that would be required, while more obscure, could conceivably be provided. The question arises, however, as to whether these configurations would devolep much speed and allow a sufficient duration of flight and adequate range to be of practical use as aircraft.

FLYING DISKS

The disk or circular planform has not been used in representative aircraft, either military or civilian, for the reason that the induced drag, as determined by the Prandtl theory of lift, would apparently be excessively high, since the aspect ratio of a circular platform is only 1.27. Extension of the Prandtl theory has also shown that the maximum possible lift coefficient to be expected from such low aspect ratio planforms should also be poor. In addition, the relatively large mean aerodynamic chord would present difficult design problems, to achieve static longitudinal stability for airfoil sections having a significant center-of-pressure travel, or for airfoil sections of so-called "stable" type, when equipped with ailerons at the trailing edge.

In the very low aspect ratio range, the Prandtl theory is probably very inaccurate. Wind-tunnel tests of very low aspect ratio airfoils indicate much less induced drag increase than expected from theory and also demonstrate very high maximum lift coefficient accompanied by extremely high stalling angles. However, in general the induced drag of very low aspect ratio wings is much larger than the induced drag of conventional aircraft wings, a condition which would adversely affect all performance values in flight conditions which require medium and high lift coefficients. Thus, performance in climb, at altitude, and for long-range conditions would be relatively poor, although high speed would be little affected.

Notwithstanding the predicted aerodynamic disadvantages of circular planform wings, quite a number of experimental efforts have been made to use this configuration—and not all of them by persons ignorant of aerodynamic fundamentals. Experimental wind-tunnel work at the NACA (1933) showed both maximum lift coefficients and stall characteristics much more favorable than could be anticipated.

The problem of static longitudinal stability could possibly be solved by the use of a stable airfoil section of the reflexed trailing edge type with wing tip ailerons (perhaps floating) aerodynamically independent of the wing.

At supersonic speeds, where the induced drag is small, the circular planform offers the probability of reduced drag, characteristic of low aspect ratio airfoils in the supersonic range. Also the circular planform presents a swept-back leading edge (of variable sweep along the span), which should result in a reduced effective Mach Number, with attendant reduced drag for a certain supersonic speed range.

No definite information has been received on the method of propulsion used on flying disks which have been sighted. However, because of distance factors involved in the sightings it is quite possible that either propellers or jet propulsion could have been employed without being noted by the observer.

FLYING FUSELAGES
(TORPEDO OR CIGAR-SHAPED BODY)

While the cigar or torpedo-shaped body represents an efficient form for the fuselage of an airplane or the body of a guided missile, in neither case has it been used as a primary lift-producing surface. However, an extension of the Prandtl theory of lift indicates that a fuselage of the dimensions reported by the Eastern Airlines pilots Whited and Chiles in the Montgomery, Alabama, incident could support a load comparable to the weight of an aircraft of this size at flying speeds in the subsonic range. The Prandtl theory probably gives very conservative values of maximum lift for bodies of this shape. German experience indicates that the maximum lift may be twice as high as that given by the theory.

Although the craft sighted by Whited and Chiles was reported to be without wings and fins, it is possible that it could have been equipped with extensible wings for take-off and landing, contained within the fuselage in cruising flight.

This type of aircraft could also be partially supported in the take-off and landing condition by the vertical component of the jet thrust, if the landing and take-off took place with the fuselage axis, or the jet stream direction in a vertical or nearly vertical altitude. The further possibility that an extensible rotor, concealed within the fuselage, could have been used, would provide another method for landing and take-off that would allow wingless flight at very high speed. Such a design could result in a relatively large duration of flight and corresponding range.

While no stabilizing fins were apparent on the "flying fuselage" reported by Whited and Chiles, it is possible that vanes within the jet, operated by a gyro-servo system, could have provided static stability, longitudinally, directionally and laterally. The same vanes could also have been used for accomplishing static balance or trim, as well as control, for maneuvering.

The above discussion regarding weight, controllability, stability, etc. is not intended to represent deductions regarding the exact nature of the torpedo or cigar-shaped aircraft which were sighted by the airline pilots, Whited and Chiles, and others. They are merely statements of possibilities, which are intended

183

to show that such an aircraft could support and control itself by aerodynamic means.

The propulsive system of this type of vehicle would appear to be a jet or rocket engine. The specific fuel consumption of engines of this type would be rather high. This, coupled with the fact that aerodynamic lift on such a body would be accompanied by high drag, places a serious limitation on the range of this aircraft for particular gross weight. If this type of unidentified aerial object has extremely long range, it is probable that the method of propulsion is one which is far in advance of presently known engines.

ROUND OBJECTS
(SPHERICAL AND BALLOON-SHAPED OBJECTS)

Spherical or balloon-shaped objects are not usually considered as efficient aircraft. Not only would the drag of such bodies be high, but the energy expenditure that would be required to develop lift by aerodynamic means would be excessive. The only conceivable means of producing lift for such a body, other than by aerostatic (simple buoyancy) means, would be by rotation of the sphere with translational motion relative to the air; or by discharging a stream of air vertically downward. Aerodynamic flight could be accomplished with a rotating sphere, provided the detailed design problems, including stability and control were worked out. The methods, using a blower system or jets, would require relatively greater amounts of energy and while they could be used for flights of very short range and duration, would not ordinarily be considered as practical by aeronautical designers.

The obvious explanation for most of the spherical shaped objects is that they are meterological or similar type balloons. This, however, does not explain reports that they travel at high speed or maneuver rapidly. It is possible that the movement of the objects was some kind of an optical illusion or that movement for a brief period due to a gas leak in the balloon was exaggerated by observers.

No reasonable hypothesis of the true nature of balls of light, such as that reported by Lt. Gorman at Fargo, N. Dakota, has been developed that explains the behavior reported. The most reasonable explanation is that the lights were suspended from balloons, or other means of support, not visible at night, and the violent maneuvers reported are due to illusion.

POSSIBILITY OF SCIENTIFIC DEVELOPMENT IN ADVANCE OF KNOWLEDGE IN THIS COUNTRY

Consideration has been given to the possibility that these unidentified aircraft represent scientific developments beyond the level of knowledge attained in this country. Since this is probably the most advanced of the industrial nations on the earth, and our interest in scientific developments throughout the world is very active, it would be necessary for any other country to conduct research and development work in extreme secrecy for any such project to have reached such an advanced state of development without a hint of its existence becoming known here. The only nation on earth with extensive technical resources which has such rigid security is the U.S.S.R. An objective evaluation of the ability of the Soviets to produce technical developments so far in advance of the rest of the world results in the conclusion that the possibility is extremely remote. Most of the successful Soviet aeronautical developments have been produced by utilizing experience of other nations, some of them being very close copies, so it is very unlikely that they have developed the propulsion and control devices necessary to make these objects perform as described.

Another possibility is that these aerial objects are visitors from another planet. Little is known of the probabilities of life on other planets, so there is no basis on which to judge the possibility that civilizations far in advance of ours exist outside the earth. The commentary on this possibility by Dr. James Lipp

185

of the Rand Project in Appendix D indicates that this solution of the mystery connected with the sighting of unidentified flying objects is extremely improbable. Pending elimination of all other solutions or definite proof of the nature of these objects, this possibility will not be further explored.

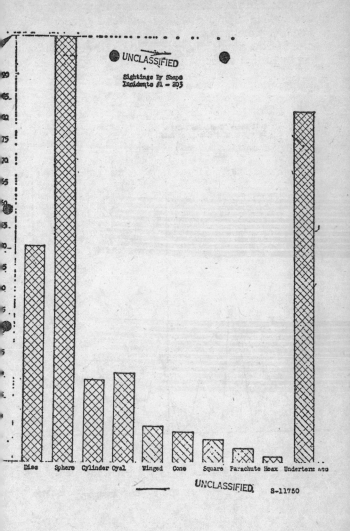

UNCLASSIFIED

Sightings By Shape
Incidents #1 - 203

| Disc | Sphere | Cylinder | Oval | Winged | Cone | Square | Parachute | Hoax | Undetermined |

UNCLASSIFIED   S-11750

187

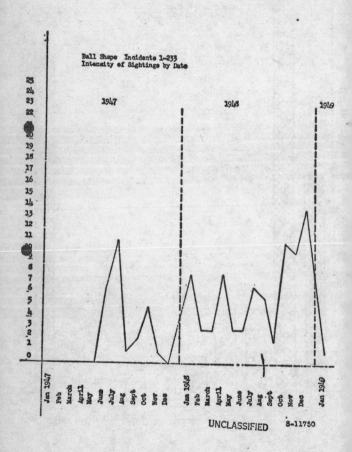

Ball Shape Incidents 1-233
Intensity of Sightings by Date

188

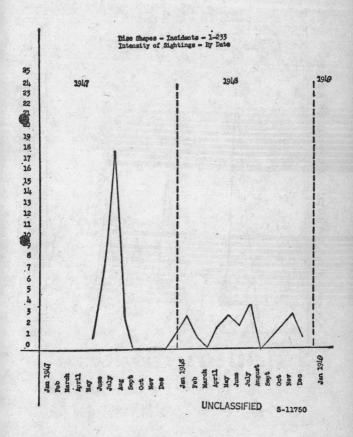

Disc Shapes - Incidents - 1-233
Intensity of Sightings - By Date

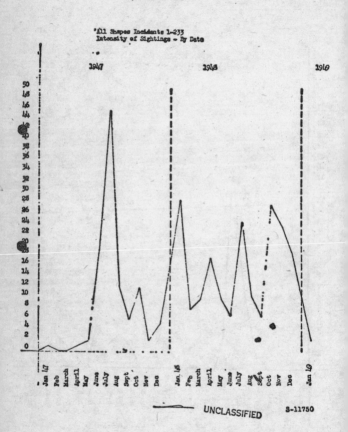

*All Shapes Incidents 1-233
Intensity of Sightings - By Date

UNCLASSIFIED

UNCLASSIFIED   S-11750

190

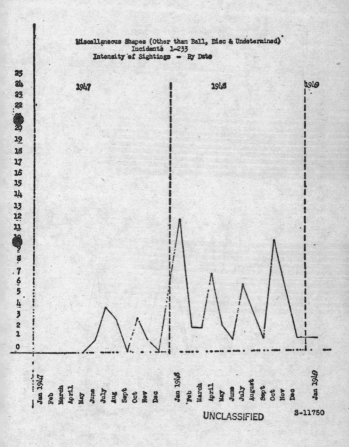

Miscellaneous Shapes (Other than Ball, Disc & Undetermined)
Incidents 1-233
Intensity of Sightings - By Date

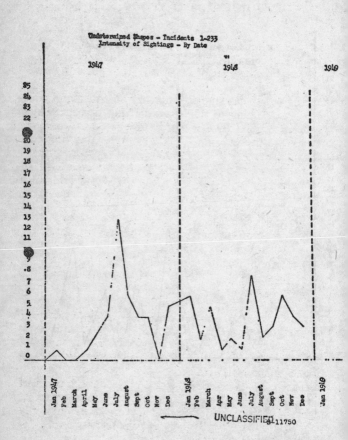

Undetermined Shapes - Incidents 1-233
Intensity of Sightings - By Date

192

Appendix "C"
Some Considerations Affecting the Interpretation of Reports of Unidentified Flying Objects
By

G. E. Valley, Member Scientific Advisory Board, Office of the Chief of Staff, United States Air Force

The writer has studied summary abstracts and comments pertaining to unidentified flying objects, which were forwarded by Air Force Intelligence. These remarks are divided into three main parts: the first part is a short *summary* of the reports; the second part consists of a general survey of various *possibilities* of accounting for the reports; the third part contains certain *recommendations* for future action.

Part I—Short Summary of Observations

The reports can be grouped as follows:

Group 1—The most numerous reports indicate the daytime observation of metallic disk-like objects, roughly in diameter ten times their thickness. There is some suggestion that the cross section is asymetrical and rather like a turtle shell. Reports agree that these objects are capable of high acceleration and velocity; they often are sighted in groups, sometimes in formation. Sometimes they flutter.

Group 2—The second group consists of reports of lights observed at night. These are also capable of high speed and acceleration. They are less commonly seen in groups. They usually appear to be sharply defined luminous objects.

Group 3—The third group consists of reports of various kinds of rockets, in general appearing somewhat like V-2 rockets.

Group 4—The fourth group contains reports of various devices which, in the writer's opinion, are sounding balloons of unusual shape such as are made by the General Mills Company to Navy contract.

Group 5—The fifth group includes reports of objects in which little credence can be placed.

General Remarks

In general, it is noted that few, if any, reports indicate that the observed objects make any noise or radio interference. Nor are there many indications of any material affects of physical damage attributable to the observed objects.

Summary—PART I

This report will consider mainly the reports of Groups 1 and 2.

Part II—On Possible Explanations of the Reports

Section A—What can be deduced concerning the nature of an unknown aerial object from a single sighting?

Here, there are two problems: first, how much can be deduced concerning the nature of the objects from geometrical calculations alone; second, how much more can be deduced if, in addition, it is assumed that the objects obey the laws of nature as we know them.

Concerning the first problem, it can be stated that only ratios of lengths, and rates of change of such ratios, can be accurately determined. Thus, the range and size of such objects cannot be determined; and it is noticeable that reports of size of the observed objects are widely at variance. However, angles, such as the angle subtended by the object, can be observed. Likewise there is fair agreement among several observers that the diameter of the objects of Group 1 is about ten times their thickness. Although velocity cannot be determined, angular velocity can be, and in particular the flutter frequency could, in principle, be determined.

All that can be concluded about the range and size of the objects, from geometrical considerations alone, is: 1) from the fact that estimated sizes vary so widely, the objects were actually either of different sizes, or more likely, that they were far enough from the observers so that binocular vision produced no stereoscopic effect; this only means that they were further off than about thirty feet; 2) since objects were seen to disappear behind trees, buildings, clouds, etc., they are large enough to be visible at the ranges of those recognizable objects.

Now, it is obviously of prime importance to estimate the size and mass of the observed objects. This may be possible to some extent if it is permissible to assume that they obey the laws of physics. Since the objects have not been observed to produce any physical effects, other than the one case in which a cloud was evaporated along the trajectory, it is not certain that the laws of mechanics, for instance, would be sufficient.

But suppose that mechanical laws alone are sufficient, then the following example is sufficient proof that at least a length could, in principle, be determined: suppose a simple pendulum were observed suspended in the sky; then after observing its frequency of oscillation, we could deduce from the laws of mechanics its precise length.

This suggests that something could be deduced from the observed fluttering motion of some of the objects of Group 1. Assume that we know the angular frequency and angular amplitude of this fluttering motion (they can be measured in principle from a motion picture). Then for purposes of calculation assume the object to be thirty feet in diameter, to be as rigid as a normal aircraft wing of 30-foot span, to be constructed of material of the optimum weight–strength ratio and to be a structure of most efficient design. It is now possible to calculate how heavy the object must be merely to remain rigid under the observed angular motion. Let the calculation be made for a plurality of assumed sizes 1, 2, 4, 8, 16, 32, 64—up to say 200 feet, and let calculated mass be plotted versus assumed size. The non-linear character of the curve should indicate an approximate upper limit to the size of the object.

If, in addition, it is assumed that the flutter is due to aerodynamic forces, it is possible that more precise information could be obtained.

The required angular data can probably be extracted from witnesses most reliably by the use of a demonstration model which can be made to oscillate or flutter in a known way.

Summary—PART II, Section A

Geometrical calculations alone cannot yield the size of objects observed from a single station; such observation together with the assumption that the objects are essentially aircraft, can be used to set reasonable limits of size.

Section B—The possibility of supporting and propelling a solid object by unusual means

Since some observers have obviously colored their reports with talk of rays, jets, beams, space-ships, and the like, it is well to examine what possibilities exist along these lines. This is also important in view of the conclusions of *PART II, Section A,* of this report.

Method I—Propulsion and support by means of "rays" or "beams."

By "rays" or "beams" are meant either purely electromagnetic radiation or else radiation which is largely corpuscular like cathode-rays or cosmic-rays or cyclotron-beams.

Now, it is obvious that any device propelled or supported by such means is fundamentally a reaction device. It is fundamental in the theory of such devices that a given amount of energy is most efficiently spent if the momentum thrown back or down is large. This means that a large mass should be given a small acceleration—a theorem well understood by helicopter designers.

The beams or rays mentioned do the contrary, a

small mass is given a very high velocity, consequently enormous powers, greater than the total world's power capacity, would be needed to support even the smallest object by such means.

Method II—Direct use of Earth's Magnetic Field

One observer (incident 68) noticed a violent motion of a hand-held compass. If we assume from this that the objects produced a magnetic field, comparable with the Earth's field; namely, 0.1 gauss, and that the observer found that the object subtended an angle θ at his position, then the ampere-turns of the required electromagnet is given by:

$$ni = \frac{30\,R}{\theta^2} \quad \text{where } R \text{ is the range of the object}$$

For instance, if R is 1 kilometer and the object is 10 meters in diameter, then $ni = 1$ billion ampere-turns.

Now, if the object were actually only 10 meters away and were correspondingly smaller, namely, 10 cm in diameter, it would still require 10 million ampere-turns.

These figures are a little in excess of what can be conveniently done on the ground. They make it seem unlikely that the effect was actually observed.

Now, the Earth's magnetic field would react on such a magnet to produce not only a torque but also a force. This force depends not directly on the Earth's field intensity but on its irregularity or gradient. This force is obviously minute since the change in field over a distance of 10 meters (assumed diameter of the object) is scarcely measurable, moreover, the gradient is not predictable but changes due to local ore deposits. Thus, even if the effect were large enough to use, it would still be unreliable and unpredictable.

Method III—Support of an electrically charged object by causing it to move transverse to the Earth's magnetic field

A positively charged body moving from west to

east, or a negatively charged body moving from east to west, will experience an upward force due to the Earth's magnetic field.

A sphere 10 meters diameter moving at a speed of one kilometer/second would experience an upward force of one pound at the equator if charged to a potential of 5×10^{12} volts. This is obviously ridiculous.

Summary—PART II, Section B

Several unorthodox means of supporting or propelling a solid object have been considered, all are impracticable. This finding lends credence to the tentative proposed assumption of Part II, that the objects are supported and propelled by some normal means or else that they are not solids. No discussion of the type of Part II, Section B, can, in principle, of course, be complete.

Section C—Possible causes for the reports
Classification I—Natural terrestrial phenomena

1. The observations may be due to some effect such as ball lightning. The writer has no suggestions on this essentially meteorological subject.

2. The objects may be some kind of animal.

Even in the celebrated case of incident 172 where the light was chased by a P51 for half an hour and which was reported by the pilot to be intelligently directed, we can make this remark. For consider that an intelligence capable of making so remarkable a device would not be likely to play around in so idle a manner as described by the pilot.

In this connection, it would be well to examine if some of the lights observed at night were not fire-flies.

3. The observed objects may be hallucinatory or psychological in origin. It is of prime importance to study this possibility because we can learn from it something of the character of the population: its response under attack; and also something about the reliability of visual observation.

One would like to assume that the positions held by many of the reported observers guarantee their observations. Unfortunately, there were many reports of curious phenomena by pilots during the war—the incident of the fire-ball fighters comes to mind. Further, mariners have been reporting sea-serpents for hundreds of years yet no one has yet produced a photograph.

It would be interesting to tabulate the responses to see how reliable were the reports on the Japanese balloons during the war. There we had a phenomenon proven to be real.

It is interesting that the reports swiftly reach a maximum frequency during the end of June 1947 and then slowly taper off. We can assume that this is actually an indication of how many objects were actually about, or, quite differently, we can take this frequency curve as indicating something about mass psychology.

This point can be tested. Suppose the population is momentarily excited; how does the frequency of reports vary with time? A study of crank letters received after the recent publicity given to the satellite program should give the required frequency distribution.

It is probably necessary but certainly not sufficient that the unidentified-object curve and the crank-letter curve should be similar in order for the flying disks to be classed as hallucinations.

A large-scale experiment was made at the time of Orson Welles' "Martian" broadcast. Some records of this must persist in newspaper files.

Classification II—Man-made terrestrial phenomena
1. The objects may be Russian aircraft. If this were so, then the considerations of Sections A and B indicate that we would have plenty to worry about. It is the author's opinion that only an accidental discovery of a degree of novelty never before achieved could suffice to explain such devices. It is doubtful whether a potential enemy would arouse our curiosity in so idle a fashion.

Classification III—Extraterrestrial objects
1. *Meteors:* It is noteworthy that the British physicist Lovell writing in "Physics Today" mentions the radar discovery of a new daytime meteorite stream

which reached its maximum during June 1947. The reported objects lose little of their interest, however, if they are of meteoritic origin.

2. *Animals:* Although the objects as described act more like animals than anything else, there are few reliable reports on extraterrestrial animals.

3. *Space Ships:* The following considerations pertain:

a. If there is an extraterrestrial civilization which can make such objects as are reported then it is most probable that its development is far in advance of ours. This argument can be supported on probability arguments alone without recourse to astronomical hypotheses.

b. Such a civilization might observe that on Earth we now have atomic bombs and are fast developing rockets. In view of the past history of mankind, they should be alarmed. We should, therefore, expect at this time above all to behold such visitations.

Since the acts of mankind most easily observed from a distance are A-bomb explosions we should expect some relation to obtain between the time of A-bomb explosions, the time at which the space ships are seen, and the time required for such ships to arrive from and return to home-base.

Section D—The anti-gravity shield

It has been proposed, by various writers, perhaps first by H. G. Wells, that it might be possible to construct a means of shielding a massive body from the influence of gravity. Such an object would then float. Recently, there appeared in the press a notice that a prominent economist has offered to support research on such an enterprise.

Obviously, conservation of energy demands that considerable energy be given the supported object in order to place it on the shield. However, this amount of energy is in no way prohibitive, and furthermore it can be gotten back when the object lands.

Aside from the fact that we have no suggestions as to how such a device is to be made, the various theories of general relativity all agree in assuming that gravitational force and force due to acceleration are indistinguishable, and from this assumption the theories predict certain effects which are in fact observed. The assumption, therefore, is probably correct, and a corollary of it is essentially that only by means of an acceleration can gravity be counteracted. This, we can successfully do for instance by making an artificial satellite, but this presumably is not what has been observed.

Part III—Recommendations

1. The file should be continued.

2. A meteorologist should compute the approximate energy required to evaporate as much cloud as shown in the incident 26 photographs. Together with an aerodynamicist he should examine whether a meteorite of unusual shape could move as observed.

3. The calculations suggested in Part II, Section A, should be estimated by an aerodynamicist with such changes as his more detailed knowledge may suggest.

4. The mass-psychology studies outlined in Part II, Section C, Classification I 3 should be carried out by a competent staff of statisticians and mass-psychologists.

5. Interviewing agents should carry objects or moving pictures for comparison with reporters' memories. These devices should be properly designed by a psychologist experienced in problems pertaining to aircraft and design of aircraft-control equipment so that he shall have some grasp of what it is that is to be found out. If the Air Force has reason to be seriously interested in these reports, it should take immediate steps to interrogate the reporters more precisely.

6. A person skilled in the optics of the eye and of the atmosphere should investigate the particular point that several reports agree in describing the objects as being about ten times as wide as they are thick; the point being to see if there is a plurality of actual shapes which appear so, under conditions approaching limiting resolution or detectable contrast.

Appendix "D"

13 December 1948   AI-1009

Brigadier General Putt
United States Air Force
Director of Research and Development
Office, Deputy Chief of Staff, Materiel

Dear General Putt:

Please refer to your letter of 18 November 1948 relative to the "flying object" problem and to Mr. Collbohm's reply dated 24 November 1948. In paragraph (b) of the reply, Mr. Collbohm promised (among other things) to send a discussion of the "special design and performance characteristics that are believed to distinguish space ships."

This present letter gives, in very general terms, a description of the likelihood of a visit from other worlds as an engineering problem and some points regarding the use of space vehicles as compared with descriptions of the flying objects. Mr. Collbohm will deliver copies to Colonel McCoy at Wright-Patterson Air Base during the RAND briefing there within the next few days.

A good beginning is to discuss some possible places of origin of visiting space ships. Astronomers are largely in agreement that only one member of the Solar system (besides Earth) can support higher forms of life. It is the planet Mars. Even Mars appears quite desolate and inhospitable so that a race would be more occupied with survival than we are on Earth. Reference 1* gives adequate descriptions on the various planets and satellites. A quotation from Ref. 1 (p. 229) can well be included here.

Whether intelligent beings exist to appreciate

---

* *Earth, Moon and Planets,* by F. L. Whipple. Harvard Books on Astronomy, Blakiston, 1941.

these splendors of the Martian landscape is pure speculation. If we have correctly reconstructed the history of Mars, there is little reason to believe that the life processes may not have followed a course similar to terrestrial evolution. With this assumption, three general possibilities emerge. Intelligent beings may have protected themselves against the excessively slow loss of atmosphere, oxygen and water, by constructing homes and cities* with the physical conditions scientifically controlled. As a second possibility, evolution may have developed a being who can withstand the rigors of the Martian climate. Or the race may have perished.

These possibilities have been sufficiently expanded in the pseudo-scientific literature to make further amplification superfluous. However, there may exist some interesting restrictions to the anatomy and physiology of a Martian. Rarity of the atmosphere, for example, may require a completely altered respiratory system for warm-blooded creatures. If the atmospheric pressure is much below the vapor pressure of water at the body temperature of the individual, the process of breathing with our type of lungs becomes impossible. On Mars the critical pressure for a body temperature of 98.6°F. occurs when a column of the atmosphere contains one sixth the mass of a similar column on the Earth. For a body temperature of 77°F. the critical mass ratio is reduced to about one twelfth, and at 60°F. to about one twenty-fourth. These critical values are of the same order as the values estimated for the Martian atmosphere. Accordingly the anatomy and physiology of a Martian may be radically different from ours—but this is all conjecture.

We do not know the origin of life, even on the Earth. We are unable to observe any signs of intelligent life on Mars. The reader may form his own opinion. If he believes that the life force is universal

---

* Not too large or they might be visible. Perhaps underground where the atmospheric pressure would be greater and where temperature extremes would be reduced.

and that intelligent beings may have once developed on Mars, he has only to imagine that they persisted for countless generations in a rare atmosphere which is nearly devoid of oxygen and water, and on a planet where the nights are much colder than our arctic winters. The existence of intelligent life on Mars is not impossible but it is completely unproven.

It is not too unreasonable to go a step further and consider Venus as a possible home for intelligent life. The atmosphere, to be sure, apparently consists mostly of carbon dioxide with deep clouds of formaldehyde droplets, and there seems to be little or no water. Yet living organisms might develop in chemical environments that are strange to us: the vegetable kingdom, for example, operates on a fundamentally different energy cycle from Man. Bodies might be constructed and operated with different chemicals and other physical principles than any of the creatures we know. One thing is evident: fishes, insects, and mammals all manufacture within their own bodies complex chemical compounds that do not exist as minerals. To this extent, life is self-sufficient and might well adapt itself to any environment within certain limits of temperature (and size of creature).

Venus has two handicaps relative to Mars. Her mass, and gravity, are nearly as large as for the Earth (Mars is smaller) and her cloudy atmosphere would discourage astronomy hence space travel. The remaining Solar planets are such poor prospects that they can be ignored.

In the next few paragraphs, we shall speak of Mars. It should be understood that most of the remarks apply equally well to Venus.

Various people have suggested that an advanced race may have been visiting Earth from Mars or Venus at intervals from decades to eons. Reports of objects in the sky seem to have been handed down through the generations. If this were true, a race of such knowledge and power would have established some form of direct contact. They could see that Earth's inhabitants would be helpless to do interplanetary harm. If afraid of carrying diseases home, they would at least try to communicate. It is hard to believe that any technically accomplished race would come here, flaunt its ability in mysterious ways and then simply go away. To this writer, long-time practice of space travel implies advanced engineering and science weapons and ways of thinking. It is not plausible (as many fiction writers do) to mix space ships with broadswords. Furthermore, a race which had enough initiative to explore among the planets would hardly be too timid to follow through when the job was accomplished.

One other hypothesis needs to be discussed. It is that the Martians have kept a long-term routine watch on Earth and have been alarmed by the sight of our A-bomb shots as evidence that we are warlike and on the threshold of space travel. (Venus is eliminated here because her cloudy atmosphere would make such a survey impractical). The first flying objects were sighted in the Spring of 1947, after a total 5 atomic bomb explosions, i.e., Alamogordo, Hiroshima, Nagasaki, Crossroads A and Crossroads B. Of these, the first two were in positions to be seen from Mars, the third was very doubtful (at the edge of Earth's disc in daylight) and the last two were on the wrong side of Earth. It is likely that Martian astronomers, with their thin atmosphere, could build telescopes big enough to see A-bomb explosions on Earth, even though we were 165 and 153 million miles away, respectively, on the Alamogordo and Hiroshima dates. The weakest point in the hypothesis is that a continual, defensive watch of Earth for long periods of time (perhaps thousands of years) would be dull sport, and no race that even remotely resembled Man would undertake it. We haven't even considered the idea for Venus or Mars, for example.

The sum and substance of this discussion is that if Martians are now visiting us without contact, it can be assumed that they have just recently succeeded in space travel and that their civilization would be practically abreast of ours.

The chance that Martians, under such widely divergent conditions, would have a civilization resembling our own is extremely remote. It is particularly unlikely that their civilization would be within a half century of our own state of advancement. Yet in the last 50 years we have just started to use aircraft and in the next 50 years we will almost certainly start exploring space.

Thus it appears that space travel from another point within the Solar system is possible but very unlikely. Odds are at least a thousand-to-one against it.

This leaves the totality of planets of other stars in the Galaxy as possible sources. Many modern astronomers believe that planets are fairly normal and logical affairs in the life history of a star (rather than cataclysmic oddities) so that many planets can be expected to exist in space.

To narrow the field a little, some loose specifications can be written for the star about which the home base planet would revolve. Let us say that the star should bear a family resemblance to the Sun, which is a member of the so-called "main-sequence" of stars, i.e., we eliminate white dwarfs, red giants and supergiants. For a description of these types, see reference 2,* chapter 5. There is no specific reason for making this assumption except to simplify discussion: we are still considering the majority of stars.

Next, true variable stars can be eliminated, since conditions on a planet attached to a variable star would fluctuate too wildly to permit life. The number of stars deleted here is negligibly small. Reference 3,† pages 76 and 85 indicate that the most common types are too bright to be in nearby space unnoticed. Lastly, we shall omit binary or multiple stars, since the conditions for stable planet orbits are obscure in such cases. About a third of the stars are eliminated by this restriction.

As our best known sample of space we can take a volume with the Sun at the center and a radius of 16

---

* Atoms, Stars and Nebulae, by Goldberg, Alter. Harvard Books on Astronomy, Blakiston, 1943.
† The Story of Variable Stars, by Campbell and Jacchia. Harvard Books on Astronomy, Blakiston, 1945.

light years. A compilation of the 47 known stars, including the Sun, within this volume is given in reference 4,* pages 52 to 57. Eliminating according to the above discussion: Three are white dwarfs, eight binaries account for 16 stars and two trinaries account for 16 stars and two trinaries account for 6 more. The remainder, 22 stars, can be considered as eligible for habitable planets.

Assuming the above volume to be typical, the contents of any other reasonable volume can be found by varying the number of stars proportionately with the volume, or with the radius cubed,

$$S_e = 22_x \frac{(r)^3}{16}$$

where S_e is number of eligible stars and r is the radius of the volume in light years. (This formula should only be used for radii greater than 16 light years. For smaller samples we call for a recount. For example, only one known eligible star other than the Sun lies within eight light years).

Having an estimate of the number of useable stars, it is now necessary to make a guess as to the number of habitable planets. We have only one observed sample, the Solar system, and the guess must be made with low confidence, since intelligent life may not be randomly distributed at all.

The Sun has nine planets, arranged in a fairly regular progression of orbits (see reference 1, Appendix 1) that lends credence to theories that many stars have planets. Of the nine planets one (the Earth) is completely suitable for life. Two more (in adjacent orbits) are near misses: Mars has extremely rigorous living conditions and Venus has an unsuitable atmosphere. Viewed very broadly indeed, this could mean that each star would have a series of planets so spaced that one, or possibly two, would have correct temperatures, correct moisture content and atmosphere to support

* The Milky Way, by Bok and Bok. Harvard Books on Astronomy, Blakiston, 1941.

civilized life. Let us assume that there is, on the average, one habitable planet per eligible star.

There is no line of reasoning or evidence which can indicate whether life will actually develop on a planet where the conditions are suitable. Here again, the Earth may be unique rather than a random sample. This writer can only inject some personal intuition into the discussion with the view that life is not unique on Earth, or even the random result of a low probability, but is practically inevitable in the right conditions. This is to say, the number of inhabited planets is equal to those that are suitable!

One more item needs to be considered. Knowing nothing at all about other races, we must assume that Man is average as to technical advancement, environmental difficulties, etc. That is, one half of the other planets are behind us and have no space travel and the other half are ahead and have various levels of space travel. We can thus imagine that in our sample volume there are 11 races of beings who have begun space explorations. The formula on page 3 above now becomes

$$R = 11 \times \frac{(r)^3}{16}$$

where R is the number of races exploring space in a spherical volume of radius $r \leqslant 16$ light years.

Arguments like those applied to Martians on page 2 need not apply to races from other star systems. Instead of being a first port of call, Earth would possibly be reached only after many centuries of development and exploration with space ships, so that a visiting race could be expected to be far in advance of Man.

To summarize the discussion thus far: the chance of space travelers existing at planets attached to neighboring stars is very much greater than the chance of space-traveling Martians. The one can be viewed almost as a certainty (if the assumptions are accepted), whereas the other is very slight indeed.

In order to estimate the relative chances that visitors from Mars or star X could come to the Earth and act

208

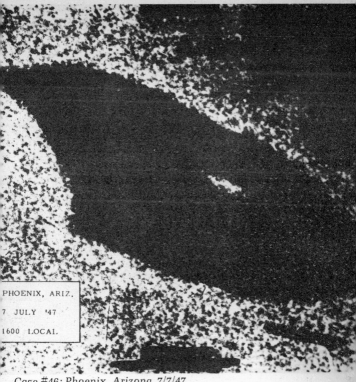

PHOENIX, ARIZ.

7 JULY '47

1600 LOCAL.

Case #46; Phoenix, Arizona, 7/7/47

**The files of Project Blue Book <u>do</u> contain a fair number
of photos showing well-defined disklike objects.
Note particularly the shots from Mt. Clemens, Michigan.**

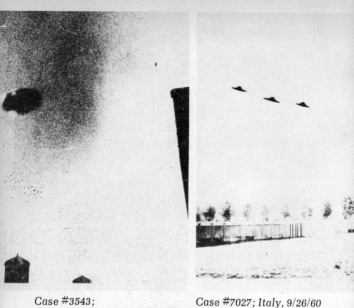

Case #3543;
New York, New York, 4/15/55

Case #7027; Italy, 9/26/60

Case #7824; Sheffield, England, 3/4/62

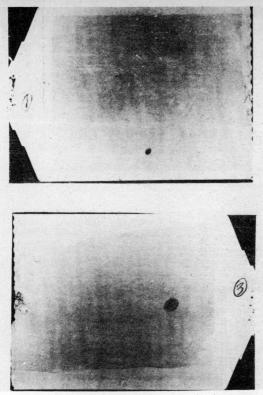

Case #7927; Burlington, Massachusetts, 5/15/62

Case #11242; St. Paul, Minnesota, 12/27/66

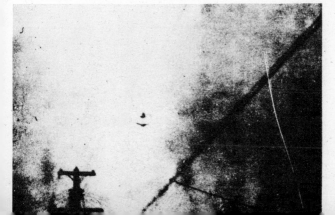

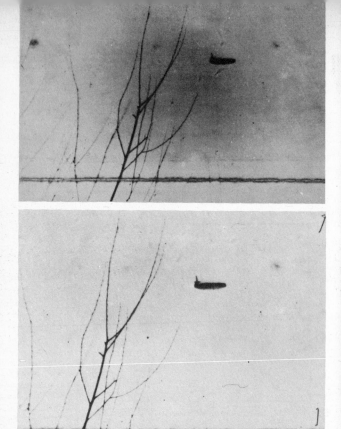

Case #11263; Mt. Clemens, Michigan, 1/9/67

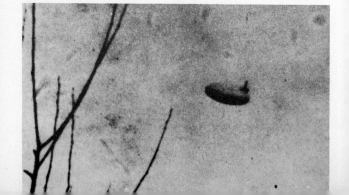

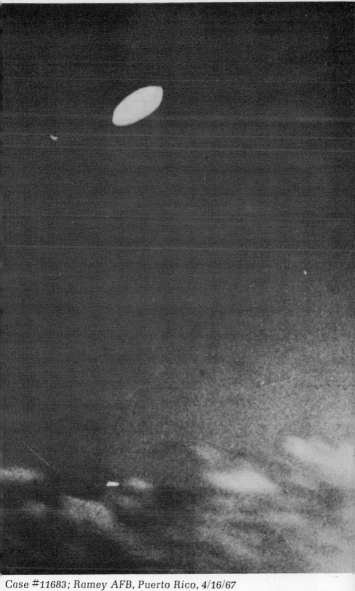

Case #11683; Ramey AFB, Puerto Rico, 4/16/67

Case #1201; San Francisco, California, 4/5/52

Some detractors allege that UFOs are never seen near large cities...

Case #6257; Washington, D.C., 2/4/59

Case #9411; New York World's Fair, Flushing Meadows,
New York, 5/30/64

Case #9666; Tulsa, Oklahoma, 8/2/65

A₁

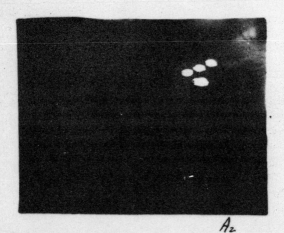

A₂

Case #1501; Salem, Massachusetts (Coast Guard facility),
7/16/52

**Critics also claim UFOs don't appear over
military bases ...**

Case #4928; Chiltose AFB, Japan, 9/1/57

Case #6724; Guantanamo Bay, Cuba, 4/21/60

Despite officials' persistent denials that UFOs were appearing on radar, such equipment in the United States and throughout the world regularly clocked UFOs. Below is just a sample of the evidence of such sightings from Blue Book files.

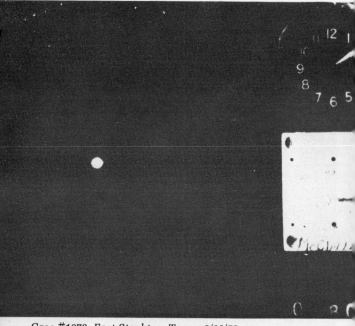

Case #1079; Fort Stockton, Texas, 3/26/52

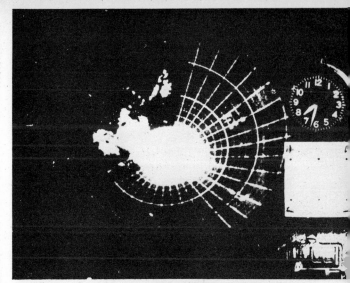

Case #1619; Osceola, Wisconsin, 7/25/52
Case #1731; Osceola, Wisconsin, 7/29/52

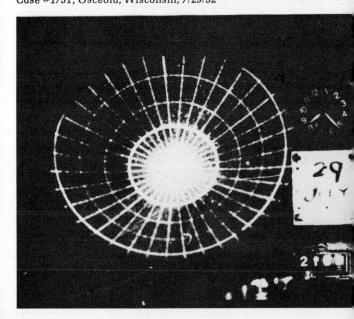

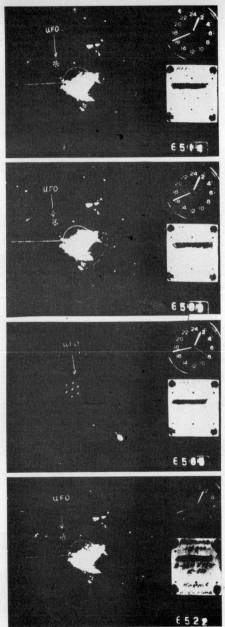

Case #3088;
Bermuda, 7/3/54

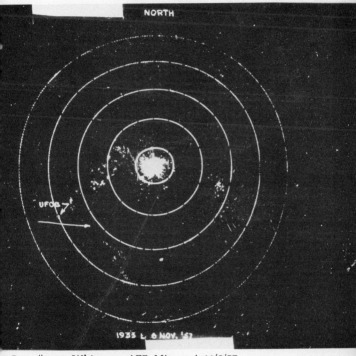

NORTH

UFOB →

1933 L. 6 NOV. '57

Case #5178; Whiteman AFB, Missouri, 11/6/57

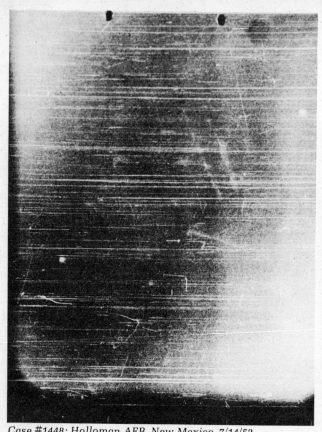

Case #1448; Holloman AFB, New Mexico, 7/14/52

**UFOs on target! Photos taken by United States
military personnel.**

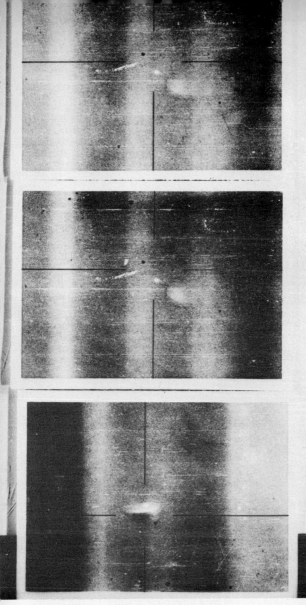

Case #4715; Edwards AFB, California, 5/2/57

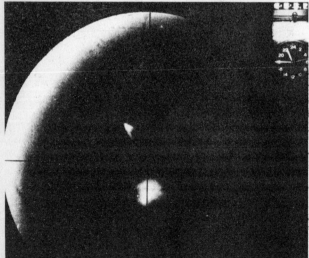

Case #10856; Minnesota, North Dakota, Wisconsin, 8/16/66

UFO caught by a telescope trained on the moon.

like "flying objects", some discussion of characteristics of space ships is necessary.

To handle the simple case first, a trip from Mars to Earth should be feasible using a rocket-powered vehicle. Once here, the rocket would probably use more fuel in slowing down for a landing than it did in initial takeoff, due to Earth's higher gravitational force.

A rough estimate of one-way performance can be found by adding the so-called "escape velocity" of Mars to that of the Earth plus the total energy change (kinetic and potential) used in changing from one planetary orbit to the other. These are 3.1, 7.0, and 10.7 miles per second, respectively, giving a total required performance of 20.8 miles per second for a one-way flight. Barring a suicide mission, the vehicle would have to land and replenish or else carry a 100% reserve for the trip home.

Let us assume the Martians have developed a nuclear, hydrogen-propelled vehicle (the most efficient basic arrangement that has been conceived here on Earth) which uses half its stages to get here and the remaining stages to return to Mars, thus completing a round trip without refueling, but slowing down enough in our atmosphere to be easily visible (i.e., practically making a landing). Since it is nuclear powered, gas temperatures will be limited to the maximum operating temperatures that materials can withstand (heat must transfer from the pile to the gas, so cooling can't be used in the pile). The highest melting point compound of uranium which we can find is uranium carbide. It has a melting point of 4560°R. Assume the Martians are capable of realizing a gas temperature of 4500°R ($=2500°K$), and that they also have alloys which make high motor pressures (3000 psi) economical. Then the specific impulse will be $I = 1035$ seconds and the exhaust velocity will be $c = 33,400$ ft/sec (reference 5*). Calculation shows that using a single stage for each leg of the journey would require a

* Calculated Properties of Hydrogen Propellant at High Temperatures. Data provided to RAND by Dr. Altman, then at JPL. Unpublished.

fuel/gross weight ratio of 0.96 (for each stage), too high to be practical. Using two stages each way (four altogether) brings the required fuel ratio down to 0.81, a value that can be realized.

If, by the development of strong alloys, the basic weight could be kept to 10% of the total weight for each stage, a residue of 9% could be used for payload. A four stage vehicle would then have a gross weight

$$\frac{(100)}{9} = 15,000$$

times as great as the payload: thus, if the payload were 2,000 pounds, the gross weight would be 30 million pounds at initial takeoff (Earth pounds).

Of course, if we allow the Martians to refuel, the vehicle could have only two stages* and the gross weight would be only

$$\frac{(100)^2}{9} = 123$$

times the payload, i.e., 250,000 pounds. This would require bringing electrolytic and refrigerating equipment and sitting at the South Pole long enough to extract fuel for the journey home, since they have not asked us for supplies. Our oceans (electrolysis to make H_2) would be obvious to Martian telescopes and they might conceivably follow such a plan, particularly if they came here without foreknowledge that Earth has a civilization.

Requirements for a trip from a planet attached to some star other than the Sun can be calculated in a similar manner. Here the energy (or velocity) required has more parts: (a) escape from the planet; (b) escape from the star; (c) enough velocity to traverse a

---

* * Actually three stages. On the trip to Earth, the first stage would be filled with fuel, the second stage would contain partial fuel, the third would be empty. The first stage would be thrown away during flight. On the trip back to Mars, the second and third stages would be filled with fuel. The gross weight of the initial vehicle would be of the order of magnitude of a two-stage rocket.

few light years of space in reasonable time; (d) deceleration toward the Sun; (e) deceleration toward the Earth. The nearest "eligible" star is an object called Wolf 359 (see reference 4, p. 52), at a distance of 8.0 light years. It is small, having an absolute magnitude of 16.6 and is typical of "red dwarfs" which make up more than half of the eligible populations. By comparison with similar stars of known mass, this star is estimated to have a mass roughly 0.03 as great as the sun. Since the star has a low luminosity (being much cooler and smaller than the Sun) a habitable planet would need to be in a small orbit for warmth.

Of the changes of energy required as listed in the preceding paragraph, item (c), velocity to traverse intervening space, is so large as to make the others completely negligible. If the visitors were long lived and could "hibernate" for 80 years both coming and going, then 1/10 the speed of light would be required, i.e., the enormous velocity of 18,000 miles per second. This is completely beyond the reach of any predicted level of rocket propulsion.

If a race were far enough advanced to make really efficient use of nuclear energy, then a large part of the mass of the nuclear material might be converted into jet energy. We have no idea how to do this, in fact reference 6* indicates that the materials required to withstand the temperatures, etc., may be fundamentally unattainable. Let us start from a jet-propellant-to-gross weight ratio of 0.75. If the total amount of expended material (nuclear plus propellent) can be 0.85 of the gross weight, then the nuclear material expended can be 0.10 of the gross. Using an efficiency of 0.5 for converting nuclear energy to jet energy and neglecting relativistic mass corrections, then a rocket velocity of half the velocity of light could be attained. This would mean a transit time of 16 years each way from the star Wolf 359, or longer times from other eligible stars. To try to go much faster would mean spending much

---

* "The Use of Atomic Power for Rockets," by R. Serber. Appendix IV Second Quarterly Report, RA-15004, Douglas Aircraft Co., Inc., Project Rand.

energy on relativistic change in mass and therefore operating at lowered efficiency.

To summarize this section of the discussion, it can be said that a trip from Mars is a logical engineering advance over our own present technical status, but that a trip from another star system requires improvements of propulsion that we have not yet conceived. Combining the efforts of all the science-fiction writers, we could conjure up a large number of hypothetical methods of transportation like gravity shields, space overdrives, teleports, simulators, energy beams and so on. Conceivably, among the myriads of stellar systems in the Galaxy, one or more races have discovered methods of travel that would be fantastic by our standards. Yet the larger the volume of space that must be included in order to strengthen this possibility, the lower will be the chance that the race involved would ever find the Earth. The Galaxy has a diameter of roughly 100,000 light years and a total mass about two hundred billion times that of the Sun (reference 4). Other galaxies have been photographed and estimated in numbers of several hundred million (reference 2, p. 4) at distances up to billions of light years (reference 7,* p. 158). The number of stars in the known universe is enormous, yet so are the distances involved. A super-race (unless they occur frequently) would not be likely to stumble upon Planet III of Sol, a fifth-magnitude star in the rarefied outskirts of the Galaxy.

A description of the probable operating characteristics of space ships must be based on the assumption that they will be rockets, since this is the only form of propulsion that we know will function in outer space. Below are listed a few of the significant factors of rocketry in relation to the "flying objects".

(a) Maneuverability. A special-purpose rocket can be made as maneuverable as we like, with very high accelerations either along or normal to the flight path. However, a high-performance space ship will certainly

* *Galaxies*, by Shapley. Harlow; Harvard Books on Astronomy, Blakiston, 1943.

be large and unwieldy and could hardly be designed to maneuver frivolously around in the Earth's atmosphere. The only economical maneuver would be to come down and go up more or less vertically.

(b) Fuel reserves. It is hard to see how a single rocket ship could carry enough extra fuel to make repeated descents into the Earth's atmosphere. The large number of flying objects reported in quick succession could only mean a large number of visiting craft.

Two possibilities thus are presented. First, a number of space ships could have come as a group. This would only be done if full-dress contact were to be established. Second, numerous small craft might descend from a mother ship which coasts around the Earth in a satellite orbit. But this could mean that the smaller craft would have to be rockets of satellite performance, and to contain them the mother ship would have to be truly enormous.

(c) Appearance. A vertically descending rocket might well appear as a luminous disk to a person directly below. Observers at a distance, however, would surely identify the rocket for what it really is. There would probably be more reports of oblique views than of end-on views. Of course, the shape need not be typical of our rockets; yet the exhaust should be easy to see.

One or two additional general remarks may be relevant to space ships as "flying objects". The distribution of flying objects is peculiar, to say the least. As far as this writer knows, all incidents have occurred within the United States, whereas visiting spacemen could be expected to scatter their visits more or less uniformly over the globe. The small area covered indicates strongly that the flying objects are of Earthly origin, whether physical or psychological.

The lack of purpose apparent in the various episodes is also puzzling. Only one motive can be assigned; that the spacemen are "feeling out" our defenses without wanting to be belligerent. If so, they must have been satisfied long ago that we can't catch them. It seems fruitless for them to keep repeating the same experiment.

Conclusions

Although visits from outer space are believed to be possible, they are believed to be very improbable. In particular, the actions attributed to the "flying objects" reported during 1947 and 1948 seem inconsistent with the requirements for space travel.

Very truly yours,
J. E. Lipp
Missiles Division

JEL:sp

Subject; AMC Opinion Concerning "Flying Discs"

TO: Commanding General
Army Air Forces
Washington 25, D. C.
ATTENTION: Brig. General George Schulgen
AC/AS-2

1. As requested by AC/AS-2 there is presented below the considered opinion of this Command concerning the so-called "Flying Discs". This opinion is based on interrogation report data furnished by AC/AS-2 and preliminary studies by personnel of T-2 and Aircraft Laboratory, Engineering Division T-3. This opinion was arrived at in a conference between personnel from the Air Institute of Technology, Intelligence T-2, Office, Chief of Engineering Division, and the Aircraft, Power Plant and Propeller Laboratories of Engineering Division T-3.

2. It is the opinion that:

a. The phenomenon reported is something real and not visionary or fictitious.

b. There are objects probably approximating the shape of a disc, of such appreciable size as to appear to be as large as man-made aircraft.

c. There is a possibility that some of the incidents may be caused by natural phenomena, such as meteors.

d. The reported operating characteristics such as extreme rates of climb, maneuverability (particularly in roll), and action which must be considered evasive when sighted or contacted by friendly aircraft and radar, lend belief to the possibility that some of the objects are controlled either manually, automatically or remotely.

e. The apparent common description of the objects is as follows:

  (1) Metallic or light reflecting surface.
  (2) Absence of trail, except in a few instances when the object apparently was operating under high performance conditions.
  (3) Circular or elliptical in shape, flat on bottom and domed on top.
  (4) Several reports of well kept formation flights varying from three to nine objects.
  (5) Normally no associated sound, except in three instances a substantial rumbling roar was noted.
  (6) Level flight speeds normally above 300 knots are estimated.

f. It is possible within the present U. S. knowledge—provided extensive detailed development is undertaken—to construct a piloted aircraft which has the general description of the object in sub-paragraph (e) above which would be capable of an approximate range of 7000 miles at subsonic speeds.

g. Any developments in this country along the lines indicated would be extremely expensive, time consuming and at the considerable expense of current projects and therefore, if directed, should be set up independently of existing projects.

h. Due consideration must be given the following:

  (1) The possibility that these objects are of domestic origin—the product of some high security project not known to AC/AS-2 or this Command.
  (2) The lack of physical evidence in the shape

215

of crash recovered exhibits which would undeniably prove the existence of these objects.

(3) The possibility that some foreign nation has a form of propulsion possibly nuclear, which is outside of our domestic knowledge.

3. It is recommended that:

a. Headquarters, Army Air Forces issue a directive assigning a priority, security classification and Code Name for a detailed study of this matter to include the preparation of complete sets of all available and pertinent data which will then be made available to the Army, Navy, Atomic Energy Commission, JRDB, the Air Force Scientific Advisory Group, NACA, and the RAND and NEPA projects for comments and recommendations, with a preliminary report to be forwarded within 15 days of receipt of the data and a detailed report thereafter every 30 days as the investigation develops. A complete interchange of data should be effected.

4. Awaiting a specific directive AMC will continue the investigation within its current resources in order to more closely define the nature of the phenomenon. Detailed Essential Elements of Information will be forwarded immediately for transmittal thru channels.

N. F. TWINING
Lieutenant General, U.S.A.
Commanding

Chapter Nine: A Summary of Project Grudge

Mapping, Charting and Reconnaissance Research Laboratory
Final Report
Project 364

Prepared by Dr. J. Allen Hynek
Assisted by Harriet R. Summerson

The Ohio State University Research Foundation
Project No. 364
for
U.S. Air Force Air Material Command
Wright-Patterson Air Force Base, Dayton, Ohio
Contract No. W33-c38-1118

Columbus, Ohio
April 30, 1949

Introduction

Perhaps the most bizarre post-war phenomenon was the sudden barrage of reports, in the summer of 1947, describing unidentified objects in the sky. The incident which evidently triggered the volley was the now-famous account by Kenneth Arnold, in which he claimed to have seen "nine peculiar-looking aircraft" without tails, which flew in a chain-like line and "swerved in and out of the high mountain peaks." The handling of this incident by the press led to the unfortunate but descriptive term "flying saucer," which caught the public imagination. From that time on, there has been a fairly steady stream of similar reports, including some of "flying saucers" seen prior to the Arnold incident, which presumably otherwise would have gone unreported. (It is pertinent therefore, to speculate whether *any* of the incidents would have been reported if Mr. Arnold had not made his observation.) Possibly, of course, we deal here with an excellent example of mass hysteria. In the interests of the defense of the country, however, it would be highly inadvisable to ignore the accounts, even though the chance be remote that they contain anything inimical to the nation's welfare. To this end, the present investigator, as an astronomer, was asked to review the data, to eliminate the patently astronomical incidents and to indicate which others might have such an explanation.

General Procedure

The method of the investigation was to examine a number of individual reports of unidentified serial and celestial objects, to determine which of them could be explained on purely astronomical lines—that is, how many cases give evidence corresponding to descriptions of meteors, fireballs or bolides, comets, the planets, or even the sun or moon. Analysis was based entirely upon these reports, furnished by Project GRUDGE offices, with no attempt to make independent interrogation of witnesses, since this was not authorized under the contract. Nor was any attempt made to deduce explanations for the non-astronomical incidents, although hypotheses which appeared possible from the evidence were noted.

The subject reports number 244 and cover, approximately, the period from January, 1947, to January, 1949. They do not, however, correspond exactly to the number of separate incidents: sometimes, two or more reports refer to the same object observed by different people (although in general such cases have been handled by affixing letters to the incident numbers, thus: 33, 33a, 33b); occasionally, subdivisions of one number patently refer to separate phenomena.

218

To avoid confusion, one report is being submitted by this investigator for each numbered incident, with cross references for identical or similar incidents, and separate discussions for those including more than one phenomenon.

Inasmuch as the avowed object of the investigation was solely to indicate the possible astronomical content of the reports at hand, in the primary analysis all evidence was accepted at face value, with no attempt to evaluate psychological factors. Frequently, however, when fairly liberal limits of tolerance were allowed, the report made sense physically, whereas the literal statement did not. (Whenever allowance was made for possible errors arising from subjective reporting, the fact was noted.) Furthermore, while some of the reports verge on the ludicrous, the attitude deliberately adopted was to assume honesty and sincerity on the part of the reporter. Among the general public, two attitudes toward "flying saucers" seem to be prevalent: one, that all are obviously hallucinations or hoaxes; the other, that "there must be something to it." From the outset, this investigator has atempted to regard each report, insofar as is logically possible, as an honest statement by the observer, and to adhere to neither of the two schools of thought.

One further comment should be made: almost all of the data dealt with in this investigation are extremely tenuous. Many of the observers' reports are incomplete and inexact, and some are distinctly contradictory. Therefore, it has obviously been impossible to reach definite, scientific conclusions. Most explanations are offered in terms of probability, the degree of which is discussed in the individual reports, but can be indicated only generally in the statistics which follow.

Summary of Results

What, in particular, was gathered from the evidence concerning the astronomical character of the objects observed?

219

Of the 244 incidents submited, 7 are excluded from all statistical reckoning: 1 is identified (in the subject report) as a hoax, 3 are duplicates, and 3 contain no information. In summarizing the findings in the remaining 237, two systems of classification are possible.

First, all incidents can be placed in one of two classes: 1) those which under no stretch of the imagination can be regarded as astronomical or extra-terrestrial (*extra-terrestrial* throughout this investigation refers solely to natural objects not originating on earth; it does not include "space ships from other planets"), and 2) those which either are definitely astronomical or can by suitable manipulation of the evidence be construed as such. The object here is to segregate all cases in which any vestige of astronomical origin is indicated. When this division is made, 111, or 47%, fall into the definitely non-astronomical category; or, conversely stated, 126, or 53%, might conceivably be considered (although the likelihood of their being so may be very small) as extra-terrestrial or astronomical in origin. The exact percentage is not important. The significant thing is that over 50% of the incidents might possibly be explained astronomically, if wide enough tolerances were allowed.

The primary purpose here, however, is to segregate incidents which have a reasonable degree of certainty of astronomical origin. Therefore, in a second, more detailed breakdown, incidents are placed in one of three classes, according to the most probable interpretation seen in the evidences offered (with a minimum of allowance for subjective observation). Class 1 includes the astronomical incidents (with degree of probability indicated). The non-astronomical incidents are divided into two classes, because it appeared as the work progressed that they fall naturally thus: in some, the evidence at hand suggested a simple explanation; in others, it did not. Listings under class 2 are not to be considered in any way decisive (with the exception of a few which, according to subject reports, have been definitely identified): they are offered as suggestions.

A summary of the results of this breakdown is shown in the following table.

CLASS	Number of incidents	Approximate percentage
1. Astronomical		
a. High probability	42	18
b. Fair or low probability	33	14
total	75	32
2. Non-astronomical but suggestive of other explanations		
a. Balloons or ordinary aircraft	48	20
b. Rockets, flares, or falling bodies	23	10
c. Miscellaneous (reflections, auroral streamers, birds, etc	13	5
total	84	35
3. Non-astronomical, with no evident explanation		
a. Lack of evidence precludes explanation	30	13
b. Evidence offered suggests no explanation	48	20
total	78	33

According to these findings, 78, or almost one-third, of the 237 incidents yet remain without an appropriate hypothesis for explanation. It is likely, of course, that with additional evidence a number of those included in class 3a would be easily explained (some of them, probably, astronomically). There are, however, at least 48 incidents in which the evidence, if correct as given, does not fit any simple explanation, and a number of these were reported by presumably well-qualified observers.

Collateral Studies

In relation to the investigation, besides the individual analyses of separate incidents, two brief studies were conducted:

Certain breakdowns of the subject reports were

made, for the purpose of determining whether they include any prevalent characteristics; for example, incidents were grouped according to the date of occurrence, the hour, the presence or lack of noise, presence or lack of trail or exhaust, number of observers, general qualifications of observers (whether with appropriate training for accurate observation of aerial phenomena—aviators, weather observers, etc.; or laymen). Although those classifications were helpful in spotting identical or similar incidents, they revealed no pertinent trends.

As a matter of general interest, the highly dubious works of Charles Fort (which, as has been stated in a previous report, are entirely reprehensible in viewpoint, but which do contain accounts of unusual aerial sightings over a period of many years) were examined, to check whether any of the reasonably authenticated incidents are similar to those recent reports. It was found, however, that Mr. Fort's accounts do not include sufficient specific evidence to reveal positive similarities, and the most that can be said of the works is that they indicate that strange objects in the sky have been reported long before this post-World War II flurry.

Recommendations

This investigator would like to offer three recommendations, one in the general interest of the nation's airmen, and two as aids toward more effective investigation of the problem of unidentified aerial objects, if such work is continued.

First and foremost, it is definitely recommended that Air Forces personnel be apprised of simple astronomical phenomena like the recurrent brilliance of Venus and the characteristics of a typical fireball, so that much confusion and alarm and even possible tragic consequences can be avoided. If, as seems possible, Lieutenant Mantell met his death while attempting to chase down Venus, certainly the need for such basic education is great.

Second, if Project GRUDGE is authorized to extend its investigations, it might be found profitable to interrogate personally varied trained personnel concerning any untoward aerial objects which they may have observed in the past. Many competent observers might hesitate to take the initiative in reporting such phenomena for fear of ridicule or criticism, yet it is only from such people that accurate and meaningful descriptions can be obtained; reliance on the general public for such observations is almost certain to prove of little value. It would be of considerable aid to know whether (aside from the few cases reported here) experienced pilots, weather observers, and other "watchers of the sky" have ever found unidentified objects there. Even negative results would prove valuable, for they would offer evidence for the belief held by many that the unexplained incidents do not really involve tangible physical objects.

Third, if this type of investigation is to be continued, men with proved scientific and technical ability should be assigned to carry out the interrogations and investigations; it would be preferable either that the interrogator and technical specialist be the same person or, at least, that they work together in class harmony. Such an arrangement would aid greatly in lessening the incompleteness and inexactness of evidence which has thus far hindered the explanation of many "flying saucer" incidents.

Engineering Division C
Memorandum Report No. CREAD-694-18D
25 April 1949

Appendix A
Psychological Analysis of Reports
of Unidentified Aerial Objects

The Inaccuracy of Human Observation

Psychologists have long known that human perception is fallible. In fact, part of the science of psychology is concerned with the measurement of errors of observation, and with the discovery of the conditions and laws that govern such phenomena.

Errors of observation may be classified as *variable* or *constant*. *Variable errors* are those in which a number of separate observations are found to differ from one another. The distribution of such errors often follows the normal probability curve. *Constant errors* are those in which observations are consistently biased in one or another direction. For example, individuals often are guilty of a constant error, in the direction of underestimation, in reporting their ages.

Errors of observation may be classified further as *precision* errors and *identification* errors. Inaccuracy in estimating the speed of an aircraft is an example of the former. Mistaking an aircraft for a "flying saucer" is an example of the latter.

It is the purpose of the present report to analyze 212 reports of observations of unidentified flying objects in order to see to what extent these reports can be explained in terms of known psychological facts and principles.

SCIENTIFIC METHOD AND A POSTERIORI DATA

A word of caution must be injected at the outset of this report. Certain conditions are necessary for drawing valid scientific conclusions. These conditions are largely lacking in the case of the data available on unidentified flying objects. It is impossible to say with any assurance what any particular individual in this series of 212 reports was actually observing at any particular time. It is only possible to examine the accumulation of available evidence or the accumulation of all reports of a given class (e.g., all reports from supposedly competent observers) and to consider them in a statistical sense. If certain characteristics appear repeatedly in reports from different people it may be possible to infer causal factors.

It will never be possible, on the other hand, to say with certainty that any given observer would not have seen a space ship or an uneasy missile, or some other object. It will only be possible to estimate the probability that he could have seen such things.

The principal hypothesis to be examined in the following discussion is that reports of unidentified flying objects have the characteristics that would be expected if they were cases of failure, on the part of typical normal individuals, to identify common or familiar phenomena.

POSSIBLE SOURCES OF INACCURATE REPORT OF FLYING OBJECTS

There are three broad classes of mistakes in human observations. These are the following: 1. Misinterpreting the nature of real stimuli, 2. Mistaking unreal (imaginary) stimuli for real ones, and 3. Deliberate falsifications. Each of these are considered briefly below.

(1) *Errors in Identifying Real Stimuli.* All normal, intelligent people experience certain errors of observation. The moon appears much larger on the horizon than when it is high in the sky. A stick looks bent when one end is in water. Distant objects appear relatively close in clear, desert atmosphere. A small point source of light, if viewed in a dark room, will appear to move about in strange gyrations . . . This is called the autokinetic illusion (see Guilford, J.P., 1929). In the accompanying figure the line *AB* looks approximately as long as the line *CD,* but when you measure them the two will be found to be of quite different lengths.

Visual stimuli originating within the eye itself also give rise to mistaken observations. Muscae volitantes or "flying gnats" are small solid particles that float about in the fluids of the eye and cast shadows on the retina. They often can be seen when you look up at the clear sky, or when you are reading. They move as your eyes move. It is sometimes possible also to

---

* Guilford, J. P. Autokinesis and the streaming phenomena, *American Journal of Psychology*, 1929, 40, 401–417.

see corpuscles or other objects that are circulating within the fluids in the retina of the eye.

Then, of course, everyone from time to time mistakes some more or less familiar object for another object. A probable explanation for many reports of unidentified aerial phenomena is that the object is really something quite familiar, such as an aircraft, a light, or a bird. The observer simply fails to identify it correctly. These errors arise chiefly as a result of inability to estimate speed and distance.

(2) *Mistaking Imaginary for Real Events.* This error of observation is usually made by children, by individuals of low intelligence (people who are very suggestible), by people who see visions, or by the mentally ill. It usually is not difficult for an expert to spot this type of person. Reports will be received by such persons especially at times when the radio and newspapers carry accounts of strange phenomena. Relatively few of the 212 investigations considered in this report are of this nature, probably because investigators interviewed only the more reliable type of witness.

(3) *Deliberate Falsifications.* It is always possible that some persons will give false reports. Circulation of false reports has been a standard psychological warfare technique from earliest times. This procedure might have some utility in wartime, but it hardly seems likely that it would be resorted to at this time. Probably, however, some individuals start false reports of "flying saucers" for the same reason that they turn in false fire alarms.

SOME CONSISTENT POINTS IN THE REPORTS OF UNIDENTIFIED OBJECTS

The following section summarizes some significant facts that come out of a tabulation of 212 reports of interrogations, by USAF Intelligence Officer, of some of the individuals who reported seeing unidentified flying objects. It is understood that these interrogations covered primarily persons that were judged to be reliable. Most of the 212 reports were made by pilots, non-flying officers, professional men, government employees, housewives and other supposedly dependable people.

1. *Number of objects.* About 79% of the people who reported on the number of objects seen said that they saw only one object.

2. *Time the object remained in sight.* About half of the persons specifying time in sight saw the object for 60 seconds or less.

3. *Altitude and distance of the object.* Of those who estimated the distance of the object, two-thirds judged it to be more than a mile away. Ninety percent also thought that it was more than 1,000 feet high.

4. *Speed.* About half judged that the speed was less than 500 miles an hour. The other half of the judgments varied from 500 miles an hour all the way to "terrific," "tremendous," "inconceivable" and "blue blazes."

5. *Background against which viewed.* The great majority of observers saw the object against a clear day or night sky.

6. *Time of day sighted.* About two-thirds as many observations were reported at night as in the day. There are, of course, many more opportunities for observing things during the day. The most popular hours were from 12 noon to 5:00 P.M. and from 7:00 P.M. at night. Very few (6 only) observations were made from 5:00 to 7:00 P.M. the usual hours of sunset.

7. *Color.* Observers almost universally reported seeing a light-colored object. Thirty observers reported "white" and twenty-five said "silver." Over 70 percent described glittering, shiny, luminescent, mirror-like, flame-like, or other very bright objects. Only six individuals said black or dark.

8. *Shape.* Over half described the object as either "round," "disc-shaped," "spherical" or "circular." Other descriptions were similar. Very few observers saw any distinctive shape.

9. *Size.* The majority of observers did not specify the objects' size. Of those who did over half said it was less than 10 feet in its largest dimension. Many

compared it with a dime, a lamp, a dot, a weather balloon, a baseball, etc.

Interpretation of the Common Points of All Reports

The words used by observors to describe the appearances of the unidentified objects fall into a surprisingly uniform pattern. The objects were usually reported as being far away, small, bright and without a distinctive shape. They were usually seen against a clear sky and were frequently seen for less than a minute.

First of all, it is obvious that it would usually be impossible for observers to make reliable estimates of the speed, distance, or size of such stimulus objects. It is not possible to estimate accurately the distance of small bright objects viewed against a clear sky, *unless the object is identified first*. If you know beforehand that an object is a weather balloon, an F-80, or a dirigible you can estimate its speed and distance with some degree of accuracy. In such situations distance is judged on the basis of known size, and speed on the basis of an estimate of distance plus the angular change in position. It must be concluded, therefore, that most of the statements of speed, distance, altitude and size are entirely unreliable and should be disregarded. This is doubly true of observations made at night. The objects seen may actually have been at very great distances, or they may have been relatively close by. In the latter case, of course, they could also have been quite small.

Secondly, it is probable, that individuals who saw objects in daylight were in many cases observing either the reflection of the sun on a shiny surface or else looking directly at a light source of high intensity. Aircraft themselves, when viewed against a clear sky, are seen as dark objects against a lighter background unless they are reflecting the sun's rays directly. This fact was recognized during the recent war by camouflage experts who placed bright lights on the leading edges of the wings of aircraft on anti-submarine patrol in order to conceal them from the eyes of submarine lookouts. If observers, during daylight hours, were actually seeing lights, or reflections of the sun, this

228

would account in large measure for their inability to identify the objects. On the other hand, if they were actually seeing enemy missiles, for example, the majority of reports of daylight sightings should have been of dark objects. It is possible, of course, that they may have thought the objects were bright because they expected all aerial objects to be bright.

On the basis of the evidence thus far considered, the best guess as to the nature of a visual stimulus that would elicit reports of unidentified flying objects is that in the daytime it would be the reflection of the sun from an aircraft, a wind-blown object, etc., and at night some direct light source, such as an engine exhaust, the light on a weather balloon, a running light on an aircraft, a meteor, etc., or light from the ground or the moon reflected back by birds or other objects in the air.

Discussion of Several Specific Reports

Discussion of a few specific reports will serve to illustrate some of the points brought up earlier, particularly some of the factors that make observations of aerial phenomena inaccurate.

Incidents No. 81 and 163.

In one case (Investigation No. 81) a civilian employee at Hickam Field at 0900 observed what looked like a balloon with a bright object suspended below it. It was estimated to be at about 6,000 ft. The bright object appeared to reflect the sun's rays at times. After a few minutes he looked away and then could not find the object again.

In another case (No. 163) a reserve officer at Van Nuys, California, about an hour before dark saw an object that looked somewhat like a weather balloon at about 2000 feet. He kept it in sight for about an hour. He later concluded that it was at a great height. At first it had the color of a fluorescent electric light but became orange as the sun went down and then rather suddenly became invisible.

Both of these objects could well have been just what they appeared to resemble most—balloons. The sun

229

was low in the sky in both cases. Reflection of the sun's rays may have given an unusual appearance to the object. The second case illustrates the uncertainty of judgments of height or distance. The object looked near, but when it remained in view for an hour the observer decided that it must be very far away. Actually he probably had nothing on which to base an accurate estimate.

Incidents 61 and 61a.

Two couples saw approximately 12 objects flying in formation at what they judged to be 2000 or 3000 feet altitude over Logan, Utah at 22:30. They were judged to be about the size of pigeons and looked white. All four observers agreed that these objects looked and acted somewhat like birds but all thought they were not birds because they appeared to travel much faster than birds.

As we have seen, it is not possible to judge speed accurately under the conditions of these observations, i.e., when looking at objects of unknown size and distance against a night sky. The objects may actually have been a flock of white birds, flying at a relatively low altitude and reflecting the lights of the city.

Incidents 30, 30b, and 48, 48a, 48b, 48c, 48d.

During the same space of time (about half an hour) on the night of 7 January 1948 observers at Look-bourne Air Force Base, observers at Clinton County AFB and the pilot of an aircraft flying from Dayton to Washington reported an unidentified object in the sky. All reports agreed as to the color and general appearance of the object, and as to the fact that the light at times was visible through a light overcast. All agreed also that it was seen to the southwest. However, persons at all three locations judged the object to be *only a few miles away*. To all of them it looked motionless at times, then appeared to gain and lose elevation. A very similar object was seen by numerous persons at Fort Knox and other towns in Kentucky a few hours earlier. All saw it *in the southwest* and many thought it was only a few miles away. The Commanding Officer at Goodman Field observed it for 1½ hours, (begining at 1445). During this time it

230

seemingly remained stationary. It was "chased" by four National Guard pilots, one of whom crashed after having been up to 20,000 feet. It was also reported by persons in Lexington, Madisonville, and Elizabethtown.

The significant fact that emerges from those reports again is the inability to estimate distance. It appears possible that persons over parts of Kentucky and Ohio may have been seeing the same astronomical phenomena which [were] a great many miles away. Nevertheless each believed it to be relatively near his own location.

Incident No. 172.

A National Guard Pilot returning to Fargo, North Dakota, in an F-51 at approximately 2100 hours saw a small light in the air below him. He was then in the traffic pattern. He dived on the light. The light gained altitude. The pilot "chased" it up to 14,000 feet, making various passes at it and attempts to run it as he climbed. He finally stalled out.

Several inferences can be drawn from the several reports about this incident. In the first place, when it is night, and a pilot is turning so steeply, and doing such violent acrobatics, that he sometimes blacks out, as was the case here, it would be very difficult if not impossible to judge at the same time what another object was doing. In the second place, if the pilot kept his eyes intently on the object, as also was the case here, he would have great difficulty in knowing and reporting later what he himself was doing. The situation is very conducive to loss of orientation. In other words, it is impossible to infer from the maneuvering or not maneuvering. It is quite possible that it was simply climbing steeply on a relatively straight course, such as would be taken by a lighted weather balloon.

As a matter of fact, a lighted weather balloon was released by the Fargo Weather Station within 10 minutes of the time the light was first sighted by the F-51 pilot. It is the opinion of the writer that this lighted balloon easily could have accounted for all of the pilot's observations. (It should be noted that the standard 30 inch and 65 inch weather balloons have a vertical speed of about 600 and 1100 ft./min. respectively.)

GENERAL DISCUSSION AND SUMMARY

In the preceeding section the hypothesis has been advanced that most reports of unidentified flying objects have been the result of persons failing to identify familiar phenomena, such as reflections from bright surfaces in the day or lights in a night sky. It is believed that this explanation will account for many of the reports. However, some reports undoubtedly have other explanation.

Vertigo. The term vertigo covers a large group of miscellaneous phenomena including air sickness, disbelief in one's instruments, and partial loss of orientation. The conditions under which some of the observations of flying objects were made were such that they could have produced loss of orientation on the part of an observer. This is especially true for those experiences occurring at night and those in which attempts were made to "chase" the object. Movement is always relative. If the only outside reference is a point of light, and both the observer and the object observed are moving, it would be practically impossible under certain conditions to tell which was moving and which was not, or to separate out the two motions. It is hard enough to fly a good pursuit curve on another aircraft in good daylight, for example, much less to close on a solitary light at night. The difficulty is due chiefly to the inability to judge distance or speed of a point source of light.

Suggestion. Suggestion works in various ways. Sensational radio and newspaper reports lead a few people to imagine they are seeing things they are not seeing. The effect on most people is to dampen their critical judgement. Under such conditions we are more likely to overlook certain factors, and find it easier to accept the suggested explanation uncritically. The expected result would be to make the reports of most observers slightly less accurate then if they had never heard reports of others seeing "flying saucers." Particularly when the stimulus object is fuzzy or ill-defined, persons tend to see it as resembling, whatever is suggested to them. Carmichael et.al.,* for example (1932) showed individuals simple designs and gave them the name of an object. When the individuals drew the design from memory, they drew it to resemble whatever the object was that had been suggested to them.

Precedent. An historical precedent can be found for most errors of human observation. Although the writer has not tried to make an historical survey of reports of earlier unidentified aerial objects, he feels sure that there have been many such reports in years past, particularly during and after World War I.

Small Wind-borne Objects. It is possible that some observers may have seen small objects carried aloft by strong winds, or objects dropped from aircraft. Bits of paper, small cartons, etc., may occasionally be carried to a considerable height by strong winds. Aircraft may sometimes jettison small articles. It would be impossible to estimate the distance, size or speed of such objects, and it would be easy to fail to recognize them.

CONCLUSIONS

It is concluded by the writer that there are sufficient psychological explanations for the reports of unidentified flying objects to provide plausible explanations for reports not otherwise explainable. These errors in identifying real stimuli result chiefly from inability to estimate speed, distance and size.

RECOMMENDATIONS

The following recommendations are offered:

1. Test the ability of pilots to estimate the course of a small lighted balloon while doing acrobatics with it at night. It is suggested that several pilots try to fly pursuit curves and collision courses on such targets

---

* Carmichael, L., Hogen, H. P., and Walter H. E. An experimental study of the effect of language on the reproduction of visually perceived form. *Journal of Experimental Psychology,* 1932, 15, 73–86.

at night and report accurately their sensations. It would be desirable, but probably impossible, to keep them from knowing the nature of the light source.

2. In all future reports of unidentified objects specify the location of the object with reference to polar coordinates (direction and degrees above the horizon) rather than asking individuals to estimate distance. If possible, obtain an estimate of size in terms of the visual angle subtended by the object.

3. In all future investigations determine the angular position of the sun with respect to the unidentified object and the observer. Also determine the approximate time during which the object was in sight (this information was not available for more than half the reports).

AIR MATERIAL COMMAND
3160 Electronics Station
Cambridge Field Station
230 Albany Street
Cambridge 39, Mass.

April 18, 1949

000.92
In reply address
both communication
and envelope to the
Commanding Officer
and attention of following
office symbol. ERH

Subject: Analysis of Project "Grudge" Reported Incidents
TO: Commanding General
Air Material Command
Wright-Patterson Air Force Base
Dayton, Ohio
ATTN: MCLAXO

1. Reference is made to the letters from your Headquarters to this station of 22 November 1948, 6 De-

cember 1948, and 14 January 1949, Subjects: "Project 'Sign'", requesting that reported incidents 1 through 172 be analyzed to determine whether or not those might have been caused by balloons launched by those laboratories.

2. A listing has been compiled of all balloons launched by those laboratoies and its contractors for special atmospheric research purposes, from the first such launching to No. 101 on 17 November 1948. Each of these launchings has been compared with the reported incidents 1 through 172. Factors of comparison were date of launching and date of recovery with respect to date of reported incidents; place of launching and place of recovery with respect to the place of reported incidents, and possible deviations from the known flight path with respect to the place of reported incidents, So that your office may make an independent analysis, three copies of the launching list are inclosed.

a. Incidents No. 5 through No. 16 reported on 4 July 1947 throughout Oregon, Idaho and Washington gave, in general, descriptions of clusters or groups of objects. The 3 July 1947 balloon launching No. 8 at Alamogordo was a cluster of balloons and was not recovered, and so might be suspected of being the cause of those reports. However, although not recovered, this flight was terminated in the New Mexico Tularosa Valley only a few miles northwest of Alamogordo. That the balloons were downed was determined both by airplane spotting and by radio direction finding upon the balloon telemetering instruments. Recovery of the balloons and instruments was prevented by the impassability of the terrain.

b. Balloon release No. 11 of 7 July 1947 could compare with respect to date with incident No. 1 through No. 4, and again with incident No. 40. This balloon flight was again a cluster. The description of incident No. 40 is inconsistent with the appearance of balloon flight No. 11. Also, in consideration of the prevailing upper winds, it is very unlikely that the balloons would have gone more than a few miles westward of Alamogordo, although it must be admitted that a long flight west of the launching point could not be ruled out as impossible.

c. Incident No. 47 compares somewhat in time with balloon launching No. 10 of 5 July 1947. However, balloon No. 10 although not recovered was known to have been downed northwest of Albuquerque, New Mexico. It was not recovered due to impassability of terrain. Incident No. 113 is a reasonable description of the 20 ft. plastic balloon and instruments used by these Laboratories. This incident was on the date of balloon release No. 46 of 9 April 1948 at Alamogordo. However, the time of the reported incident (1506 CST) is about ½ hour before the time of balloon release (1432 MST), thus the incident could not have been that balloon.

d. It is of interest to note that incident No. 122 was reported by an employee of these Laboratories who had considerable experience in the use of balloons of all kinds, and could have been depended upon to know the appearance and behavior of a balloon if it was this he saw.

e. Incident No. 163 bears a fair description of the appearance of a large plastic balloon in sunset light. The object's disappearance could be accounted for either by its movement into the earth's sunset shadow or by natural defocusing of the observer's eyes. This incident could possibly have been balloon release No. 75 or No. 76 on 20 and 21 July 48 from Alamogordo. Balloon No. 75 was recovered at Hollistor, California, which is in the Monterey Bay area, on 22 July 1948 and could have easily had a trajectory which would have been within sight of the Los Angeles area. Balloon No. 76 was never recovered. It is possible that it had a trajectory similar to No. 75.

f. All other reported incidents from 1 to 172 do not seem to have reasonable comparison with balloons launched by those Laboratories.

3. The balloons used by those Laboratories are now somewhat standardized. They are 20 feet long, plastic, white in color, and has sphere-on-cone in shape. Nearly all launchings are made at the Holloman AFB at Alamogordo, New Mexico. Two photo-

236

graph prints are enclosed showing the appearance and size of these balloons. The larger photograph shows the typical flight appearance at any altitudes where it would be visible. It is hoped that this information may be of some use to you in identifying future reports of incidents.

4. It is believed that certain of the items in the questionnaire "Checklist–Unidentified Flying Objects" produce insignificant and unreliable data from an observer. These are: 9. Distance of object from observer; 11. Altitude; 12. Speed; and 16. Size. For any unfamiliar object beyond the focal range of the human eyes (about 60 ft.), those four factors are mutually interdependent and therefore indeterminant unless at least one of them (and some observed angles) are known. Directly asking an observer about these indeterminants not only gets unreliable data but induces wild answers because the observer is led into making a statement about quantities for which he has no basis in fact. He will unconsciously assume knowledge of some one of these factors and so give incorrect information on all. That people (many of whom should know better) will arbitrarily give answers to two significant figures on these questions, which really cannot be answered at all, is proof of the unreliability of their information.

5. It is suggested that these four items on the questionnaire be replaced by questions which will yield answers possible of being independent facts in terms of the observer's best estimates of angles and time. From such data given by observers of the same object at two different places, a reliable calculated estimate could be made of the object's size, altitude, speed, and path. These data should include:

a. *An estimate of the angular size of the object.* A quick but reasonable estimate can be made by comparing the angle subtended by the index finger at arms length. The finger ⅞″ wide) of an average man held at 26″ to 30″ (arm's length) will subtend an angle of approximately two degrees. In this way angular size from about ½° to about 8° can be estimated.

b. *The range of the object's flight in terms of the*

237

angle subtended by the observed path. If the object moves in a reasonably straight course it is important to observe the position at the beginning and the end of its course. After the flight has been completed a person can extend his arms toward the two points and also at 90° or 180° and by comparison estimate the angular extent of the flight. It is also important that information which will determine those directions relative to a compass point be given. If the angular course is associated with objects on the horizon, with roads, with the sun (if the time of day is also noted) or by the north star, the orientation can be rechecked at any later time.

c. *The time required for the object to traverse the observed course.* This is probably the most difficult estimate to make. Timing with a watch is the most satisfactory, but an observer is seldom prepared to do so. Seconds can be counted with good accuracy by saying, "one flying saucer; two flying saucers, three flying saucers"—etc., at a normal speaking speed. On the other hand it is not easy to count seconds and at the same time made all the other desirable observations. It must be remembered that when a person is excited his estimates of time are apt to be rather inaccurate.

d. *Estimation of the elevation angle of the object.* Almost all persons will overestimate elevation angles. This tendency can be reduced by the observer extending one arm vertically and the other horizontally to observe a 90° angle. The vertical arm can then be lowered to point to the observed object. In this way the observed angle can be compared with a 90° angle and a more accurate estimate obtained.

6. It is realized that it might not be possible for an observer to perform the operations suggested in the preceding paragraph, during the period the object is sighted. If he would immediately reconsider what he saw and then estimate such measurements, he should be able to give quantitative answers accurate to at least 25%. In interrogating observers, they should also be asked to reconstruct their observations and then estimate these same factors. It is suggested that instruc-

tions for making such quick and estimated observations be given to weather observers, control tower operators, civil police, forest and fire rangers, and other such people who might have good chance of seeing unidentified flying objects. If any information concerning unidentified flying objects is given to the public, instructions for reliable observation should be included.

7. This organization will be pleased to be of any further assistance required in connection with this matter.

UNITED STATES DEPARTMENT OF COMMERCE WEATHER BUREAU

Report Information on "Ball Lightning"

I. Origin

Various theories and suggestions have been proposed to explain ball lightning, most of them being without well-established physical foundation. There is still doubt in scientific circles regarding the origin of a number of reported cases of ball lightning.

Briefly, the explanations of the origin of ball lightning may be broken down as follows:

(1) Brush discharge (St. Elmo's fire.)

(May be stationary over sharp-pointed objects, or moving along or near the surface of wires, roofs, rocks, etc., especially on mountains. Conditions most favorable for brush discharge occur during thunderstorms, but the phenomenon may occur even during clear, dry, dusty weather. When a lightning stroke is approaching an object, the brush discharge becomes especially intense.)

(2) Intensely ionized, incandescent volume of air forming end of lightning stroke and lasting for short interval of time.

(This would occur mainly during thunderstorms following the passage of a lightning stroke. At the ground end, the terminal flash is intense, and vapors, smoke or molten material from objects fused at points struck may enhance and extend the duration of incandescence. After-image formed on the retinas of the eyes of a person looking at the brilliant flash at the point of discharge may give spurious effects.)

(3) Brush discharge in air containing high concentration of dust or other aerosols, during thunderstorms.

(If this occurs, it probably is associated with the path taken by a real lightning stroke, and presumably involves corona discharges from suspended particles and possibly combustion in some cases.)

(4) Jumping of gap by lightning indoors.

(When lightning strikes a house, lightning streamers may jump gaps such as between pipes within the house, thus causing a bright flash of limited extent. After-image is generally formed on the retina and movements of eye produce apparent movements of the illuminated region.)

(5) A cloud-to-ground lightning stroke with an associate, horizontally-directed, moving potential wave may possibly produce a transient horizontal potential gradient sufficiently intense to initiate electrical discharges.

(Such discharges would involve luminous darts moving at high speed and may move over irregular trajectories, producing, in some cases at least, more-or-less horizontally directed, sinuous, ribbon-like or tubular paths. If there is a heavy concentration of electrical charges near the earth beneath the thunderstorm the triggering of a discharge by the transient potential gradient may yield horizontal lightning streamers having a relatively slow propagation rate and long duration.)

(6) A lightning discharge that strikes and runs along a conductor such as power or telephone lines and flashes-over or jumps the gaps at breaks produces

a brilliant illumination at the gaps that may be mistaken for ball lightning.

(7) A piece of wire with attached light object that is carried aloft by the gusty winds and turbulence attending a thunderstorm or tornado may serve to facilitate conduction of lightning currents and yield streamers at its ends during discharges.

    (g) Spurious cases.
        (a) After-image (persistence of vision)
        (b) Will-o'-the Wisp
        (c) Meteorites
        (d) Reflections of lightning observed on highly polished objects, such as door knobs
        (e) Falling molten metal
        (f) Lightning channel seen on end

II. Appearance

(a) *Forms*

Spherical, roughly globular, egg-shaped, or pear-shaped; many times with projecting streamers; or flame-like irregular "masses of light." Appearance of outer boundary is generally hazy or ill-defined. Photographs of the phenomenon may show one or several sinuous, tubular propagation paths (trajectories taken by luminous darts), which may have associated with them broader luminous spaces of irregular configuration. (These latter spaces probably are regions where the sinuosities of path became involved and tortuous or are areas of major discharge where darts originated or terminated.) Some paths show a beaded structure (alternate luminous and dark spaces).

(b) *Color*

Luminous in appearance, described in individual cases by different colors but mostly reported as deep red and often as glaring white. One scientist described the color in a certain case as similar to that he has noted in the laboratory on observing active nitrogen, or possibly slightly darker. Another observed one of

241

yellow and still another of lavender or rose color. Others have reported some of blue appearance. The luminous mass is occasionally stated to be surrounded by a border, weakly but differently-colored than the main body.

(c) *Degrees of Brilliance*
Brilliance at most glaring white and incandescent. Minimum brilliance equal to that of feeble St. Elmo's Fire.

(d) *Movement through Space*
1. *Possible directions.*
Generally downward, inclined or horizontal, in straight, curved, or tortuous paths. Mostly observed near the surface, but may originate in thunderclouds, and so take a trajectory from cloud to earth.
2. *Maneuverability*
May appear stationary, or moving. Range of speed is zero to values of the order of 107 cm./sec. In the latter, extreme case, the luminous darts observed are probably of the same general nature as the lightning streamer, although the path taken may be very irregular and even show reversals in direction. In some cases, long sections of paths of such luminous darts may show slight curvature. Near the ground or in closed spaces a much smaller speed is often said to be observed, mostly about 1–2 meters/sec. The "ball of fire" may seem to move or float along in a room, or to roll along the floor. In a thunderstorm, as may be experienced on a mountain top, an observer has reported "seeing balls of fire roll along the rocks and drop from one to another." Intense St. Elmo's Fire on sharp objects beneath thunderstorms may fluctuate rapidly in size, intensity, and orientation, or show displacements from one point to another, hence the flame may appear to whirl and dance, or move. When a lightning flashover at a point produces an after-image on the observer's retina, movements of the eyes cause corresponding movements of the image which the untrained observer attributes to the movement of a luminous "ball of fire" or flame. Ball

242

lightning observed by Jensen * in the wake of a lightning flash through dust-laden air during a thunderstorm "appeared as a shapeless mass of lavender color which seemed to float slowly downward." Jensen states: "The rose-colored mass seemed most brilliant near the ground and gave the impression of a gigantic pyrotechnic display. Two or three of the globular structures seemed to roll along a pair of 2300 volt power lines for 100 feet or more, then bounded down on the ground and disappeared with a loud report."

When a lightning streamer from a thundercloud terminates in the air, the leader stroke is sometimes so faintly luminous in portions that only a segment of the path is observed. This may conceivably give the impression of elongated "ball of lightning," but is a natural cloud–air lightning stroke.

3. *Nearby Air or other Craft*

There have been numerous cases of aircraft struck by lightning. When the aircraft is all-metallic, it serves as a Faraday cage, and provides electrical protection to the crew and passengers. Just preceding the onset of a lightning stroke to an aircraft, pilots have reported observing a streamer of corona discharge build up on the nose, propellers or other extremity of the craft.** The movement of the streamer accompanies that of a lightning stroke nearly or through the aircraft. Corona discharges on sharply convex surfaces of aircraft have also been observed during flight between masses of clouds strongly charged with electrical charges of opposite sign (positive and negative). Autogenous charging of the aircraft by tribo-electric and other effects during flight through snow or other precipitation particles intensifies the corona discharges. These are of the same nature as St. Elmo's Fire.

St. Elmo's Fire has been observed numerous times on the mastheads of ships and generally moves with them during passage beneath thunderclouds or other

---

* Jensen, J. C. *Physics*, vol. 4, p. 371 (1933).
** Harrison, L. P. "Lightning Discharges to Aircraft and Associated Meteorological Conditions," N.A.C.A. Technical Note 1001 (1946).

meteorological conditions where intense electrical potential gradients exist.

III. Effect on Surrounding Atmosphere

1. Clouds

Lightning of any kind can occur in clouds only if the dielectric properties of the air are broken down when the sparking potential gradient is reached. In clear air this amounts to about 30,000 volts per cm. at sea level and about 21,000 volts per cm. at 10,000 ft. altitude. In clouds, or in the presence of precipitation particles the sparking potential gradient is less, depending on the size of the particles. For example, in the presence of raindrops ⅛ inch in diameter it is about 10,000 volts/cm.

As shown by Macky,* droplets of water suspended in an electrical field sufficiently intense to induce breakdown will display sparking-over phenomena and will become deformed. Under very strong fields, the droplets become drawn out into filaments and disrupt with attendant electrical discharges along their surfaces or through them.

It is probable that these phenomena occur along the channel of a lightning stroke through a cloud, and that some evaporation and disruptive breakdown of droplets occur in consequence of the intense heat and flow of electrical charges. These major effects on cloud or precipitation particles are believed to be confined to the lightning channel, although minor effects such as glow or brush discharges from particles in other portions of the cloud possibly occur in connection with the development of lightning strokes. These discharges from countless particles may yield a general illumination within the cloud under strong electrical field conditions, especially during propagation of lightning strokes.

Effects of "ball lightning" on clouds are unknown. Since "ball lightning," if real, is presumably less severe than an ordinary lightning stroke or at most

* Macky, W. A., *Proc. Roy. Soc.*, London, Ser. A., vol. 133, pp. 565–567 (1931).

is probably a dart streamer of such a stroke, we may assume that the effects of "ball lightning" on clouds are not more severe than those outlined above in connection with lightning.

2. Increased Ionization

The formation of corona discharge at any point leads to a considerable increase in ionization of the surrounding air. Any case of so-called "ball lightning" which is actually a corona discharge will have a similar effect.

Ordinary lightning strokes distribute heavy concentrations of electrons and ions or charged nuclei along and near their channels during the passage of the stepped leader or dart leader. These particles form a space charge surrounding the channel. After the leader reaches the earth, the return stroke occurs from earth to cloud. When this develops, the space charge tends to migrate rapidly to the channel, producing a rush of charges within it. The flow of these charges in the channel yields the brilliant, return lightning stroke. Within the channel ionziation is exceeding heavy.

"Ball lightning" associated with a true lightning stroke will probably involve a flow of space charges to its channel and so leads to a diminution of space charge from the environment of the path but an immediate increase of ionization along its path. Following the passage of the phenomenon, ionization will decay by recombination.

3. Nearby Air or Other Craft

All metallic aircraft which are struck by true lightning generally have scorch marks, pits, or holes burned through the skin. The holes rarely exceed one inch in diameter. (See N.A.C.A. Technical Note 1001.) Portions of non-metallic material in contact with the area struck may be burnt or explosively separated from the metal to which the material is attached. When radio antennae are struck or the lightning arrester does not function as desired, damage to radio equipment often occurs.

Temporary blinding of pilots looking directly at the flash due to the stroke to some exterior portion of the aircraft such as the nose of the fuselage may introduce some hazard. As a rule the temporary blinding is effective from about 10 seconds to a larger fraction of a minute, but in one extreme case a co-pilot was reported to have been temporarily blinded for about 8 minutes. Several cases of temporary blinding of about 3 minutes have been reported.

The Weather Bureau has not received any reports of accidents in which an airplane was said to have suffered contact with "ball lightning." Judging by the phenomenon called by that name and experienced at the surface, the aircraft damage to be expected by such contact would probably be less severe than that caused by a typical genuine lightning stroke. That type of so-called "ball lightning" which is actually an intense corona discharge would not cause any mechanical damage to non-inflammable exposed materials, but would hamper radio communications by producing static similar to the kind termed "precipitation static."

A real lightning stroke to a non-metallic object on the ground often causes an explosive disruptive effect on the object and will cause burning of inflammable materials.

Contact of so-called "ball lightning" may have physical effects on exposed persons varying from negligible to fatal. In the cases of fatalities resulting from this cause, it is believed that genuine lightning was involved. Physical effects of electrical origin on persons enclosed in all-metallic aircraft are negligible, owing to the Faraday cage protection afforded by the conducting skin. However, a slight electrical shock may be experienced by a crew member aboard an aircraft if he is making good contact at the well separated points during passage of the steep wavefront of potential through the area of contact at the time of a real lightning stroke.

IV. Accompanying Phenomena

1. *Sound*

The origination and dissipation of "ball lightning" at the surface are often attended by a sharp report, but not invariably. Very frequently the beginning or end, respectively, of "ball lightning" is accompanied by a positively identified stroke of streak lightning to or very nearly to the point of observation. The thunder produced by such a stroke will naturally be considered by many observers to have been associated with the "ball lightning." "Ball lightning" which is in the form of the corona discharge makes very little sound, since the current carried is very low and the explosive heating effects on the air negligible. Lightning of the continuing-current type, with low-wave-front, will not produce intense sounds, and this is to be more or less expected, also, of isolated luminous dart streamers traversing the channels of preceding or succeeding lightning strokes. Such streamers have been included in the category of "ball lightning."

2. *Chemical Effects*

The odor of ozone in connection with "ball lightning" has been reported by some observers. This is to be expected in cases where the phenomenon is a brush discharge which produces ozone in air. When actual streak lightning is involved, the formation of oxides of nitrogen and ozone is a normal occurrence.

3. *Thermal Effects*

Fires have been caused in combustible material, such as straw, by discharges reported to have been "ball lightning."

4. *Electrical Effects*

"Ball lightning" will certainly be accompanied by radio static in some form. Electrical shock to persons is possible when the phenomenon stems from streak lightning. Disruptive mechanical effects on non-conductors especially if containing moisture, or crushing effects on hollow conducting tubes, may occur in cases where actual steep wave-front, lightning currents pass through the objects.

5. *Optical Appearances*

Some of the cases of "ball lightning" observed have displayed excrescences of the appearance of little flames emanating from the main body of the luminous mass, or luminous streamers have developed from it and propagated slant-wise toward the ground.

In rare instances, it has been reported that the luminous body may break up into a number of smaller balls which may appear to fall towards the earth like a rain of sparks. It has even been reported that the ball has suddenly ejected a whole bundle of many luminous, radiating streamers toward the earth, and then disappeared.

Jensen * has quoted the following report of electrical discharges appearing in a violent storm: "A tornado which occurred on the evening of July 9, 1932, near Rock Rapids, Iowa, gave evidence of a closely related type of luminous display according to the report of Mr. George Raveling, U.S. Weather Bureau observer. From the sides of the boiling, dust-laden cloud a fiery stream poured out like water through a sieve, breaking into spheres of irregular shapes as they descended. No streak lightning of the usual type was observed and no noise attended the fire-balls other than the usual roar of the storm."

(g) *Possible Objects to Which Attracted*

Lightning strokes are more likely to hit at or near the top of high, pointed objects, than on the surfaces of low objects with flat or concave exteriors. If the tips of the high objects are grounded via conductors such as wires or metal pipes, they will tend to show a higher frequency to strokes than ungrounded objects. This is especially true if, in the former case, the ground is well moistened or possesses an extensive network of conducting elements (water pipes, telephone and electric cables, etc.).

It follows that the lightning flash will be observed more frequently at these relatively high points than elsewhere, and hence probably that "ball lightning" will appear to develop quite commonly at such points.

Brush discharges tend to form at sharply convex extremities of objects, and align themselves in the direction of the potential gradient. Well-grounded and conducting objects would generally receive preference. These considerations apply to cases which were class-

* Jensen, J. C., *Physics,* vol. 4, p. 374 (1933).

ified by the layman as "ball lightning" but actually were cases of St. Elmo's Fire (bright glow or brush discharges).

There have been reports by observers of "ball lightning" to the effect that the phenomenon appeared to float through a room or other space for a brief interval of time without making contact with or being attracted by objects. Holzer and Workman * have published a reproduction of moving film camera photographs of unusual discharges during thunderstorms. In the case of the phenomenon observed at Santa Fe, New Mexico (elevation 7000 feet) on the night of September 3, 1936, these authors state: "The cameras were mounted rigidly on a bench in a portable laboratory. The discharge was probably about 100 feet from the cameras, although the exact distance is not known since no thunder associated with this flash could be distinguished from the general background of thunder. The discharge occurred within less than one-thousandth of a second after an intense cloud ground stroke not shown on this portion of the film. Analysis of the photographs indicates that the discharge consisted of at least four luminous darts moving with a projected velocity of the order of 10^7 cm/sec. The most notable features of this discharge are: (1) its irregularity of path and rapid reversals in direction, (2) its proximity to ground objects with no apparent contact with the ground, (3) the beaded nature of the path, and (4) the progress of the discharge in two directions from a single point."

Note should be made of the fact that the luminous darts did not appear to be attracted to available ground objects even though they were in the vicinity of the ground. On this basis it cannot be stated whether there are any definite objects to which all cases of "ball lightning" would be attracted. We should think that sharp-pointed, grounded objects are most likely to attract "ball lightning."

* Holzer, R. E., and Workman, E. J., *Jour. of Applied Physics*, vol. 10, p. 659 (1939).

(h) *Methods of Terminal Dissipation*

As a rule so-called "ball lightning" of the variety which we judge to be intense brush discharge dissipates when the potential gradient diminishes to a value below the critical one for maintenance of the discharge. This generally occurs following lightning strokes which largely discharge the heavy concentrations of electric charges of opposite sign in the overlying thundercloud.

"Ball lightning" which appears to form at sharp-pointed objects as a lightning stroke approaches disappears when (a) the main lightning currents cease flowing just after contact of the stroke or (b) the space charge around the lightning channel is largely collected into the channel and transported to earth or cloud.

"Ball lightning" which appears to be a luminous dart like a meteorite rapidly falling (or rising) along the path of an immediately preceding or succeeding lightning stroke disappears into the earth (or cloud).

"Ball lightning" in the form of a luminous ball apparently moving through a space or rolling along the ground dissipates eventually, perhaps on making contact with some object. Some observers have stated that the ball collapses with a noise resembling that of a big firecracker, leaving an odor of ozone. It seems probable that in these cases also the dissipation takes place when the potential gradient has diminished below the critical value for maintenance of the discharge, simultaneously with the occurance of a genuine lightning stroke to the area involved.

As indicated previously, reports have also been given that the main body of the "ball lightning" has appeared to have broken up into a number of smaller "balls" which have fallen to earth, or to have emitted small streaks, like lightning, projected towards the earth, and thus dissipated.

A sound of thunder, of greater or lesser intensity, may accompany the dissipation. It is not possible to be certain that the sound is always intimately connected with the phenomenon, for it may have been the thunder associated with a nearby lightning stroke.

Abstract

Early in 1950 the Geophysics Research Division received a directive to investigate peculiar light phenomena that had been observed in the skies of the southwestern United States. Project Twinkle was established to check into these phenomena and their explanation.

The gist of the findings is essentially negative. The period of observations covers a little over a year. Some unusual phenomena were observed during that period; most of them can be attributed to such man-made objects as airplanes, balloons, rockets, etc. Others can be attributed to natural phenomena such as flying birds, small clouds, and meteorites. There has been no indication that even the somewhat strange observations often called "Green Fireballs" are anything but natural phenomena.

Our recommendations are in essence that there is no use in sinking any more funds into this at the present time and that we will keep in connection with one of our meteor studies a sharp eye on anything unusual along this line.

1. *Background*

In accordance with instructions contained in a classified letter from Chief of Staff, USAF to CG, AMC, subject "Light Phenomena," on 14 September 1949, Lt. Col. Frederic C. E. Oder of CRD attended a conference at Los Alamos, 14 October 1949 on the subject of "Green Fireballs" observed in the Northern New Mexico area. Since the phenomena had been observed only in this area and only since 1947, it had caused considerable concern among security agencies in the area. It was the conclusion of the scientists present at this meeting that the information available was not sufficiently quantitative. Instrumental observations—photographic, triangulation, and spectroscopic—were considered essential.

Dr. L. La Paz of the Department of Meteoritics of University of New Mexico was present at the Los

251

Alamos meeting and subsequently was invited to submit proposals for studying this phenomena under GRD sponsorship. On 2 February 1950, Dr. La Paz advised that due to difficulties with academic arrangements, he was unable to undertake this study.

During February 1950, the frequent reports of unexplained serial phenomena in the vicinity of Holloman Air Force Base and Vaughn, New Mexico prompted the Commanding Officer of Holloman Air Force Base to initiate a program to gather factual data. These data then would be used to demonstrate the need for initiating a study of the phenomena. On 21 February 1950, an observation outlook post was set up at Holloman Air Force Base manned by two personnel. Observations with theodolight, telescope and camera were undertaken between the hours of sunrise and sunset.

On March 5, 1950 a conference was held at Wright-Patterson Air Force Base which included Holloman Air Force Base and GRD personnel. Action was taken to initiate a three point program which was confirmed by AMC in the form of a letter directive on 16 March 1950, subject "Light Phenomena."

a. Askania instrument triangulation by Land-Air Inc.
b. Observations with Mitchell camera using spectrum grating by Holloman Air Force Base personnel.
c. Electromagnetic frequency measurements using Signal Corps Engineering Laboratory equipment.

Under contract to GRD, Land-Air Inc. was required to maintain constant watch at two Askania stations for a six-month period. Since an abnormal number of reports had been received from Vaughn, New Mexico, it was decided to install the instrumentations at Vaughn.

2. *Contractual period—1 April 1950 to 15 September 1950.*
Some photographic activity occurred on 27 April

and 24 May, but simultaneous sightings by both cameras were not made, so that no information was gained. On 30 August 1950, during a Bell aircraft missile launching, aerial phenomena were observed over Holloman Air Force Base by several individuals; however, neither Land-Air nor Project personnel were notified and, therefore, no results were acquired. On 31 August 1950, the phenomena were again observed after a V-2 launching. Although much film was expended, proper triangulation was not effected, so that again no information was acquired. On 11 September, arrangements were made by Holloman AFB for Major Gover, Commander 93rd Fighter Squadron at Kirtland AFB, to be on call so that aerial objects might be pursued. This would make possible more intimate visual observation and photography at close range. Major Gover was not authorized to shoot at the phenomena.

Generally, the results of the six-month contractual period may be described as negative. Although the photographic theodolites functioned continuously, the grating cameras functioned very little, since the military personnel assigned to operate them had been withdrawn due to the needs concerned with the Korean situation. The facilities for the electromagnetic frequency measurements that were to be provided by the Signal Corps Engineering Laboratories were not utilized due to the fact that the frequency of occurrence of these phenomena did not justify the $50,000 a year transfer of funds to the Signal Corps which would be required to carry out such a monitoring facility. However, the phenomena activity over Holloman AFB 150 miles south of Vaughn, New Mexico during the latter part of August 1950 was considered sufficiently significant so that the contract with Land-Air (Askania cameras only) was extended for six months ending 31 March 1951.

3. *Contractual Period—1 October 1950 to 31 March 1951*

Because of the diminution of phenomena activity in the vicinity of Vaughn and the resumption of activity near HAFB, the Askania cameras again were overhauled and installed at HAFB. This installation was completed about 5 November 1950. On 16 October 1950, arrangements were made by Lt. Albert of HAFB that Northrup Aircraft pilots engaged in frequent flying of B-45 and QF-80 aircraft in the Holloman vicinity would report all observations of aerial phenomena.

During this period, occasional reports were received of individuals seeing strange aerial phenomena, but these reports were sketchy, inconclusive, and were considered to be of no scientific value. No sightings were made by the Askania cameras. Nothing whatsoever was reported by the Northrup pilots. Popular interest seemed abated, at least in the southwest. On 31 March 1951, due to the expiration of the contract, Land-Air ceased constant vigilance at the two Askania stations. In summary, the results during this period were negative.

4. *Post Contractual Inquiry*

In view of the unproductive nature of the contract with Land-Air, it was decided to make further inquiry concerning recent aerial object developments in New Mexico. On 9 August 1951, the situation was discussed with Lt. Col. Cox of the 17th OSI District (Kirtland AFB). Until 15 March 1950 the District had been diligent in forwarding copies of their reports on aerial object phenomena. Since then, no reports have been received by the Geophysics Research Division. Colonel Cox advised that reports of strange aerial phenomena were still received by the 17th OSI office, at the rate of once or twice a month, but little attention was being given to this matter. Most of the reports originated from personnel at Los Alamos. The OSI files were reviewed. (A summary covering recent reports is attached.) It was learned that representatives from LIFE and also from ARGOSY were interested in publishing articles on aerial object phenomena.

On 27 August 1951, development concerning aerial phenomena were discussed at Holloman AFB. Lt. John Alber previously associated with the project had now been transferred from Holloman. Therefore, the project was discussed with Major Edward A. Doty who had assumed responsibility. Major Doty, who seemed to be thoroughly acquainted with the situation, advised that there have been very few reports of aerial phenomena in the vicinity of Holloman since September 1950. The populace around HAFB seem to have lost their sensitivity as observers. Even during the meteor shower of 11–12 August 1951, no alarming reports were received. However, on 14 March 1951, nine Bell personnel reported sighting between fourteen and twenty bodies "not unlike a flock of geese." On 9 July a "red glowing ball" was sighted by a sergeant stationed at the Corona Experimental Radar Site at Corona, New Mexico. (Copies of both reports are attached.) More recently, a pilot reported some aerial objects which, after investigation, were identified as planets.

Mr. B. Guildenberg, who is an assistant to Major Doty and an active amateur astronomer, commented that he has been spending several hours at his telescope almost every night for the past few years and never once observed an unexplainable object; that on one occasion, an excited acquaintance was pacified when a "strange object" showed up as an eagle in the telescope; that Clyde Tombaugh, discoverer of the planet Pluto and now engaged in activities at White Sands, never observed an unexplainable aerial object despite his continuous and extensive observations of the sky; that Fred Whipple in his work photographing meteors at Las Cruces never detected a strange aerial object with his Schmidt cameras; and that the A and M College at Las Cruces engages in astronomical observations but had never observed strange aerial phenomena.

It was learned from Major Doty, that Col. Baynes, C.O. at HAFB, no longer felt there was any justification for the allocation of funds for maintaining systematic investigation. Rather, he provided that the project be maintained on a standby basis and without official Air Force status. This entails assignment of an officer (Major Doty) to collect incoming reports, make periodic review of the files "for patterns or persistent characteristics in the reports," maintain liaison with OSI, Provost Marshall's Office and any other agencies whose activities may serve to provide information concerning future aerial phenomena developments. Land-Air has agreed to report and if possible photograph any abnormal sightings made during their scheduled periods of operation (about eight hours each day). The weather station will function similarly. Also, all pilots have been briefed to report any unusual observations. If necessary, the project can be activated very quickly, even to the extent where funds will be made available, for the purchase of equipment.

Major Doty also arranged a conference with Mr. Warren Kott, who is in charge of Land-Air operations. Mr. Kott pointed out that a formal report covering the year's vigilance period had not been issued since the contract contained no such provision. Actually, a time correlation study should be made covering the film and verbal recordings at both Askania stations. This would assure that these records did not contain significant material. However, such a study is quite laborious, and would require about thirty man days to complete. Again, no provisions are contained in the contract for this study, but Mr. Kott felt that this could be done by Land-Air at the additional expense in the near future when the work load diminished. Mr. Kott requested formal authorization to do this and Major Doty agreed to issue this letter of authorization. It was arranged further that at such time when the study is completed all photographic and tape recordings would be sent to the Geophysics Research Division. Prior to departing HAFB, the project files were reviewed. Major Doty advised that access to the files had not been requested by any periodicals.

On 28 August 1951, the subject was discussed informally with Dr. Lincoln La Paz, who expressed disbelief in all aerial phenomena except for the green fire-balls. The red fire-ball occasionally reported he believed was the visual after-effect of the green. Their recent origin (1947) and peculiar trajectories did not permit, according to Dr. La Paz, them to be classed as natural phenomena. The most recent that has come to his attention occurred over Detroit on 7 July 1951. It crossed the city from Northwest to Southeast with a sharply descending trajectory which leveled out and was observed by many residents of the city. Dr. La Paz expressed the opinion that the fireballs may be of our own military origin, but if not, they are a matter of serious concern.

5. Conclusions

Undoubtedly, a good many of the observations reported are attributable to ordinary man-made objects such as airplanes, balloons, smoke rockets, etc. It appears that balloon observations especially are responsible for a large number of the reports. The possibility of small emissive clouds issuing from atomic installations also has been proposed.

Many of the sightings are attributable to natural phenomena such as flight of birds, planets, meteors, and possibly cloudiness. Dr. Fred L. Whipple of Harvard, in a memorandum to this laboratory dated 9 August 1950 relative to this problem, indicated that he had observed a tendency for the occurrence of small detached clouds in New Mexico which might have been mistaken for an aerial object when illuminated by the reflected light of the moon. Dr. Whipple investigated the possibility of a correlation between the frequency of aerial phenomena observations and weather conditions—specifically cloudiness. A rough analysis of available weather data indicated that on the 53 nights (between 5 December 1948 and 5 March 1951) when observations were reported, 10 were clear, 24 partially cloudy, 5 completely overcast and 14 had no record. The number of cloudy nights involved seems unsually high for New Mexico. The weather reports were for the Las Cruces area only whereas many of the observations were a considerable distance from Las Cruces. Further investigation is therefore necessary to determine correlations with cloudiness.

Dr. Whipple also conducted a study as to whether the age of the moon was related to the frequency of aerial phenomena observations. The results did not indicate that the phenomena were observed largely at full moon. The statistics show that of the 72 observations reported, 45 occurred when the moon was up and 27 when it was down with many of the observations occurring at the time of the moon's first quarter. From the statistical study, Dr. Whipple suggests that the existence of moonlight is correlated with the phenomena. Dr. Whipple's frequency diagram of observations vs. age of moon is included in this report.

It should be noted that Dr. Whipple made a careful study of meteor photographs taken in New Mexico on 35 nights when observations were reported. None of the photographs revealed the presence of unusual sky phenomena.

Finally, the overall picture obtained from the year of vigilance and inquiry does not permit a conclusive opinion concerning the aerial phenomena of interest. The comparatively high incidence of the phenomena since 1948 does not necessarily indicate that the objects are man-made. It is conceivable that the earth may be passing through a region in space of high meteoric population. Also, the sun-spot maxima in 1948 perhaps in some way may be a contributing factor.

6. *Recommendations*

Since the findings to date cannot be considered conclusive, it appears that the following recommendations would be pertinent:

(1) No further fiscal expenditure be made in pursuing the problem. This opinion is prompted partly by the fruitless expenditure during the past year, the uncertainty of existence of unexplainable aerial objects, and by the inactive position currently taken by Holloman AFB as indicated by the "stand-by status" of the project. The arrangements by HAFB for continued vigilance by Land-Air, the weather station as well as the briefing of pilots on the problem in part relieves the need for a systematic instrumentation program.

(2) Within the next few months, Dr. Whipple will have completed the installation of two 18-inch Schmidt

cameras for meteor studies. The cameras will be stationed about 20 miles apart in the vicinity of Las Cruces, New Mexico. Since these studies will be sponsored by the GRD, arrangements can be made for examining the film for evidence of aerial object phenomena.

Chapter Ten: The USAF Guide to UFO Identification

UFOB Guide

This guide is designed for use in determining the feasibility of follow-up investigation of Unidentified Flying Object reports and in identifying the objects or phenomena concerned.

Air Technical Intelligence Center
Wright-Patterson Air Force Base, Ohio

Part I
Follow-up Investigations

GENERAL

A UFOB report is worthy of follow-up investigation when it contains information to suggest that a positive identification with a well known phenomenon may be made or when it characterizes an unusual phenomenon. The report should suggest almost immediately, largely by the coherency and clarity of the data, that there is something of identification value and/or scientific value.

In general, reports which should be given consideration are those which involve several reliable observers, together or separately, and which concern sightings of greater duration than one quarter minute. Exception should be made to this when circumstances attending the report are considered to be extraordinary.

Special attention should be given to reports which give promise to a "fix" on the position and to those reports involving unusual trajectories.

RULES OF THUMB

Every UFOB case should be judged individually but there are a number of "rules of thumb," under each of the following headings, which should prove helpful in determining the necessity for follow-up investigation.

1. *Duration of Sighting*

When the duration of a sighting is less than 15 seconds, the probabilities are great that it is not worthy of follow-up. As a word of caution, however, should a large number of individual observers concur on an unusual sighting of a few seconds duration, it should not be dismissed.

When a sighting has covered just a few seconds, the incident, when followed-up in the past, has almost always proved to be a meteor or a gross mis-identification of a common object owing to lack of time in which to observe.

2. *Number of Persons Reporting the Sighting*

Short duration sightings by single individuals are seldom worthy of follow-up.

Two or three competent independent observations carry the weight of 10 or more simultaneous individual observations. As an example, 25 people at one spot may observe a strange light in the sky. This, however, has less weight than two reliable people observing the same light from different locations. In the latter case a position-fix is indicated.

3. *Distance from Location of Sighting to Nearest Field Unit*

Reports which meet the preliminary criterion stated above should all be investigated if their occurrence is in the immediate operating vicinity of the squadron concerned.

For reports involving greater distances, follow-up necessity might be judged as being inversely proportional to the square of the distances concerned. For example, an occurrence 150 miles away might be considered to have four times the importance (other things being equal) than one that is 300 miles away.

4. *Reliability of Person or Persons Reporting*

In establishing the necessity of follow-up investigations only "short term" reliability of individuals can be employed. Short term reliability is judged from the logic and coherency of the original report and by the age and occupation of the person. Particular attention should be given to whether the occupation involves observation reporting or technical knowledge.

5. *Number of Individual Sightings Reported*

Two completely individual sightings, especially when separated by a mile or more, constitutes sufficient cause for follow-up, assuming previous criterion have not been violated.

6. *The Value of Obtaining Additional Information Immediately*

If the information cannot be obtained within seven days, the value of such information is greatly decreased.

It is of great value to obtain additional information immediately if previously stated criteria have been met. Often, if gathered quickly, two or three items (weather conditions, angular speed, changes in trajectory, duration, etc.) are sufficient for immediate evaluation.

If investigation is undertaken after weeks or months the original observers cease to be of value as far as additional new information is concerned. Generally, late interrogation yields only bare repetition of facts originally reported plus an inability on the part of the observer to be objective.

7. *Existence of Physical Evidence (Photographs, Material, Hardware)*

In cases where any physical evidence exists, a

follow-up should be made even if some of the above criteria have not been meet.

CONCLUSION—PART I

It is understood that all above criteria must be evaluated in terms of "common sense." The original report, from its wording and clarity, will almost always suggest to the reader whether there is any "paydirt" in the report.

Part II
Identification Criteria

GENERAL

When a UFO report meets, in large measure, the criteria projected in Part I and a follow-up investigation is instituted, then the interrogator should ask what physical object or objects might have served as the original stimulus for the report. The word "object" here includes optical phenomena such as reflections from clouds, sundogs, etc.

Frequently one or perhaps two solutions will be immediately suggested by the nature of the report. The word "solution" cannot be used here in the scientific sense. A solution in UFOB work means that a hypothesis has been arrived at which appears to have the greatest probability of having given rise to the given report.

Following is a group of hypotheses or examples which should prove helpful in arriving at solutions. A check should be made to see how many of the items are satisfied by the report and how many are missing. An effort should be made to obtain any missing items as soon as possible.

Each typical hypothesis is listed on a separate page.

1. *PURPOSE:* This publication is designed for the use of Ground Observer Corps personnel and is published to familiarize observers with common phenomena which are sometimes misinterpreted as Unidentified Flying Objects (UFOB's).

2. *DEFINITIONS:*

a. *Unidentified Flying Object (UFOB)*—Relates to any airborne object which by performance, aerodynamic characteristics, or unusual features does not conform to any presently known aircraft or missile type, or which cannot be positively identified as a familiar object.

b. *Familiar Objects*—Include balloons, astronomical bodies, birds, etc.

3. *OBJECTIVE:* Due to the prolonged observation of the sky during both daylight and night time hours, familiar objects such as meteors, aircraft, balloons, astronomical bodies, searchlights, birds, etc., will be frequently observed by GOC personnel. Due to atmospheric conditions (temperature inversions, dust, clouds, etc.), reflections, sound (or lack of sound), speed, position, etc., common phenomena may sometimes be misinterpreted as UFOB's. It is highly desirable that all UFO phenomena be identified or explained. In this respect, the observer requires some "rule-of-thumb" to assist him in this identification.

The object of this publication is to familiarize the Ground Observer with the appearance(s) of common objects under one or more of the circumstances listed above.

4. *GUIDANCE:* Attached is a list of common phenomena to which Ground Observers may be exposed during their tours of duty. It is recommended that you

become thoroughly familiar with these criteria, as they may enable you to identify objects with a greater degree of accuracy.

Identification Criteria
Balloons

1. *Shape:* Round, cigar, pinpoint, or bowling pin.
2. *Size:* Balloons up to a hundred feet will generally appear from pinpoint to size of a pea held at arm-length.
3. *Color:* Silver, white or many tints. It may possibly appear dark as when projected against the clouds. Sometimes transparent.
4. *Speed:* Large scale erratic speed ruled out. In general hovering to slow apparent speed.
5. *Formation:* Single to cluster.
6. *Trail:* None.
7. *Sound:* None.
8. *Course:* Straight with a general gradual ascent, unless falling.
9. *Time in Sight:* Generally long. Note: Balloon may suddenly burst and disappear.
10. *Lighting Conditions:* Night or day but especially at sunset or sunrise.

Aircraft

1. *Shape:* From conventional to circular or elliptical.
2. *Size:* Pinpoint to actual.
3. *Color:* Silver to bright yellow (night—black or color of lights). Jet exhaust yellow to red. Under certain conditions aircraft too far distant to be visible to the naked eye, will reflect sunlight from wings to fuselage.
4. *Speed:* Generally only angular speed can be observed. This depends on distance but small objects crossing major portion of sky in less than a minute can be ruled out. Aircraft will not cross

major portion of sky in less than a minute whereas a meteor certainly will.

5. *Formation:* Two to twenty. Numbers greater than 20 more likely birds than aircraft.
6. *Trails:* May or may not have (vapor and exhaust).
7. *Sound:* Zero to loud shrill or low depending on altitude and winds aloft. Under certain conditions, aircraft may be observed at high altitudes, without making any sound.
8. *Course:* Steady, straight or gently curving (not erratic—may appear still if approaching head-on). Right angle turns and sudden reversals, abrupt changes in altitude ruled out.
9. *Time in Sight:* More than 15 seconds, generally of the order of a minute or two.
10. *Lighting Conditions:* Night or day.

Meteor

1. *Shape:* Round to elongated.
2. *Size:* Pinpoint to size of moon.
3. *Color:* Flaming yellow with red, green or blue possible.
4. *Speed:* Crosses large portion of sky in few seconds except if coming head-on.
5. *Formation:* Generally single—can break into shower at end of trajectory. Occasionally (but rare) small groups.
6. *Trail:* As night almost always a luminous train which can persist as long as a half hour (rarely). Daytime meteors are much less frequently observed. In daytime, leaves a whitish to dark smoke trail.
7. *Sound:* None.
8. *Course:* Generally streaking downward, but not necessarily sharply downward. Can on rare occasion give impression of slight rise.
9. *Time in Sight:* Longest reported about 30 seconds, generally less than 10.
10. *Lighting Conditions:* Day or night. Mostly night.
11. *Other:* An exceptionally bright meteor is called a

265

fire-ball. These are rare but extremely spectacular and on occasion have been known to light surroundings to the brightness of daylight.

Stars or Planets

General
The planets, Venus, Mars, Jupiter, and Saturn are generally brighter than any star, but they twinkle very much less (unless very close to horizon). Stars twinkle a great deal and when near the horizon can give impression of flashing light in many colors.

1. *Shape:* Pinpoint—starlike.
2. *Size:* Never appreciable.
3. *Color:* Yellow with rainbow variations.
4. *Speed:* Stars' apparent speeds carry them from east to west in the course of the night but they are often reported as erratic. The effect is psychological, most people being unable to consider a point as being stationary. Occasionally turbulence in the upper atmosphere can cause a star to appear to jump (rare) but somehow twinkling gives the impression of movement to many people.
5. *Formation:* There are no clusters of very bright stars but faint stars are grouped in their familiar constellations. Note: A report of 4 or 5 bright clustering lights would rule out stars.
6. *Trail:* None.
7. *Sound:* None.
8. *Course:* Always describe 24 hour circle around pole or sky from east to west.
9. *Time in Sight:* When clear, stars are always visible. Most stars rise or set during the course of the night. Stars low in western sky set within an hour or two. Stars in east always go higher in sky.
10. *Lighting Conditions:* Night—twilight.

Searchlights

1. *Shape:* Round to elliptical.
2. *Size:* Pea at arm's length to large luminous glow,

dependent upon cloud height.
3. *Color:* White fluorescent.
4. *Speed:* Stationary to fantastic.
5. *Formation:* Usually only one but occasionally two or three.
6. *Trail:* None.
7. *Sound:* None.
8. *Course:* Circling, straight, stationary or erratic. Note: Scattered clouds can give impression of object disappearing and reappearing in a different portion of the sky in a few seconds.
9. *Time in Sight:* Generally long.
10. *Lighting Conditions:* Night.

Optical Phenomena

General

This can cover a multitude of things.

Optical phenomena which have been reported as UFOBs run from reflections on clouds and layers of ice crystals (sundogs) to the many types of mirages. No one set of optical phenomena can be set down as representation for the whole class.

There is no limit to the speed of optical phenomena. Reflections can travel from incredible speed, as in the case of a search-beacon on high clouds, to stationary.

1. *Shape:* Generally round but can be elliptical or linear.
2. *Size:* Starlike to large luminous glow.
3. *Color:* Generally yellow.
4. *Speed:* Stationary to fantastic.
5. *Formation:* Any.
6. *Trail:* None
7. *Sound:* None.
8. *Course:* Any.
9. *Time in Sight:* Any.
10. *Lighting Conditions:* Day and night.
11. *Other:* One of the standard types is the "sundog." In this a large luminous halo is seen around the sun with one to four images of the sun placed

along the halo circle at intervals of 90 degrees. Another report often has to do with a bright planet or even the moon shining through a light overcast. Mirage reflections are said to occur frequently when temperature inversions exist in the atmosphere.

Chapter Eleven: Dr. Hynek's Conferences with Astronomers

Special Report on Conferences with Astronomers on Unidentified Aerial Objects to Air Technical Intelligence Center Wright-Patterson Air Force Base

by
J. Allen Hynek
August 6, 1952

This special report was prepared to describe the results of a series of conferences with astronomers during and following a meeting of the American Astronomical Society in Victoria, B. C., in June, 1952. It recounts personal opinions of a large number of professionally trained astronomical observers regarding unidentified aerial objects. In addition, it reports sightings by five professional astronomers that were not explainable by them. Representing the opinions of highly trained scientists, these comments should prove particularly helpful in assessing the present status of our knowledge of unknown objects in the skies.

Purpose of Interviews

The desirability has been established of inquiring of professionally trained astronomers of considerable scientific background as to whether they had ever made sightings of unidentified aerial objects. At the same time, it is felt that it would be profitable to obtain the informal opinions and advice of high-ranking astronomers on the entire subject of unidentified aerial objects, of the manner in which the investigation of these objects was being conducted by the Air Force, and of their own inner feelings about the possibility that such objects were real and might constitute either a threat to national security or new natural phenomena worthy of scientific investigation.

Accordingly it was planned that a tour would be made of several of the nation's observatories, not in the guise of an official investigator, but rather as an astronomer traveling about to discuss scientific problems. It was felt that this mild deception was necessary, that an artificial barrier to communication might not be set up which would invalidate the assumption that truly representative opinions were being obtained. Therefore, to maintain good faith, the names of the astronomers interviewed are withheld from this report.

In all, 45 astronomers were interviewed, nearly always individually except in a few cases where this was impossible. Eight observatories were visited and the National Meeting of the American Astronomical Society in Victoria, British Columbia, was attended on June 25 to June 28.

Because of the confidential and highly personal manner in which the interviews quoted below were made, and to keep faith with the many astronomers interviewed, who, generally, were not aware that anything more than a personal private talk between astronomers was going on, the names of the astronomers will be withheld. They will be assigned letters, but the code will not be included in this report.

Table 1 gives an informal evaluation of each astronomer as an observer, and, for some, their rating as a professional astronomer. These ratings are based on my own personal opinion; they do not represent any fixed levels of achievement in the general field of astronomy.

TABLE 1. INFORMAL EVALUATION OF ASTRONOMERS PROVIDING DATA FOR THIS REPORT

Astronomer	Rating as an observer	Rating as a professional astronomer	Astronomer	Rating as an observer	Rating as a professional astronomer
A	3	–	V	3	2
B	1	–	W	3	–
C	3	–	X	3	1
D	2	–	Y	1	–
E	3	–	Z	–	–
F	3	–	AA	–	–
G	1	–	BB	–	–
H	2	–	CC	–	–
I	1	–	DD	1	1
J	1		EE	1	–
K	–	–	FF	–	–
L	1	–	GG	1	1
M	1	–	HH	2	1
N	3	1	II	2	2
O	2	3	JJ	–	–
P	3	3	KK	1	–
Q	1	1	LL	–	–
R	1	–	MM	2	–
S	2	–	NN	–	–
T	–	–	OO	–	–
U	1	–	PP	–	–

Key to ratings: 1. Excellent
2. Above average
3. Average

Interviews with Astronomers

There follows a simple narrative of the interview, after which the opinions and advice of the astronomer will be summarized.

Astronomer *A* has never made any sightings and knows of none in his immediate acquaintance who have.

Astronomer *B* has made sightings of things which people would call "flying saucers" but hasn't seen anything that he couldn't explain. He has seen birds at night flying in formation illuminated by city lights, but probably not bright enough to have been photographed because they were traveling "pretty fast." Astronomer *B* wonders if some of the sightings are not due to Navy secret weapons, since only the Navy has officially said nothing about flying saucers. Astronomer *B* was quite outspoken and feels that past methods of handling the subject have been "stupid." He feels pilots should not be hushed up, and that secrecy only whets the public appetite.

Astronomer *C* has made no sightings, and is quite reluctant to discuss the subject. It is evident that he regards it as a fairly silly proceeding and subject. Difficult to bring the conversation around to the subject.

Astronomer *D* has made no such sightings and does not know any associate who has. He is fairly sympathetic in the matter and appears open minded on the subject.

Astronomer *E* has made no sightings, but heard the great Seattle meteorite of May 11 at 1:30 a.m. Apparently, he is not much interested in the subject.

Astronomer *F*, from England, has made no sightings, but tells of the reports of unidentified objects in England.

Astronomer *G* has made no sightings, nor have his associates. Reasonably interested in talking about the subject, he clearly does not consider it a topic of any real importance as compared with the problems he is interested in at the moment.

Astronomer *H* has been associated with systematic meteor observation, but not for any great length of time. He has made no sightings nor have his associates. His meteor cameras have not picked up any objects.

Astronomer *I* has made no sightings and it was rather difficult to get him to talk about the subject at all. Clearly he does not regard it as a problem of importance.

Astronomer *J*, who has had long experience at a

meteor observatory, has made no sightings but clearly is very interested in the problem. He has promised cooperation should any items come to his attention. He is very much interested in seeing this problem cleared up. His professional rating is excellent.

Astronomer L has made no sightings nor, as far as he knows, have any of his associates.

Astronomer M has made no sightings. Politely interested, but he clearly does not regard it as a major problem.

Astronomer N, with an excellent professional rating, has made no sightings nor does he know of any associates who have. He said that astronomer Whipple thinks the green fireballs observed in New Mexico are small asteroids, whereas the ordinary meteors are cometary fragments. There is a further discussion of this point later with reference to La Paz.

Astronomer O, whose professional rating is only moderate, has seen none.

Astronomer P, whose professional rating also is only moderate, has seen none and does not consider the problem very important.*

Astronomer Q, with an excellent professional rating, has seen no unidentified objects but says that reports come in occasionally from the Fraser River Valley northeast of Vancouver. Apparently these sightings have been concerned with lights similar to the Lubbock lights.

Astronomer R has personally sighted an unidentified object, a light which loomed across his range of vision, which was obstructed by an observatory dome, much faster than a plane and much slower than a meteor. If it had been a plane, then its rapid motion could be accounted for only by closeness, but since no motors were heard, this explanation was essentially ruled out. Light was steadier than that of a meteor and was observed for about three seconds. Astronomer R does not ascribe any particular significance to this sighting,

---

* The professional ratings given here show that "sightings" and interest in the problem do not run inversely proportional to the professional rating of the astronomer.

except as it constitutes one of the many incomplete and unexplained sightings. Astronomer R was not reluctant to talk about the subject of flying saucers and pointed out that we must not fall into the error of believing that we understand all physical phenomena. As late as the year 1800, it was thought impossible that meteorites, "stones from heaven," could fall from the sky. There is no reason to believe that a century and a half later *all* the physical phenomena that exist have been discovered. Astronomer R is, however, violently opposed to the sensational approach to this problem. He points out that many scientists, or at least some scientists, have approached these sightings for the sake of personal glory and publicity but not for the benefit of the country. He is also opposed to magazines such as *Life* setting themselves up as scientific arbiters and passing scientific judgment on sightings when not qualified to do so. In short, Astronomer R believes this subject is serious enough to be considered as a scientific problem, and that it should be taken entirely out of the sensational realm. He believes, for instance, that a group of serious scientists should aim to help investigators by starting with a thorough-going investigation of the "Lubbock lights." This investigation would comprise not only a rehash of previous sightings, but an intelligent cooperative effort to examine the world of physical phenomena and to see which of those, and which scientific or physical principles, might conceivably have led to these observations. He feels that the Lubbock incident is a particularly propitious one to start with since the observations were made by reliable observers in a scientific atmosphere, and that, therefore, these qualified observers could discuss with other scientists their sightings in a dispassionate manner. Astronomer R turned over the record of his sighting made at the instant of the sighting, for whatever use it may be. He is interested in the problem and eminently cooperative.

Astronomer S has seen none and is not particularly interested in the problem.

Astronomer T has personally seen nothing, but recounted the incident at Selfridge Field which occurred early in June, 1952, in which a group of fliers from Selfridge Field was sent out to attack a target over Lake Erie. As they were approaching the target, the shore observers radioed "Why don't you shoot? You are already in the target." This apparently is another example of the fairly frequent radar "sightings."

Astronomer *U*, Hugh Pruett, who does not mind having his name used, is Northwest Regional Director of the American Meteor Society. Although getting on in years, he has had a great deal of experience with meteor observation. He evinced considerable interest and cooperation in the problem, and I took the liberty of asking him to cooperate with this endeavor in tracking down meteor sightings which might be associated with reports on flying saucers. He is well acquainted with all the officers and members of the American Meteor Society, and he could provide considerable help in assembling a panel of consulting astronomers. Pruett plotted the flight of the great Seattle meteor from hundreds of reports. He is an avid "trackerdowner" of such things, and he can be of considerable assistance in these matters. He himself has not made any unexplained sightings. I checked my knowledge of meteors with him and corroborated the points that there are many meteors that are green, that some drop vertically, that some wobble, some have noise associated with them, and some have been seen as long as 25 seconds. There is one record in the literature of a meteor that lasted 50 seconds, but this seems hardly possible. Pruett, although he observed no objects, did hear a very loud noise above the clouds early one morning which he does not believe was aircraft. He asked the local radio station to help; his phone was busy for four hours. There is no question that the noise existed, but no one saw anything.

Astronomer *V* has made no sightings. He was so interested in speaking of his own troubles that it was impossible to bring the conversation around to scientific problems. His professional rating is only intermediate.

Astronomer W was difficult to interest in the subject and did not admit to having seen anything.

Astronomer X, with a high professional rating, has made no sightings and exhibits an extremely negative attitude toward the whole problem. He feels that all sightings except the green fireballs are merely misrepresentations of familiar objects, and he has no patience with the subject. He believes that La Paz should have enough data to get the heights of the green fireballs, and therefore settle the question. La Paz, when questioned later, said he did have sufficient observations and the objects were eight to ten miles high. Astronomer R, who happened to be present when Astronomer X was "sounding off," again reiterated that it would be a good idea for some astronomer to take a reasonable attitude toward this problem, and that we will get no place by merely pooh-poohing it.

Astronomer Y has made no sightings but has stated, "If I saw one, I wouldn't say anything about it." This statement led the conversation into the question of what conditions would have to be met before he would report it. The answer from him was the same as from several other astronomers, that if they were promised complete anonymity and if they could report their sightings to a group of serious respected scientists who would regard the problem as a scientific one, then they would be willing to cooperate to the very fullest extent. Astronomer Y suggested that an article be written in some astronomical journal informing the astronomical world that a reliable clearing house for such information exists.* Astronomer Y, and others, were of the strong opinion that the astronomical world should be informed through reliable channels as to what the Air Force is doing in tracking down these stories, and what is being done to put the investigation of such incidents on a scientific basis.

Astronomer Z, from Germany, has sighted none him-

---

* The writer does not agree with this as it would almost immediately fall into the hands of the press and the ensuing publicity would be a strong deterrent to the receipt of reports.

self but tells that flying saucer reports also exist in Germany, but he believes that many may have been introduced by the Occupation Forces. He reports that rumors are frequent that the flying saucers might be from Mars, but that these reports are taken by the intelligent simply as American propaganda to cover up the existence of secret weapons. Or, they say, if not the Americans, then the Soviets.

Astronomer *AA*, from England, has made no sightings himself. He tells that such sightings are talked about in England, however. The only specific case he knows anything about is that of the falling ice which killed the sheep. These very handy "flying saucers" served a very good purpose in getting around meat rationing because when the sheep was killed, obviously for table use, the blame was put to falling ice. The stories ended when a chemical examination of the only authentic case of such a fall showed the ice to have uric acid in it. This led to a change in the sanitation routines aboard the BOAC planes!

Astronomer *BB* has made no sightings personally, but informed the writer that he would talk to a reputable committee of scientists if he did see anything.

Astronomer *CC* has made no sightings himself although he has been in a very good position to do so. He was reluctant to discuss the matter to any extent.

Astronomer *DD*, with a top professional rating, has seen nothing personally, nor does he know of any of his associates who have. Interested in the problem, he feels that a scientific panel could provide the answer.

Astronomer *EE* has never seen any unexplainable objects. He has seen a phenomenon which most people would have said was a "flying saucer." This turned out to be a beacon light describing a cone of light, part of which intercepted a high cirrus cloud. This led to a series of elliptical lights moving in one direction and never coming back.

Astronomer *FF* has seen none himself, but recently received a report from a ranger who said he was an amateur astronomer; he reported a bright light but said that it was not a meteor. Astronomer *FF* said his recitation of the incident was very dramatic. Astronomer *FF* suggested sending up a control "flying saucer" to see how many reports come back. Apparently he had in mind an extremely bright rocket or perhaps a spectacular balloon.*

Astronomer *GG*, with an excellent professional standing, and cooperative and highly respected, has made no sightings personally. He concurs with others that a committee of scientists to approach the problem of flying saucers would be a good idea. Astronomer *GG* had the suggestion that St. Elmo's fire should be induced artificially to see if this is one of the causes of the numerous sightings of lights by pilots.

Astronomer *HH*, whose professional rating is excellent, has made no sightings personally. He agreed that the conditions under which he would talk would be complete anonymity in reporting to a committee or even to one reputable astronomer in whom he had full confidence.

Astronomer *II*, with an adequate professional rating, has made two sightings personally. The sightings were two years apart. The first sighting, which was witnessed also by an astronomer not interviewed on this trip, occurred in this manner: A transport plane travelling

---

* Again, I do not think much of this astronomer's suggestion. It would serve to tell us how many people will report an unusual incident, which number can be compared with the number of people who report a typical sighting; if the numbers agree then this would be some proof that an actual object had been sighted in the latter cases. The confusion that would be created by this maneuver is hardly worth the while. Recently, the balloon sighting over Columbus gives us, in effect, the same results that Astronomer *FF* suggested. Certainly in this case hundreds, if not thousands or more people saw the balloons which, incidentally, were not spectacularly bright and could easily have escaped detection. It is interesting to note that the public at large is bcoming more aware of things which might pass for flying saucers and are becoming less gullible and trigger happy. The quality of reports should be going up, and it seems that greater degree of credence can be given to sightings reported by a group of people in each case. It is becoming less likely that any large group of people will be fooled by ordinary or even unusual aircraft, balloons, or meteors. This was not the case before the turn of the half century.

west made quite a bit of noise and Astronomer *II* looked up to watch it. He then noticed, above the transport and going north, a cluster of five ball-bearing-like objects. They moved rapidly and were not in sight very long. Two years after this sighting, he sighted a single such object which disappeared from sight by accelerating, probably by turning but not by going up quickly. Astronomer *II* is willing to cooperate but does not wish to have notoriety. Nevertheless, he would furnish further details, and Observer's Questionnaires should be sent to him.

Astronomer *JJ* has made no sightings himself, but agrees on the policy of reporting to a duly constituted panel if he should see any.

Astronomer *KK* has made no sightings and was not particularly interested in the problem.

Astronomer *LL*, Dr. La Paz, has already had so much publicity in *Life* magazine that there appears to be no reason for keeping his name secret. He is the Director of the Institute of Meteoritics at the University of New Mexico, and is cooperative in the extreme. One sighting of his has been described in *Life* magazine and also fully in OSI reports. He has made extensive reports about the green fireball sightings in New Mexico in OSI reports also.

The discussion of green fireballs with many astronomers disclosed that most of them were of the opinion that these were natural objects. However, close questioning revealed that they knew nothing of the actual sightings, of their frequency or anything much about them, and therefore cannot be taken seriously. This is characteristic of scientists in general when speaking about subjects which are not in their own immediate field of concern. Dr. La Paz has seen only one green fireball himself, but has been avid in collecting reports on the others. Because his full reports are in the OSI files, only the salient points will be discussed here. It appears that the green fireballs can be characterized by being extremely bright, most of them lighting up the sky in the daytime, estimated magnitude -12, which is extremely bright. They appear to come in bunches and at one time 10 were observed in 13 days.

No noise is associated with them despite their brightness. The light appears to be homogeneous, and their light curve resembles a square wave, that is, it comes on abruptly, remains constant while burning, and goes out exceedingly abruptly, as though it is snapped out by a push-button. They leave no trails or trains. As to their color, La Paz is aware of the fact that other meteors have a green color, but he insists that this is a different green, corresponding to the green line in the copper spectrum (5218 Angstrom units). These objects generally move in a preferential north-south, south-north direction.

If these data are correct, that is, if this many objects actually were seen, all extremely bright, all having this particular green color, all exhibiting no noise, all showing a preferential direction, all being homogeneous in light intensity, all snapping out very quickly, and all leaving no trails, then we can say with assurance that these were not astronomical objects. In the first place, any object as bright as this should have been reported from all over the world. This does not mean that any one object could have been seen all over the world, but if the earth in its orbit encountered, for some strange reason, a group of very large meteors, there is no reason that they should all show up in New Mexico. Besides, copper is not a plentiful element in meteors, and the typical fireball goes from dim to bright to very bright to bright and then fades out fairly fast, often breaking into many parts. They frequently leave a trail of smoke in the daytime and of luminescence at night. It is recommended that the OSI reports be obtained, and that the sightings of these fireballs be examined in detail. If the data as reported by La Paz are correct, then we do have a strange phenomena here indeed.

Astronomer *MM* has not seen any. He happened to be with me, however, while I interviewed some laymen who had seen some aluminum-colored discs. He was most impressed by the consistency of their stories.

Astronomer *NN* is Clyde Tombaugh, who has already been identified in the *Life* article. He has made two sightings, the first of which is the one reported in

Life magazine and the second was reported to me. The details can be obtained by sending him a questionnaire, as he is willing to cooperate. Briefly, while at Telescope No. 3 at White Sands, he observed an object of −6 magnitude (four times brighter than the planet Venus at its brightest) traveling from the zenith to the southern horizon in about three seconds. The object executed the same maneuvers as the nighttime luminous object which was reported in *Life* magazine. No sound was associated with either of the sightings.

Mr. Tombaugh is in charge of optics design and rocket tracking at White Sands Proving Ground. He said that if he is requested officially, which can be done by a letter to the Commanding General, Flight Determination Laboratory, White Sands Proving Ground, Las Cruces, New Mexico, he will be able to put his telescopes at White Sands at the disposal of the Air Force. He can have observers alerted and ready to take photographs should some object appear. I strongly recommend that this letter be sent.

Astronomer *OO* is a meteor observer at the Harvard Meteor Station in New Mexico. Although relatively new on the job, he observed two lights while on watch at 1:30 a.m. that moved much too fast for a plane and much too slow for a meteor. The two lights were white and moved in a parallel direction. It is recommended that an Observer's Questionnaire be sent to this observer, as his sighting bears a resemblance to the sighting made by Astronomer *R*. It was impossible to obtain full details of those sightings because this would have classed me as an official investigator. The details of these sightings should be obtained by official questionnaires.

A meteorologist at the Lowell Observatory is identified here as observer *PP*. He was not interviewed, but a clipping was obtained from a Flagstaff newspaper covering his observations made on May 27, 1950. The object was observed between 12:15 and 12:20 p.m. on Saturday, May 20, from the grounds of the Lowell Observatory. The object presented a bright visible disc to the naked eye and passed moderately rapidly in front of a fractocumulus cloud in the northwest. Upon passing in front of the cloud its appearance changed from that of a bright object to a dark object, due to the change in contrast. No engine noise was heard, nor was there any exhaust. It seems that this might have been a weather balloon but in this case it would be strange if this meteorologist would become confused by it. He reports that it was not moving with the wind, but across the wind.

Finally, in this survey of astronomers, my associates and I at the Perkins Observatory should be included. There are six of us there, and to the best of my knowledge, none of us has ever seen any unexplainable object in the skies.

While in Albuquerque, I met, through Dr. La Paz, a Dr. Everton Conger, Instructor in Journalism at the University of New Mexico. On July 27, 1948, between 8:35 and 8:45 a.m. he noticed a disc-shaped object in the sky. It was flat and round like a flat plate. It appeared to be made of duraluminum and gave off reflected light very similar to the light reflected from a highly polished airplane wing. The full details of his sighting are in my notes. I obtained his cooperation and he would be very glad to fill out an official questionnaire.

I also interviewed, while in Albuquerque, Mr. Redman and Mr. Morris, the two gentlemen whose picture appeared in *Life* magazine in the now-famous article on flying saucers. I questioned them separately and found that their stories were remarkably consistent. Indeed, since they viewed the object from widely different parts of the city, there is some possibility that the parallax of the object can be obtained by making theodolite sightings now on where the object appeared to them. The position of the object can be identified now because it was viewed close to a canyon in the mountains. Dr. La Paz has kindly offered to obtain the parallax of this object for us.

Summary and Discussion

Over 40 astronomers were interviewed of which five had made sightings of one sort or another. This is a higher percentage than among the populace at large. Perhaps this is to be expected, since astronomers do, after all, watch the skies. On the other hand, they will not likely be fooled by balloons, aircraft, and similar objects, as may the general populace.

It is interesting to remark upon the attitude of the astronomers interviewed. The great majority were neither hostile nor overly interested; they gave one the general feeling that all flying saucer reports could be explained as misrepresentations of well-known objects and that there was nothing intrinsic in the situation to cause concern. I took the time to talk rather seriously with a few of them, and to acquaint them with the fact that some of the sightings were truly puzzling and not at all easily explainable. Their interest was almost immediately aroused, indicating that their general lethargy is due to lack of information on the subject. And certainly another contributing factor to their desire not to talk about these things is their overwhelming fear of publicity. One headline in the nation's papers to the effect that "Astronomer Sees Flying Saucer" would be enough to brand the astronomer as questionable among his colleagues. Since I was able to talk with the men in confidence, I was able to gather very much more of their inner thoughts on the subject than a reporter or an interrogator would have been able to do. Actually hostility is rare; concern with their own immediate scientific problems is too great. There seems to be no convenient method by which to attack this problem, and most astronomers do not wish to become involved, not only because of the danger of publicity but because the data seem tenuous and unreliable.

Therefore, it is my considered recommendation that the following procedure be adopted by the Air Force.

First, the problem of unidentified aerial objects should be given the status of a scientific problem. In any scientific problem, the data are gathered with meticulous care and are weighed and considered, without rush, by entirely competent men. Therefore, it is proposed that some reputable group of scientists be asked to examine recent sightings which have already

282

gone through one or two screenings. If this group becomes convinced that the data are worthy of being treated as a scientific problem, that is, that the sightings are valid and that unexplained phenomena really do exist, then they should be asked to vouch that these data are "worthy of being admitted into court." Armed with this scientific opinion, various scientific societies should be approached. The American Physical Society, the American Astronomical Society, and the Optical Society of America are suggested, in particular. These Societies should be asked, in view of the validity of the data, to appoint one or more members to constitute a panel to advise ATIC and perhaps to direct the necessary researches into the phenomena. This would serve not only to work toward an ultimate solution of the problem, but in the meantime would lend dignity to the project.

In short, either the phenomena which have been observed are worthy of scientific attention or they are not. If they are, then the entire problem should be treated scientifically and without fanfare. It is presumed that the scientific panel would work with the full knowledge and cooperation of the general contractor, but would not be bound by secrecy, which would tend to hamper their work. It is possible that this panel might be a panel in the RDB, similar to those in geodesy, infrared, or upper atmospheric research.

In the meantime, it is recommended that the Air Force approach the Joint Chiefs of Staff for endorsement of a considered statement of philosophy and policy for presentation to the public press. There is much confusion in the public mind as to what is being done about the situation, and a great deal of needless criticism is being directed toward the Air Forces for "trying to cover up" or "dismissing the whole thing." The considered statement to the public press that the problem is being considered as a scientific one and is being referred to competent scientists in various fields should do a very great deal in satisfying the public clamour.

It may be, of course, that this proposal will not get

beyond the first step. The scientist, or scientists, who examine the carefully screened evidence may decide there still is not enough evidence to admit the problem into the court of scientific appeal. Personally, I hardly think that this will be the case, since the number of truly puzzling incidents is now impressive.

The second stage may be a long one. The first effort should be to determine with great accuracy what the phenomena to be explained really are and to establish their reality beyond all question.

Third stage would be the eventual publication of the findings of the scientific panel. This might take the form of a progress report. If, for instance, the scientific chase is led into a detailed examination of atmospheric optics, one can envision, perhaps, many years of work. This, however, is the price one pays for a truly scientific investigation.

One final item is that the flying-saucer sightings have not died down, as was confidently predicted some years ago when the first deluge of sightings was regarded as mass hysteria. Unless the problem is attacked scientifically, we can look forward to periodic recurrences of flying-saucer reports. It appears, indeed, that the flying saucer along with the automobile is here to stay, and if we can't shoo it away, we must try to understand it.

Appendix

While in Los Angeles, I was asked to appear in a TV program with Gerald Herd, the BBC science analyst; with Walter Riddel, the rocket expert; and with Aldous Huxley. They were to have a round-table discussion on flying saucers. I declined immediately but was prevailed upon to be in the studio when the program was in progress. I am afraid that my presence as an astronomer "cramped their style" to a great degree, but nonetheless the program had the general effect of convincing the hearers that flying saucers did exist. There was very little constructive about the program. It consisted of a rehash of all the things we have heard so much about already. It might be profitable, for instance, to have a TV program, sponsored by the Air Force, acquainting the public with the problem of flying saucers as a scientific problem. Though suggested jokingly, there might be some point to this, if this investigation ever gets to the scientific panel stage.

Chapter Twelve: The Soviet Effort to Contact Extraterrestrial Life

Section I
History of the Problem

The idea that intelligent beings might exist outside of the earth was debated in antiquity (Anaxagoras, Plutarch, Lucian, etc.). This speculation was frowned upon by the Catholic Church as contradictory to the Christian dogma of the uniqueness of man and his relation to the universe. During the Renaissance the idea of habitable worlds was again revived (Nicolaus, Cusanus, Giordano, Bruno, Kepler, etc.).

The telescope showed many details on the surface of the planets which generally favored the idea of habitability. It was assumed that man was the goal to which all creation moves and consequently, the celestial bodies did not have any reason to exist unless they served as homes for intelligent beings. In the 18th Century, such scientists as Huygens, Fontenelle, Swedenborg, and others wrote elaborate treatises on the supposed inhabitants of other planets, and even the great philosopher Kant thought that at least some of the planets besides the earth might be inhabited.

Further development of this idea occurred in the early 19th Century. Sir William Hershel, perhaps the greatest observational astronomer of all times, deduced from his own observations that the sun was really a dark body which very well might be inhabited. He theorized that the brilliant surface of the sun was actually its atmosphere and the so-called sunspots were simply the solid dark surface showing through the rifts of the atmosphere. The very influential French astronomer Arago, as late as 1850, could not find anything wrong with this theory.

In 1832, Von Littrow accepted the idea of J. Lambert (1750) that comets were undoubtedly inhabited and their extensive atmospheres had the purpose of mitigating and preserving the heat of the sun, which must vary greatly along the eccentric orbits of those bodies. Both men were leaders in the mathematical theory of comets.

On the moon the German astronomer Gruithuisen could see cities and railroads, and other astronomers speculated what function the rings of Saturn might have to make conditions there more comfortable for the intelligent beings which were undoubtedly there.

In the second half of the 19th Century the science of astrophysics was born and quickly showed that the conditions of the sun, moon, comets, and the majority of the planets were such as to preclude the existence of any life there. The only possibly habitable planets were Venus and Mars, and life on these was highly problematical. It became unfashionable to talk about inhabitants of other planets, and Lowell's ideas about the artificial origin of the canals on Mars was generally ridiculed.

A few hardy souls here and there continued to maintain that Mars must be habitable regardless of what scientists' observations indicated. In the U.S. such were E. C. Slipher and W. H. Pickering, in the USSR, G. A. Tikhov and especially K. E. Tsiolkovskiy. Tikhov remained essentially a scientist and only tried to prove that terrestrial plants can adapt themselves to the conditions on Mars. Tsiolkovskiy was a dreamer who threw caution to the winds. One of his books, constantly quoted by Soviet astronomers, has the revealing title "Dreams about the Earth and the

Heavens." With the development of rocket technology Tsiolkovskiy became in the USSR an almost infallible authority to be quoted alongside Lenin and Marx.

The novelists, as usual, were years behind the scientists. H. G. Wells' "The War of the Worlds" appeared in 1905. It was (and still is) extremely popular throughout the world, and many remember the panic in 1938 when this story was dramatized on the radio. Millions of people believed the Martians were landing in New Jersey and marching on New York City.

However, the scientists were rather cool toward the possibility of life on Mars or elsewhere outside the earth. Perhaps the lowest point in the belief of extraterrestrial life was reached in the 1920's when Sir James Jeans showed that the collision of two stars, according to him the only possible mode of the formation of a planetary system, is an extremely improbable event, and it may well be that the earth is a cosmic freak with some kind of mold on it called life.

Doubts were soon thrown on Jeans' theory of the origin of the solar system, and quiet investigations on the origin of life on the earth and other celestial bodies continued. In this respect, A. I. Oparin's work deserves to be mentioned. He is still Director of the Institute of Biochemistry, Academy of Sciences, USSR, and is the author of many articles and several books on this problem.

The situation changed radically with the postwar development of radio astronomy when it became possible to think of a direct contact with extraterrestrial civilizations by means of radio. The beginning of the new approach was sharply marked by the appearance in the British periodical "Nature" of a letter by two U.S. scientists, G. Cocconi and P. Morrison, "Searching for Interstellar Communications" (1959). This letter fired the imagination of many people including one of the remarkable Soviet scientists, I. S. Shklovskiy, the author of numerous articles and several books on the subject.

Shklovskiy's first book, "The Universe, Life, and Intelligence," appeared in 1962, its second edition in 1965. The first edition was revised by the author, translated by Paula Fern, annotated by the U.S. astronomer C. Sagan, and published in the U.S. in 1966 as "Intelligent Life in the Universe" by I. S. Shklovskiy and C. Sagan.

With the First Conference on "Extraterrestrial Civilizations" (Byurakan Observatory, May 20–23, 1964) which included all the leaders in radio astronomy and some optical astronomers, the problem can be said to have obtained the official recognition of the Soviet Union.

Before proceeding to the details of Soviet schemes for the establishment of contact with extraterrestrial civilizations it is important to realize that the whole problem hinges on the answers to three general questions:

(1) What is the origin of the solar system? Without knowing this answer it is not possible to decide whether planets are rare or common around the stars.

(2) What is the nature of life?

(3) What is the origin of life on the surface of the earth?

In spite of a very large amount of work, in both the East and West, no definite answers to these questions are available. We have to fall back on vague arguments such as "with so many stars some of them at least must have planets," etc. It is impossible at the present time to prove or disprove the existence of planets of the size of the earth even around the nearest stars, let alone life on these planets. Therefore, the existence of intelligent life elsewhere in the universe is at the present time an article of faith rather than a scientific fact. In this respect, scientists are in exactly the same position as their predecessors were in the 18th Century, or even the ancient Greeks 2,000 years ago. The only difference considered extremely significant by the proponents of life in the universe is modern man's possession of radio communication techniques capable of reaching out to 1,000 light years and more. How to utilize this capability is the subject of animated discussion among the radio astronomers in the West and the USSR.

Section II
Existence of Extraterrestrial Life

1. General Attitude

The Soviets are emphatic that their materialistic philosophy is in complete agreement with the idea of extraterrestrial civilizations. According to this philosophy, life is a normal and inevitable consequence of the development of matter, and intelligence is a normal consequence of the existence of life.

Even the best-informed scientists in the USSR, like Oparin and Shklovskiy, must necessarily subscribe to this crude philosophy promulgated more than 100 years ago by Marx and Engels. However, once having stated their materialistic point of view they often introduce reservations. Thus Oparin thinks that the presence of oceans was the necessary factor in the appearance of life on earth, and Shklovskiy is willing to accept the existence of life only on the earth, but this would be a "miracle."

2. What Kind of Life?

The Soviets seem to be committed to life based on the hydrocarbon compounds, that is essentially the same kind of life that exists on the earth, from bacteria to man. Oparin considers any other basis of life sheer impossibility, and at any rate devoid of any physical meaning. Shklovskiy goes into considerable detail to show by energy considerations that life must necessarily be based on hydrocarbon reactions.

Speculations common in the West about the possibility of life based on ammonia, or even inorganic compounds (as in Hoyle's novel "The Black Cloud" which appears to be not only alive but even intelligent) do not occur in Soviet literature.

3. Persistence of Terrestrial Type of Life

As conditions on the Moon, Venus, and Mars are known to be severe in terrestrial terms, the problem arises whether even the simplest terrestrial organisms like bacteria can exist there. Experiments to test bacteria and other simple organisms under these conditions are conducted in both the East and West, on a comparable scale. In the USSR, this is done in the Institute of Microbiology, Academy of Sciences, USSR, and probably other places. There is a recent report of the simulation of conditions on Mars for microbial growth by A. I. Zhukova and I. I. Kondrat'yev (1965) of that institute.

The problem has assumed considerable importance as terrestrial bacteria have been shown to possess remarkable endurance and adaptability in planetary conditions. The danger of contamination of planets by terrestrial micro-organisms exists and has required international cooperation since the introduction of space exploration.

4. Search for Life on Mars

Mars is the only planet where conditions remotely approach those on the earth. It was therefore natural that Mars became the focus of attention of astronomers and biologists looking for evidence of life elsewhere in the solar system.

In the U.S., the center of the study of Mars for a long time was the Lowell Observatory, Arizona, where Percival Lowell's work was continued by E. C. Slipher. In the USSR, an indefatigable searcher for evidence of life on Mars was Tikhov.

Tikhov (1875–1960) was a Pulkovo astronomer who had attained considerable international reputation for the excellence of his observational work. In 1909, during one of the great oppositions of Mars, he studied that planet through filters and proved the existence of snow near its poles and clouds in its atmosphere, in spite of the low position of the planet during observations. This work remained little known in the West, and was repeated at the next great opposition in 1924 with substantially the same results by W. H. Wright at Lick Observatory, California.

After his retirement from Pulkovo, Tikhov settled down in Alma-Ata, Kazakh S.S.R., and in 1947 formed there a "Sector of Astrobotany" at the Institute of Physics and Astronomy of the Academy of the Kazakh S.S.R. The idea of this sector (or section) was to study the behavior of plants in conditions approaching those of the Planet Mars, that is the Arctic tundra and high mountains.

Many astronomers and botanists worked at this section, which published five volumes of its proceedings (1947–1960). Although this work did not resolve the question of life on Mars, it nevertheless uncovered many remarkable instances of adaptation of plants to extreme climatic conditions. Tikhov's method of obtaining spectra of plants in reflected light to compare with the spectrum of Mars was later employed in the West, especially with the development of the infrared techniques.

With Tikhov's death his section was absorbed by the Institute of Astronomy. Tikhov's works were published in five volumes by the Academy of Sciences, Kazakh S.S.R. They contain 33 of his own papers on the problems of terrestrial plants and existence of life on Mars.

The results of investigations by Tikhov and his collaborators were indecisive so far as the existence of plants on Mars was concerned, paralleling similar results in the West. They simply increased the probability in favor of the existence of such life. The occurrence of intelligent life on Mars is even more difficult to prove than the existence of plants. Shklovskiy's point of view is that Mars once had a civilization which launched its artificial satellites, but is now a dead body.

The question of life on Mars will be resolved only with an actual visit there either of instrumented or manned vehicles. For this reason, emphasis is being given to the development of techniques for detecting the existence of life on Mars in both the U.S. and the USSR planetary exploration program. The discovery by Mariner 4 of craters on the surface of Mars, however, has little direct bearing on the problem of life there. The same can be said of the presumed absence of the Martian Canals.

Few astronomers believe that there can be any life on Venus or the moon. An exception is N. A. Kozyrev, a Soviet astronomer famous for his observations of the moon, who thinks that the high temperature of Venus refers to its ionosphere, and the surface may be in a condition to allow the development of life.

But even the moon cannot be assumed to be entirely devoid of life. Such is the opinion of A. I. Oparin, the greatest authority on such matters in the USSR. According to the TASS Agency (December 29, 1966), Oparin thinks that organic substances either alive or dead are possible on the moon.

Such an idea would probably be unacceptable in the West, but it was only 30 or 40 years ago that W. H. Pickering, an American astronomer, tried to explain various changes of tint in the moon by colonies of insects appearing and disappearing during the progress of the lunar day.

5. Meteorites and Life

Meteorites are the only bodies of extraterrestial origin that are available for a study in our laboratories. In connection with the problem of extraterrestrial life, a large number of mineralogists, physicists, biologists, etc., everywhere are studying meteorites. The proof of the existence of organic substances in meteorites would support the existence of life outside the earth, no matter what the ultimate origin of meteorites might be. But in this problem, as in all other problems concerning extraterrestrial life, there is no simple answer and no convincing proof of the existence of life. The problem has recently been reviewed by A. A. Imshenetskiy (1966), Director of the Institute of Micro-biology, Academy of Sciences, USSR, where many investigations of such nature are being carried out.

There are three items in meteorites which must be considered in this connection:

(a) Carbonaceous chondrites are stony meteorites which have some carbon matter (up to five per cent of weight) of possible organic origin. At the present time there are 30 meteorites of this class, which can be divided into three subclasses quite different from each other. At first it seemed that this is indisputable proof of the cosmic origin of organic matter, but later researches proved this improbable. The carbon-aceous matter is now considered to be of inorganic origin and similar to matter found in the terrestrial rocks.

(b) "Organized elements" in the same meteorites are small round grains which have been considered as possibly produced by plant spores. The best author-ity in the USSR on these problems, G. P. Vdovykin, does not think they are of organic origin at all.

(c) Bacteria in meteorites have been reported time and again both in the East and West. In every case they were proved to be introduced into the meteorite after its fall on the surface of the earth.

6. Soviet Attitude Toward Science Fiction

The idea of inhabited worlds naturally evokes in people all sorts of emotions which are not always amenable to scientific treatment. In the Soviet phi-losophy, scientific fiction occupies an honorable place provided that it is not represented as solid achieve-ments of science. Much of what Tsiolkovskiy wrote, for instance, can be characterized as science fiction, and one of the famous Soviet writers, Alexis Tolstoy, was famous for his fantastic stories. Academican Ob-ruchev, the explorer of Siberia, was also a science fiction writer.

However, the Soviets have attempted to draw a line separating science fiction from deliberate fraud and distortion of facts well established by science, and some Soviet scientists, principally astronomers, are busy refuting and criticizing sensationalism by writers who exhibit more exuberance than knowledge. One such writer is Kazantsev, the author of a fantastic tale, "Guest Out Of Cosmos" (1959), which has had its repercussions abroad also. The main idea is that the Tunguska meteor, which landed in Russia in 1908, was in reality a spaceship from Mars supplied with a hydrogen bomb. This ship blew up over Siberia, thus saving the earth from conquest by the Martians. Astronomer Yu. G. Perel' (1959) concedes that a fiction writer may invent anything he pleases, but Kazantsev represents his wild surmises and ignorant theories as scientifically established facts. Kazantsev, however, proceeded to attack official science as concealing from the public the true situations, etc., thus closely paralleling the UFO enthusiasts in the U.S. who accuse the Air Force of suppressing evidence supporting flying-saucer visitations.

Another line of pseudo-scientific effort is directed toward the discovery of traces of contacts of higher civilization with the earth. In the USSR, M. M. Agrest in 1959 put forward an idea that classical myths and biblical stories contain in them vague reminiscences of visits by extraterrestrial highly civilized beings. These are gods coming down to earth, angels flying through the air, destruction of Sodom and Gomorrah (evidently by an atomic bomb), kidnapping of people (the biblical Enoch) by the intruders, etc.

The search for information, however, is not restricted to the Bible. Anything is good if it points toward the existence of extraterrestrial civilizations; crude images on rocks in the Sahara, mythical small men in China, Peruvian fairy tales, are examples. More recently, in the Soviet popular magazine, "Sputnik," 1967, Nr. 1, there is an article by Vyacheslav Zaytsev, "Visitors from Outer Space," which is full of such stories. It is stated that the author spent 30 years of his life collecting this information.

To the credit of Shklovskiy (second edition of his

book, Chapter 23) he refutes many of the ridiculous stories which have been propagated very assiduously in the West, particularly in the U.S., where they have been adopted by the adherents of the UFO cult. Other serious Soviet writer-scientists like V. N. Komarov ("Man and Mysteries of the Universe," 1966) also exhibit an exemplary caution.

In general, it appears that the problem of sensationalism in science is exactly the same both in the USSR and the U.S. There are scientists interested in the problem of extraterrestrial civilizations and there are writers who want to publish a breathtaking book. There are even combinations of the two. In the USSR, Shklovskiy is not averse to publicizing his own wild ideas. In the West, there are F. Hoyle and George Gamow of the same type. Modern science is so fantastic that the boundary between possible and impossible is fairly indistinct. Some people, sometimes even bona fide scientists, simply cannot discern this boundary and mix up solid science, their unconscious desires, and fairy tales into a nightmarish whole. The Soviets cannot escape this situation any more than the Americans and West Europeans.

Section III
Possibility of Establishing Contact

In view of the complete absence of concrete data on extraterrestrial civilizations the only possible formulation of the problem is this: Assuming that there are extraterrestrial civilizations, what would be the best way of getting in touch with them? This problem is twofold: (1) How can understandable signals be transmitted and (2) how can signals from outer space be detected and interpreted?

Radio signals from other civilizations, no matter how clear and strong, would have had no significance 50 years ago, since nobody on earth could intercept them, let alone interpret. According to modern astrophysics the development of stars is a continuous process and they certainly were not all created at the same time. If there are planets around them, and if there is life on these planets, and if there are civilizations, they must be in various stages of development. The extraterrestrial civilizations obviously must be in a similar or higher state of development than our own in order to make a contact possible.

On the earth, life has existed for something like two or three billion years. Written documents can be traced for some 6,000 years, while in contrast the use of radio for interstellar communications is less than 20 years old. In other words, the time during which a civilization like ours is in a position to communicate with other civilizations is infinitesimally short in comparison with the duration of life on the planet, and age of the stars.

The next question is how long shall we have this ability to communicate with other civilizations, that is, how long is our civilization likely to endure? The answer to this can be based only on faith and temperament. Shklovskiy thinks that a civilization cannot last longer than 10,000 years, for which he is taken to task by his Soviet colleagues. According to the Communist conception our civilization, once reorganized by the adherents of Marx and Lenin, will go on forever as all sources of internal friction will be removed. Therefore, the duration of a civilization should be put down as 10^9 rather than 10^4 years. Western writers would tend to the longer time scale. It is, however, clear that the duration of a civilization is something that cannot be decided a priori. Our own civilization may be said to be 6,000 years old, and whether it will survive for another 4,000 years, or 400 years, or even 40 years is anybody's guess. Some thinkers, notably H. G. Wells and O. Spengler, were very pessimistic in this respect. It is well known that our civilization has had its ups and downs. The ancient Romans, for instance, were much more highly civilized than their descendants a thousand years later. Therefore, there is no need to postulate a complete distruction of our civilization in order to lose our ability for interstellar communication.

The duration of any civilization is accordingly a guess, and this factor makes all discussions about interstellar contacts very nearly a pure exchange of verbiage. Shklovskiy, for instance, develops a formula for the average distance between civilizations, d, depending on the time, T, of the duration of the existence of stars and, t, the duration of civilization:

$$d = 5.2 \ (T/t)^{1/3} \text{ parsecs}$$

If we put $T = 10^{10}$ years as commonly accepted and $t = 10^4$ years we compute the average distance between two civilizations in our galaxy to be 520 parsecs or about 1,700 light years. Shklovskiy is evidently afraid of his own result and is willing to take $t = 10^5$ to 10^6 years. Even in this case the distances come out on the order of 100 parsecs or 300 light years.

Similar calculations by L. M. Gindilis, reported in an article entitled, "The Possibilities of Communication with Extraterrestrial Civilizations" (Zemlya I Vselennaya, No. 1, 1965), are summarzied in Appendix I. Although the assumptions used in Gindilis's calculations are different from Shklovskiy's, Gindilis concludes that the distance between civilizations in a galaxy is not less than several hundred lights years and is probably more than a thousand light years.

Although the results of these two calculations differ, the important feature is that both calculations indicate the extremely large distance involved in attempting to establish communications with extraterrestrial civilizations.

The tremendous distance between the stars is another serious difficulty; they average out to about 3 parsecs or 10 light years, not to speak of the millions of light years separating us from other galaxies. The situation is thus not very encouraging even with the most favorable assmptions about the frequency of the planets and a simultaneous existence of highly developed civilizations on these planets. (Some of the planetary requirements for civilizations to evolve are given in Appendix II.) Soviet radio astronomers such as Troitskiy and Kotel'nikov think that 1,000 light years is the maximum distance at which interstellar communications have any meaning at all, and at this distance the existence of only one civilization similar to ours can be expected.

As is well known, Project Ozma in the U.S. was based on a much greater restriction of the problem. Only the nearest stars were considered and among these only those that were more or less in the same physical class as our sun. Only two stars γ Ceti and ϵ Eridani about 11 light years distant were tried. Signals in the hydrogen line 1420 Mc were sent to these stars from the National Radio Observatory in May–July 1960, and characteristics of the radio emission from these stars analyzed. No evidence of any artificial signals was discovered, and the answer to our own signals, if any, cannot be expected until 1982.

It is not known whether the Soviets ever attempted a similar experiment. They all quote the Ozma project, and the book "Interstellar Communications" published by the NASA in 1963 (in which the Ozma project is described) appears to be one of their fundamental information sources, although the Soviet expert Khaykin considers Ozma a waste of time and resources (Byurakan conference, p 90). The inference in most of the Soviet papers, however, seems to be that the Soviets have nothing to offer in the experimental line comparable even to the modest Project Ozma. Experience, however, with Soviet scientific practice, notably their withholding of information on recent scientific activities for several years as was the case with their radio telescope development, makes it advisable to exercise caution in ascertaining their status from published literature alone.

How can the existence of civilizations like ours be discovered? Shklovskiy points out that at least one indication of intelligent activity is available, i.e., the generation of electromagnetic energy by planets which, of course, at stellar distances would merge with their stars. He notes that there are several thousand radio and television stations on the earth, and taking their power into consideration concludes that the brightness

298

temperature of the earth in television wavelengths is some millions of degrees. Moreover, this temperature started rapidly increasing since about 1940. He speculates, therefore, that if a similar situation can be associated with one of the nearest stars it would be prima facie evidence of existence of intelligent life there. He cautions, however, that this possibility requires a long and careful survey of all sources of cosmic origin, something that is not very easy to organize.

Developing the idea of energy criterion, Kardashev points out that the earth civilization is currently utilizing 4×10^{19} ergs/sec and this quantity is rapidly increasing in an exponential way. By extrapolation he concludes that by the year 5000 A.D. humanity will consume 4×10^{33} ergs/sec, which is equal to the output of the sun and by the year 8000 A.D. to the energy output of the whole galaxy, that is 4×10^{44} ergs/sec.

Obviously such possibilities require the harnessing of the whole energy of the sun, of which the earth intercepts now only one part in two billion. Projects of this sort are in existence, one of them being Dyson's Sphere to capture and retain the energy of the sun. The utilization of the galaxy will then be the next problem.

Kardashev sets up a classification of civilizations according to the energy criteria as follows:

(1) Technological level approaches that of terrestrial civilization; consumption of energy 4×10^{19} ergs/sec.

(2) Civilization utilizing the whole energy of the star, that is, of the order 4×10^{33} ergs/sec.

(3) Civilization, having at its disposal the energy of its galaxy, is about 4×10^{44} ergs/sec.

Further, Kardashev, basing his argument on our own experience, thinks that Stage 1 is reached in a few billion years. Stage 2, according to him, should develop within several thousand years after Stage 1 had been reached. Stage 3 should be developed in not more than 10 million years after Stage 2. Thus indicating that the 10,000 years postulated by Shklovskiy for the existence of a civilization is not satisfactory to at least some Soviet astronomers.

The evidence of the existence of a civilization of Type 3 would consist of radio phenomena which could not be explained in any rational way. All this setting up of criteria is highly arbitrary as it presupposes complete understanding of radio astronomical processes, which is hardly the case.

An illustration of this humble truth is the controversy produced by Soviet astronomers over STA-21 and STA-102, that is, Nrs. 21 and 102 in the California Institute of Technology Catalogue of Cosmic Radio Sources. They were hastily declared as satisfying the requirements of civilizations of Type 3, and some more of such, LHE-210, LHE-459, and LHE-523, were found at GAISh.

So far as the situation with STA-102 is concerned much doubt has been thrown on Kardashev's claim that its period variation in radio frequency should be considered as an artificial signal with a period of 100 days, drawing our attention to this galaxy. Astronomers in the West failed to confirm its periodic variation and it is generally considered now of the quasar type, that is, a perfectly natural, although not yet perfectly understood, object.

Yu. N. Pariyskiy investigated, on Kardashev's request, sources STA-21 and STA-102 with the great Pulkovo radio telescope (Byurakan Conference, pp 54–60), but his conclusions are hardly in favor of the artificial origin of the radio emission from these two sources. He finds that their radio properties are similar to those of some other cosmic sources and the strength of the signals under the most favorable assumption exceeds by several orders of magnitude the strength that we can reasonably expect from civilizations of Class 2 or 3.

The criteria which an artificial signal from another civilization should satisfy, according to Kardashev, are:

(1) The small angular size of the source. This he considers an extremely important if not a

300

decisive indication of the artificiality of the source.

(2) Maximum intensity of signal in the range of 3-10 cm.

(3) Variability of the signal in time.

Much of the discussion at the Byurakan Conference was centered on these criteria, some participants declaring that many natural objects could satisfy them. V. I. Slysh (Byurakan Conference, pp 61–67) thinks that a simultaneous fulfillment of these criteria by a cosmic source would constitute a presumption (but not a proof) of its cosmic origin. The question whether a cosmic source is artificial or not can be settled according to Slysh only by a systematic survey of the whole sky by means of a radio interferometer with a resolving power 0.1″. This at least would eliminate all sources that are clearly natural, so that attention could be concentrated on a few suspicious objects. He does not indicate whether the Soviet technical capacity is adequate to meet this challenge.

1. Means of Communication

Assuming that there are extraterrestrial civilizations willing to communicate, consideration must be given to how this may be accomplished. There are three possible ways of doing this:

(a) Direct contact, that is, interstellar travel, seems to be excluded from serious consideration despite the fact that this mode of communication is the most appealing to human imagination. Even assuming that physiological requirements of inhabitants of various planets are identical, the problem of travel, aggravated by tremendous distances, still remains. The various proposals of photon rockets, etc. (for which Dr. Stanyukovich is famous in the USSR) taking advantage of the relativity dilatation of time will not be of much use even when they are technically possible. According to Sagan the flight with acceleration of 10 m/sec² would allow a trip to the Andromeda galaxy in 28 years so far as the passengers in the rocket are concerned. However, for the home civilization that sent them this would be equivalent to 1.5 million years. A round trip taking three million years is of doubtful value. The information returned may have been made obsolete by better systems developed after the mission departed.

(b) Radio contact is a method for exchange of signals which is now technically possible but the distances at which it is effective are very small in comparison with the size of the universe.

Only one way radio contact, of course, is not limited by distance. We may imagine a civilization in the Andromeda galaxy that sent out signals "to whom it may concern" a million and a half years ago. We would just now be receiving them.

(c) Possible contact by means of masers, lasers and other modern electronic means.

L. N. Gindilis (1965) in his survey of the problem gives a tabulation summarizing the present situation. This tabulation is shown in Table I, where d denotes the distance between civilizations in light years, and t_c the life-time of a civilization. This t_c as has already been remarked is of a highly speculative nature. Shklovskiy takes it to be of the order of 10,000 years. Gindilis thinks it should be billions of years, that is comparable to the life-time of the planets themselves.

TABLE I
TYPES OF CONTACT BETWEEN CIVILIZATIONS

Distance Between Civilizations, light years	Possible Types of Contact
$d < 100$	All types are possible.
$100 < d < 1,000$	(1) One-way radio communication
	(2) Two way radio communication possible
	(3) Direct contacts by bodily visit possible but unlikely
$1,000 < d < t_c$	(1) One-way radio communication
	(2) Direct contacts, if possible, will be only one way
$d > t_c$	Only one-way radio communication possible.

The bulk of discussion in the USSR (as well as in the West) is on the selection of suitable radio frequencies and other characteristics of radio waves for interstellar communications. The hydrogen wavelength 21 cm originally proposed as having a universal meaning and actually used in the Ozma project is objected to by many scientists both East and West. The reason for this is the abundance of interstellar hydrogen which places the high threshold of radio noise exactly in this line.

The choice of the wavelength for communication is, of course, badly restricted by the known properties of the earth's atmosphere. Moreover, it is equally restricted by the unknown properties of other bodies' atmospheres. It is easy to imagine a planetary atmosphere suitable for life having argon instead of nitrogen, which would radically change its transmission properties.

Perhaps the most thorough discussion of this problem was given by Kotel'nikov in the Byurakan Symposium (pp 113–120). The hydrogen wavelength 21 cm is assumed to be impractical for the above-mentioned reasons. He proposes a multi-channel receiver containing a large number of narrow-band filters. If a monochromatic signal of a certain frequency reaches the antenna it will be automatically recorded and an appropriate channel tuned to that frequency.

Even with this device the coverage of the whole sky is not an easy undertaking. Assuming a limiting distance of 1,000 light years, the number of stars in this space will be of the order of 10 million. To cover the whole sky including all these stars will take exactly one year utilizing antennas and recorders recommended by Kotel'nikov. Further, what guarantee is there that the signal will be detectable on exactly the date programmed for observation? Kotel-nikov's final conclusion is that it may be possible to discover a civilization of our type by our present radio means if it exists on one star out of 10^6. If this figure is one star out of 10^7 the discovery will be almost impossible, and if a civilization exists only on one star out of 10^8 its discovery will be impossible unless the radio apparatus becomes much more efficient. The criteria of one civilization per 10^6 stars corresponds statistically to the limiting distance of 500 light years. Thus a distance of only 500 to 1,000 light years must be considered as the limiting distance for interstellar communications.

V. S. Troitskiy (ibid., pp 97–112) by an entirely different line of reasoning comes to the same conclusion that even with a narrow direction signal the limiting distance of a civilization detectable by radio is about 1,000 light years. He estimates a power requirement for this distance on the order of 1.6×10^{16} watts. A brief discussion of power requirements from a Soviet reference is contained in Appendix III.

The problem of what to transmit to stellar civilizations and how to interpret signals received from them was only briefly treated at the Byurakan Conference. A. V. Gladkiy (pp 145–146) expressed only general ideas as to the form a language can take under different conditions. He is a member of the Institute of Mathematics, Siberian Section of the Academy of Sciences, USSR, and being a mathematician he declares that it should not be assumed that mathematics of our stellar correspondents will be the same as ours. A short discussion of the artificial language Lincos developed by the Dutch mathematician Hans Freudenthal does not indicate any Soviet originality in this direction. The attempt to unravel the meaning of the Mayan inscriptions of Yucatan by a mathematical analysis carried out by the same Mathematical Institute of Siberia was not well received in the West, and the Mayan language is probably much simpler than the language of a planet X attached to star Y in galaxy Z. The understanding of stellar language may possibly turn out to be a harder problem than sending or receiving stellar communications. Resolutions of the Byurakan Conference emphasize the importance of linguisitic studies in this connection.

As to the other than radio communications with stellar civilizations, the only promising means is an apparatus of the laser type. Shklovskiy discusses it in considerable detail (second edition, Chapter 20), but he cautions that it requires space platforms for its use which are not yet available. As Shklovskiy notes in the introduction to his book, the present rapid development of radio astronomy, gamma-ray astronomy, X-ray astronomy, etc., indicates possibilities never dreamed of just a few years ago. What is said about stellar civilizations today may become obsolete tomorrow.

The fundamental question whether extraterrestrial civilizations (or even life in general) exist at all has not been answered in these papers nor in similar papers in the West. Nor the next question, whether mankind is willing to put so much effort into a search which may well prove futile, likewise has not been settled.

The Soviets have something to say about this. They rationalize by noting that the development of methods for interstellar communications will be of the greatest advantage to radio technology in general regardless of what the radio technology was originally designed for.

There is also a curious utilitarian streak running through Soviet discussions. In the Soviet periodical ("Sputnik") (1967, Nr. 1, p. 179), e.g., the Nobel prize winner, Physical chemist, N. Semyonov, declares that the present knowledge and technology makes possible the regeneration of the atmosphere of Mars which could make Mars a suitable home for humans. Also, some Soviet writers are optimistic that the more advanced civilizations are very anxious to communicate their knowledge to us, even though the Soviets are at times quite unwilling to reveal many of their scientific advancements.

2. Associated Programs, Facilities and Personalities

The only solid basis for the estimate of the Soviet effort in establishing interstellar communications is the book "Extraterrestrial Civilizations" published by the Armenian Academy of Sciences in 1965. It consists of 13 papers delivered on this problem at a conference on May 20–23, 1964, at the Byurakan Observatory.

The titles of these papers, in many cases self-explanatory, are given in Appendix IV. There are other indications of the Soviet activity as noted in the text of this report but the total amount of information is very small. The Conference was titled the "First All-Union Conference devoted to the Problem of Extraterrestrial Civilizations." The second Conference was to be called in 1965 but there is no further reference to it in available Soviet scientific literature.

A condensed translation of the resolutions of the Byurakan Conference is given in Appendix V. In it there are a number of institutions in the USSR mentioned as suitable centers for the development of various problems connected with contacting extraterrestrial civilizations. Appendix VI shows two of the large radio antennas in the USSR.

One of the centers listed by the Byurakan Conference is GAISh (Shternberg Institute), where one of the most influential of the workers on these problems, I. S. Shklovskiy, is located. In a citation in connection with his election to the corresponding membership of the Academy of Sciences and award of the Lenin prize it is stated that he is in charge of a large theoretical and experimental section of the GAISh. Members of this section carry out astrophysical investigations utilizing the largest optical and radio telescopes, cosmic rockets, and artificial satellites ("Zemla i Vselennaya," 1966, Nr. 5, p. 3).

Research at the GAISh of interest in the present connection is carried out by N. S. Kardashev, G. B. Shalomtskiy and other associates of Shklovskiy. They are observing radio galaxies of the quasar type with radio instruments of FIAN (Physical Institute of the Academy of Sciences) on the wavelength 32.5 cm with a view of locating artificial sources.

Quasars are very small objects appearing like stars but with masses approaching those of galaxies. All this is not certain at all and there is no agreement in the interpretation of the observations. The smallness of the apparent size of quasars, which is of the order of 1", is according to Kardashev, a good indication of the possibility of their artificial origin.

It is impossible to say just what practical results of a program like this could be. Kardashev's attempt to explain the periodic fluctuations in the radio emission of source STA-102 (as has already been mentioned) as a communication signal has not been accepted in the West. At any rate, this research may be expected to shed some light on the nature of quasars.

Also, Kardashev and Pashchenko at GAISh (Shklovskiy-Sagan, p. 478) will be attempting to detect artificial signals on the 21 cm hydrogen wavelength. The anticipated power of the signals should be relatively great. A negative result from this search would indicate that in our galaxy there are no civilizations with power resources of the order 10^{33} ergs/sec. The investigations on the Andromeda galaxy, M31, will also be conducted. It is perhaps noteworthy that nothing of this can be found in the second edition of Shklovskiy's book, and Sagan inserted this paragraph evidently from direct contact with Shklovskiy. Also, an equivalent to this program does not exist in the West.

Nothing is known of the research programs in this connection at the Pulkovo Observatory or at any other institution named in the resolutions of the Byurakan conference.

In a book "Radio for 70 years" (1965), Siforov (pp 11–23) in an article titled "Radio Role in Space Exploration" fails to include in his scheme of five steps in the development of radio communications the problem of interstellar communication where it logically belongs. He devotes to this problem exactly two lines:

It is not impossible that by radio electronic means the problem of contact with intelligent beings elsewhere in the Universe will be solved.

Pariyskiy and Khaykin of Pulkovo in their review of the development of radio astronomy (ibid, pp 140–153) do mention the problem of interstellar communications in a few lines, but put their faith in the international radio telescope discussed at a meeting of International Radio Union (Tokyo, 1963). No concrete program at Pulkovo or any other place in the USSR is mentioned.

Also nothing is said about observational programs in the detailed review article by L. M. Gindilis (1965), although the picture of the Pulkovo (see Appendix VI) radio telescope is given with a caption:

Certain peculiar sources of radio emission that are suspected to be artificial have been investigated with this instrument.

This probably refers to resources STA-21 and STA-102, which were investigated on request from Kardashev (as discussed above), but not to any particular program of investigation.

The only practical approach to this problem would be the organization of a continuous radio survey of all objects within a certain distance, such as 1,000 light years, as indeed is recommended by the Byurakan Conference. This will be a gigantic program requiring monitoring some 10 million objects. Obviously an international cooperation is called for, especially so in the southern hemisphere, part of which is inaccessible to the Soviet astronomers. As the Soviets are already doing astronomical work in Chile this would be the logical place for the establishment of such a radio telescope for the purposes of such a survey.

Nothing illustrates better the importance of the subject of extraterrestrial civilizations in the USSR than a list of attendants at the Byurakan Conference of 1964 who either delivered papers themselves or participated in the ensuing discussion:

*1. V. A. Ambartsumyan, President, Academy of Sciences Armenian S.S.R.; Director, Byurakan Observatory.
*2. I. S. Shklovskiy, GAISh.
 3. G. A. Gurdzadyan, Byurakan.
 4. Ya. B. Zel'dovich, Member Academy of Sciences, USSR.
*5. V. A. Kotel'nikov, IRE, Member Academy of Sciences, USSR.

6. B. V. Kukarkin, Astronomical Council, Academy of Sciences, USSR, GAISh.
7. D. Ya. Martynov, GAISh.
*8. N. S. Kardashev, GAISh.
9. E. G. Mirzabekyan, Byurakan.
10. G. M. Ayvazan, Armenian Academy of Sciences.
11. P. M. Geruni, IRE, Armenian Academy of Sciences, USSR.
*12 Yu. N. Pariyskiy, Pulkovo·
13. I. D. Novikov, Mathematics Institute, Academy of Sciences, USSR.
14. Ye. Ya. Boguslavskiy, NII 885.
*15. V. I. Slysh, GAISh.
*16. L. I. Gudzenko, FIAN.
*17. B. N. Panovkin, Council for Radio Astronomy, Academy of Sciences, USSR.
18. A. A. Pistol'kors, Corresponding Member, Academy of Sciences, USSR.
*19. V. I. Siforov, Corresponding Member, Academy of Sciences, USSR; IRE.
20. V. A. Razin, NIRFI.
21. L. M. Gindilis, GAISh.
22. G. S. Saakyan, Byurakan.
*23. S. E. Khaykin, Pulkovo.
*24. G. M. Tovmasyan, Byurakan.
*25. V. S. Troitskiy, NIRFI, Director.
*26. N. A. Smirnova, Pulkovo.
*27. N. L. Kaydanovskiy, Pulkovo.
28. E. Ye. Khachikyan, Byurakan.
29. A. V. Gladkiy, Institute of Mathematics, Siberian Section, Academy of Sciences, USSR.

A few remarks can be made about these people.

* Denotes authors of the reports read at the Conference. The large number of radio astronomers from Byurakan Observatory may be explained by the fact that the Conference was held there. Otherwise, the largest number of representatives (6) was from the GAISh, that is, the Shternberg Astronomical Institute of Moscow University, which is an important organizational and observational center of all astronomical work in the USSR.

(1) *V. A. Ambartsumyan* is the best known theoretical astrophysicist in the USSR, highly respected at home and abroad. He is the past president of the International Astronomical Union, and a member of the Academy of Sciences, USSR. This is the first intimation of his interest in the problem of extraterrestrial civilizations, and his remarks at the meeting were of a general character, apparently made in his capacity as the host of the conference. As a serious worker in the problem he can probably be dismissed.

(2) *I. S. Shklovskiy* is the most picturesque figure in the above list. He is highly respected abroad for his contributions to theoretical astrophysics and radio astronomy, yet there is a streak in his make-up that baffles observers.

He enthusiastically accepted the idea of extraterrestrial civilizations, criticizing his predecessors Oparin and Fesenkov for their lack of imagination and "pedestrian" attitudes. His work is generally brilliant with a few odd ideas here and there.

One of these was his theory that the Martian satellites are artificial hollow bodies put up by the Martians some half a billion years ago before the Martian civilization expired. This reasoning is based on so many wild assumptions that some astronomers were convinced that it was a deliberate hoax to see how much nonsense they could swallow. Such hoaxes have occurred now and then in the history of science.

Anyway, Shklovskiy cannot ever claim priority in this idea. In 1950, a book was published in the U. S. by Gerald Heard under the title "Is Another World Watching?" The author believes the UFO's are coming from Mars, and its satellites are platforms for launching Martian flying saucers. There is more than one contact between the world of UFO's and scientific discussions of extraterrestrial civilizations.

But Shklovskiy's reputation apparently has not been damaged in spite of violent criticism of some of his work both at home and abroad. Last fall he was elected corresponding member of the Academy of Sciences, USSR. It is known also that he heads a large research group at the GAISh.

(6) and (7) are well known astronomers at the GAISh. Both, and especially Kukarkin, are political figures who get into everything in the way of astronomy at home and abroad.

(8) *N. S. Kardashev,* a pupil of Shklovskiy, is one of the ablest men at GAISh and is particularly interested in the problem.

(4) *Ya. B. Zel'dovich* is a theoretical physicist who has been connected with the FIAN and later with the Institute of Chemical Physics.

(5) *V. A. Kotel'nikov* is the Director of IRE (Institute of Radio Technics and Electronics) of the Academy of Sciences, USSR. He is known for his radar measurements of the planets. *V. I. Siforov* (19) is Director of the laboratories of IRE.

(25) *V. S. Troitskiy* is Director of NIRFI (Radio-Physics Institute at Gor'kiy University). He is the author of many papers on radio astronomy, and especially on the moon.

(12) *Yu. N. Pariyskiy,* (26) *N. A. Smirnova,* (23) *S. E. Khaykin,* and (27) *N. L. Kaydanovskiy* are Pulkovo radio astronomers.

(16) *L. I. Gudzenko* at the FIAN (Physical Institute of the Academy of Sciences, USSR) is prominent in radio astronomy work.

To the above mentioned persons we can add K. P. Stanyukovich, a rocket expert, who frequently writes on interstellar travel by means of photon rockets; V. I. Krasovskiy, an upper atmospheric specialist; V. A. Bronshten, and some others. The total number of scientists in the USSR actively interested in the problem of interstellar communications and extraterrestrial civilizations is probably in the neighborhood of 50.

Of special significance is the participation of Kotel'nikov and Siforov of IRE, both of whom are not only radio scientists of considerable standing but also (especially Siforov) influential political figures. Their activity in the problem of extraterrestrial civilizations indicates the degree of importance that the Soviet government attaches to it. If recommendations of the Byurakan Conference in regard to construction of new instruments, establishing special sections for the study

311

of the problem at various specified institutes, establishment of a special commission to deal with it, etc., are to be implemented (about which no recent information is available), Siforov and Kotel'nikov will play key roles. The presence of participants like Boguslavskiy, connected with Research Institute Nr 885, and a strange reference (in the resolutions) to P. Ya. 2427 may be indicative of a military interest in this topic.

Appendix I
Calculations by Gindilis *

The possibilities of communication with other civilizations depend upon the distances between them. This distance in turn is a function of the size of the universe and the number of civilizations in it.

Restricting himself to our own galaxy, Gindilis (1965) attempts to calculate the number of civilizations coexisting in time with our own. The following equation is used:

$$N_c = N k_1 k_2 p_1 p_2^r (t_c) \tag{1}$$

Where N_c = number of civilizations in our galaxy coexisting in time with our own.

N = total number of stars in our galaxy.

k_1 = factor that specifies the presence of planetary systems (therefore, Nk_1 is the number of planetary systems in the galaxy).

† k_2 = factor that specifies the planetary systems with conditions that are suitable for life to begin.

---

* "The Possibilities of Communication with Extraterrestrial Civilizations," by L. M. Gindilis. Foreign Technology Division translation number FTD-HT-66-517/1+2+4 dated 27 September 1966.

† Gindilis apparently has not defined this term accurately. In his calculations this term k_2 also includes a factor of the probability of how many planets within a planetary system have conditions suitable for life to begin. This second factor is not necessarily equal to one as is discussed in Appendix II.

p_1 = probability that life will begin on a planet with suitable conditions.

p_2 = probability that in the process of evolution of living matter on a given planet intelligent beings will develop that are capable of congregating into a society and creating their own civilization.

t_c = lifetime of technologically developed civilizations.

According to Gindilis only the factor k_1 can presently be evaluated more or less reliably. The evaluation is based on a study of the rotational velocity of stars of different spectral classes.

"As we move along the spectral sequence from stars of type 0 to stars of type M the temperature of the surface layers changes continuously. Other characteristics of stars, for example, their mass, their luminosity, etc., also change continuously. But the rotational velocity changes continuously only for stars of the early spectral classes from 0 to F2. Around the F2 class the rotational velocity changes sharply, almost stepwise. The equatorial regions of those stars that are hotter than the F2 class rotate with a velocity greater than 100 km/sec. Stars of the later spectral classes G, K and M practically do not rotate at all: their equatorial velocity is several km/sec. We have the impression that, for some reason, in the process of their development the stars of these spectral classes have lost their initial angular momentum, due to which their velocity is significantly reduced. It is curious that the magnitude of the lost momentum for the stars of the same type as the sun corresponds to the angular momentum of our planetary system. From this we can make a very plausible conclusion that the loss of angular momentum is connected with the formation of planetary systems around the stars in a definite stage of their evolution. One possible mechanism for transferring the angular momentum from a star to the forming planets, in which the role of the transfer agent is played by a magnetic field, was proposed by the English astrophysicist Hoyle. If these presentations are valid, then we can assume that there are planetary systems around all the stars whose spectral classes are

313

later than F2. The overwhelming majority of the stars of the galaxy satisfy this condition, i.e., the k_1 factor in formula (1) must be close to unity."

Gindilis also points out that another important argument in favor of a large number of planetary systems in the galaxy results from observations of "Barnard's Flying Star." Because this star is very close to the solar system (closest to us after Proxima and Alpha Centauri) it moves rapidly along the celestial sphere in comparison with other stars. Barnard's Flying Star is a red dwarf of the M5 spectral class with a mass of 0.15 that of the sun. Van de Kamp (American) observed that the proper motion (path across the celestial sphere) of this star has periodic oscillations caused by the presence of an invisible dark satellite. The satellite is dark because its mass is only about 1.5 times that of Jupiter and therefore cannot be self-luminous. This could be a giant planet rotating around the star along a strongly elongated orbit.

Professor B. V. Kukarkin (USSR) has noted that wobbling could also be caused by a system of several planets similar to our planetary system, provided the periods of rotation of the planets are approximately commensurate. Kukarkin suggests that the proper motion of our sun would appear to another civilization's astronomers to be satisfied by the presence of one giant dark satellite with a period of about 60 years. This is explained by the approximate commensurability of the periods of rotation of the two largest planets of our solar system: five periods of Jupiter correspond to 59.3 years, two periods of Saturn correspond to 58.9 years.

Gindilis continues, "These arguments are not, of course, strong proof of the existence of planetary systems around many stars. However, they indicate that there is a weighty basis for such an assumption. Most investigators consider that planetary systems are well spread throughout the galaxy and that their number can attain one hundred billion ($k_1 \sim 1$).

"Of course, not all planets are suitable for the evolution of life. Evaluating the number of planets with conditions suitable for life is a rather difficult problem,

314

if only because we know nothing about the life forms that can develop on other planets. We shall not consider this question. The reader can find details about this in the exceptional book of I. S. Shklovskiy 'Universe, Life, Intelligence,' in the books of A. I. Oparin and V. G. Fesenkov, 'Life in the Universe,' and Kh. Shepli, 'Stars and People.' The limits for the factor k_2 given there lie in the range from 10^{-6} to 0.06. From this the number of planets in the galaxy with conditions suitable for life is from 10^5 to 10^{10}."

If the element of randomness is excluded, and it is assumed that life must arise in the presence of the necessary conditions (according to Gindilis many scientists think so) then $p_1 = 1$.

Even with the above assumption there is no guarantee that once life has begun it will necessarily evolve into intelligent life. According to Professor A. A. Neyfakh (USSR) even insignificant difference in the physical conditions on different planets in comparison to terrestrial conditions can cause difference in the period of evolution by one or two orders of magnitude.

Because intelligent life developed on earth, the factor p_2 is greater than zero, but from the above discussion not necessarily equal to unity. Thus there is a definite probability that on a planet where some life has developed, this life at sometime in the future will have evolved into intelligent thinking beings. As evident from the preceding discussion, it is not possible to determine this probability p_2.

As described in the main text there is no agreement as to the time span of a civilization. One view is that the lifetime of a civilization t_c is limited and regardless of its length (hundreds, thousands, or millions of years) is small when compared to the cosmic time scale T. Another view is that the lifetime of a technologically developed civilization is indefinitely large and can be only compared with the age of the oldest objects in the universe.

The form of the function $f(t_c)$ depends upon the point of view with regard to the time span of a civilization.

315

If $t_c << T$,

   then $f(t_c) = \dfrac{t_c}{T}$

If $t_c \sim T$,

   then $f(t_c) = \dfrac{(T - T_0)}{T}$

where T_0 is the time between the formation of a planetary system and the appearance of a technologically developed civilization on it.

Assuming the lifetime of a civilization is limited, the following variables may be substituted into equation (1):

Nk_1k_2 = between 10^5 and 10^{10}

P_1 and P_2 unknown but greater than zero and less than or equal to one.

$f(t_c) = \dfrac{t_c}{T}$ where T is generally accepted in 10^{10}

Upon substituting into equation (1) under the premise that one wishes to calculate the maximum number of civilizations, the following result is obtained:

$N_c \sim t_c$

Therefore in the most favorable case the number of civilizations coexisting with ours in the galaxy is equal in order of magnitude to their lifetime t_c in years.

Gindilis then quotes two evaluations of the number of civilizations, the first evaluation is that there are not less than one per 10^{12} stars (not less than one civilization in five neighboring galaxies). The second evaluation, more optimistic, is that there is one civilization per 10^6 stars or on the order of 10^5 civilizations in the galaxy.

Gindilis then calculates the average distance d between civilizations in the galaxy by using the following formula:

$d = d_0 \ (N/N_c)^{\frac{1}{3}}$

where d_0 is the average distance between neighboring stars, then assuming $d_0 = 7$ light years one may calculate the average distance d, given values of N and t_c. These results are shown in Table II.

Based on Table II and his discussion about the possible number of civilizations in the galaxy, Gindilis concludes that the distance between civilizations is not less than several hundreds of light years, and it is probably more than a thousand light years.

TABLE II
Distance between civilizations as a function of the number of civilizations.

N/N_c	N_c	d (in light years)
10^2	10^9	32
10^3	10^8	70
10^4	10^7	150
10^5	10^6	320
10^6	10^5	700
10^7	10^4	1500
10^8	10^3	3200
10^9	10^2	7000

Appendix II
Planetary Requirements

If one assumes that the process of the beginning and evolution of life on other planets must be similar to the Earth's (as maintained by Soviet astrophysicist I. S. Shklovskiy), the following series of planetary requirements must be met.

1. "Planets on which life may begin and develop may not evolve too close to or too far away from their star, and their surface temperatures must be favorable to the development of life. However, taking into account that a comparatively large number of planets, say about ten, can originate simultaneously with the star, it may be reasonably expected that at least one or two of them may rotate at distances at which the temperature range remains within the required limits. It is very unlikely that the red dwarfs of the spectral

class M, and even later subclasses K, would sustain life on their planets since their radiation energy is insufficient.

2. The mass of an inhabitable planet must be neither too large nor too small. If the gravitational field of a planet is too strong, the original hydrogen-rich atmosphere will not be able to evolve (by a process involving the escape of hydrogen into space) into the oxygen-containing air on which the advanced terrestrial type of life depends; if the gravitational field is too weak, the atmosphere will escape into space early in the planet's history (Mercury is such an example).

3. A highly organized life may be found only on planets circling sufficiently old stars whose ages may be estimated at several billion years, since enormous intervals of time are necessary for the appearance of any intelligent species on a suitable planet.

4. The star must not vary significantly in its brightness for several billion years. During this time it must reliably and continuously pour forth a steady stream of light and energy, never once pulsating or altering its output to any significant degree. Most stars meet this condition.

5. The star must not be of multiple type, otherwise the orbital motion of its planets would be substantially different from the circular, and the resulting sharp, if not catastrophic, temperature variations on the planet's surface would preclude the possibility of life developing." *

Not all Soviet scientists completely agree with the listed requirement. F. A. Tsilsin (of the State Astronomical Institute), for example, does not agree that only single stars are capable of having planets which fulfill the other outlined requirements. Tsilsin goes on to point out three instances where a binary star system could have an inhabited planet. In the first of these the two stars are very close together and the planet rotates around their common center of gravity. In the second instance the two stars are far apart and one

---

* The quotation taken from ATD Report 66–57.

or both have a planet rotating around them in the favorable temperature zone. In the last case a planet is considered to be in the libration point of the binary star.

Although it's not agreed that each factor listed must be met for intelligent life to develop, as evidenced by the preceding discussion, the list does serve to indicate some of the considerations necessary in trying to accurately determine the probability that intelligent life exists elsewhere.

Appendix III
Power Requirements

In considering a radio communication link between our civilization and another civilization, it is of interest to determine the power which must be radiated in the direction of the other civilization.

The power requirement can be calculated by the following equation:

$$W = I_r \left(\frac{\lambda}{d_1}\right)^2 2 \left(\frac{\lambda}{d_2}\right)^2 2R^2 \qquad (1)$$

where d_1 = diameter of the transmitting reflector
d_2 = diameter of the receiving reflector
R = distance between reflectors
Equation (1) reduces to:

$$W = I_r \left(\frac{\lambda}{d_1}\right)^2 2 \left(\frac{\lambda}{d_2}\right) R^2 =$$

$$10^{-24.2} \frac{R^2}{d_1^2 \ d_2^2} \ \text{watt/cps} \qquad (2)$$

under the assumption that the hydrogen radio frequency line is used and that the other civilization is at a rather high galactic latitude where the level of interference (determined by the cosmic radiation background) is much smaller. Two types of interference which have to be considered are radio emissions from the star around which the inhabited planet revolves and background cosmic radiation. The intensity of

319

this interstellar interference in the radio-frequency line is not greater than that of the continuous galaxy radio-frequency emission in the same spectral range, which is equal to $10^{-21.5}$ cw/m^2 ster/cps for comparatively large angular distances from the Milky Way band. In the Milky Way the intensity of the hydrogen radio-frequency line is several dozen times greater than the magnitude at the higher galactic latitudes.

As an example, assume that $d_1 = d_2 = 80$ m and that the other civilization is 10 lights years away ($R = 10$). Substituting these values into equation (2), W must be greater than or equal to 100 watts/cps, which is already feasible. It is quite possible that the other civilizations could have a much greater transmission capability and much larger antenna systems than does our civilization. Either or both of these conditions would allow communications over larger distances. Much larger reflectors are being considered which could also increase the radius of communication possibilities. The calculation has shown that communications with other civilizations can be accomplished with modern equipment.

Appendix IV
Papers Read at the Byurakan Conference

1. V. A. Ambartsumyan, Introduction, pp 7–11.
2. I. S. Shklovskiy, "Multiplicity of Inhabited Worlds and the Problem of Establishing Contacts Between Them," pp 15–34.
3. N. S. Kardashev, "Transmittal of Information by the Extraterrestrial Civilizations," pp 37–53.
4. Yu. N. Pariyskiy, "Observations of Peculiar Radio Sources STA-21 and STA-102 in Pulkovo," pp 54–60.
5. V. I. Slysh, "Radio Astronomy Criteria of Artificiality of Radio Sources," pp 61–67.
6. L. I. Gudzenko and B. N. Panovkin, "On the Problem of Reception of Signals From Extraterrestrial Civilizations," pp 58–61.

Appendix V
Resolutions of the Byurakan Conference
May 20–23, 1964

1. Although materialistic philosophy favors the existence of intelligent extraterrestrial life, at the present time there is no valid proof of such life. However, there are strong indications that such life might exist and might develop civilizations.

A contact with extraterrestrial civilizations would be of the highest importance and interest but until very recently such a contact was clearly impossible. At the present time, however, there is a possibility of establishing interstellar communications by means of electromagnetic waves. The best range for this purpose are frequencies 10^9 to 10^{11}, that is the region of centimeter and decimeter waves.

The present-day technology allows the registration of radio signals across stellar distances. A rapid development of cybernetics makes it possible to formulate the problem of cosmic linguistics. The rapid growth of scientific literature on these subjects, and the first practical steps made in the U.S. to contact extraterrestrial civilizations, clearly show that interstellar communication is an actual scientific problem.

2. It is therefore necessary to undertake the development of an experimental as well as theoretical approach to this problem.

A. Experimental work should be conducted along the following two lines of effort:

(a) A systematic survey of the sky in order to detect signals from objects within 1,000 light years, and sending signals within that distance to possible cosmic correspondents.

(b) A search for signals from the substantially more developed civilizations than our own by applying a careful analysis to discrete cosmic radio sources suspected to be of artificial origin.

To carry out these projects, it is necessary to utilize the already existing apparatus and set up radio interferometers with long base lines of the order of 10^6 to 10^7 λ's, in the centimeter wavelengths.

B. It is necessary to continue and intensify optical investigations having a bearing on the above-mentioned programs. This would include work on planetary and stellar cosmogony, a search for planetary systems, identification of radio sources, and an organization of special investigations outside the atmosphere of the earth.

C. Along with these programs there should be organized studies in adjacent fields:

(a) A theoretical study of statistical properties of artificial radio sources, that is, the establishment of criteria for the artificiality of signals and the development of methods for the discovery of artificial signals. Further, it is necessary to develop methods of analysis of the statistical properties of radio signals and apply these methods to cosmic sources of suspected artificial origin.

(b) Development of methods of establishing contact and of a cosmic language on the basis of the general theory of linguistics. Also, the development of the theory of decipherment and of the basic principles of the theory of learning.

3. To carry out these programs it is desirable to establish in a number of scientific organizations special working groups. The institutions recommended for this purpose are:

GAISh (Shternberg Astronomical Institute, Moscow University)

GAOAN SSSR (Pulkovo Astronomical Observatory)

BAO AN ArmSSR (Byurakan Astronomical Observatory)

NIRFI (Radio-Physical Institute at Gor'kiy University)

IRE (Institute of Radio Technology and Electronics, AN SSSR)

Siberian Section of the Academy of Sciences, USSR

Mechanical-mathematical Faculty of Moscow University

P. Ya. 2427 (Post Office Box 2427, of some unidentified radio institute).

4. For coordination of research work in various organizations the Astronomical Council and the Council for Radio Astronomy of the Academy of Sciences, USSR, are asked to organize a special Commission for Interstellar Communications. This Commission should be empowered:

(a) Using the available optical and radio astronomy information to work out for the next conference a program of search for the artificial cosmic sources. A possibility of international cooperation in this task should be considered.

(b) Paying attention to the recommendations of the present conference to work out during 1964–1965 a plan for technical and financial assistance in the problem of interstellar communications. This plan should include the construction of appropriate radio telescopes and of receiving and analyzing apparatus.

The personnel of the proposed commission is recommended as follows:

I. S. Shklovskiy, GAISh, MGU

V. S. Troitskiy, NIRFI, Gor'kiy University

G. M. Tovmasyan, Byurakan Observatory, Armenian AN

Yu. P. Pariyskiy, GAO AN SSR (Pulkovo)

N. S. Kardashev, GAISh, MGU

L. M. Gindilis, GAISh, MGU

B. N. Panovkin, Council for Radio Astronomy, AN SSSr

5. It is considered desirable to call the next conference on the problem of extraterrestrial civilizations and interstellar communications in 1965.

6. It is proposed to ask the Academy of Sciences, Armenian SSR, to publish the proceedings of the present conference as a separate book.

Chapter Thirteen: UFO Research Today—from Condon toward 2001

It no doubt came as something of a surprise when a demand that UFOs be studied seriously issued from the pen of astronomer Dr. J. Allen Hynek, the Air Force's chief debunker of saucer sightings for so many years.

In an open letter to the editor of Science magazine, dated August 1, 1966, Dr. Hynek criticized the American scientific establishment for failing to properly investigate the persistent reports of UFOs.

. . . Each wave of sightings adds to the accumulation of both the misidentifications of otherwise familiar things (still the great majority) and to the reports which, by present methods of attack, defy analysis. All this has increased my own concern and sense of personal responsibility and motivated me to urge the initiation of a meaningful scientific investigation of the UFO phenomenon by physical and social scientists.

324

I had guardedly raised this suggestion in the past . . . and at various official hearings, but with little success. UFO was a term that called forth buffoonery and caustic banter; hence no scientist would look at it. It remained a topic for buffoonery and caustic banter precisely because scientists paid no attention to the raw data—the reports themselves.

Hynek expressed his pleasure that the Air Force had made funds available for a respectable, scholarly study of the UFO phenomenon (he was referring to a $313,000 grant to the University of Colorado initiated in October, 1966) and stated that he felt he could be of greater service to his colleagues by

setting forth something of what I have learned during my "travels," particularly as it relates to frequently made statements about UFOs which may lead to misconceptions they may unwittingly subscribe to. Some of these statements are:

Only UFO 'buffs' report UFOs: The exact opposite is much nearer the truth. Only a negligible handful of reports submitted to the Air Force, or to any other organization so far as I know, are from the 'true believer,' the same who attend UFO conventions and who are members of the 'gee-whiz' groups . . . It has been my experience that quite generally the truly puzzling reports come from people who have *not* given much or any thought to UFOs, generally considering them "bunk" until shaken by their own experience.

UFOs are reported by unreliable, unstable, and uneducated people: . . . UFOs are reported in even greater numbers by reliable, stable, and educated people. The better, more articulate and coherent reports predicate a fairly high threshold of intelligence; dullards rarely overcome the inertia inherent in gettting down to making a written report.

UFOs are never reported by scientifically trained people: This is unequivocally false. Some of the very best, most coherent reports have come from scientifically trained people. It is true, however, that scientists are among the most reluctant to make a report, and to have it made public . . .

UFOs never are seen clearly or at close range, but are seen under conditions of great uncertainty and always reported vaguely: . . . this is precisely the reason I called for scientific attention to the UFO phenomenon. It is such reports, and only such reports, that I have felt deserved the attention of physical and social scientists of stature with a respectable and scholarly study. I have in my files several hundred reports which are real brain teasers and could easily be made the subject of profitable discussion among physical and social scientists alike.

The Air Force has no evidence that UFOs are extraterrestrial or represent advanced technology of any kind: This is a true statement, and an honest one, but which is widely interpreted to mean that there is evidence against the two hypotheses . . .

UFO reports are generated by publicity: Positive feedback is undoubtedly at work when sightings are widely publicized. On the other hand, some of the sightings that are reported at times of high publicity come from reliable people who request anonymity, and who state that if they had not heard of reports from other ostensibly reliable persons, they would never have mentioned their own experience for fear of ridicule . . .

UFOs have never been sighted on radar or photographed by meteor or satellite tracking cameras: This statement is not equivalent to saying that radars, meteor cameras, and satellite tracking stations have not picked up "oddities" on their scopes or films that have remained unidentified. It has been lightly assumed that although unidentified, the oddities were not *unidentifiable* as conventional objects. One should consider, however, the existence of such odd photographs as those of a "retrograde satellite," taken in 1958, and the puzzling reports from several Moonwatch Teams during the IGY. I have seen photographs taken with the Baker-Nunn tracking cameras that contained unexplained "satellite" trails . . .

Dr. Hynek concluded by stating that his concern for serious study of UFOs had become intensified by "noting a pattern emerge after many years of 'monitoring the phenomenon.' This pattern suggests that 'something is going on.'

"I cannot dismiss the UFO phenomenon with a shrug. I have begun to feel that there is a tendency in 20th century science to forget that there will be a 21st century science, and, indeed, a 30th century science, from which vantage points our knowledge of the universe may appear quite diferent than it does to us. We suffer, perhaps, from temporal provincialism, a form of arrogance that has always irritated posterity."

It seemed as though the demand for a serious scientific investigation of UFOs might be at last realized when the Air Force Office of Scientific Research awarded that $313,000 grant to the University of Colorado for an eighteen-month study of the enigma. Dr. Edward U. Condon, former director of the National Bureau of Standards, then a professor of physics at the university, was to head the "totally independent study."

Major Hector Quintanella, Director of Project Blue Book at that time, stressed in his press releases that the Air Force was passing the ball to the University of Colorado and would neither interfere with nor influence the study in any way: "The only involvement of Project Blue Book with the Colorado contract is to provide them with duplicates of all current UFO reports and such material from our files as they may ask for," Major Quintanella stated.

The following "UFO Investigator's Conference Trip Report" was made by USAF Capt. C. H. Van Diver, Chief of Safety, after his attendance at a meeting held at the University of Colorado on June 12–13, 1967, nine months after Condon's committee had received the project from the Air Force:

a. Dr. E. V. Condon—head of the University of Colorado's UFO Investigative Program—opened the session with a brief history of UFO's:

(1) The first reported sighting was at Mt. Rainier in 1947; the object sighted was described as being saucer shaped, hence, the present name.

(2) In December of the same year, the DOD delegated all investigative responsibility to the Air Force since it was felt that if a threat existed, either from outer space or a foreign government, the Air Force would be best equipped to handle it.

(3) In 1952, the CIA established a panel for review of all sightings to date. Their report was classified, for unknown reasons, but is essentially declassified now and was mostly routine with explanations of the sightings in the large majority of the cases.

(4) In 1966, due to much criticism of Air Force handling, i.e., a small part of the populace felt the Air Force was concealing the facts, etc., the University of Colorado received a grant from the DOD to investigate—in conjunction with the Air Force—and determine if there was any valid evidence to support the hypothesis that we are receiving extra terrestrial visitors. (Item of interest: Religious cults/sects have been established that believe Jesus lives on Venus. Some persons claim they have made round trips—on inter-planetary vehicles—to that planet and made direct contact with Him).

b. Dr. R. J. Low followed Dr. Condon and discussed the UFO problem in general:

(1) The University of Colorado first thought a methodology of study on the UFO problem could be established after an initial 90 day analysis period; at the end of 180 days, a valid methodology had not yet been produced. Primarily, this was due to their inability to correlate the sightings with science, i.e., controlled experiments which produce valid data or unconfirmed sightings. (One would think, after 20 years, that one of these supposedly extra-terrestrial visitors would have been captured.)

(2) Dr. Low continued by stating that because of the inconclusive and inadequate facts available, an

328

attorney has been hired to produce a judgment—on those facts available—to determine whether we should continue to investigate and spend large amounts of taxpayers' money or to discontinue the project at the end of the University of Colorado's investigative period in the early spring of 1968.

(3) Dr. Low stated other studies include:

(a) Human perception.

(b) Press coverage. (Is there an interconnection or correlation between press coverage and the sightings?)

(c) Optical mirage problems. (Refraction/simulation effects.)

(d) Instrumentation. (Is present instrumentation and personnel sufficient, i.e., radar, FAA, weather observers, astronomers, etc.)

(e) To what extent do the reports of UFO's reflect the culture of the times.

(f) Radioactive charge gasses emitted from the sun.

(g) The production of valid photographic evidence.

(h) Possible conspiracy. (Yes or no. If not, how do you convince the public?)

Between 1947 and 1965, the mean unidentified sightings represent 6.4% of the total; however, nearly 20% were unidentified because of "other" and "insufficient data."

Those which are astronomical were not reported by qualified astronomers. The astronomical sightings break down thusly:

Meteors	1,295
Stars, planets	805
Other	67
Total	2,167

The miscellaneous sighting include missiles, hoaxes, flares, fireworks, mirages, searchlights, chaff, birds, satellite decay, radar analysis, reflections, clouds, and contrails, etc.

* * *

d. Dr. M. M. Wertheimer, psychologist, next presented problems of human perception starting with the transmitted energy from the distal event to the proximal stimulus, sensation, perception, cognition and hence to the report to someone, i.e., police, Air Force, etc., and eventually to the University of Colorado. He discussed the following perception stimuli and relationships:

(1) Dust on the cornea of the eye.

(2) Pressure, either external by the fingers or by electrical means, can cause unusual visual images.

(3) After-images from staring at a light source.

(4) Auto kinetics.

(5) Apparent size of image or after-image. (This varies with distance, that is to say, the various sizes can appear the same size with varying distances).

(6) Distortions and illusions.

(7) Gamma movement. (A light the size of a searchlight does not go out or disappear all at once when turned off, but rather seems to fade away).

(8) Personnel error in estimation of celestial angles. (This is consistently wrong when near zero degrees or ninety degrees.)

(9) Persons who read about UFO's are more likely to report a UFO.

(10) Non-scientific personalities are more likely to report UFO's.

(11) All "personal recollection" very unreliable.

(12) Photos. (Hoaxes and defects in developing, i.e., reflection and refraction of light source.)

e. Drs. D. R. Saunders and J. H. Rush followed with examples of some of the instrumentation required for the conducting of UFO investigaitons. They compared gaseous light sources to incandescent or tungsten light sources with interpretations of their various spectras. Their presentation included the various types of films available and their usage, and the various angles from which photographs should be made—if we ever have the opportunity to witness this phenomenon. Dr. Saunders also covered routine investigative techniques including the witness interview, compilation of data, analysis, and validity of the sighting, etc. (This technique is the same as that used in aircraft accident investigations.)

2. And last, but not least, we were instructed to keep "open minds" at all times during our investigations. Since we are now in a period in which space travel lies just ahead, it is within the realm of possibility that others (extra-terrestrial in nature) may also have the same capability. (Did I tell you about the individual who came into the Safety Office last week and wanted to know whom he could contact to obtain information on how to build a flying saucer?)

From certain comments and parenthetical asides in the above report, it would seem that a sense of levity must have been interjected from time to time at the conference. This seems quite proper. No one wants to listen to hours of reports and statistics without the welcome leavening of an occasional bit of humor. But it is also apparent that many of the UFO myths which Dr. Hynek sought to dissipate in his open letter were being steadfastly perpetuated.

From the beginning of the Condon Committee's research there were rumors that the whole affair was designed to be nothing more than an official whitewash and cover-up that would, hopefully, extirpate the entire matter of UFOs forever from the American public's consciousness and concern. The optimists in the civilian UFO research groups tried to discount such allegations as the paranoid mumblings of the eternally discontented in their ranks.

But even the most determined and cooperative UFOlogists were dismayed when author John G. Fuller reprinted the damning and controversial memo that Project Coordinator Robert J. Low issued on August 9, 1966, two months before the University of Colorado had been officially awarded the Air Force contract:

"The trick would be, I think, to describe the project so that, to the public, it would appear a totally objective study but, to the scientific community, would present the image of a group of nonbelievers trying their best to be objective but having an almost zero expectation of finding a saucer."

Can a scientific investigative group that sets out on a research project with "almost" zero expectation be considered either scientific or objective? And, of course, the use of the word "trick" is especially lamentable and damaging.

Low goes on to state that one way of carrying on the charade for the gullible public, while winking a knowing eye at the scientific community, would be to "stress investigation, not of the physical phenomena, but rather of the people who do the observing—the psychology and sociology of persons and groups who report seeing UFOs. If the emphasis were put there, rather than on examination of the old question of the physical reality of the saucer, I think the scientific community would quickly get the message."

And the message would be that people who report seeing UFOs are either kooks, crackpots, cultists, or scientifically unsophisticated dolts who misinterpret natural phenomena. The Condon Committee would, therefore, conduct a study peopled almost exclusively "by nonbelievers who, although they couldn't possibly prove a negative result, could, and probably would, add an impressive body of evidence that there is no reality to the [UFO] observations."

While the aware and interested public and the optimistic UFOlogists were awaiting the release of the Condon Committee's two-year study, Fuller's article reproducing the damaging memo was published in the May 14, 1968, issue of Look magazine. David R. Saunders, formerly a Condon Committee Co-Principal Investigator, also beat Condon's **Scientific Study of Unidentified Flying Objects** * to the newsstands with his **UFOs? Yes!**

* Bantam Books, January 1969.

Where The Condon Committee Went Wrong.*
If the Condon Committee had deliberately sought
to smother UFO research or had simply been too
biased from the outset to conduct any semblance
of an objective investigation, the informed public
was not accepting the insulting tone of their
simplistic dismissal of the UFO phenomenon. As
author John Keel wrote at the time:

A large part of the University of Colorado Report,
Scientific Study of Unidentified Flying Objects, is
neither scientific nor objective. "It was the report of
a scientific project commissioned by the U.S. Air
Force at a cost of over $600,000. Many UFO re-
searchers, such as Major Donald Keyhoe, James Mc-
Donald and John Fuller, are attacked in the text.
And Edward Condon, head of the project, has used
the report for personal vindictiveness.

Over fifty per cent of the Condon Report consists
of reprints of old Air Force releases and often ir-
relevant papers and essays on astronomical, meteorological, and other mundane phenomena. These
materials were obtained at little or no cost to the project
and serve only as 'padding.' Many of the charts and
graphs included date back to the early 1950's. *No*
effort was made to update these materials.

No effort was made to collect, correlate and present
accurate data on the thousands of UFO reports received and allegedly studied by the projects during
the 1966–68 period. The deletion of even a basic
total of the number of reports received is inexcus-
able.

The individual sections of the report are filled with
contradictions. It is obvious that the various contrib-
utors were unfamiliar with the research and findings
of their own colleagues. The report is very poorly
organized and appears to have been thrown together
at the last minute by a group neither informed nor
interested in the subject.

* David R. Saunders with R. Roger Harkins. Signet Books,
Desember 1968.

The contents of the report do not justify the great expense involved. The same kind of report could probably have been assembled by any publishing house for a few thousand dollars.

The Colorado Project clearly represents a conscious effort to satisfy the needs of the Air Force contract, but does not indicate a sincere effort to collect and examine the basic UFO data. Its main theme is the criticism of the extraterrestrial thesis. A genuinely scientific study would have first collected sufficient data to determine whether or not a phenomenon existed at all. Then *all* the various theories would have been studied and compared with the available data. Sighting factors of time, geography, terrestrial features, the correlative aspects in the witnesses' backgrounds and features in their reports, must all be sifted and weighed before any theory can be considered. This type of systematic study was not undertaken. Instead, the project treated the reports individually. They repeated the common mistake of the civilian UFO groups and tried to prove or disprove the individual events. Doctors seeking a cure for cancer do not study individual cases.*

J. Allen Hynek's review of **Scientific Study of Unidentified Flying Objects** appeared in the April 1969 **Bulletin of the Atomic Scientists:**

While devoted in large part to exposing hoaxes or revealing many UFOs as mis-identifications of common occurrences, the book leaves the same strange, inexplicable residue of unknowns which has plagued the U.S. Air Force investigation for 20 years. In fact, the percentage of "unknowns" in the Condon report appears to be even higher than in the Air Force investigation . . . which led to the Condon investigation in the first place. Every contributor to the report finds in his particular area of examination (photos, radar-visual sightings, physical evidence, etc.) something that

* From *Anomaly*, 1969 (a privately circulated newsletter published by Mr. Keel—ed.).

cannot be dismissed as a misidentification of known phenomena.

On the basis of many years experience with the UFO phenomenon, I would have deleted nearly two-thirds of the cases included in the report as potentially profitless for the avowed purposes of the project . . . Examining reports that stem from obvious . . . mis-identification of planets, stars, etc., can add little to scientific knowledge. Far greater care should have been taken in screening cases to be studied . . .

Both the public and the project staff . . . have confused the UFO problem with the ETI (extra-terrestrial intelligence) hypothesis. This may hold the greatest popular interest, but it is not the issue. The issue is: Does a legitimate UFO phenomenon exist?

Let us suppose that a committee of nineteenth century scientists had been asked to investigate the phenomenon of the aurora borealis as a single project. It would not have been responsible to state that the polar phenomenon gave no evidence of the existence of some meta-terrestrial intelligence. The issue would have been whether the aurora could be explained in terms of nineteenth century physics.

It may be that UFO phenomena are just as inexplicable in terms of twentieth century physics . . . [how does] the Condon Report serve science when it suggests that a phenomenon which has been reported by many thousands of people over so long a time is unworthy of further scientific attention?

Surely part of the reason why the Condon Committee's denial of the UFO as a matter for serious scientific investigation was not accepted as an official decree was the statistical fact that more and more people throughout the world were having sightings of their own. In 1967, public opinion polls indicated that more than fifty million Americans believed in UFOs. In 1974, public opinion polls reported that more than 15 million Americans claimed to have seen a UFO.

In the early days of UFOlogy, the various civilian

groups had been regarded as centers of bizarre hobbyist activity. Their literature was considered a perverse offshoot of science fiction for either the war-of-the-worlds paranoids or the there's-a-heavenly-place-somewhere escapists. In 1965, however, when **Look** magazine assigned author John Fuller to investigate a series of sightings in Exeter, New Hampshire, a publishing and public opinion breakthrough was in the making. Fuller's rational approach to the subject was published in **Look**'s high-circulation pages and later issued in book form.*

While Fuller was researching the UFO phenomena in Exeter, he learned the amazing story of Betty and Barney Hill, a couple who had suffered lacunar amnesia while on a motor trip in 1961. Later, when hypnotized by psychiatrist Benjamin Simon, they related an account of having been taken aboard a UFO and subjected to a physical examination by small UFOnauts. A condensed version of the story was again printed in **Look**, and excerpts of [Hills'] **The Interrupted Journey** (1966) were later carried by syndicated feature services in dozens of newspapers throughout the nation. Such a wide circulation of UFO material, which formerly had been considered fodder for the flying saucer freaks, created both a demand for more knowledge of the subject and a more serious approach to the matter by the scientific and academic sorts who had been steadfastly pooh-poohing the UFO.

Broadcaster Frank Edwards' **Flying Saucers: Serious Business** was released at the peak of the 1966 UFO flap. In a matter of weeks, the book had sold over fifty thousand hardcover copies. If nothing else, the newly alerted publishers were deciding that UFOs really were "serious business" at the cash registers. By mid-1967 **Paperbound Books in Print** listed thirty UFO titles.

Among the potboilers and paperback quickies, a

* *Incident at Exeter*, 1966.

serious UFO literature was in the process of evolution. Jacques Vallee's statistical and scientific analysis of UFOs, **Anatomy of a Phenomenon,** had appeared with little fanfare in 1965, but it was quickly reissued in paperback. Longtime strange-phenomena writer Vincent Gaddis published **Mysterious Fires and Lights** (1967), an interesting compilation of electromagnetic and UFO-related phenomena. Gaddis's friend and associate, zoologist Ivan T. Sanderson, turned his considerable talents to bear on the mystery with **Uninvited Visitors** (1967).

British author John Mitchell contributed two provocative studies. The **Flying Saucer Vision** dealt with UFOs as a modern myth, and **The View Over Atlantis** (1969) set forth his study of "ley lines," an ancient grid of trails which appear to link Great Britain's megalithic monuments. Mitchell gave birth to a whole new aspect of the mystery when, in the course of his research, he found that other ancient peoples had established grid works along the paths supposedly followed by mysterious aerial objects.

Closely associated with the question of ley lines is the phenomenon of Orthoteny, a term coined by French researcher-writer Aimé Michel. An authority on psychic research, Michel began an intensive study of UFOs after many sightings and landings in France in 1952–54. It became his contention that the UFOs followed straight lines for great distances. **Flying Saucers and the Straight-Line Mystery** appeared in 1956 and created interest only among the more scientifically minded UFO buffs. Michel's theories did not receive wide circulation until the UFO publishing explosion in 1966–67.

Aviation Week & Space Technology editor Philip J. Klass made his bid for the role of chief UFO debunker with **UFOs Identified** (1968). His assertion that nearly all UFO reports could be attributed to sightings of "natural plasmas of ionized air" resurrected a concept that had been studied by the USAF in 1948 and dismissed as untenable.

As Senior Physicist of the Institute of Atmo-

337

spheric physics and Professor in the Department of Meteorology at the University of Arizona, the late Dr. James McDonald commented before the House Committee on Space and Astronautics on the possibility that UFOs might be attributed to ball lightning or plasma: "It is true that a very small fraction of all the raw reports involve misidentified atmospheric phenomena . . . but in my opinion we cannot explain away UFOs on either meteorological or astronomical grounds . . . Klass has, in my opinion, ignored most of what is known about ball lightning and most of what is known about plasmas and also most of what is known about interesting UFOs in developing his curious thesis. It cannot be regarded as a scientifically significant contribution or illuminating the UFO problem."

In **Passport to Magonia** (1969) Dr. Jacques Vallee dropped the "nuts and bolts" aspect of statistically evaluating UFOs and considered how very much the fairy lore of Europe compared to contemporary UFO reports. Dr. Vallee suggested that it was not unreasonable to draw parallels between accounts of religious apparitions, reports of dwarflike beings with supernatural powers, and earlier accounts of miraculous airships with the modern tales of UFO landings. It was Vallee's argument that "the mechanisms that have generated these various beliefs are identical."

Brinsley Le Poer Trench, an early editor of Great Britain's fine **Flying Saucer Review,** had some years before begun an important study of historical material and myths in relationship to the UFO enigma. His **The Sky People** (1906) and **Men Among Mankind** (1963) broke ground that would later be effectively seeded by Englishman Raymond W. Drake and Frenchman Paul Misraki. Along with Trench, Drake and Misraki sought to demonstrate how ancient writers had left a literary legacy of mysterious objects sighted in the skies, of historic religious and occult events that had been influenced by the UFO phenomenon in ways ranging from subtle to overt.

It was not until Erich von Däniken's **Chariots of the Gods?** was published in 1970 that the concept of "ancient astronauts" became acceptable in the United States. Aided by the popularity of a television special and a later adaptation of theatrical release, **Chariots** soared to the top of the best-seller charts and prompted instant imitators and the reissuance of earlier books on the subject.

At the time of the 1966 UFO flap, television writer John A. Keel began to turn his keen research talents to the enigma. Through a series of articles in **Saga, True,** and **Flying Saucer Review,** Keel established a reputation as a man who was following his own path, a path that was leading away from the generally accepted extraterrestrial hypothesis.

Keel combined mysticism, psychic phenomena, esoteric occult practices, monster sightings, and a veritable catalog of the bizarre and unexplained for a landmark book entitled **UFOs: Operation Trojan Horse** (1970). Keel suggested that the purpose of the UFO mystery was other than it appeared and that those several, ostensibly disparate phenomena, which man has forever categorized in widely different areas, might well have a common single source, regardless of the frame of reference in which they may have occurred.

Neither the buffs nor the UFOlogical establishment were ready for Keel's thesis. His **Strange Creatures From Time and Space** was issued that same year in an original paperback format. Because his monumental **Trojan Horse** had become unmanageable in terms of sheer bulk, **Creatures** consisted largely of material culled from the larger work. It was more successful because, shorn of most of Keel's theorizing, it could be judged as one of the many "stranger-than" paperbacks which were flourishing at that time.

Keel's **Mothman Prophecies** (1975), a personal memoir of his experiences investigating a weird

339

winged entity, UFOs, men-in-black "silencers," and the tragic collapse of the Silver Bridge at Point Pleasant, West Virginia, was considered too "far-out." His **The Eighth Tower** (1975) was judged too dour, somber, and pessimistic for safe consumption, and Keel's detractors contented themselves with calling him "unscientific" rather than confronting his hypotheses.

But, whether universally acknowledged or not among hardcore UFO researchers, the course had been set for a New UFOlogy devoted to understanding the mechanisms of belief rather than perpetuating the beliefs generated by those mechanisms.

"In recent times I have come to support less and less the idea that UFOs are 'nuts and bolts' spacecraft from other worlds," Dr. Hynek stated in the August 1976 issue of **UFO Report**. "There are just too many things going against this theory . . . I think we must begin to re-examine the evidence. We must begin to look closer to home."

When interviewer Timothy Green Beckley asked Hynek how he reacted to the suggestion that UFOs might originate from another time-space continuum or dimension, the former Project Blue Book astronomer answered by stating that he would now assess the extraterrestrial theory as "naive."

It's the simplest of all hypotheses, but not a very likely explanation for the phenomenon we have seen manifesting itself over centuries . . . We should take into consideration the various factors which strongly suggest a linkage, or at least a parallelism, with occurrences of a paranormal nature.

Among the factors which belie the interplanetary theory is the proneness of certain individuals to have reported UFO experiences.

Another peculiarity is the alleged ability of certain UFOs to dematerialize . . . There are quite a few reported instances where two distinctly different UFOs hovering in a clear sky will converge and eventually fuse into one object.

These are the types of psychic phenomena that are confronting us in the UFO mystery.

Today Hynek, one-time chief official UFO debunker for Project Blue Book, is Director of the Center for UFO Studies, 924 Chicago Avenue, Evanston, Illinois 60201. All reports by UFO witnesses are welcomed. No names will be used in any published account without prior consent having been issued.

"I'm anxiously waiting for the curtain to rise and the next act to begin," Hynek told **UFO Report**. "I do not know what they [UFOs] have in store for us, but it should be interesting.

"We have behaved quite foolishly in the past. For several decades, there has been a tremendous amount of buffoonery. We've been party to a three-ring circus.

"Anything that is as farfetched as flying saucers will always be laughed at, out of hand.

"What we really need to do is change our whole attitude and manner of thinking. Remember what George Bernard Shaw once said, 'All great ideas begin as heresies!' "

One important lesson that quantum physics is teaching us is that we cannot observe reality without changing reality. As John Wheeler of Princeton University states is: "In some strange sense, this is a participatory universe. What we have been accustomed to call 'physical reality' turns out to be largely a papier mâché construction of our imagination plastered in between the solid iron pillars of our observations. These observations constitute the only reality. Until we see why the universe is built this way, we have not understood the first thing about it . . . We will first understand how simple the universe is when we recognize how strange it is."

We might say the same things of the UFO

341

mystery. It may at last be revealed as a remarkably simple construct when once we recognize how wonderfully strange it is and that it involves our participation and our interaction as integral elements of our greater reality.

My first published works in the paranormal and UFO research field appeared in 1956. **Gods of Aquarius: UFOs and the Transformation of Man*** presents both my current theories and the hypotheses of others as to what the UFO phenomenon is really all about and what its central purpose really is.

I have come to the conclusion that some **external intelligence** has interacted with mankind throughout history in an effort to learn more about us—or in an effort to communicate certain basic truths and concepts to our species. I am also convinced that there is a subtle kind of symbiotic relationship which exists between mankind and the UFO intelligences. I think that in some way, which we have yet to determine, they need us as much as we need them. It is quite possible that either one or both of our species might once have had an extraterrestrial origin, but the important thing is that the very biological and spiritual evolution of Earth may depend upon the establishment of equilibrium between us and our cosmic cousins.

I do not dogmatically rule out the extraterrestrial hypothesis, but I do lean toward the theory that UFOs may be our neighbors right around the corner in another space-time continuum. What we have thus far been labeling "space ships" may be, in reality, multidimensional mechanisms or psychic constructs of our paraphysical companions.

I have even come to suspect that, in some instances, what we have been terming "spaceships" may actually be a form of higher intelligence, rather than vehicles transporting occupants.

I feel, too, that these intelligences have the ability to influence the human mind telepathically

* Harcourt Brace Jovanovich, 1976.

in order to project what may appear to be three-dimensional images to the witnesses of UFO activity. The image seen may depend in large part upon the preconceptions which the witness has about alien life forms, and thus our reported accounts of occupants run the gamut from Bug-Eyed Monster types to Little Green Men to Metaphysical Space Brothers.

The mechanism employed by the UFO entities is always relevant to the witness's time context. At the same time, the form in which the UFO construct appears—and the symbology it employs—are always timeless, archetypal, and instantly recognizable at one level of the beholder's consciousness. Elves, fairies, and angelic beings, it would seem, have been popular in all cultures and in all recorded time. The complete experience of any witness to UFO activity is quite probably part of the natural process whose actual purpose is simply too staggeringly complex for our desperately throbbing brains to deal with at this moment in time and space.

Jerome Clark and Loren Coleman, in their excellent **The Unidentified** (1975), state as their "First Law of Paraufology" that the UFO mystery is primarily subjective and symbolic. While they admit that the phenomenon is not without objective aspects, they maintain that such manifestations are only "subsidiary" displays "whose cause can be traced to certain extrasensory functions of the brain."

Their "Second Law of Paraufology" says that the objective manifestations associated with UFOs are "Psychokinetically-generated byproducts of those unconscious processes which shape a culture's vision of the Otherworld. Existing only temporarily, they are at best only quasi-physical."

What Clark and Coleman are saying here is that certain of mankind's psychic needs tap psychokinetic and other psi energy and fashion fairies, apparitions of the Virgin Mary, and UFOs—archetypes which we can experience only as images and

343

symbols. "The forms they assume are both ancient and modern," Clark and Coleman assert: "Ancient in the sense that they always have been instrinsic parts of the psyche; modern in that we perceive them in the context of ideas the conscious mind has acquired."

What the UFO myth is telling us, according to Clark and Coleman, is the following: "Man is on the brink of catastrophe because our age has denied him the capacity for belief in the magical and the wonderful. It has destroyed the mystical, nonrational elements which traditionally tied him to nature and his fellows. It has emphasized rationality to the exclusion of intuition, equations to the exclusion of dreams, male to the exclusion of female, machines to the exclusion of mysteries."

The UFO phenomenon has absorbed many of the ancient archetypes which spiritually evolving man has needed to believe in so that he might complete his world. If man does not once again achieve a balance within both his own and the collective psyche, the UFO myth tells us, nature will have its way.

"The collective unconscious, too long repressed, will burst free, overwhelm the world and usher in an era of madness, superstition and terror—with all their socio-political accounterments: war, anarchy, fascism," state Clark and Coleman.

There are several theories as to the UFOnauts' actual place of origin and their true identity. Every investigator, regardless of how open-minded he may hope to be, has his favorite location, whether physical or ethereal, for the agents of the apparently universal and timeless UFO phenomenon. Generally, these arguments are distilled to the central isue of whether the UFO intelligences are essentially nonphysical entities from an invisible realm in our own world or physical beings who have the ability to attain a state of invisibility and to materialize and dematerialize both their bodies and their vehicles.

Perhaps both theories are correct. We may be

344

confronted by both kinds of intelligence in our spiritual, intellectual, biological, evolutionary process.

Or we may be dealing with an intelligence that has a physical structure so totally unlike ours that it presents itself in a variety of guises and at times employs invisibility, materialization, and dematerialization in order to accomplish its goal of communication with our species.

UFO contactees often speak of an impending New Age wherein mankind will attain a new consciousness, a new awareness, and a higher state—or frequency—of vibration. They speak of each physical body being in a state of vibration and of all things vibrating at their individual frequencies.

The UFO intelligences, they say, come from higher dimensions all around us which function on different vibratory levels, just as there are various radio frequencies operating simultaneously in our environment. We can attune ourselves to these higher dimensions in much the same manner as a radio receiver tunes into the frequencies of broadcasting stations. Different entities travel on various frequencies, according to their vibratory rate.

In **Mysteries of Time and Space** [Dell, 1976], I suggested that some undeclared paraphysical opponents have engaged our species in what I call the Reality Game. When we have apprehended the true significance of this contest, we will attain such control of our life and our abilities that we will confront all aspects of existence with the same ease and freedom with which we would enter a game. I believe that this is a glorious way to approach life, truly reflective of mankind's noble, star-seeded heritage.

The distinguished scholar Joseph Campbell has observed that the most important function of a living mythological symbol is to waken and give guidance to the energies of life. Such a mythological symbol not only "turns a person on," but turns him in a specific direction which enables him to participate effectively in a functioning social group.

345

Dr. John W. Perry has identified the living mythological symbol as an "affect image"—an image which speaks directly to the feeling system and instantly elicits a response. If a symbol must first be "read" by the brain, it is already a dead symbol and will not produce a responding resonance within the reader. When the vital symbols of any given social group are able to evoke such resonances within all its members, ". . . a sort of magical accord unites them as one spirittual organism, functioning through members, who, through separate in space, are yet one in being and belief."

In my introduction to **Gods of Aquarius** I put forth my contention that the UFO provides contemporary man with a vital, living mythological symbol, an "affect image," which communicates directly to his essential self, bypassing the brain, evading acculturation, manipulating historical conditioning. I believe that the UFO will serve mankind as a transformative symbol that will unite our entire species as one spiritual organism, "functioning through members, who, though separate in space, are yet one in being and belief."

To suggest that the UFO is a living mythological symbol does not diminish its reality in an objective, physical sense. Indeed, the UFO may ultimately be more real than the transitory realities of computers, machines, associations, political parties, or détentes. Through the cosmic catharsis of dreams, visions, and inspirations, the UFO will serve as spiritual midwife to bring about manind's starbirth into the universe.

346

Appendix A: The Unidentified

Case No.	Date(s)	Witness(es)	Location
12	June 24, 1947		Portland, Oregon
27	July 3, 1947		South Brookville, Maine
34	July 4, 1947		Emmett, Idaho
36	July 6, 1947		Fairfield-Suisan AFB, California
50	July 8, 1947		Muroc AFB, California
69	July 29, 1947		Hamilton Field, California
85	September 3, 1947		Oswego, Oregon
91	October 1947	Civilian	Dodgeville, Wisconsin
95	October 14, 1947		Proenix, Arizona
139	April 5, 1948		Holloman AFB, New Mexico
185	July 29, 1948		Indianapolis, Indiana
190	July 31, 1948		Indianapolis, Indiana
191	July–August 1948		Marion, Virginia
208	September 23, 1948		San Pablo, California
218	October 15, 1948	Air visual and radio	Kyushu, Japan
257	December 3, 1948		Fairfield-Suisan AFB, California
275	January 4, 1949		Hickam Field Hawaii
284	January 27, 1949		Cortex, Florida
319	March 17–18, 1949	Multiple	Killeen Base, Camp Hood, Texas
358	April 24, 1949	Multiple	Arrey, New Mexico
361	April 28, 1949		Tucson, Arizona
376	May 5, 1949		Fort Bliss, Texas
379	May 6, 1949		Livermore, California
384	May 9, 1949		Tucson, Arizona
404	May 27, 1949		Southern, Oregon

483	July 24, 1949	Mountain Home, Idaho
496	July 30, 1949	Mount Hood, Oregon
642	February 24, 1950	Albuquerque, New Mexico
645	February 25, 1950 AESS personnel	Los Alamos, New Mexico
650	March 3, 1950	Selfridge AFB, Michigan
671	March 20, 1950	Stuttgart, Arkansas
678	March 27, 1950 Military radar	Motobu, Okinawa
680	March 28, 1950	Santiago, Chile
682	March 29, 1950	Marrowhode Lake, Tennessee
706	April 8, 1950	Kokomo, Indiana
711	April 14, 1950	Fort Monmouth, New Jersey
721	May 7, 1950	East Ely, Nevada
738	June 27, 1950	Texarkana, Texas
758	July 13, 1950	Redstone Arsenal, Georgia
773	August 4, 1950	North Atlantic
793	August 20, 1950	Nicosia, Cyprus
787	August 24, 1950 Air radar	Bermuda
790	August 30, 1950	Sandy Point, Newfoundland
797	September 3, 1950	Spokane, Washington
807	September 20, 1950	Kit Carson, Colorado
809	September 21, 1950	Provincetown, Massachusetts
819	October 15, 1950 "Reliable Observer"	Knoxville, Tennessee
821	October 15, 1950 Ground radar	Pope AFB, North Carolina
824	October 23, 1950	Bonlee, North Carolina
829	November 5, 1950	Oak Ridge, Tennessee
845	December 2, 1950	Nanyika, Kenya, Africa

Case No.	Date(s)	Witness(es)	Location
848	December 6, 1950	Air visual, military and civilian	Fort Meyers, Florida
849	December 11, 1950		Alaska
864	January 8, 1951		South of Fort Worth, Texas
868	January 12, 1951	Military	Fort Benning, Georgia
886	February 1, 1951	Military	Johnson AB, Japan
896	February 26, 1951	Multi (civilian)	Durban, South Africa
897	February 26, 1951		Ladd AFB, Alaska
907	March 13, 1951	Military and civilian	McClellan AFB, California
908	March 15, 1951		New Delhi, India
928	May 31, 1951	Military (multi)	Niagara Falls, New York
943	July 24, 1951		Portsmouth, New Hampshire
955	August 25, 1951	Military	Albuquerque, New Mexico
962	August 31, 1951		Matador, Texas
964	September 6, 1951	Military	Claremont, California
969	September 13, 1951	Ground radar	Goose AFB, Labrador
980	October 2, 1951	Graduate physicist	Columbus, Ohio
984	October 3, 1951	Military radar	Kadena, Okinawa
985	October 9, 1951		Terre Haute, Indiana
989	October 11, 1951	Multiple (ground and air)	Minneapolis, Minnesota
1011	December 18, 1951	Civilian (pilot)	Andrews AFB, Washington
1013	December 24, 1951	Military	Mankato, Minnesota
1021	December 7, 1951		Oak Ridge, Tennessee
1023	December 7, 1951		Sunbury, Ohio
1037	January 16, 1952	General Mills Research	Artesia, New Mexico

1052	February 11, 1952	Military	Pittsburgh, Pennsylvania
1061	February 23, 1952	Military	Sinuiju, North Korea
1074	March 20, 1952		Queen Annes City, Maryland
1076	March 22, 1952	Military (air visual)	Yakima, Washington
1077	March 24, 1952	Military radar	Point Conception, California
1082	March 29, 1952	Military	Misawa AFB, Japan
1095	April 5, 1952	Military radar	Duncanville, Texas
1097	April 5, 1952		Miami, Florida
1099	April 6, 1952		Temple, Texas
1108	April 12, 1952		North Bay, Ontario
1112	April 14, 1952		Memphis, Tennessee
1113	April 14, 1952	Central Airlines	La Crosse, Wisconsin
1115	April 15, 1952		Santa Cruz, California
1124	April 17, 1952		Longmeadow, Massachusetts
1127	April 17–18, 1952	Civilian	Yuma Test Station, Arizona
1128	April 18, 1952		Bethesda, Maryland
1129	April 18, 1952		Corner Brook, Newfoundland
1130	April 18, 1952	Military radar	Japan
1131	April 18, 1952		Corner Brook, Newfoundland
1144	April 22, 1952	Military	Okinawa
1147	April 24, 1952	Military	Bellevue Hill, Vermont
1148	April 24, 1952		Milton, Massachusetts
1151	April 24, 1952	Military	Clovis, New Mexico
1160	April 27, 1952		Roseville, Michigan
1163	April 27, 1952	Military	Yuma, Arizona
1167	April 29, 1952		Marshall, Texas

Case No.	Date(s)	Witness(es)	Location
1168	April 29, 1952	Military	North of Goodland, Kansas
1174	May 1, 1952		Moses Lake, Washington
1176	May 1, 952	Military	George AFB, California
1183	May 5, 1952		Tenafly, New Jersey
1185	May 7, 1952	Military	Keesler AFB, Mississippi
1194	May 9, 1952	Military	George AFB, California
1198	May 10, 1952	Civilian	Ellenton, South Carolina
1213	May 14, 1952		Puerto Rico
1219	May 20, 1952		Houston, Texas
1227	May 25, 1952		Walnut Lake, Michigan
1232	May 28, 1952	Multiple	Saigon, Indochina
1233	May 28, 1952		Albuquerque, New Mexico
1236	May 29, 1952	Military	San Antonio, Texas
1243	June 1, 1952	Military	Rapid City, South Dakota
1245	June 1, 1952		Walla Walla, Washington
1246	June 1, 1952		Soap Lake, Washington
1249	June 2, 1952		Bayview, Washington
1250	June 2, 1952	Military	Fulda, Germany
1255	June 5, 1952		Lubbock, Texas
1256	June 5, 1952	Military	Albuquerque, New Mexico
1257	June 5, 1952	Military	Offutt AFB, Nebraska
(Case missing)	June 6, 1952		Kimpo AB, Korea
1260	June 7, 1952	Military	Albuquerque, New Mexico
1263	June 8, 1952	Military	Albuquerque, New Mexico
(Case missing)	June 9, 1952		Minneapolis, Minnesota

352

1269	June 12, 1952	Military	Forth Smith, Arkansas
1270	June 12, 1952	Military radar	Marrakech, Morrocco
1273	June 13, 1952		Middletown, Pennsylvania
1285	June 15, 1952		Louisville, Kentucky
1295	June 16, 1952	Military	Walker AFB, New Mexico
1298	June 17, 1952	Multiple	McChord AFB, Washington
1299	June 17, 1952	Military	Cape Cod, Massachusetts
1302	June 18, 1952		Columbus, Wisconsin
1305	June 18, 1952		Pontiac, Michigan
1308	June 19, 1952	Military radar	Goose AFB, Labrador
1310	June 19, 1952	Military	Yuma, Arizona
1313	June 20, 1952	Military	Korea
1319	June 21, 1952	Military	Kelly AFB, Texas
1323	June 22, 1952	Military	Korea
1331	June 23, 1952		Spokane, Washington
1332	June 23, 1952	Military	McChord AFB, Washington
(Case missing)	June 23, 1952		Kirksville, Missouri
1334	June 23, 1952		Oak Ridge, Tennessee
1335	June 23, 1952		Near Owensboro, Kentucky
1340	June 25, 1952	Military	Tokyo, Japan
1344	June 25, 1952	Multiple	Chicago, Illinois
1347	June 25, 1952	Military	Japan, Korea Area
1348	June 26, 1952	Military	Terre Haute, Indiana
1351	June 26, 1952		Pottstown, Pennsylvania
1355	June 27, 1952	Military	Topeka, Kansas
1361	June 28, 1952	Civilian	Lake Kishkonoug, Wisconsin

Case No.	Date(s)	Witness(es)	Location
1363	June 28, 1952	Military	Nagoya, Honshu, Japan
1364	June 29, 1951	Military	O'Hare Airport, Chicago, Illinois
1380	July 3, 1952	Civilian	Selfridge AFB, Michigan
1382	July 3, 1952	Civilian	Chicago, Illinois
1390	July 5, 1952		Norman, Oklahoma
1397	July 6–12, 1952	Photos	Governors Island, New York
1405	July 9, 1952	Military	Colorado Springs, Colorado
1409	July 9, 1952	Military (photos)	Kutztown, Pennsylvania
1431	July 12, 1952		Annapolis, Maryland
1436	July 13, 1952	Military radar and scope photos	Kirksville, Missouri
1444	July 14, 1952		Norfolk, Virginia
1451	July 15, 1952		West Palm Beach, Florida
1476	July 17, 1952	Military	Lockbourne AFB, Ohio
1479	July 17, 1952	Military	Rapid City, South Dakota
1482	July 18, 1952	Military	Lockbourne AFB, Ohio
1483	July 18, 1952		Miami, Florida
1485	July 18, 1952	Multiple	Patrick AFB, Florida
1492	July 19, 1952	Civilian	Williston, North Dakota
1494	July 19, 1952	Military	Elkins Park, Pennsylvania
1501	July 16, 1952	Military (photos)	Beverlym, Massachusetts
1502	July 17, 1952		White Plains, New York
1504	July 20, 1952		Lavalette, New Jersey
1514	July 21, 1952	Military	Wiesbaden, Germany
1516	July 21, 1952	Military	San Marcos AFB, Texas

1522	July 21, 1952		Randolph AFB, Texas
1524	July 21, 1952		Holyoke, Massachusetts
1533	July 22, 1952	Military	Rockville, Indiana
1536	July 22, 1952		Uvalde, Texas
1538	July 22, 1952	Military	Los Alamos, New Mexico
1554	July 23, 1952		Pottstown, Pennsylvania
1556	July 23, 1952		Boston-Provincetown, Massachusetts
1567	July 23, 1952		Altoona, Pennsylvania
1572	July 23, 1952		Trenton, New Jersey
1578	July 23, 1952		South Bend, Indiana
1584	July 24, 1952		Carson Sink, Nevada
1588	July 24, 1952		Travis AFB, California
1628	July 26, 1952	Military	Kansas City, Missouri
1637	July 26, 1952	Military	Kirtland AFB, New Mexico
	July 26, 1952		Williams, California
1654	July 22, 1952	Military	Stafford, Virginia
1661	July 26, 1952	Civilian/military	Washington, D.C.; Andrews AFB
1664	July 27, 1952		Wilmington, Delaware
1680	July 27, 1952	Military	Selfridge AFB, Michigan
1684	July 27, 1952		Witchita Falls, Texas
1700	July 28, 1952	Military	Heidelberg, Germany
1707	July 28, 1952	Military radar	McGuire AFB, New Jersey
1708	July 28, 1952	Military	McChord AFB, Washington
1731	July 29, 1952	Multiple (photo)	Osceola, Wisconsin
1732	July 29, 1952		Langley AFB, Virginia
1738	July 29, 1952		Merced, California

Case No.	Date(s)	Witness(es)	Location
1739	July 29, 1952		Witchita, Kansas
1747	July 29, 1952		Ennis, Montana
1755	July 30, 1952		Albuquerque, New Mexico
1758	July 30, 1952		San Antonio, Texas
1771	August 1, 1952		Lancaster, California
1783	August 2, 1952		Lake Charles, Louisiana
1812	August 4, 1952		Phoenix, Arizona
1813	August 4, 1952	Civilian	Mount Vernon, New York
1827	August 5, 1952		Haneda AFB, Japan
1841	August 6, 1952		Tokyo
1843	August 6, 1952	Military	Belleville, Michigan
1845	August 6, 1952		Fort Austin, Michigan
1855	August 7, 1952		San Antonio, Texas
1870	August 9, 1952		Lake Charles AFB, Louisiana
1889	August 13, 1952		Tokyo, Japan
1920	August 18, 1952	Military	Fairfield, California
1928	August 19, 1952		Red Bluff, California
1938	August 20, 1952		Neffesville, Pennsylvania
1944	August 21, 1952		Dallas, Texas
1956	August 23, 1952		Akron, Ohio
1961	August 24, 1952		Hermanas, New Mexico
1964	August 24, 1952		Tucson, Arizona
1969	August 24, 1952	Multiple	Leveland, Texas
1972	August 25, 1952	Multiple	Pittsburg, Kansas
1975	August 25, 1952		Delaware, Ohio

1979	August 25, 1952		Holloman AFB, New Mexico
1986	August 26, 1952		Lathrop Wells, Nevada
1987	August 26, 1952		Biloxi, Mississippi
1994	August 26, 27, 30, 1952		Mexico
2006	August 28, 1952	Multiple	Chickasaw, Alabama
2013	August 29, 1952	Military	Colorado Springs, Colorado
2022	September 1, 1952	Multiple	Marietta, Georgia
2023	September 1, 1952	Military	Yaak, Montana
2025	September 2, 1952	Military	Chicago, Illinois
2045	September 6, 1952	Multiple	Lake Charles AFB, Louisiana
2048	September 6, 1952		Tucson, Arizona
2049	September 7, 1952		San Antonio, Texas
2052	September 7, 1952		San Antonio, Texas
2062	September 9, 1952		Rabat, French Morocco
2077	September 12, 1952		Allen, Maryland
2085	September 13, 1952	Military	Allentown, Pennsylvania
2086	September 14, 1952	Multiple	Santa Barbara, California
2087	September 14, 1952		Operation Mainbrace
2089	September 14, 1952		White Lake, South Dakota
2092	September 14, 1952	Multiple	El Paso, Texas
2093	September 14, 1952	Civilian	Olmsted AFB, Pennsylvania
2099	September 16, 1952	Military	Portland, Maine
2100	September 16, 1952	Multiple	Warner Robins, Georgia
2105	September 17, 1952		Tucson, Arizona
2119	September 23, 1952		Gander Lake, Newfoundland
2124	September 24, 1952	Military	Charleston, West Virginia

357

Case No.	Date(s)	Witness(es)	Location
2126	September 26, 1952	Military	41°N–35°W (Atlantic)
2128	September 27, 1952	Multiple	Inyokern, California
2136	September 29, 1952	Military	England
2138	September 30, 1952		Denver, California
2140	September 29, 1952	Civilians	Southern Pines, North Carolina
2142	October 1, 1952		Shaw AFB, South Carolina
2143	October 1, 1952	Multiple	Pascagoula, Mississippi
2150	October 7, 1952		Alamogordo, New Mexico
2155	October 10, 1952	Multiple	Otis AFB, Massachusetts
2171	October 17, 1952		Taos, New Mexico
2172	October 17, 1952	Multiple	Killeen, Texas
2173	October 17, 1952	Military	Tierra Amarilla, New Mexico
2175	October 19, 1952	Military	12°17′ N 155°35′ W (Pacific)
2177	October 19, 1952		San Antonio, Texas
2179	October 21, 1952	Civilian	Knoxville, Tennessee
2184	October 24, 1952	Military	Elberton, Alabama
2196	October 29, 1952	Military	Erding Air Depot, Germany
2200	October 31, 1952		Fayetteville, Georgia
2202	November 3, 1952	Multiple	Laredo AFB, Texas
2206	November 4, 1952		Vineland, New Jersey
2219	November 12, 1952	Military	Los Alamos, New Mexico
2220	November 13, 1952		Clasgow and Opheim, Montana
2224	November 15, 1952		Wichita, Kansas
2246	November 24, 1952		Annandle, Virginia
2248	November 27, 1952	Military	Albuquerque, New Mexico

2253	November 30, 1952	Military	Washington, D.C.
2266	December 8, 1952		Ladd AFB, Alaska
2267	December 9, 1952		Madison, Wisconsin
2302	December 28, 1952	Civilian	Marysville, California
2315	January 1, 1953		Craig, Montana
2323	January 8, 1953	Military	Larson AFB, Washington
2326	January 10, 1953		Sonoma, California
2337	January 17, 1953		Guatemala
2361	January 28, 1953		Point Mugu, California
2364	January 28, 1953		Corona, California
2365	January 28, 1953	Ground radar	Albany, Georgia Area
2384	February 3, 1953	Ground radar	Iceland
2388	February 4, 1953		Yuma, Arizona
2419	February 17, 1953	Ground radar	Port Austin, Michigan
2426	February 20, 1953	Air visual	Stockton, California
2441	February 24, 1953		Sherman, Texas
2543	February 27, 1953	Military	Shreveport, Louisiana
2490	March 10–11, 1953	Military air and air intercept (radar)	Hackettstown, New Jersey
2496	March 14, 1953		37°25′ N 132°25′ E (Sea of Japan)
2511	March 21, 1953	Four GOC observers	Elmira, New York
2521	March 25, 1953	Military	San Antonio, Texas
2524	March 27, 1953	Military air	Mount Taylor, New Mexico
2526	March 29, 1953		Spooner, Wisconsin
2535	April 8, 1953	Military air	Fukuoka, Japan
2542	April 15, 1953		Tucson, Arizona

Case No.	Date(s)	Witness(es)	Location
2555	May 1, 1953	Ground and air visual	Goose AFB, Labrador
2577	May 27, 1953		San Antonio, Texas
2601	June 22, 1953	Pilot and radar observer	Goose AFB, Labrador
2605	June 24, 1953	Air intercept (radar)	Iwo Jima
2606	June 24, 1953	Military	Simiutak, Greenland
2663	August 3, 1953	Control tower operator	Amarillo, Texas
2686	August 20, 1953	Military air	California Area
2692	August 27, 1953	Military	Greenville, Mississippi
2838	December 17, 1953		Hasseholm, Sweden
2840	December 24, 1953		El Cajon, California
2844	December 28, 1954		Marysville, California
2913	February 26, 1954	Multi civilian	Newburyport, Massachusetts
2923	March 2, 1954	Military and civilian	Pennsylvania
2926	March 5, 1954	Air visual	Nouasseur, French Morocco
2937	March 12, 1954	Military	Nouasseur, French Morocco
2962	April 8, 1954		Chicago, Illinois
2974	April 23, 1954		Pittsfield, Maine
2976	April 24, 1954		Hartland, Maine
2983	April 26, 1954		Athens, Georgia
2994	May 10, 1954	Military	Elsinore, California
2997	May 11, 1954	Military	Washington, D.C.
3009	May 22, 1954		La Porte, Indiana
3020	May 31, 1954		Concord, New Hampshire
3029	June 1, 1954	Military	Minneapolis, Minnesota
3037	June 8, 1954		Texarkana, Texas

ID	Date	Type	Location
3042	June 18, 1954	Military	Laredo, Texas
3062	June 22, 1954	Military	Miami Beach, Florida
3067	June 24, 1954		Danvers, Massachusetts
3072	June 25, 1954		Indian Lake, Ohio
3116	July 18, 1954		Normandy, Missouri
3140	July 30, 1954		Los Angeles, California
3149	August 2, 1954		Westlake, Ohio
3155	August 6, 1954		San Antonio, Texas
3162	August 11, 1954		Pacific Ocean
3166	August 15, 1954	Military	San Marcos, Texas
3180	August 24, 1954	Multi civilian	Lagarfjot River, Iceland
3182	August 26, 1954		Danville, Virginia
3185	August 27, 1954		Dorchester, Massachusetts
3189	August 29, 1954		Prince Christian, Greenland
3196	September 5, 1954		Butler, Missouri
3198	September 5, 1954		Butler, Missouri
3213	September 18, 1954	Military	Kimpo AB, Korea
3222	September 21, 1954	Multi civilian	Barstow, California
3224	September 21, 1954	Multi civilian	Santa Maria Airport, Azores
3226	September 22, 1954		Marshfield, Missouri
3227	September 23, 1954		Gatlinburg, Tennessee
3260	October 13, 1954	Military	Nouasseur, French Morocco
3269	October 15, 16, 17, 1954	Civilian unknown	Kingfisher, Oklahoma
3281	October 28, 1954	Military	Miho AB, Japan
3287	October 29, 1954	Multi civilian	Azores
3326	November 15, 1954		Augusta, Maine

Case No.	Date(s)	Witness(es)	Location
3331	November 19, 1954		Corvallis, Oregon
3341	November 28, 1954		Manila, Philippines
3352	December 3, 1954	Medical doctor	Gulfport, Mississippi
3356	December 7, 1954		Cape Province, South Africa
3382	January 1, 1955	Civilian	Cochise, New Mexico
3401	January 26, 1955	Military	Lakeland, Florida
3414	February 1, 1955		Cochise, New Mexico
3416	February 2, 1955	Military air	Miramar NAS, California
3427	February 10, 1955	Military	Bethesda, Maryland
3517	April 30, 1955		Travis County, Texas
3523	May 4, 1955		Keflavik Airport, Iceland
3565	May 23, 1955	Military	Cheyenne, Wyoming
3673	July 29, 1955	Military	Columbus, Nebraska
3699	August 11, 1955		Iceland
3720	August 23, 1955		Arlington, Virginia
3743	September 3, 1955		Bellingham, Washington
3750	September 7, 1955		Washington, D.C.
3757	September 9, 1955		Rock Garden, Tennessee
3800	October 8, 1955		Loogootee, Indiana
3810	October 11, 1955		Point Lookout, Maryland
3860	November 17, 1955		St. Louis, Missouri
3862	November 20, 1955	Multi civilian and military	Lake City, Tennessee
3869	November 25, 1955		LaVeta, Colorado
3893	December 21, 1955		Caribou, Maine

3977	February 19, 1956	Civilian pilot	Houston, Texas
4050	April 4, 1956		McKinney, Texas
4127	June 6, 1956		Banning, California
4270	August 8, 1956		20 miles south of Quartsite, Arizona
4348	August 27, 1956		Juniata, Pennsylvania
4379	September 4, 1956	Military	Dallas, Texas
4399	September 14, 1956		Highland, North Carolina
4489	November 1, 1956		60 miles east of St. Louis, Missouri
4543	November 30, 1956	Multi	Charleston AFB, South Carolina
4577	December 31, 1956	Military	Guam
4706	April 25, 1957		Ringgold, Louisiana
4760	June 12, 1957		Milan, Italy
4841	July 27, 1957		Longmont, Colorado
4847	July 29, 1957		Cleveland, Ohio
4848	July 29, 1957	Capitol Airlines	Oldsmar, Florida
4959	September 20, 1957	Military	Kadena AFB, Okinawa
5003	October 8, 1957	Military	Seattle, Washington
5205	November 6, 1957	Tape	Boerne, Texas
5227	November 6, 1957	Multi	Radium Springs, New Mexico
5254	November 8, 1957		Merrick, Long Island, New York
5419	November 26, 1957	Multi	Robins AFB, Georgia
5445	November 30, 1957	Military	New Orleans, Louisiana
5545	December 13, 1957		Col Anahuac, Mexico
5559	December 17, 1957		Fruita, Colorado
5716	March 14, 1958		Healdsburg, California

Case No.	Date(s)	Witness(es)	Location
5763	April 14, 1958	Military	Lynchburg, Virginia
5800	May 9, 1958	Military air visual	Bohol Island, Philippines
5852	June 14, 1958		Pueblo, Colorado
5857	June 20, 1958		Fort Bragg, North Carolina
5999	August 17, 1958	Military	Warren, Michigan
6027	September 1, 1958		Wheelus AFB, Tripoli
6089	October 2, 1958		Stroudsburg, Pennsylvania
6148	October 27, 1958		Lock Raven Dam, Maryland
6153	November 3, 1958	Military	Minot, North Dakota
6317	March 26 or 27, 1959		Corsica, Pennsylvania
6400	June 18, 1959		Edmonton, Alberta, Canada
6409	June 30, 1959	Military	Patuxent River, Maryland
6446	July 25, 1959		Irondequoit, New York
6462	August 10, 1959	Military	Goose AFB, Labrador
6506	September 13, 1959		Gills Rock, Wisconsin
6507	September 13, 1959	Military	Bunker Hill AFB, Indiana
6534	October 1, 1959		Telephone Ridge, Oregon
6538	October 4, 1959	Military	Philippines
6543	October 6, 1959	Military	Lincoln, Nebraska
6563	October 19, 1959	Military	Plainville, Kansas
6600	November 18, 1959		South of Crystal Springs, Mississippi
6663	February 27, 1960	Military	Rome, New York
6667	March 4, 1960	Photo	Dubuque, Iowa
6681	March 23, 1960		Indianapolis, Indiana
6711	April 12, 1960	Physical scientist	La Camp, Louisiana

364

			...ity, Kansas
6914	August 23, 1960		Wichita, Kansas
6929	August 29, 1960		Crete, Illinois
6962	September 10, 1960	Film	Ridgecrest, California
7057	October 5, 1960		Mount Kisco, New York
7133	November 27, 1960		Chula Vista, California
7134	November 29, 1960	Military air	South of Kyushu, Japan
7284	February 27, 1961		Bark River, Michigan
7321	Spring 1961		Kemah, Texas
7359	April 24, 1961	Military	35°50' N 125°40' W (Pacific)
7417	May 22, 1961		Tyndall AFB, Florida
7437	June 2, 1961	Multiple	Miyako Jima Air Station, Japan
7491	July 7, 1961		Copemiah, Michigan
7499	July 11, 1961		Springfield, Ohio
7510	July 20, 1961	Civil airplane, ground radar, audio tape	Houston, Texas
7579	August 12, 1961		Kansas City, Kansas
7741	November 21, 1961		Oldtown, Florida
7742	November 23, 1961		Sioux City, Iowa
7754	December 13, 1961		Washington, D.C.
7818	February 25, 1962	Military	Kotzebue, Alaska
7823	March 1, 1962		Salem, New York
7840	March 26, 1962		Ramstain AFB, Germany
7841	March 26, 1962		Naperville, Illinois
7851	April 4, 1962		Wurtland, Kentucky
7930	May 26, 1962	Multi	Westfield, Massachusetts

Case No.	Date(s)	Witness(es)	Location
7931	May 27, 1962	Multi	Palmer, Alaska
7957	June 21, 1962	Military	Indianapolis, Indiana
7968	June 30–1 July, 1962		Richmond, Virginia
8020	July 19, 1962		Metuchen, New Jersey
8034	July 30, 1962		Ocean Springs, Mississippi
8064	August 18, 1962		Bermuda
8133	September 21, 1962		WSW of Biloxi, Mississippi
8182	October 23, 1962		Farmington, Utah, ("Duck Hunter Case")
8215	November 17, 1962		Tampa, Florida
8360	May 18, 1963		New Plymouth, New Zealand
8363	May 22, 1963		Pequannock, New Jersey
8371	Summer		Middletown, New York
8388	June 15, 1963		14°17′ N 69°57′ E (Indian Ocean)
8434	July 1, 1963		Glen Ellyn, Illinois
8506	August 11, 1963		Warrenville, Illinois
8514	August 13–14, 1963		St. Calen, Switzerland
8548	September 14, 1963		Susanville, California
8549	September 15, 1963		Vandalia, Ohio
8581	October 4, 1963		Bedford, Ohio
8603	October 23, 1963		Meridian, Idaho
8604	October 24, 1963		Cupar Fife, Scotland
8647	December 11, 1963	Military	McMinnville, Oregon
8654	December 16, 1963		40°00′ N 175°54′ W (Pacific)
8729	April 3, 1964		Monticello, Wisconsin

8787	May 9, 1964	Multiple civilian	Asheville, North Carolina
8788	May 9, 1964		Chicago, Illinois
8811	May 18, 1964		Mount Vernon, Virginia
8836	May 26, 1964		Cambridge, Massachusetts
8839	May 26, 1964		Pleasantview, Pennsylvania
8870	June 13, 1964		Toledo, Ohio
8924	July 16, 1964		15 miles south of Houghton Lake, Michigan
8942	July 20, 1964	Civilian and military	Clinton, Iowa–Littleton, Illinois
8969	July 27, 1964		Norwich, New York
8973	July 27, 1964		Denver, Colorado
9031	August 10, 1964	Military	Wake Island
9048	August 15, 1964		New York City, New York
9049	August 15, 1964		Yosemite Park, California
9053	August 18, 1964		200 miles east of Dover (Atlantic)
9104	September 10, 1964	Military air	Cedar Grove, New Jersey
9170	November 14, 1964		Menomonee Falls, Wisconsin
9183	November 19, 1964		34°55' N 164°05' E (Pacific)
9242	January 23, 1965	Military	Williamsburg, Virginia
9301	March 4, 1965	Physical specimen	Corvallis, Oregon
9305	March 8, 1965		Mount Airy, Maryland
9345	April 4, 1965		Keesler AFB, Mississippi
9389	May 7, 1965		Oxford, Michigan
9474	July 6, 1965		Kiel, Wisconsin
9550	July 25, 1965		Castalia, Ohio
9675	August 4, 1965		Dallas, Texas

9680	August 4, 1965		Tinley Park, Illinois
9806	August 19, 1965	Two witnesses	Cherry Creek, New York
9864	August 30, 1965		Urbana, Ohio
9890	September 2–3, 1965	Three witnesses	Exeter, New Hampshire
9915	September 3, 1965	Two witnesses	Damon, Texas
9970	September 25, 1965	Three witnesses	Chisholm, Minnesota
9971	September 25, 1965	Two witnesses	Rodio, New Mexico
10066	November 4, 1965		Middletown, Ohio
10193	February 2, 1966		Salisbury, North Carolina
10196	February 6, 1966		Nederland, Texas
10247	March 20, 1966		Mims, Florida
10262	March 22, 1966		Houston, Texas
10270	March 23, 1966		Temple, Oklahoma
10291	March 26, 1966		Texahoma, Oklahoma
10329	March 30, 1966		Ottawa, Ohio
10384	April 5, 1966	Illustrated photo	Alto, Tennessee
10385	April 5, 1966		Lycoming, New York
10535	May 7, 1966	Military	Goodfellow AFB, Texas
10626	June 6, 1966		Spooner, Wisconsin
10629	June 8, 1966		Kansas, Ohio
10663	June 18, 1966		Burnsville, North Carolina
10693	June 27, 1966		19° N 172° E (Pacific)
10739	July 11, 1966		Union, Pennsylvania
10781	July 25, 1966		Vanceboro, North Carolina
10798	July 31, 1966	Multiple	Presque Isle State Park, Pennsylvania

10872	August 19, 1966		Donnybrook, North Dakota
10888	August 23, 1966		Columbus, Ohio
10899	August 26, 1966		Gaylesville, Alabama
10917	September 1, 1966		Willsboro, New York
10933	September 6, 1966		Suffolk County AFB, New York
10942	September 9, 1966		Franklin Springs, New York
10944	September 13, 1966	Photos	Gwinner, North Dakota
10973	September 28, 1966		Wilmington, Ohio
10996	October 5, 1966	Multiple	Osceola, Wisconsin
11092	October 26, 1966		Cold Bay AFS, Alaska
11135	November 8, 1966		Saginaw, Minnesota
11239	December 25, 1966	Multiple	Monroe, Oregon
11350	February 9, 1967	Civilian	Odessa, Delaware
11355	February 12, 1967		Grand Rapids, Michigan
11383	February 16, 1967		Stoughton, Wisconsin
11394	February 20, 1967		Oxford, Wisconsin
11419	February 27, 1967	Multiple	Grand Haven, Michigan
11454	March 6, 1967		Benton Harbor, Michigan
11460	March 6-11, 1967		Galesburg, Moline, Illinois
11480	March 9, 1967		Onawa, Iowa
11541	March 22, 1967		Wapello, Iowa
11551	March 24, 1967	Civilian	Belt, Montana
11559	March 26, 1967	Multiple	New Winchester, Ohio
11677	April 21, 1967		South Hill, Virginia
11744	May 17, 1967		Rural Hall, North Carolina
11815	June 24, 1967		Austin, Texas

11831	June 29, 1967	Scotch Plains, New Jersey
11869	July 10, 1967	Lizelia, Mississippi
12235	February 9, 1968	Groveton, Missouri
12498	September 15, 1968	Ocala, Florida
12567	November 23, 1968	Newton, Georgia
12607	January 17, 1969	Crittendon, Virginia

370

Appendix B: USAF Technical Information Sheet

U. S. AIR FORCE TECHNICAL INFORMATION SHEET

This questionnaire has been prepared so that you can give the U. S. Air Force as much information as possible concerning the unidentified aerial phenomenon that you have observed. Please try to answer as many questions as you possibly can. The information that you give will be used for research purposes, and will be regarded as confidential material. Your name will not be used in connection with any statements, conclusions, or publications without your permission. We request this personal information so that, if it is deemed necessary, we may contact you for further details.

---

1. When did you see the object?

_____ _____ _____
Day   Month   Year

2. Time of day: _____ _____
                    Hour   Minutes

(Circle One):   A.M.   or   P.M.

---

3. Time zone:

(Circle One): a. Eastern
           b. Central
           c. Mountain
           d. Pacific
           e. Other _____

(Circle One): a. Daylight Saving
           b. Standard

---

4. Where were you when you saw the object?

_____ _____ _____
Nearest Postal Address   City or Town   State or Country

Additional remarks: _____

---

5. Estimate how long you saw the object. _____ _____ _____
                                     Hours   Minutes   Seconds

5.1 Circle one of the following to indicate how certain you are of your answer to Question **5.**

     a. Certain
     b. Fairly certain

     c. Not very sure
     d. Just a guess

---

6. What was the condition of the sky?

(Circle One): a. Bright daylight
           b. Dull daylight
           c. Bright twilight

     d. Just a trace of daylight
     e. No trace of daylight
     f. Don't remember

---

7. IF you saw the object during DAYLIGHT, TWILIGHT, or DAWN, where was the SUN located as you looked at the object?

(Circle One): a. In front of you
           b. In back of you
           c. To your right

     d. To your left
     e. Overhead
     f. Don't remember

8. IF you saw the object at NIGHT, TWILIGHT, or DAWN, what did you notice concerning the STARS and MOON?

8.1 STARS *(Circle One):*

a. None
b. A few
c. Many
d. Don't remember

8.2 MOON *(Circle One):*

a. Bright moonlight
b. Dull moonlight
c. No moonlight — pitch dark
d. Don't remember

9. Was the object brighter than the background of the sky?

(Circle One):   a. Yes   b. No   c. Don't remember

10. IF it was BRIGHTER THAN the sky background, was the brightness like that of an automobile headlight?:

(Circle One) a. A mile or more away (a distant car)?
b. Several blocks away?
c. A block away?
d. Several yards away?
e. Other _____

11. Did the object: *(Circle One for each question)*

		Yes	No	Don't Know
a.	Appear to stand still at any time?	Yes	No	Don't Know
b.	Suddenly speed up and rush away at any time?	Yes	No	Don't Know
c.	Break up into parts or explode?	Yes	No	Don't Know
d.	Give off smoke?	Yes	No	Don't Know
e.	Change brightness?	Yes	No	Don't Know
f.	Change shape?	Yes	No	Don't Know
g.	Flicker, throb, or pulsate?	Yes	No	Don't Know

12. Did the object move behind something at anytime, particularly a cloud?

(Circle One):   Yes   No   Don't Know.   IF you answered YES, then tell what it moved behind: _____

13. Did the object move in front of something at anytime, particularly a cloud?

(Circle One):   Yes   No   Don't Know.   IF you answered YES, then tell what it moved in front of: _____

14. Did the object appear: *(Circle One):*   a. Solid?   b. Transparent?   c. Don't Know.

15. Did you observe the object through any of the following?

a. Eyeglasses	Yes	No		e. Binoculars	Yes	No	
b. Sun glasses	Yes	No		f. Telescope	Yes	No	
c. Windshield	Yes	No		g. Theodolite	Yes	No	
d. Window glass	Yes	No		h. Other			_____

16. Tell in a few words the following things about the object.

a. Sound _____

b. Color _____

17. Draw a picture that will show the shape of the object or objects. Label and include in your sketch any details of the object that you saw such as wings, protrusions, etc., and especially exhaust trails or vapor trails. Place an arrow beside the drawing to show the direction the object was moving.

18. The edges of the object were:

(Circle One): a. Fuzzy or blurred   e. Other _____
               b. Like a bright star   _____
               c. Sharply outlined   _____
               d. Don't remember

19. IF there was MORE THAN ONE object, then how many were there? _____.
Draw a picture of how they were arranged, and put an arrow to show the direction that they were traveling.

374

20. Draw a picture that will show the motion that the object or objects made. Place an "A" at the beginning of the path, a "B" at the end of the path, and show any changes in direction during the course.

21. IF POSSIBLE, try to guess or estimate what the real size of the object was in its longest dimension. _____ feet.

22. How large did the object or objects appear as compared with one of the following objects *held in the hand* and at about arm's length?

   (Circle One):   a. Head of a pin   g. Silver dollar
                       b. Pea   h. Baseball
                       c. Dime   i. Grapefruit
                       d. Nickel   j. Basketball
                       e. Quarter   k. Other _____
                       f. Half dollar

   22.1 *(Circle One* of the following to indicate how certain you are of your answer to Question 22.
                       a. Certain   c. Not very sure
                       b. Fairly certain   d. Uncertain

23. How did the object or objects disappear from view? _____
_____.

24. In order that you can give as clear a picture as possible of what you saw, we would like for you to imagine that you could construct the object that you saw. Of what type material would you make it? How large would it be, and what shape would it have? Describe in your own words a common object or objects which when placed up in the sky would give the same appearance as the object which you saw.

25. Where were you located when you saw the object? (Circle One):

a. Inside a building
b. In a car
c. Outdoors
d. In an airplane
e. At sea
f. Other _____

26. Were you (Circle One)

a. In the business section of a city?
b. In the residential section of a city?
c. In open countryside?
d. Flying near an airfield? ·
e. Flying over a city?
f. Flying over open country?
g. Other _____

27. What were you doing at the time you saw the object, and how did you happen to notice it?

_____

_____

_____

28. IF you were MOVING IN AN AUTOMOBILE or other vehicle at the time, then complete the following questions:

28.1 What direction were you moving? (Circle One)

a. North   c. East   e. South   g. West
b. Northeast d. Southeast f. Southwest h. Northwest

28.2 How fast were you moving? _____ miles per hour.

28.3 Did you stop at any time while you were looking at the object?
(Circle One)   Yes   No

29. What direction were you looking when you first saw the object? (Circle One)

a. North   c. East   e. South   g. West
b. Northeast d. Southeast f. Southwest h. Northwest

30. What direction were you looking when you last saw the object? (Circle One)

a. North   c. East   e. South   g. West
b. Northeast d. Southeast f. Southwest h. Northwest

31. If you are familiar with bearing terms (angular direction), try to estimate the number of degrees the object was from true North and also the number of degrees it was upward from the horizon (elevation).

31.1 When it first appeared:
a. From true North _____ degrees.
b. From horizon _____ degrees.

31.2 When it disappeared:
a. From true North _____ degrees.
b. From horizon _____ degrees.

376

In the following sketch, imagine that you are at the point shown. Place an "A" on the curved line to show how high the object was above the horizon (skyline) when you *first* saw it. Place a "B" on the same curved line to show how high the object was above the horizon (skyline) when you *last* saw it.

In the following larger sketch place an "A" at the position the object was when you *first* saw it, and a "B" at its position when you *last* saw it. Refer to smaller sketch as an example of how to complete the larger sketch.

34. What were the weather conditions at the time you saw the object?

34.1 CLOUDS *(Circle One)*
    a. Clear sky
    b. Hazy
    c. Scattered clouds
    d. Thick or heavy clouds
    e. Don't remember

34.2 WIND *(Circle One)*
    a. No wind
    b. Slight breeze
    c. Strong wind
    d. Don't remember

34.3 WEATHER *(Circle One)*
    a. Dry
    b. Fog, mist, or light rain
    c. Moderate or heavy rain
    d. Snow
    e. Don't remember

34.4 TEMPERATURE *(Circle One)*
    a. Cold
    b. Cool
    c. Warm
    d. Hot
    e. Don't remember

35. When did you report to some official that you had seen the object?

    Day   Month   Year

36. Was anyone else with you at the time you saw the object?

    (Circle One)   Yes   No

    36.1 IF you answered YES, did they see the object too?
        (Circle One)   Yes   No

    36.2 Please list their names and addresses:

37. Was this the first time that you had seen an object or objects like this?

    (Circle One)   Yes   No

    37.1 IF you answered NO, then when, where, and under what circumstances did you see other ones?

38. In your opinion what do you think the object was and what might have caused it?

39. Do you think you can estimate the *speed* of the object?

       (Circle One)   Yes   No

IF you answered YES, then what speed would you estimate?   _____ m.p.h.

40. Do you think you can estimate how far away from you the object was?

       (Circle One)   Yes   No

IF you answered YES, then how far away would you say it was?   _____ feet.

41. Please give the following information about yourself:

NAME _____   _____   _____
            Last Name   First Name   Middle Name

ADDRESS _____   _____   _____   _____
               Street   City   Zone   State

TELEPHONE NUMBER _____

What is your present job? _____

Age _____   Sex _____

Please indicate any special educational training that you have had.

    a. Grade school _____   e. e. Technical school _____
    b. High school _____   (Type) _____
    c. College _____   f. Other special training _____
    d. Post graduate _____

42. Date you completed this questionnaire: _____   _____   _____
                                         Day   Month   Year

U. S. AIR FORCE TECHNICAL INFORMATION SHEET
(SUMMARY DATA)

In order that your information may be filed and coded as accurately as possible, please use the following space to write out a short description of the event that you observed. You may repeat information that you have already given in the questionnaire, and add any further comments, statements, or sketches that you believe are important. Try to present the details of the observation in the order in which they occurred. Additional pages of the same size paper may be attached if they are needed.

NAME _____
(Please Print)

SIGNATURE _____

DATE _____

(Do Not Write in This Space)

CODE:

Appendix C: UFO Incident Maps, Charts, Graphs

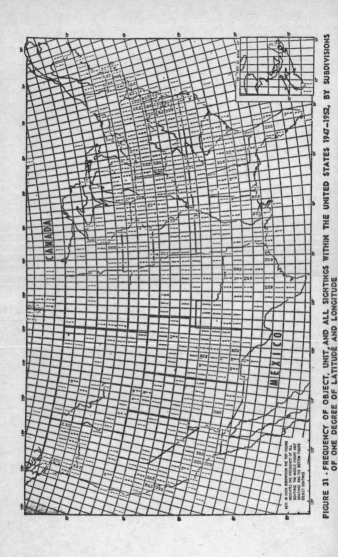

KEY: IN EACH SUBDIVISION THE TOP FIGURE
INDICATES THE FREQUENCY OF ALL
SIGHTINGS. THE MIDDLE FIGURE UNIT
SIGHTINGS AND THE BOTTOM FIGURE
OBJECT SIGHTINGS.

FIGURE 31 - FREQUENCY OF OBJECT, UNIT, AND ALL SIGHTINGS WITHIN THE UNITED STATES 1947-1952, BY SUBDIVISIONS
OF ONE DEGREE OF LATITUDE AND LONGITUDE

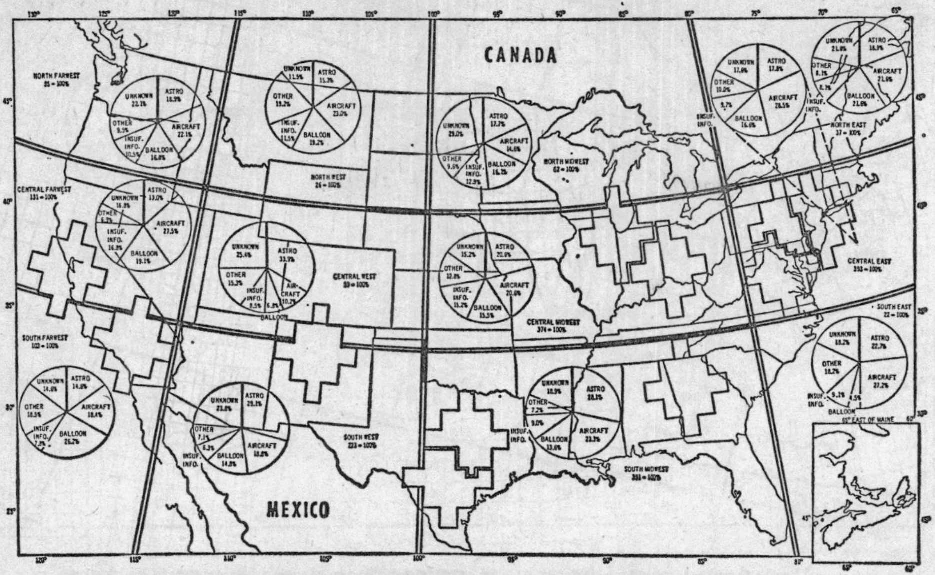

FIGURE 32 DISTRIBUTION OF OBJECT SIGHTINGS BY EVALUATION FOR THE TWELVE REGIONAL AREAS OF THE UNITED STATES, WITH THE EXPANDED AREAS LOCATED (EXPLAINED

383

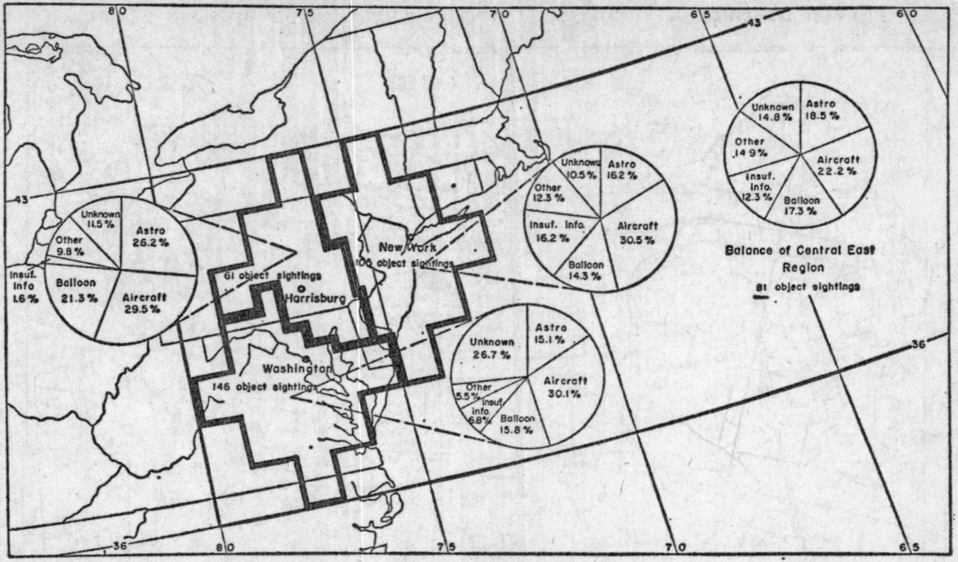
80
75
70
65
60
43
36
Unknown 11.5%
Astro 26.2%
Other 9.8%
Insuf. Info 1.6%
Balloon 21.3%
Aircraft 29.5%
61 object sightings
Harrisburg
New York
106 object sightings
Washington
146 object sightings
Unknown 10.5%
Astro 16.2%
Other 12.3%
Insuf. Info. 16.2%
Aircraft 30.5%
Balloon 14.3%
Unknown 26.7%
Astro 15.1%
Aircraft 30.1%
Other 5.5%
Insuf. Info. 6.8%
Balloon 15.8%
Unknown 14.8%
Astro 18.5%
Other 14.9%
Aircraft 22.2%
Insuf. Info. 12.3%
Balloon 17.3%
Balance of Central East Region
81 object sightings

FIGURE 33 COMPARISON OF EVALUATION OF OBJECT SIGHTINGS IN THE STRATEGIC AREAS OF THE CENTRAL EAST REGION

B-7511

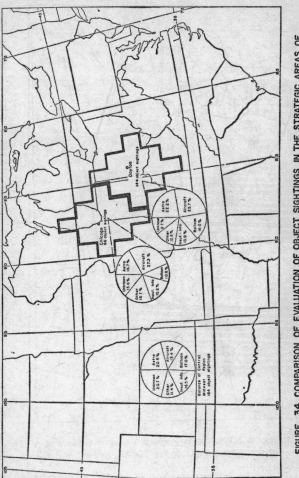

FIGURE 34 COMPARISON OF EVALUATION OF OBJECT SIGHTINGS IN THE STRATEGIC AREAS OF THE CENTRAL MIDWEST REGION

385

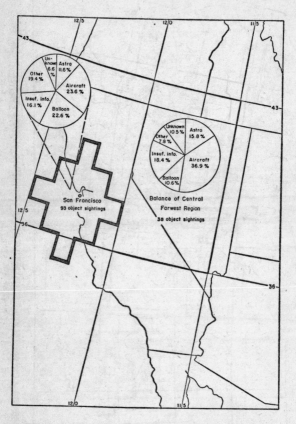

FIGURE 35 COMPARISON OF EVALUATION OF OBJECT SIGHTINGS
IN THE STRATEGIC AREAS OF THE CENTRAL FARWEST REGION

B-7513

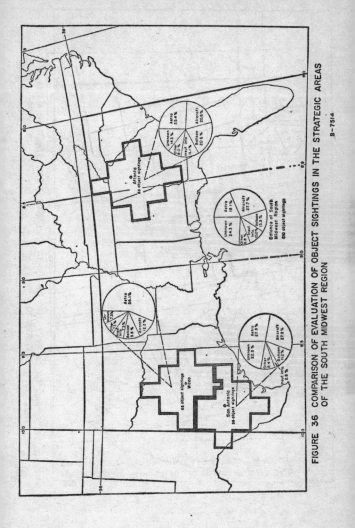

Astro
25.4%

Aircraft
20.6%

Unknown
14.3%

Insuf. info
11.1%

Balloon
20.6%

Antonio
63 object sightings

Astro
18.1%

Aircraft
27.7%

Unknown
24.5%

Other
6.8%

Insuf. Info/
OOV/balloon
13.3%

Balance of South
Midwest Region
810 object sightings

Astro
56.1%

Unknown
23%

Insuf. info 3.3%

Other
2.3%

Balloon
12.1%

Aircraft
<2.2%

96 object sightings
WGSD

Astro
27.6%

Aircraft
27.6%

Unknown
22.2%

Other
8.4%

Balloon
11.2%

Insuf. info
2.8%

San Antonio
36 object sightings

FIGURE 36 COMPARISON OF EVALUATION OF OBJECT SIGHTINGS IN THE STRATEGIC AREAS
OF THE SOUTH MIDWEST REGION

B-7514

387

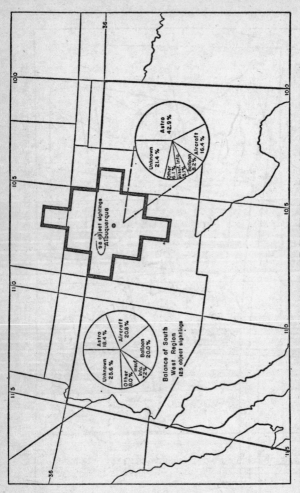

FIGURE 37 COMPARISON OF EVALUATION OF OBJECT SIGHTINGS IN THE STRATEGIC AREAS OF THE SOUTH WEST REGION

A-7515

98 object sightings
Albuquerque

Astro 42.9%
Aircraft 16.4%
Balloon 8.2%
Insuf. Info. 5.1%
Other 6.1%
Unknown 21.4%

Balance of South West Region
125 object sightings

Astro 18.4%
Aircraft 20.8%
Balloon 20.0%
Insuf. Info. 7.2%
Other 8.0%
Unknown 25.6%

388

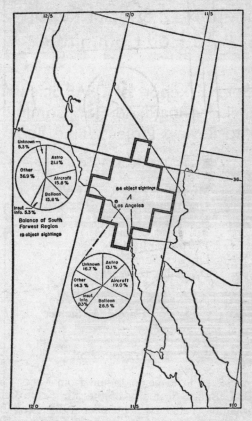

FIGURE 38 COMPARISON OF EVALUATION OF OBJECT SIGHTINGS IN
THE STRATEGIC AREAS OF THE SOUTH FARWEST REGION

B-7516

Appendix D: Special Report USAF Ad Hoc Committee

Special Report of USAF Scientific Advisory Board Ad Hoc Committee to Review Project "Blue Book"

MARCH 1966

MEMBERS PARTICIPATING
Dr. Brian O'Brien (Chairman)
Dr. Launor F. Carter
Mr. Jesse Orlansky
Dr. Richard Porter
Dr. Carl Sagan
Dr. Willis H. Ware

SAB SECRETARIAT
Lt. Col. Harold A. Steiner

I. Introduction

As requested in a memorandum from Major General E. B. LeBailly, Secretary of the Air Force Office of Information, dated 28 September 1965 (Tab A), an SAB Ad Hoc Committee met on 3 February 1966 to review Project "Blue Book." The objectives of the Committee are to review the resources and methods of investigation prescribed by Project "Blue Book" and to advise the Air Force of any improvements that can be made in the program to enhance the Air Force's capability in carrying out its responsibility.

In order to bring themselves up to date, the members of the Committee initially reviewed the findings of previous scientific panels charged with looking into the UFO problem. Particular attention was given to the report of the Robertson panel which was rendered in January 1953. The Committee next heard briefings from the AFSC Foreign Technology Division, which is the cognizant Air Force agency that collates information on UFO sightings and monitors investigations of individual cases. Finally, the Committee reviewed selected case histories of UFO sightings with particular emphasis on those that have not been identified.

II. Discussion

Although about 6% (646) of all sightings (10,147) in the years 1947 through 1965 are listed by the Air Force as "Unidentified," it appears to the Committee that most of the cases so listed are simply those in which the information available does not provide an adequate basis for analysis. In this connection it is important also to note that no unidentified objects other than those of an astronomical nature have ever been observed during routine astronomical studies, in spite of the large number of observing hours which have been devoted to the sky. As examples of this the Palomar Observatory Sky Atlas contains some 5,000 plates made with large instruments with wide field of view; the Harvard Meteor Project of 1954–1958 provided some 3300 hours of observation; the Smithsonian Visual Prairie Network provided 2500 observing hours. Not a single unidentified object has been reported as appearing on any of these plates or been sighted visually in all these observations.

The Committee concluded that in the 19 years since the first UFO was sighted there has been no evidence that unidentified flying objects are a threat to our national security. Having arrived at this conclusion the Committee then turned its attention to considering how the Air Force should handle the scientific aspects of the UFO problem. Unavoidably these are also related to Air Force public relations, a subject on which the

Committee is not expert. Thus the recommendations which follow are made simply from the scientific point of view.

III. Conclusions and Recommendations

It is the opinion of the Committee that the present Air Force program dealing with UFO sightings has been well organized, although the resources assigned to it (only one officer, a sergeant, and secretary) have been quite limited. In 19 years and more than 10,000 sightings recorded and classified, there appears to be no verified and fully satisfactory evidence of any case that is clearly outside the framework of presently known science and technology. Nevertheless, there is always the possibility that analysis of new sightings may provide some additions to scientific knowledge of value to the Air Force. Moreover, some of the case records which the Committee looked at that were listed as "identified" were sightings where the evidence collected was too meager or too indefinite to permit positive listing in the identified category. Because of this the Committee recommends that the present program be strengthened to provide opportunity for scientific investigation of selected sightings in more detail and depth than has been possible to date.

To accomplish this it is recommended that:

A. Contracts be negotiated with a few selected universities to provide scientific teams to investigate promptly and in depth certain selected sightings of UFO's. Each team should include at least one psychologist, preferably one interested in clinical psychology, and at least one physical scientist, preferably an astronomer or geophysicist familiar with atmospheric physics. The universities should be chosen to provide good geographical distribution, and should be within convenient distance of a base of the Air Force Systems Command (AFSC).

B. At each AFSC base an officer skilled in investigation (but not necessarily with scientific training) should be designated to work with the corresponding university team for that geographical section. The

ocal representative of the Air Force Office of Special
Investigations (OSI) might be a logical choice for this.

C. One university or one not-for-profit organization should be selected to coordinate the work of the
teams mentioned under A above, and also to make
certain of very close communication and coordination
with the office of Project Blue Book.

It is thought that perhaps 100 sightings a year might
be subjected to this close study, and that possibly an
average of 10 man days might be required per sighting
so studied. The information provided by such a program might bring to light new facts of scientific value,
and would almost certainly provide a far better basis
than we have today for decision on a long term UFO
program.

The scientific reports on these selected sightings,
supplementing the present program of the Project
Blue Book Office, should strengthen the public position of the Air Force on UFO's. It is, therefore, recommended that:

A. These reports be printed in full and be
available on request.

B. Suitable abstracts or condensed versions be
printed and included in, or as supplements to, the
published reports of Project Blue Book.

C. The form of report (as typified by "Project
Blue Book" dated 1 February 1966) be expanded,
and anything which might suggest that information is
being withheld (such as the wording on page 5 of the
above cited reference) be deleted. The form of this report can be of great importance in securing public
understanding and should be given detailed study by
an appropriate Air Force office.

D. The reports "Project Blue Book" should be
given wide unsolicited circulation among prominent
members of the Congress and other public persons as
a further aid to public understanding of the scientific
approach being taken by the Air Force in attacking
the UFO problem.

Appendix E: Excerpts from Blue Book Briefing for Air Defense Command

This briefing has been prepared specially for A[ir] Defense Command units. Its purpose is to present a[ll] aspects of Project Blue Book so ADC personnel wi[ll] have a better understanding of the goals of the projec[t], be able to more accurately evaluate reports of unide[n]tified flying objects, and increase the quality of thos[e] reports that are forwarded.

A copy of this briefing will be given to each AD[C] unit and should be given wide distribution.

As you have been told, this briefing is about Un[i]dentified Flying Objects or "flying saucers" if you in[sist]. We don't like the name "flying saucers" and on[ly] rarely use it because it seems to represent weird storie[s] hoaxes, etc., sort of a joke.

We don't take "flying saucers" too seriously eithe[r] but we do take the problem of Unidentified Flyin[g] Objects seriously. The definition of an Unidentifie[d] Flying Object is any airborne object that by perform[ance], aerodynamic characteristics or unusual feature[s] does not conform to any presently known type of ai[r]craft or missile, or which cannot be identified as [a] known object or phenomenon.

The mission of the Air Defense Command is suc[h] that you are in a position to be recipients of the be[st] reports of Unidentified Flying Objects. For that reaso[n] this briefing is being presented today. Three mai[n] points will be covered in this briefing.

    a. The general aspects of Project Blue Book [to] clear up any misconceptions that anyone may have.

    b. How reports can be evaluated in the units.

    c. How to increase the quality of reports that a[re] forwarded.

Security Classification

First of all I would like to tell you about the security of this project. The majority of the information currently being carried as Restricted. This is merely protect the names of the people who have given us reports; it is not any attempt to cover up any information that we have. The required security classification admittance to this briefing is Secret, however. The reason for this is that in some instances we may get to a discussion of classified equipment, classified locations, or classified projects during the question and answer period that follows this briefing. When the project was first started, it was classified as Top Secret. This *is* probably the reason for the rumors that the Air Force has Top Secret information on this subject; it does not. The only reason for the original classification was that when the project first started the people on the project did not know what they were dealing with and, therefore, unknowingly put on this high classification.

We release all information to the press that they ask for, except the names of persons involved in the sighting, methods used to obtain information when this involves intelligence methods and anything else such as locations of radar sites, types of radar sets, performance of aircraft, etc., that may be classified.

The Air Technical Intelligence Center

Many people are not familiar with the Air Technical Intelligence Center. The Air Technical Intelligence Center was at one time part of Air Material Command, however, in mid 1952 the command was changed and it is now a field activity of the Directorate of Intelligence, Headquarters Air Force. Our chief, Brigadier General Garland, is directly responsible to Major General Samford, the Director of Intelligence, Headquarters USAF. The prime function of the Air Technical Intelligence Center is not to investigate "flying saucer" reports, it is charged with the prevention of technological surprise by a foreign country. This means that all enemy aircraft, guided missiles, etc., and any equipment related to these articles, studied at the Air Technical Intelligence Center.

History of the Project

To give you a brief history of this project, it started in 1947, when on 24 June 1947 a Mr. Kenneth Arnold sighted several disc-like objects nears Mt. Rainier in the State of Washington. From that time until August 1949, 375 reports were collected and analyzed. In August 1949, a report was written on these 375 incidents and it was concluded that all sightings were due to:

1. Mass hysteria or war nerves.
2. Hoaxes or persons seeking publicity.
3. Psychopathological persons.
4. Misinterpretation of known objects.

These conclusions have been given a great deal of study and it is now concluded that the vast majority of the reports received are not due to hysteria, war nerves, hoaxes, publicity seekers, psychopathological persons, etc., but they are reports made by persons who have definitely seen something that they themselves could not explain at the time of the sighting and have very sincerely made their report to the Air Force. This does not mean that these reports could not have been misinterpretations of known objects, as not all of us are familiar with the many different ways known objects can appear under various conditions.

In the Summer of 1951 the project was reviewed at the request of Headquarters USAF and Project Blue Book was established. Between 1949 and 1951 the project had not been dropped, but it was being carried on a low priority basis. The reason for the renewed interest in the project was that between 1949 and 1951 very little publicity had been given this subject, however, reports continued to come in. These reports were mainly from military personnel, and could be classed as good reports. I would like to stop here a minute and explain what we mean by a good report. To us, a good report is one in which several people were involved and the motives of these people in making the report cannot be questioned. They have made con-

aratively careful observations and have reported
verything that they observed. Very few, if any, of the
eports in ATIC files could be classed as an excellent
eport, since everyone is familiar with the frailties of
uman powers of observation and with the necessity
or obtaining readings by instruments to get exact
alculations.

After reorganization of the project in the summer
f 1951, reports continued to come in at the rate of
bout ten a month. In the spring of 1952 there was an
ncrease in the number of reports and they hit a peak
f 70 per day in July 1952. At the present time they
ave dropped off to about five a week. There is no
oubt that the emphasis placed on this subject by the
ress caused this big up-sweep in reports.

Current Situation

It can be stated now that as far as the current
ituation is concerned, there are no indications that
he reported objects are a direct threat to the United
tates nor is there any proof that the reported objects
re any foreign body over the United States or, as far
s we know, the rest of the world. This always brings
p the question of space travel. We have gone into
his with many people and it is the opinion of most
cientists or people that should know that it is not
mpossible for some other planet to be inhabited and
or this planet to send beings down to the earth. How-
ver, there is no, and I want to emphasize and repeat
he word "No", evidence of this in any report the Air
orce has received.

We have arrived at the conclusion that these reported
bjects are no direct threat to the United States for
everal different reasons. One, we have never picked
p any "hardware." By that we mean any pieces,
arts, whole articles, or anything that would indicate
n unknown material or object. We have received
any pieces of material to be analyzed but in every
ase there was no doubt as to what this material was.

Photographs

We have photographs of some unusual things, but

in all of those that show any amount of detail, there i
a varying amount of doubt as to their authenticity
Still photographs are very easy to fake, without re
touching the negative. Our files contain many photo
that were submitted in good faith. Some have turne
out to be flaws in the negative, light flares or photos o
some relatively rare known natural phenomena. W
have some that cannot be readily explained since the
are merely "blobs" of light and could be variou
things. None of the photos on file that cannot be ex
plained show any detail in the object or are cause fo
any undue speculation.

Statistical Study

We have made a statistical study of the data that w
have collected in order to attempt to determin
whether or not there is any common pattern in th
sightings but we have had no success in finding an
such pattern. The statistical study made by ATIC wa
made on cross-index cards with 16 items, such as
reported shape, a reported direction, color, etc., bein
cross-indexed in an attempt to find a pattern, but w
found none. In order to make a more detailed stud
and since it is very difficult to handle 3,000 reports o
cross-index cards, an IBM study is now being made.

A Few Statistics

Two points that are of interest but are not in them
selves greatly significant are plots of the distributio
of our unknown sightings and a plot of the frequenc
of reports. A definition of the term "unknown" will b
given later.

1. Slide of Location of Unknowns

You will notice that the unknown reports do tend t
cluster around critical areas in the United States. On
explanation might be that the people in these areas ar
aware of the fact that they are in a critical area an
are more aware of unusual things.

2. Slide on Frequency of Reports

A plot of the frequency of reports shows a series o
peaks in July of each year. We cannot account for thi
Some people have offered the explanation that there

tter weather in July, more clear skies. We have
ecked this and there seems to be no correlation;
her months also have clear skies. The fact that July
ghts are warmer and more people are outdoors has
so been advanced, this doesn't appear to have any
earing on the problem either.

You might be interested in a breakdown of our
ports for 1952. In breaking down these reports, we
se several degrees of certainty under each category.
'e'll take balloons, for example. We will classify
em as a known balloon, a probable balloon, or a
ossible balloon. A known balloon means that we were
efinitely able to correlate the facts of the sighting
ith the data on a balloon track and there is no doubt
at the object was a balloon. Probably a balloon
eans that we were not able to correlate all the data,
ut there is no doubt in our minds but what the re-
orted object was a balloon. A possible balloon is
here we check the report with balloon data and
annot find a correlation yet we still believe the object
as a balloon.

3. Slide showing Breakdown of Conclusions

In analyzing 1021 reports, and those are reports
at have been received through military channels and
o not include several hundred reports from civilians
irect to ATIC, the following is the breakdown of
onclusions as of 22 December 52:

Balloons		18.51%
Known	1.57	
Probable	4.99	
Possible	11.95	
Aircraft		11.76%
Known	0.98	
Probable	7.74	
Possible	3.04	
Astronomical Bodies		14.20%
Known	2.79	
Probable	4.01	
Possible	7.40	
Other (Ducks over drive-in movies, searchlights on clouds, etc.)		4.21%

Hoaxes	1.66%
Radar (Explanation not proven)	6.84%
Insufficient Data to Evaluate	22.72%
Unknown	20.1 %

This leaves a balance of 20.1% of the reports which are classified as unknown. At this point, a definition of the term "unknown" is in order. Usually there is more than one source or observer. Again, this does not mean that just because a person is alone, sees something he cannot explain to himself and reports it his account of what he saw is laughed off. Normally one person just cannot supply the necessary data. For this reason, we dwell more on reports where the data can be substantiated by others. To go a step further in a report we classify as unknown there can be no doubt as to the reliability of the persons making the observation. If the report contains a relatively good amount of data, it is then checked against the location of known objects, phenomena, etc. If none of these explain the sighting, it is classed as unknown. It might well be that if we had more data on the sighting, it could easily be explained.

Why Continue The Project?

I might state now that the project will be continued and the subject will continue to be treated seriously. There are several reasons why the project will be continued.

a. There are reports we cannot explain. We believe we can explain all but about 20%, but if you note the breakdown of conclusions, we only can positively identify about 7%. With the world situation what it is and with the present advances in science, it behooves the Air Force to have a system whereby they can receive reports of, evaluate, and determine the identity of objects reportedly flying over the United States.

b. There is no assurance that at some future date some foreign power could not develop some object that by present day standards is unconventional in appearance or performance. Due to the fact that the term "flying saucer" has become almost a household word

400

for anything that cannot be identified as a conventional object, it might be reported as a flying saucer. The Japanese paper balloons of World War II are an example of this.

c. The third reason is related to the first. The Air Force is responsible for the aerial protection of the United States. It is our responsibility to assure ourselves and the public that these continuing reports, and we believe they will continue, are not a threat.

To give you a little better idea of the project, I would like to tell you how we operate. Air Force Letter 200-5 is the basis for our operation. It states that the Air Technical Intelligence Center is responsible for analyzing all reports of unidentified flying objects and that each Air Force unit is responsible for forwarding reports that they receive to the Air Technical Intelligence Center. It further states that all reports will be forwarded by wire, then followed up within three days by a written AF Form 112. This reporting requirement in AFL 200-5 does not mean that the officer receiving the report from the source or the observer does not have the prerogative to make his own evaluation and determine whether or not the observation is worth forwarding.

Cross Check With The GOC

Another ready source of possible information that may shed some light on a report of an unidentified flying object is the Ground Observer Corps. The GOC can be used in two ways, they may make reports and they can cross-check reports.

Summary on Report Evaluations

It would be impossible to give you all the checks that can be made on reports since each report requires a different approach. I've given you a few ideas and you can undoubtedly think of more. One thing we do ask is that when you make a check on a report you obtain enough data to substantiate your conclusion. Just because someone reported four objects near a city and there were four aircraft in formation near the same city, don't quickly assume they were one and the same. Get some information on the location of the reported object, the time and course, then check this against the flight of the aircraft. If it correlates to a reasonable degree, they were very probably the same thing.

Reporting Solutions

If, during an investigation of a sighting, after a TWX has been sent reporting the incident, the investigating officer should identify the reported object, ATIC should be immediately notified as to the solution.

Popular Theories

Many theories have been advanced that all of the reports are due to mirages, sun dogs, ice clouds and what-have-you. Some of our reports are caused by such things. We have received excellent photos of sun dogs and descriptions of mirages. These are definitely in the minority, however, and cause only a small percentage of the sightings.

Another popular solution is that all "flying saucers" are "skyhook" balloons. To check this a study of about 55 cross-country balloon tracks were made. To remove any doubt, the tracks were taken of flights made during July and August 1952 when reports were coming in at the rate of 50 per day. These balloons were seen and reported as "flying saucers" at only 8 points.

Video Cameras

You may have heard about a camera that has been modified for use on this project. At the present time, we have 100 of these cameras. They are a commercial model stereo camera with one lens fitted with a diffraction grating. The grating serves as a prism to separate the light source into its various components. Any light source that is made up of an element or combination of elements has a distinctive spectrum. This spectrum is similar to a finger print. A file of the spectra of known objects, stars, meteors, etc., is being assembled and this file spectra can be compared to the spectra obtained from photos from the cameras.

402

These cameras will be placed in control towers and a few selected radar stations throughout the United States. We are having some difficulty with the gratings on these cameras, however, and consequently have not put them out in the field. The grating is a rather touchy piece of equipment and we are having trouble getting it to stand up under certain conditions.

We realize that this is not a fool-proof measure. These cameras are not a piece of highly developed scientific equipment, but we do hope that we may be able to obtain some information.

Other Instrumentation

The possibilities of more extensive instrumentation has been discussed in detail. Many suggestions for more complete cameras, special aircraft instrumentation, and other detection devices have been studied. It is possible that a study contract for such instrumentation may be let, but no actual program will be started now. The cost of such a program would out-weigh the results.

Sample Incidents

You might be interested in some of the reports we get. I'll give you a brief description of two or three.

On the night of 13 May 1952 about 10 P.M. four amateur astronomers were making observations through a small telescope on a college campus. All of a sudden they noticed four oval shaped objects in a diamond-shape formation. The objects appeared nearly overhead and disappeared at an angle of 12° above the horizon in about 3 seconds. The objects or lights were reddish brown in color and about the size of a half dollar, quarter turned, at arm's length.

Our evaluation of this was unknown. It could possibly have been ducks or geese reflecting light, except the observers pointed out that they had purposely set up their telescope in an area that was completely dark so that there would be no ground lights to hinder their observations.

Another interesting sighting occurred at Patrick AFB in July 1952. Seven people, all AF personnel, observed five different lights near the base during a period of 15 seconds. The first one was hovering in the west, three traveled very swiftly over the base on a west to east heading, and the fifth light came over the base from the west, made a turn, and went back to the west. All of the lights appeared to be much brighter than a star and amber-red in color and there was no sound. No aircraft were in the area.

A balloon had been launched prior to the sighting and could account for the hovering light. It is possible that the three fast-moving lights were meteors, although to see three meteors all traveling the same direction only seconds apart is doubtful. The fifth light that was observed is the one that makes the sighting interesting, no meteor comes in, makes a 180° turn, and departs.

On 14 July 1952 at 2012 EST two Pan American pilots flying on a heading of 60° near Norfolk, Virginia, observed eight objects over Chesapeake Bay near Old Point Comfort, Virginia. The DC-4 aircraft was at 8,000'. When the aircraft was about 20 to 25 miles out on the NE leg of the Norfolk beam, six objects in trail were observed below and coming toward the DC-4. When they reached a point under and slightly below the aircraft, they appeared to roll on edge and without any radius of turn, shoot off on a heading of about 270° rolling back into a flat position. Immediately after the change in direction the formation was joined by two other objects.

When first seen the objects were glowing on the top side with an intense amber-red light, many times more brilliant than the lights of the city below, they resembled a glowing red hot coal. They appeared circular. As they approached the DC-4 they appeared to decelerate just before they changed direction. During their approach they held a good formation but just before the turn, they appeared to tend to overrun the leader. With the deceleration the glow seemed to dim. Immediately after turning and flattening out, the glow disappeared entirely. They reappeared at once, glowing brilliantly again. As they began to climb, the lights went out one by one.

They were in view long enough for the pilot to get out of the left seat after he first observed the objects, cross the cockpit, pick them up just as they completed their turn and watch them disappear. It was estimated that this was between 10 and 20 seconds.

The only "clue" as to a possible identification of the objects is a part of the intial report that stated that there were five jet aircraft in the vicinity of Langley AFB, Va., at the time of the sighting. (Note: The incident took place about 10 miles NE of Langley AFB.) Efforts to obtain more data on these jets were unsuccessful.

Since aircraft were in the area, it is possible that they were observed. The in-trail formation could have been a "rat race" although doing this in jet, at night, below 8,000', is difficult to believe. The almost instantaneous turn could have been some type of an illusion. The diminishing light could have been the jets pulling off power before the turn. This again is a doubtful point since there is no data available on the appearance of the tailpipe of a jet head-on from above.

Since there were jet aircraft in the area, it is possible that the two Pan American pilots saw these jets. Therefore, we have written this off as "possibly aircraft."

Conclusion

In concluding this briefing it can again be stated that in none of the reports so far received are there any indications that the reported objects are a direct threat to the United States, nor is there any proof that any of the reports received have been reports of any radically new unknown material objects. We admit we cannot explain every report but we believe we know enough about the unknowns to say they are not anything to invoke undue speculation.

The project will be continued. Even if a system for the foolproof explanation of every sighting is developed it will continue because you never know what may happen in the future.

The one threat that could come out of this problem of "flying saucers" is a "wolf, wolf" situation. Some people take an exceedingly "dim view" of such reports and use no logic in trying to explain them. We do not want to clutter communications channels with worthless reports. If you can logically explain a report, fine, there is no need to waste your time and effort forwarding it. All we ask is that you do use logic in writing it off a report as a "flying saucer."

Secret

AUTH: CG, ATIC
BY: E. J. RUPPELT
Capt., USAF
DATE: 23 Dec. 52

FROM: CG ATIC   231400Z DEC 52
TO: CG AIR DEFENSE COMMAND ENT
       AFB COLO
FROM: AFOIN-ATIAA   FOR DCS/I

Reference telephone call from Maj. Sadowski to Capt. Ruppelt on 22 Dec. 52. Proposed tour to brief your forces and divisions has been postponed and is tentatively scheduled to start in late January or early February. Postponement was necessary due to time being taken up by meetings with and preparing data for CIA. CIA has made survey of some of the sightings in the ATIC file and has arranged for a panel of several top U.S. scientists to review them. Although plans are not completely firm, this meeting is tentatively scheduled to take place in early January. CIA's interest is from standpoint of reports similar to present reports of unidentified flying objects being used as psychological warfare and to add confusion in possible attack. They believe a system for rapidly sorting out false reports or reports of known objects and phenomena should be established. Referenced briefing tour is being given high priority and you will be notified as soon as it can be started and of the planned itinerary.

ROBERT E. KENNEDY, MAJOR, USAF
AIR ADJUTANT GENERAL

Appendix F: Excerpts from Article in *Air Intelligence Digest* by Captain Edward J. Ruppelt*

* * *

It should be stressed that USAF intelligence has no indications that any foreign nation has a super-weapon capable of flying anywhere in the world at will, nor that craft from outer space are coming near our planet Earth. It would be foolish, however, to say that either is impossible, no matter how highly improbable it may sound. Fifteen years ago, the atomic bomb was highly improbable.

The impact of the atom bomb on the entire world is well known, and it immediately posed a problem to any nation that held dreams of conquest. It would seem natural for a nation with the apparent plans of the Soviet Union to use any means possible to negate the leadership strength that possession of the bomb has given the U.S.

It is possible to suppose that UAOs ["Unidentified Aerial Objects," i.e., UFOs] might be a Soviet propaganda weapon, in which case, they could be either 1) planted fakes or 2) a clever use of natural phenomena designed to create mass hysteria. If this be true, it has been as miserable a failure as the balloons upon which the Japanese placed so much reliance during World War II.

If UAOs are being used for propaganda, it would be reasonable to assume that the USSR would choose first to frighten pro-American nations in Europe with the appearance of a radically new weapon, to compensate for the atom bomb. To support this theory, it will be remembered that strange objects appeared over

* From August 1952 *Air Intelligence Digest*.

the Scandinavian countries in 1946. The objects observed there were reported to have unusual range and unusual performance characteristics. When these incidents subsided, strange objects were reported to be flying over the U. S. The hypothesis here is that the Soviets could be attempting to frighten both the European nations and the U. S. by a new device that they hope will be construed to mean that the Soviets are far ahead of the rest of the world in technical know-how.

The above theory, however, runs into one big stumbling block. If these objects are weapons or advanced types of aircraft, they are, of necessity, man-made. How is it then possible that, in the four years that the USAF has been studying UAOs, not one has crashed? Man-made devices are not infallible.

To recapitulate, the USAF will maintain an open mind and study all UAO reports until enough information has been gathered to explain the unexplained 15%. By continually receiving reports, devising further methods of evaluating them, and collating them with other reports, a continual watch is being kept.

II. *UAOs OVER USA*

United States Air Force Headquarters continues to receive an increasing number of reports about weird objects in the sky. These reports—carefully checked at the Air Technical Intelligence Center, and when possible, evaluated—range from balloons to unidentified aerial objects of all conceivable shapes, sizes, speeds, and motions.

The dramatic scope of the subject of unidentified aerial objects has piqued America's interest for years. In this atomic age there is fascination in the weird and unknown, since man's inventions themselves approach the incredible. The public press has nurtured and sustained our interest in UAOs whenever it could find the slightest excuse to keep the story alive.

Since the USAF has been keeping books, over [several thousand] UAO sightings have been reported. Many of these reports have come from trained and experienced U. S. Weather Bureau personnel, USAF rated officers, well-qualified civilian pilots, technicians associated with various research projects, and, in one case, a group of professors from a Texas university.

Of these sightings, enough remain that cannot be explained by any known cause to justify the USAF in continuing to pursue its investigations.

On 24 June 1947, Kenneth Arnold, a businessman of Boise, Idaho, reported seeing a chain of nine saucer-like objects whipping in and out of mountain peaks at 1,200 mph, near Mount Rainier in the state of Washington. Mr. Arnold, who was flying his private aircraft that day, was so impressed that he contacted the press and the incident was played up across the country. Because of the wide publicity this sighting received, many persons consider this the first UAO sighting. Nothing could be further from the truth.

III. *Sightings*

There can be no attempt, in this article, to cover all the sightings on file at the Air Technical Intelligence Center. Generally speaking, the configuration of these objects fall into three categories 1) balls of fire, 2) disc-shaped, 3) roughly cigar-shaped.

OTHERS MIGHT BE SPACE SHIPS
CRAFT FROM OUT YONDER COULD BE DISCS, SPHERES, OR BIG V-2s WITH WINGS

It is just possible that some of the unidentified objects may be space ships from another planet. The idea of space travel is no longer the fantastic subject it was in the years before World War II. In the USAF's study of unidentified objects, space ships have been given serious consideration.

Although we do not know what a space ship from another planet will look like, we do know approximately what a space ship built on Earth will look like.

Willy Ley, the rocket expert, says the ship will look like a large rocket—like a V-2, but taller. Its height will be 10 to 12 times its largest diameter. It will have short wings, placed far back. The wings will be either sharply swept back, or will have a delta configuration.

409

Such a ship will have an atomic power plant. Thrust for take-off will be provided by a chemical booster, to avoid making the take-off area radioactive, and the atomic power will be used shortly afterward.

However, a transport from another planet might have the shape of a sphere, or a disc. For travel through the Earth's atmosphere, the sphere would not be nearly as efficient as a thin disc. The sphere could have tremendous strength, but its aerodynamic characteristics would not match those of the disc. In the vacuum of outer space, however, the shape of a space ship would not affect its flight at all.

If the unidentified objects are space ships from outside the Earth's orbit, the strange behavior of some of them (hovering, flying in jerky bursts of speed, changing direction at high speed, spinning and accelerating suddenly to high speeds) can be explained only by 1) a source of power unknown to Earthlings; 2) materials possessing greater strength and greater ability to resist heat than any now known on Earth; 3) physically superior beings or robots capable of withstanding enormous G forces—or; 4) new, radical means of overcoming or screening gravity.

Two Possibilities: Mars and Venus

Space ships could come here from either Mars or Venus. Other planets in the solar system are considered poor prospects for life to exist. Because of the climatic and atmospheric conditions believed to exist on Mars, it is thought by astronomers that a race of intelligent beings would be more likely to be found on that planet than on Venus. Mars has a rare atmosphere, nearly devoid of oxygen and water, and its nights are much colder than our Arctic winters. The atmosphere of Venus appears to be cloudy, and apparently consists mainly of carbon dioxide with deep clouds of formaldehyde droplets. Venus seems to have little or no water.

Despite these environmental characteristics, it is possible that intelligent beings exist on both planets. Such beings could be types whose body chemistry, size, appearance, and basic requirements for maintenance of life are entirely different from our own.

When Mars is nearest Earth, it is about 35,000,000 miles away. When Venus is nearest Earth, it is about 26,000,000 miles away. Venus is nearly as large as Earth; Mars is smaller than Venus.

Space Ships Might Come from Other Solar Systems

Arguments such as those applied to Mars and Venus need not necessarily apply to planets orbiting stars other than our sun, according to J. E. Lipp, of the Rand Corporation.

Many planets outside our solar system may have the environmental characteristics of Earth. The existence of life on planets which have the "right conditions" is not only possible, Lipp firmly believes, but inevitable. He assumes, for the sake of his argument, that man is "average," and thus that half the beings on such planets are ahead of us in knowledge, and have reached various levels of space travel experience. Conceivably, as Lipp suggests, among the myriads of other solar systems in space, one or more races of intelligent beings on planets far removed from our solar system *HAVE* discovered methods of travel that we could regard only as fantastic. Yet, the greater the astronomical distances that would have to be traversed by space travelers to reach our Earth from outside our solar system, the slighter the chance that space travelers would ever find this planet. The galaxy we are in has a diameter of about 100,000 light years, and a total mass of about 200 billion times that of our sun. Other galaxies, at distances up to billions of light years, have been photographed, numbering several hundred million and each containing millions of individual stars. A race of superior intelligence, unless it occurs frequently in outer space, would not be likely to stumble upon Planet III of Sol, a fifty-magnitude star in the outskirts of our local, or Milky Way, galaxy.

VII. PRE-1947 UAO REPORTS

Early—meaning pre-1947—reports are rich and varied, and fall consistently, like modern sightings, into three categories: luminous balls; saucer-shaped objects; cigar-shaped objects.

EDITOR'S NOTE: *Time*, in a recent article, mentioned the celebrated "airship" reported seen in 1896–97 by thousands of people from Oakland, Calif. to Chicago, and printed part of a clipping about it from the New York *Herald* of 11 April 1897. *Readers Digest*, in an article in its July 1952 issue, "Flying Saucers Are New in Name Only," mentioned reported UAO sightings in 1913, 1904, 1897 (the same one mentioned by *Time*), 1882, and 1870. These references gave a superficial impression that *Time* and *Readers Digest* had extensively researched the subject of UAO sightings. These eminent magazines, however, for all their reputations for thoroughness and their large research staffs, barely scratched the surface of this rich and extraordinarily interesting subject.

It is rather widely believed that the now-famous "Arnold Report" of 24 June 1927 was the first UAO report. Actually, reported UAO sightings go way, way back—well over a century and possibly to Old Testament days. Almost all "early sightings," as they have been short-titled by the Air Force, fall into the same main categories that the modern sightings fall into: luminous balls, saucer-shaped objects, or cigar-shaped objects.

The AIR INTELLIGENCE DIGEST requests its readers to make their own evaluations of these early reports. Were they—as many modern sightings have turned out to be—illusions, mistaken identifications, or hoaxes? Or were they real, and of terrestrial origin? Or real, and of celestial origin, possibly transplanetary or even transtellar?

There are many hundreds of reported early sightings on record, but, after careful screening, the DIGEST has selected for presentation *only those* discussed and/or reproduced (see accompanying artwork) in this article.

A large percentage of the early reports were in the form of letters to such sober and reputable journals as the London *Times; Scientific American Nature; American Meteorological Journal; U. S. and Canada Monthly Weather Review; l'Astronomie; Astronomische Nachrichten; London, Edinburgh, and Dublin Philosophical*

Magazine and Journal of Science; The Observatory—Monthly Review of Astronomy; etc. This proves, if it proves nothing else, that the witnesses were deeply moved and excited by what they saw—or thought they saw. M. Lincoln Schuster wrote in his introduction to the book, *A Treasury of the World's Great Letters:* "When any person has a soul-shaking experience, he usually can—and frequently does—write a letter about it."

Appendix G: Excerpts from Radio Interview with Colonel Lawrence J. Tacker

FOR RELEASE: 9 P.M., EST, Tuesday, December 20, 1960

"WASHINGTON VIEWPOINT"

CORRICK: Good evening. This is Ann Corrick with Sid Davis at the Pentagon in Washington. Washington Viewpoint tonight is concerned with a curious controversy—flying saucers. Are they real or imagined?

Our guest on Washington Viewpoint has devoted many years of study to this question. He is Lieutenant Colonel Lawrence J. Tacker, a war combat veteran and master navigator with the United States Air Force. Colonel Tacker currently is Chief of the Magazine and Book Branch of the Air Force Office of Information. His long-time interest in reports of flying saucers, or unidentified flying objects as they're called, led him to publish a book earlier this month which describes just what the Air Force is doing about persistent reports that someone somewhere has actually spotted flying saucers. The title of Colonel Tacker's book, by the way, is *Flying*

Saucers and the U. S. Air Force, published by Van Nostrand, and it represents the official Air Force position on the question of whether they are real or imagined.

Well, Colonel, just what is the official Air Force position; are there actually little people from a celestial culture flying around spying on us?

COLONEL TACKER: Definitely not, Ann. The official Air Force position on flying saucers or space ships from other planets is that we do not deny the possibility that life could exist out there some place and that a visit from outer space could happen. What we say is that to date it has not happened. That is, we have no evidence on hand to prove the existence of space ships or the fact that space travel in reverse is fait accompli.

CORRICK: And yet a lot of people who are intelligent and alert people claim that they actually have seen what must be a space ship from some other planet.

COLONEL TACKER: Well, if they believe this, Ann, it's a pure act of faith. Actually the Air Force does not deny the fact that many solid citizens have seen objects or phenomena in the sky which have mystified them for a time. In most instances when they reported these sightings to the Air Force we have been able to identify the object or the phenomena that they viewed and in most instances the reporting persons are satisfied with our interpretation.

CORRICK: Sid Davis.

DAVIS: Colonel, in your book you say "there are just not any manned space ships yet." How are you so sure?

COLONEL TACKER: Because to date, Sid, there is no evidence to substantiate such a fantastic claim.

DAVIS: Well, you have a lot of reports that are unexplained and this is the way you list them in your book. What about the unexplained ones, the unknown ones?

COLONEL TACKER: Well, the unknown or unexplained cases in the last few years have run about two per cent of the total number of sightings; and in most of these instances the Air Force feels that if more immediate data had been gathered initially at the scene of the sighting, these too could have been explained.

However, we can't go along with the theory of the UFO groups and many of the persons associated with these groups that because we have not come up with a definite answer in a very few cases, that this is an argument for the existence of space ships.

CORRICK: Well, Colonel Tacker, what do most of these sightings turn out to be?

COLONEL TACKER: Well, in most cases, Ann, they are either conventional objects seen under extenuating circumstances like high-flying aircraft under odd lighting conditions or in unusual cloud formations, or aircraft seen through a mist or rain, or they are serial phenomena or astrophysical phenomena such as a mock sun or a bolide, or fireball, meteor, or a planet seen by refraction due to a temperature inversion—something along these lines.

CORRICK: What is the source of most of these reports? What kind of people call them in to you?

COLONEL TACKER: Oh, a great many people call them in. As I said before, the great majority of these people are patriotic and honest citizens who are mystified by what they see initially and they make their reports to the Air Force to try to find out, number one, I think most of them are motivated, as I said, patriotically—try to help us. You must remember that the UFO Program or the Flying Saucer Program, as some people prefer to call it, is a small integral part of our overall air defense mission. By law the U. S. Air Force is charged with the air defense of the United States; and when we get a report of a sighting visually, maybe at some town a few miles away from an air base or on a radar scope, and we do get returns on radar scopes now and then that look as though they are actual objects in the sky; we might scramble an aircraft. By "scramble" I mean get it off immedi-

415

ately, it's an aircraft that's on fighter alert and it goes up to investigate.

In all instances they come back either with a known identification of an airliner or a balloon, or they come back with a negative result, that is they found nothing. Well this is where the UFO program begins, and the technical intelligence people begin at this point and try to identify or come up with an answer for what caused the sighting; either to the observer on the ground or what caused the return on the radar scope.

DAVIS: Colonel, what about all the charges and speculation that the Air Force has secret documents on file that are conclusions to the UFO situation and refuses to release the information?

COLONEL TACKER: This is pure rubbish, Sid. There are no such documents. I've gone through the files, I've looked thoroughly for any such an Air Force conclusion. I've never found anything to this subject, 200-2, paragraph 18 to be exact, cites specifically that UFO sightings will not be classified.

DAVIS: What other countries have frequent flying saucer reports?

COLONEL TACKER: Well, just from my experience and reading many of the reports from our own Aero-Space Technical Intelligence Center, I would say that, really, the countries that have most of the reports would be Australia, New Zealand, England and the South American or Spanish-speaking countries.

DAVIS: What about Russia?

COLONEL TACKER: That's a different question. We have received on occasion through our own sources over there, people stationed within Russia at various times, second-hand reports of the fact that UFO's or flying saucers have been seen there, but naturally we receive no direct result from Russian authorities on this subject.

DAVIS: Well, do Russian scientists tell you anything about their investigations of these things? Do they do anything about these reports in Russia that you know of?

COLONEL TACKER: Not that I know of, Sid; no.

CORRICK: Colonel Tacker, since the Air Force has begun investigating these sightings have these reports increased or decreased?

COLONEL TACKER: Well, I'd say they've been definitely on the decrease, Ann. We had a couple of peak years, as I pointed out in the book, fifty-two and fifty-seven. In 1952 we had quite a rash of sightings that seemed to start with the famous Washington, D. C. sightings, in 1952, and in 1957 we had a tremendous rash of sightings all over the country right after Sputnik I was launched.

CORRICK: I see. Well, how many have you had, say this year, as compared to last year?

COLONEL TACKER: Well—

CORRICK: A great decrease, a great increase?

COLONEL TACKER: I'd say a great decrease. I believe to date we've had under two hundred reports for this year.

CORRICK: Earlier you mentioned that the unexplained sightings ranged in the two per cent area . . .

COLONEL TACKER: Approximately two per cent for the last four or five years. Let me go out— this is a claim, really, of some of the UFO groups in claiming that the Air Force withholds information on this subject. They say that we give an erroneous figure when we give two per cent and I have been very careful to stress that that is in the last five years. Initially in the program, I'd say that UFO unknowns ran as high as twenty per cent back in the 1940's. Again this was due to the fact that it was an entirely new area to explore, our investigative techniques weren't up to what they are now, we didn't have facilities at our disposal then like— let me give you a real good example: the National Space Surveillance Center at Bedford, Massachusetts which can tell you on the first orbit if Russia or the United States have put something up. And certainly this unit at Bedford would be able to tell us if space ships were in our skies.

DAVIS: Colonel, you're very positive about your feeling that if there's no evidence to substantiate these sightings, there is no such thing. This two per cent figure—isn't it entirely possible that life on other planets has progressed beyond ours, and that perhaps they have invented a space ship that is capable of coming to planet earth and of zooming around here and then going back? Isn't this in the realm of possibility?

COLONEL TACKER: It is absolutely possible, Sid, that life exists on other planets; it's also possible that it could be of a higher order of intelligence than our own; but the last point you make about them visiting our atmosphere and zooming around and looking us over, I'd say again it's not possible up to now; that is, we have no evidence to date. And let me reiterate that that's the problem— not if it could happen or in the future, definitely we can see that it could, that there definitely is a possibility of life out there. What we say is that up until now we have no evidence to say we have been visited from other planets.

CORRICK: Well, Colonel, there have been many clubs and organizations established of people who really and honestly believe that there are these space ships zooming around, as Sid says. I'm sure you're familiar with most of them. Who are these people, who are the believers?

COLONEL TACKER: Well, Dr. Allen Hynek, our civilian consultant on this subject, and he happens to be the head of astrophysics at Northwestern University and the head of the observatory there, he calls them "cosmic romantics" and I think that's a good name. I think it's a fascinating subject myself; and as Dr. Hynek says, he'd like to see a space ship show up and be able to announce it. And there again I feel that if this did happen the Government would announce it immediately. In fact, an event of this significance I feel positive that one agency in the Government, like the Air Force, could not repress such information. I feel that it would be in the public domain almost immediately if an event of this significance did take place.

As to the people that make up these groups, a lot of them are people like you and I that are interested in this technological age of ours. I was talking to Willy Ley, the famous rocket researcher, the day before yesterday and he pointed out that we have over thirty-three pieces of hardware circling the earth right now, which is a tremendous number of artifacts to be up there whirling around. They're not all satellites; some of them are second-stage, third-stage pieces of rockets, but they're up there. And I think the public itself is getting very used to this type of thing. That's why I prophesied in the book that the flying saucer era itself is coming to an end.

CORRICK: How do you mean that?

COLONEL TACKER: Well, I believe, really, that the flying saucer era is similar to the great accent on spiritualism which took place at the turn of the century; and I believe that the public will find some other romantic subject to become imbued in and go on to it, rather than flying saucers. We're becoming used to space and it looks as though we're going to put a man into space real soon and I think this will really signify the end of the so-called saucer era.

DAVIS: Can we get back to the flying saucer clubs, et cetera? What's in it for people who become avid fans of the UFO? The people who promote the reports, the people who constantly write you letters?

COLONEL TACKER: Well, I believe, Sid, that there's a big dollar sign involved in this subject. I think that—well, I know—that many books and many articles are written on this subject; dues are paid to these clubs; although most of the clubs do say that they are nonprofit in nature, that they are simply dedicated to public knowledge, really, getting the information out. The groups themselves, as I said, are composed to a large extent of interested

419

people like you and I in this scientific age that we happen to be in.

DAVIS: Some of these people, some of these so-called flying saucer buffs, or fans, or fanaticists, have tape-recordings, they have statements that they've talked to people on Venus—Mars—they make lectures saying that they've seen lovely women up there; what about these people? Are you going to use the term "crackpot" to describe them?

COLONEL TACKER: Oh, I think there are crackpots involved, Sid, as there are in any belief of this nature; but here's a real interesting fact about these groups. They're strongly divided between the so-called "contactees," the people that actually rush off and visit Venus and Mars at the drop of a hat, and the so-called "euphologists," the people who say that they've had no contact to date but they're sure that there are space ships from other planets looking us over. These groups even fight amongst themselves and the euphology group, the groups that investigate flying saucers, actually call the contactees crackpots. It's real interesting.

CORRICK: Colonel Tacker, just exactly what is the objective of these groups, these people? What do they want the Government to do?

COLONEL TACKER: Well, that's hard to say. They say that there's been a great deal of secrecy in Government; they absolutely overlook the need for intelligence, intelligence classification in Government; and they feel that really we could be in great danger from space ships, maybe a greater danger than any that exists on earth.

Actually at this point I guess I should say again what I've said many times—that there is nothing in the Air Force files, either classified or unclassified, which prove or tends to prove the existence of space ships from other planets.

CORRICK: Do you think the Air Force—or this Government—is now doing everything it possibly can to track down this controversy?

COLONEL TACKER: I'm absolutely positive in my own mind that our Government is doing everything it can and as an instance let me cite the vast scientific scientific resources that the Government itself has at its disposal and by this I'm talking about the Air Research and Development Command which would include our basic research laboratories, the Air Material Command, scientific consultants from many different laboratories of our colleges and universities, industrial laboratories, instantaneous communications world-wide; anywhere in the world that there is a sighting, we can be talking to them in a matter of minutes.

And then compare this, really, to the really pathetic effort of a small group of euphologists who have a typewriter and read a newspaper account of the thing, and—you see you can't really compare. It's an extreme contrast, really. And the Government does go out and investigate these things in meticulous detail; it gives its answers; and of course here's where we're questioned in our interpretation by these groups who are convinced that they're space ships. I'm sure we're not going to change the mind of a person who believes in space ships and we don't want to necessarily try. We do want to convince them that the United States Government and the Air Force is not withholding any information on the subject.

DAVIS: Right now we're sitting in the Pentagon. Now supposing I leave here, I go outside, and I see something that looks like a cigar up in the sky. What happens? I run back inside here and I tell somebody. What do you do?

COLONEL TACKER: Well, if you came back into the Pentagon and reported it to me, I would immediately report it to the nearest air base, which is the initial course of action that any citizen should take. The air base will conduct a preliminary investigation and if in the preliminary investigation they cannot identify the object, it will be referred immediately to the Air Defense Command and the Aero Space Technical Intelligence Center, where it will be run down eventually by their investigators.

DAVIS: What prompts a scramble, then? If I'm

the only person that saw this, would there be a scramble just on the basis of what I saw?

COLONEL TACKER: No, not on the basis of just one individual sighting. The air base would be alerted immediately, as I said, the nearest air base. And they in turn would immediately ascertain if many people had seen it.

DAVIS: How long does it take to run something like that down? A matter of minutes—hours, days? Weeks?

COLONEL TACKER: Well, I'd say the initial preliminary investigation would be done very quickly in this particular case, in this area, it would be a matter of minutes. Because we probably have many aircraft in the air over Washington both from Andrews Air Force Base and Bolling Air Force Base; possibly some of our interceptors would be up on a training mission and could be diverted very quickly to the area; we could probably pin this down in a matter of minutes.

CORRICK: Is there any particular time of year, Colonel Tacker, when these sightings are more frequent?

COLONEL TACKER: Well, yes, Ann; in the spring and summertime when people are outside and are looking up. I don't imagine we had many reports on this Eastern seaboard in the last two or three days because most people have been inside next to their fires.

CORRICK: Is there any particular area of the country that you get greater numbers of reports . . . ?

COLONEL TACKER: No, it seems to be rather evenly spread throughout the country.

CORRICK: I know we've had quite a few stories from our station in Cleveland, Ohio, and it seems to me they are seeing an awful lot of flying saucers in Cleveland.

COLONEL TACKER: I don't think Cleveland is more guilty than any other of the cities. Cleveland and Akron do have rather active UFO groups out there which are probably stressing again and again, and again, the fact that space travel in reverse is an accomplished fact. But I don't think we could take any one section or one city and pin it down and say that they reported more UFO's than anybody else.

DAVIS: What about phases of the moon? Does that have any effect on reports of UFO's?

COLONEL TACKER: Not noticeably, Sid. This has been looked into.

DAVIS: Is that right?

COLONEL TACKER: Yes, Sir.